Prophet, Priest, and King shows theologians from around the world unified in their pursuit of the whole teaching of the Christian faith. Readers aiming to better understand Christ, to see how his threefold office helps us appreciate him whole, and to glean from many serving thoughtfully in his body today can read with great anticipation and profit.

—MICHAEL ALLEN, John Dyer Trimble
Professor of Systematic Theology, academic dean,
Reformed Theological Seminary, Orlando

Most of the authors in this path-setting book received their advanced theological training in the United States or the United Kingdom, but their thoughtful reflections on the person and work of Christ reflect viewpoints from around the world (Brazil, China, Egypt, Guatemala, India, Indonesia, Kenya, Taiwan). Sensitivity to those diverse local cultures, combined with common faithfulness to Scripture, makes for a compelling book. The authors articulate—but also fruitfully discuss among themselves—a range of important subjects, including standards of personal and communal purity, struggle between spiritual and terrestrial authorities, and relations between human and divine governments. "Theology in context" is the goal, and the goal is won.

—MARK NOLL, coauthor of *Clouds of Witnesses:*
Christian Voices from Africa and Asia

Prophet, Priest, and King, as well as the Theology Together series it introduces, brings us "global theology" at its best. The authors draw from the riches of the Western theological tradition and bring them into genuine conversation with majority world contexts and concerns. The result is a set of constructive essays that are neither slavish reiterations of Western theology nor faddish "contextual" theologies, but rather beautiful expressions of the catholicity of the church. I commend the authors and editors for offering an exemplary model of theology as dialogue.

—UCHE ANIZOR, professor of theology,
Talbot School of Theology, Biola University

Prophet, Priest, and King: Christology in Global Perspective, a project of Theo Global, which the organization I lead has been privileged to host the Africa regional gathering for close to ten years, is a groundbreaking work that aims to engage with historic Christian faith while respecting contextual diversity. Its noble vision, "From Every People to Every People," underpins this effort. By bringing together scholars from Africa, Asia, Latin America, and the United States, the book provides a rich tapestry of insights into the multifaceted roles of Christ as prophet, priest, and king with remarkable depth. What sets this volume apart is its commitment to amplifying diverse voices in a spirit of respect for one another's work; each essay invites readers into a truly global conversation that germinates and grows in context. This is a must-read for theologians, pastors, and students seeking to understand Christ's significance in a globalized world. The authors have delivered a scholarly yet accessible resource for our time.

—DAVID TARUS, PHD, executive director, Association for
Christian Theological Education in Africa (ACTEA)

Prophet, Priest, and King masterfully bridges deep theological insight with diverse global perspectives, enriching our understanding of Christ's offices. This work celebrates the unity and diversity of the global church. A must-read for scholars and practitioners alike.

—REV. AUGUSTUS NICODEMUS LOPES, PHD,
pastor at Esperança Bible Presbyterian Church, Orlando

This book is a profound, transformative, exploration of Christology showcasing the global, catholic faith through groundbreaking insights of Majority World scholars.

—RT. REV. DR. ALFRED OLWA, bishop,
professor, Diocese of Lango, Uganda

Here are theologians from around the world confessing Christ from their own locations in ways that edify the whole church. This first volume of the Theology Together series epitomizes the marriage of contextuality and catholicity the global church so desperately needs, wonderfully fulfilling the promise of the series name.

—KEVIN J. VANHOOZER, research professor of systematic
theology, Trinity Evangelical Divinity School

Delightful intercultural theological conversations on a significant doctrine. Useful to all those who seek to relate biblical teachings to cultural insights.

—DR. MOHAN CHACKO, principal emeritus,
Presbyterian Theological Seminary, Dehradun, India

Coming from diverse contexts, theological backgrounds, and traditions, the contributors to this esteemed volume—the first of its kind, published by Theo Global—unanimously affirm the unique status of Christ as prophet, priest, and king. In the twenty-first century, where confusion abounds regarding the person and work of Jesus Christ both inside and outside the church, this book offers a much-needed clarity, shedding light on how we can better understand and relate to our Savior and Lord, as expressed by thoughtful global voices.

—FREW TAMRAT, PHD, principal, Evangelical
Theological College of Addis Ababa, Ethiopia

Prophet, Priest, and King is an invitation to a treasury of global theological conversation. Each voice, speaking from its unique cultural context, presents a critically compelling, biblically faithful, spiritually refreshing perspective on the person and work of the Lord Jesus at the heart of "the faith once for all delivered to the saints." I highly recommend it.

—IVOR POOBALAN, PHD, principal, Colombo Theological
Seminary, cochair, Theology Working Group, Lausanne Movement

While many studies on Christology exist, this text distinguishes itself by two defining features: First, it is written by a group of global scholars, and second, most remarkably, there is a constant dialogue between the various authors. As a result, a most diverse and coherent global Christology is emerging based on the threefold office of Christ. A significant contribution to an important conversation!

—VELI-MATTI KÄRKKÄINEN, professor of
systematic theology, Fuller Theological Seminary

It is exciting to see the Theology Together project beginning to bear fruit in this volume. Theological scholarship from the majority world has often been marginalized because it has been seen as written for those margins rather than for the church as a whole. This project negates that view, showing how theological voices from the majority world bring fresh and creative insights to the one faith shared by all Christians everywhere. This volume begins at the very heart of that faith, with the person and work of Christ as prophet, priest, and king. It also provides a timely opportunity to approach those concepts in new and life giving ways, for Western and non-Western Christians alike, as they journey together in discipleship and mission.

—ANTHONY POGGO, secretary general of the Anglican Communion,
former bishop of Kajo-Keji in the Episcopal Church of South Sudan

This book is a winsome introduction to a promising new series. Its content commends Christ's threefold office as a biblical framework that is full of global relevance. And its format creatively embodies the type of theological dialogue for which many of us hope. The inset boxes are not interruptions; they are helpful supplements that add contextual illustrations and doctrinal insight. Thus readers can learn a great deal about Christology—and everything else that the risen Lord holds together.

—DANIEL J. TREIER, PHD, Gunther H. Knoedler Professor
of Theology, PhD program director, Wheaton College

In this volume, gifted authors from around the globe help us see the Lord Jesus Christ with fresh eyes. Here we have Christology as it should be: thoughtful reflection on the biblical witness with a keen eye for how cultural contexts and Christian tradition can enrich our love and worship of the risen Christ. Take up and read, and join the throng of Revelation 5.

—STEPHEN T. PARDUE, PHD, program director, ThM/PhD
in Theological Studies, Asia Graduate School of Theology

Prophet, Priest, and King offers a *tour de force* of biblical, theological, historical, and sociolinguistic reflections on Jesus Christ's three offices. Beautifully written in elegant, accessible prose, the contributors explain the biblical text and their own culture's understanding of government (king), religion (priest) and ethics (prophets) within non-Christian religious constructs, including Islam, Hinduism, Confucianism, and Korean shamanism. The reader is treated to a banquet of culturally diverse dishes, each nourishing the soul, expanding the mind, and strengthening faith. Contributors dialogue with each other through embedded comments within the essays, allowing readers to listen in on a fascinating conversation—I could not put the book down!

—LYNN COHICK, distinguished professor of New Testament
and director, Houston Theological Seminary

With *Prophet, Priest, and King*, Theo Global introduces an exciting publishing project for the global church. By bringing together gifted theologians from diverse contexts to present a unified understanding of the biblical text, this book expands our understanding of Christ's saving work and empowers Christians in all callings to fulfill their own prophetic, priestly, and kingly ministry.

—PHILIP RYKEN, president, Wheaton College

PROPHET, PRIEST, AND KING

VOLUME EDITORS

Michael S. Horton
Elizabeth W. Mburu
Justin S. Holcomb

MANAGING EDITOR

Adam P. Smith

CONTRIBUTORS

Sofanit T. Abebe
Heber Carlos de Campos Jr.
Havilah Dharamraj
Nelson Morales Fredes
Wilson Jeremiah
Aruthuckal Varughese John
Wageeh Mikhail
Thomas Park
Shao Kai Tseng

PROPHET, PRIEST, AND KING

CHRISTOLOGY IN GLOBAL PERSPECTIVE

MICHAEL S. HORTON, ELIZABETH W. MBURU,
AND JUSTIN S. HOLCOMB, EDITORS

ZONDERVAN
ACADEMIC

This volume is dedicated to Mark Anthony Green, who envisioned and, together with Adam Smith, executed the dream.

ZONDERVAN ACADEMIC

Prophet, Priest, and King
Copyright © 2025 by Michael S. Horton, Elizabeth W. Mburu, and Justin S. Holcomb

Published in Grand Rapids, Michigan, by Zondervan. Zondervan is a registered trademark of The Zondervan Corporation, L.L.C., a wholly owned subsidiary of HarperCollins Christian Publishing, Inc.

Requests for information should be addressed to customercare@harpercollins.com.

Zondervan titles may be purchased in bulk for educational, business, fundraising, or sales promotional use. For information, please email SpecialMarkets@Zondervan.com.

Names: Horton, Michael Scott, editor. | Mburu, Elizabeth W., 1968– editor. | Holcomb, Justin S., 1973– editor.

Title: Prophet, Priest, and King : Christology in global perspective / Michael Horton, Elizabeth W. Mburu, and Justin S. Holcomb, editors.
Description: Grand Rapids, Michigan : Zondervan Academic, [2024] | Series: Theology together series | Includes bibliographical references and index.
Identifiers: LCCN 2024032538 (print) | LCCN 2024032539 (ebook) | ISBN 9780310142928 (softcover) | ISBN 9780310142935 (ebook) | ISBN 9780310142959 (audio)
Subjects: LCSH: Jesus Christ—Person and offices. | BISAC: RELIGION / Christian Theology / Christology | RELIGION / Biblical Studies / New Testament / Jesus, the Gospels & Acts
Classification: LCC BT198 .P73 2024 (print) | LCC BT198 (ebook) | DDC 232/.8—dc23/ eng/20240906
LC record available at https://lccn.loc.gov/2024032538
LC ebook record available at https://lccn.loc.gov/2024032539

Cover design: Tammy Johnson
Cover art: Getty Images
Interior design: Kait Lamphere

Printed in the United States of America
25 26 27 28 29 LBC 5 4 3 2 1

CONTENTS

Introduction: Theology Together Series xi

Volume Introduction xvii
    Michael S. Horton, Elizabeth W. Mburu, and Justin S. Holcomb

PART I: CHRIST AS PROPHET

Introduction 3
Elizabeth W. Mburu and Michael S. Horton

1. The Church as Christ's Prophetess 21
    Wilson Jeremiah

2. More than a Prophet: Arab Christians and the Question of
   Christology 45
    Wageeh Mikhail

3. Jesus and God's Prophetic Imagination 62
    Nelson Morales Fredes

PART II: CHRIST AS PRIEST

Introduction 81
Elizabeth W. Mburu and Michael S. Horton

4. Christ's Priestly Office in Confucian Contexts.................. 93
    Shao Kai Tseng

5. Jesus the High Priest: A South Asian Reading 120
   Havilah Dharamraj
6. Christ as the High Priest and Asian Shamanism.................. 144
   Thomas Park

PART III: CHRIST AS KING

Introduction 169
Elizabeth W. Mburu and Michael S. Horton
7. Christ's Sovereignty and His Present Kingdom.................. 182
   Aruthuckal Varughese John
8. Mission Accomplished, though King Forever 207
   Heber Carlos de Campos Jr.
9. In Step with the King: Participation and the Reign of Christ 230
   Sofanit T. Abebe

Conclusion... 255
Michael S. Horton, Elizabeth W. Mburu, and Justin S. Holcomb

For Further Reading 262
List of Contributors 264
Scrpiture Index 268
Subject Index 276

INTRODUCTION:
THEOLOGY TOGETHER SERIES

From Every People to Every People: Theology in Context

Christians in the West might assume that missionaries, especially those from Britain and the United States, brought the gospel to Asia and Africa. Sharing this broad assumption, some Christians risk throwing out the baby of essential Christian faith and practice with the bathwater of Western prejudice, while others see "contextualization" as a pretext for relativism and syncretism. The authors in this series seek a third way that is sensitive to regional diversity as well as to unity in "the faith that was once and for all delivered to the saints" (Jude 1:3 ESV).

As these chapters reflect at least indirectly, Christianity not only emerged in the Middle East, but spread quickly through central Asia, Africa, and India, beginning with the apostles. Armenia was the first country to adopt Christianity officially in 301. About a decade later the Christian apologist Arnobius could celebrate that the gospel "has subdued the fires of passion, and caused races and peoples and nations most diverse in character to hasten with one accord to accept the same faith." He adds, "For the deeds can be reckoned up and numbered which have been done in India, among the Seres [China], Persians, and Medes; in Arabia, Egypt, in Asia, Syria; among the Galatians, Parthians, Phrygians; in Achaia, Macedonia, Epirus; in all islands and provinces on which the rising and setting sun shines."[1] A wide

---

1. Angelo Di Berardino, ed., *Encyclopedia of Ancient Christianity*, vol. 1 (Downers Grove, IL: IVP Academic, 2014), 500.

door was opened in China by Emperor Taizong in the seventh century when he embraced Christ through an Assyrian missionary, Alopen, who gave him the Scriptures.[2]

During roughly the same period, missionaries were making inroads among European tribes. Consequently, our collective memory is (or should be) broader and deeper than the history of Western Christianity. This is not in any way to diminish the significance of the modern missionary movement but is to affirm that being catholic and evangelical today requires appreciation for the diversity of voices that have propagated it from the beginning.

Thus, when Asian and African Christians bear witness to this evangelical catholicity, they neither adopt wholesale nor reject distinctively Western developments of Christian faith and practice. The global church has its own stories to bring to the family reunion, both ancient and contemporary, not only receiving important legacies of Western Christianity but enriching the whole body of Christ in our day. The goal of this volume, the first in the Theology Together series, is expressed well by Arnobius above: to draw upon that fruit of more ancient missionary movements that "caused races and peoples and *nations most diverse in character* to hasten with one accord to accept the *same faith.*"

INTRODUCTION TO THE PROJECT

The Theology Together series is the fruit of in-person conversations over days of fellowship and friendship. Since 2015, Theo Global has gathered scholars from around the world for theological conversation. The fruit of these regional conferences was a meeting in Istanbul in 2023, where face-to-face conversations produced much of the material in this volume. As much "work" is done over meals and tea as is done in hearing, giving, and responding to papers. Besides its regional gatherings, Theo Global brings salient voices to other venues for still richer cross-cultural conversations. Often responsible for a variety of practical duties supporting and executing the church's mission,

---

2. Di Berardino, ed., *Encyclopedia of Ancient Christianity*, 1:501.

participants find these concentrated interactions to be a refreshing oasis and a stimulation to their ongoing academic interests. We want readers to join us, as it were, in this published version of stimulating conversation.

The team of editors and contributors at the Hagia Irene in Istanbul, Turkey, where the Council of Constantinople (381) authorized the final version of the Nicene Creed. From left to right: Justin Holcomb, Sofanit Abebe, Nelson Morales, Heber Campos Jr., Elizabeth Mburu, Havilah Dharamraj, Varughese John, Tom Park, Shao Kai Tseng, Wageeh Mikhail, Michael Horton, Adam Smith.

The lodestar for our vision is the scene in Revelation 5:9–10:

And they sang a new song, saying,

> "Worthy are you to take the scroll
>   and to open its seals,
> for you were slain, and by your blood you ransomed people
>   for God
>   from every tribe and language and people and nation,

and you have made them a kingdom and priests to our God,
    and they shall reign on the earth." (ESV)

It is noteworthy, first and foremost, that the song celebrates the Lamb whose blood ransomed people from every tribe on earth (cf. Dan 7:14; Rev 7:9; 14:6). God the Son assumed human nature to be the savior of the whole world, and he is building new humanity around himself through the preaching of the gospel, making disciples from "all nations" (Matt 28:19). Soteriology and ecclesiology are bound up together. It is a hymn of praise that leads to mission. They have not made themselves anything, but "you have made them a kingdom and priests to our God." Doctrine is for doxology, and doxology fuels discipleship. In jubilation we find the proper voice for our mission. At present, Christ's kingdom may appear weak, divided, and oppressed not only by external threats but within the church itself. Yet the eschatological goal is settled: "They shall reign on the earth."

OUR VISION:
FROM EVERY PEOPLE TO EVERY PEOPLE

Our vision is focused on savoring the rich biblical truths that unite Christ's body in all times and places while understanding how those truths are mediated through very different cultural-linguistic horizons. This dual concern is evident in our vision to offer a series that is "From Every People to Every People." Even at the interpersonal level, we know that doctrines such as original sin or Christ's vicarious atonement can be misunderstood because of widely divergent experiences. How are they heard in a shame-based culture as opposed to one that is individualistic and relativistic? In an increasingly globalized environment, one does not need to travel great distances to have many cross-cultural encounters. And while the cross-pressures may be different, we know that our confession of Christ clashes with all our cultures. Believers share more in common with each other, across all distances and eras, than they do with their non-Christian neighbors.

"From Every People" underscores that framing sound doctrine cannot be left up to one part of Christ's body in one part of the world at one moment in time. The antidote to an overreliance on Western sources is not rejection but participation. Given the legacy of colonialism, such participation has been too often more an appearance than a reality. Yet the health of the whole church and its global mission depends on this becoming a more evident reality. Many cultures in the majority world are closer to the world of the New Testament than Western societies. Our different contexts help us to engage in that mutual edification and reproof to which Christ's body is called.

Furthermore, we encourage diversity with respect to specialization. The contributors are recognized for their contributions to exegetical, biblical, systematic, and historical theology. The editors make every effort to ensure that each volume is balanced with insights from all these fields.

OUR METHOD: THEOLOGY IN CONTEXT

Rather than the category "contextual theology," we prefer "theology in context." Our primary goal is not to apply theology *to* our cultural contexts (as important as that is) but to exegete Scripture and its doctrines together *from* our distinct cultural backgrounds. Much of modern theology simply assumes its northern European and American contexts. International partners often write for this audience. Even "contextualization" tends sometimes to conform to Western anthropological and hermeneutical models that elide the specificity of both one's cultural context and Christian theological discourse. The hermeneutical relationship is often described as a "fusion of horizons."[3] But we have sufficient warnings from the apostles to expect that the encounter will be often more like a "clash of horizons."[4] Scripture itself warrants a "hermeneutics of suspicion," reminding us that we are all not only as individuals but as cultures prone to suppress the truth, consciously or unconsciously, in favor of our prejudices.[5] Yet because of God's common grace, no culture

---

3. See Hans-Georg Gadamer, *Truth and Method*, trans. J. Weinsheimer and D. G. Marshall (New York: Continuum, 2006), 305.

4. See Paul Ricoeur, "The Hermeneutic Function of Distanciation," in *Hermeneutics and the Human Sciences*, ed. and trans. John B. Thompson (New York: Cambridge University Press, 1981), esp. 132–38.

5. As Merold Westphal writes, "In order to take seriously the noetic effects of sin, Christians need

is as corrupt as it can possibly be. Our differences allow us to see weaknesses in each other's expressions of faith, as well as our own, and to glean wisdom from brothers and sisters whose contributions we may have overlooked.

On the one hand, we seek to avoid the illusion of a "theology from nowhere." Only when we acknowledge our cultural biases can we test them by the authority of God's word, the only infallible rule of faith and practice. Some of these biases will be seen to nourish healthy correctives to the biases of other cultures; others will have to be challenged. Not only analysis of our own time and place is required but also the rationale of the great teachers of the past for doctrines we hold together. Rooted in the sixteenth-century Reformation, evangelicals have historically sought again and again to return to the wells of the Jewish prophets and apostles, drinking deeply from the wisdom of the ancient Christian teachers, many of whom were from the Middle East and Africa.

On the other hand, we seek at all costs to avoid reversing the authority of Scripture and culture. We are not aiming for an African theology, an Indian theology, a Middle Eastern theology, an Asian theology, a Latin American theology, an American theology, and so on, but for a catholic and evangelical theology that exhibits clearly the particular cultural obstacles, as well as correctives to reception, interpretation, and application of Christian doctrines. For example, rather than a theology of liberation (with its myriad subgroups), we are interested in the liberating theology of the Trinity, Christology, ecclesiology, and eschatology. We will hear the distinct voices of Christian scholars testifying to the one object of our faith: the triune God who speaks and acts. None of us can presume to speak for the cultural context of a nation, much less a whole continent or even the diverse theological traditions in our own neighborhoods. We are not aiming for comprehensiveness in either global representation or doctrinal breadth but in sparking global conversations with many voices seeking to grow together in our common faith.

---

to incorporate a hermeneutic of suspicion into their thinking, and in such an effort, postmodern analyses can be helpful and illuminating (without being atheistic)." See Merold Westphal, ed., *Postmodern Philosophy and Christian Thought* (Bloomington, IN: Indiana University Press, 1999), 3. Also see Justin S. Holcomb, "Investigating Metanarratives and Theology," in *For the World*, ed. Justin S. Holcomb and Glenn Lucke (Phillipsburg, NJ: P&R, 2014).

VOLUME INTRODUCTION

An excellent example of the catholicity toward which we aim in the Theology Together series is Christ's threefold office of prophet, priest, and king. Arising naturally from Scripture and developed richly in patristic sources from both the East and the West, North and South, it has been given a prominent place in evangelical confessions since the Reformation and, more recently, in non-Western contexts. This rubric encourages integration of Christ's person with the many-faceted aspects of Christ's work. While our eyes are fixed on "Jesus, the pioneer and perfecter of our faith" (Heb 12:2), we will point to dissonances and challenges to understanding the scriptural images because of cultural presuppositions of prophets, priests, and rulers, and we will testify to Jesus as Word, as sacrifice, and as Lord. We will also offer examples of how our contexts suggest connections, bridges, and opportunities to correct misunderstandings that can correct and enrich interpretation.

There is ample precedent for organizing Christology around his threefold office as prophet, priest, and king. Many in the Christian tradition have appealed to this threefold office: Origen, Eusebius, John of Damascus, Aquinas, John Calvin, Herman Bavinck, and more. Obviously, the rubric of prophet, priest, and king comes from the Bible, so it draws the focus of contributors to biblical and theological reflection. In the spirit of the in-person conversations from which this series arises, we include short responses along the way from scholars in other parts of the world.

We begin each section with a biblical-theological essay that traces the development of the doctrine in Scripture. The chapters that follow focus on a particular aspect of that motif and its significance for Christian faith and practice. Along the way, authors continue their conversations by inserting comments in response to the text. We offer this volume as a feast from the nations for the nations.

Doxology being the proper end of theology, this project is conceived as a global anthem of appreciation of Jesus Christ in his triple office of prophet, priest, and king—an anthem raised by regional voices united by the desire to do theology together for the edification of the universal church and for the greater glory of God.

Michael S. Horton
Elizabeth W. Mburu
Justin S. Holcomb

PART I

CHRIST AS PROPHET

INTRODUCTION: CHRIST AS PROPHET

THE PROPHET GREATER THAN MOSES

ELIZABETH W. MBURU

Old Testament: Deuteronomy 18:14–22

The Old Testament text that gives the clearest image of a prophet that would arise, one who would be like Moses but who would actually be greater than Moses, is found in Deuteronomy 18, the last book of the Pentateuch. The setting of the story of Moses and the Israelites in this season of their history is the territory of Moab, east of the Jordan, across from Jericho (Deut 1:5; Num 36:13; Josh 1:2). Deuteronomy recounts Moses's farewell addresses to the Israelites as he prepared a new generation to enter into the promised land. The Sinaitic covenant is essentially renewed, and, for a brief moment, the flow of salvific history pauses.

The theme of transition permeates the entire book. Moses, as God's appointed prophet, is readying himself to pass on the banner to Joshua. However, Deuteronomy 18:14–22, which is found in the larger section of covenant stipulations, clarifies that the transition is not just about Joshua but also about the prophetic office.

Surrounding this text are requirements for human leaders in various civic and religious spheres. In chapter 18, Moses gives the stipulations for priests and prophets. Those for prophets are given so "that the prophetic order should be fully accredited by the side of the other state authorities, and its operations regulated by a definite law (vv. 9–22)."[1] In other words, the prophetic office was divinely authorized to challenge the status quo, to remind God's people to keep the covenant, and to warn them of the punishment that they would face if they didn't.[2]

Prophets existed in the ancient world beyond Israel, as can be seen from prophetic utterances documented in texts from Mesopotamia, Syria, and Anatolia.[3] However, prophets in Israel were not to be like the prophets of the pagan nations. *Ve'atah* ("but as for you") is placed first for the sake of emphasis. They did not need to practice sorcery and divination like the pagan nations they were to conquer. Moses himself warned the Israelites against listening to those who relied on such practices (18:14). God regarded their practices as so evil that they were to be rejected totally.[4] This was because "Pagan magic was identified with pagan religion. So any practice of the occult was an expression of rebellion against the basic demand of Yahweh for Israel's loyalty to the covenant."[5]

Instead, God himself would raise up a prophet like Moses from among them (Deut 18:15). The phrase *kamni* ("like me") spoken by Moses is not meant to imply that he would resemble Moses in all ways. Nor does it mean that it applied only to messianic expectations, as some commentators wrongly concluded from their interpretation of certain supporting texts such as Numbers 12:6–8; Deuteronomy 34:10; and Hebrews 3:2, 5.[6] Rather, like Moses, he would also speak God's words on his behalf (Deut 18:18), he would be a mediator between God and the people, and the Israelites were to listen to him as they had done to Moses. If they failed to do so, they would be accountable to God.

The prohibition (18:14), as well as the test that follows, which validates God's true prophet (18:22), shows that although *nabi'* ("a prophet") is in the

---

1. Carl Friedrich Keil and Franz Delitzsch, *Commentary on the Old Testament*, vol. 1 (Peabody, MA: Hendrickson, 1996), 931.

2. Victor Harold Matthews, Mark W. Chavalas, and John H. Walton, *The IVP Bible Background Commentary: Old Testament* (Downers Grove, IL: InterVarsity Press, 2000), s.v. Deut 18:14–22.

3. Matthews, Chavalas, and Walton, *IVP Bible Background Commentary: Old Testament*, Deut 18:14–22.

4. Eugene H. Merrill, "The Pentateuch," in *Holman Concise Bible Commentary*, ed. David S. Dockery (Nashville: B&H, 1998), 67.

5. Paul R. Gilchrist, "Deuteronomy," in *Evangelical Commentary on the Bible*, vol. 3, Baker Reference Library (Grand Rapids: Baker, 1995), 122.

6. Keil and Delitzsch, *Commentary on the Old Testament*, 934.

singular, the context points to a series of prophets who would come after Moses, not just the Messiah. The Israelites' original request at Horeb (18:16) confirms that God would provide succeeding generations of Israelites with a spokesman to carry on what he had started through Moses (Exod 20:19).

Nevertheless, even though this prophecy does not apply exclusively to Jesus Christ, it certainly includes him. Messianic expectations were already a reality by that time (cf. Gen 3:15), and later messianic expectations pointed back to this promise. Ultimately, this prophetic office was fulfilled in Jesus Christ. Indeed, only he measured up to—and surpassed—the ministry of Moses (cf. Deut 34:10). As Keil and Delitzsch righty point out,

> All the prophets of the Old Testament stood within the sphere of the economy of the law, which was founded through the mediatorial office of Moses; and even in their predictions of the future, they simply continued to build upon the foundation which was laid by Moses, and therefore prophesied of the coming of the servant of the Lord, who, as the Prophet of all prophets, would restore Jacob, and carry out the law and right of the Lord to the nations, even to the end of the world (Isa. 42, 49, 40, 61).[7]

Witnesses in the New Testament that point back to Deuteronomy 18 and apply it to Jesus include Philip (John 1:45), Peter (Acts 3:22–23), Stephen (Acts 7:37), the Samaritans (John 4:25), and even Christ himself (John 5:45–47).

New Testament: Mark 9:2–13

The event in the New Testament that reveals Jesus's identity as a prophet like and even greater than Moses is the transfiguration (Mark 9:2–13; cf. Matt 17:1–13; Luke 9:28–36). Mark begins with the phrase "after six days" to give us the temporal setting (9:2). Some commentators suggest that this time marker may refer to the six days that God worked in Genesis before the divine rest or that it parallels the six days that Moses waited for a Revelation

---

7. Keil and Delitzsch, *Commentary on the Old Testament*, 935–36.

(Exod 24:16).[8] However, as R. Alan Cole points out, it may merely reflect the eyewitness nature of the story and could just be an approximate number, given that Luke cites eight days in his account (9:28).[9]

In Mark's story up to this point, readers have taken note that Jesus's messiahship entailed suffering. Now, Mark shows us Jesus's divine glory. He went to a high mountain and took with him three disciples: Peter, James and John. The adjective *high* implies contact with heaven.[10] Jesus, like Moses before him (Exod 34:29), was transfigured before them, his clothes dazzling white (Mark 9:3). Although Greek myths and Jewish apocalyptic literature have stories of transfigurations, the most likely background is Moses.[11] The whiteness is also reminiscent of Daniel's vision of the "Ancient of Days."[12] The word *metemorphōthē* ("he was transfigured") means that his appearance was changed, in that his true glory was revealed.

This is the first fulfilment of the words Jesus had uttered in the previous scene (8:38; 9:1). The second part of the fulfilment would be seen after the resurrection. Indeed, "the transfiguration is a foretaste of the final triumph of Jesus, whether it is seen in itself as a fulfilment of this prophecy or promise of Jesus."[13] The presence of Moses and Elijah confirms the witness of Law and Prophets to Christ (9:4). However, it is more. Moses had spoken of Christ prophetically, and Elijah was expected to come as the Messiah's forerunner to restore all things (9:11–12; Luke 24:27; John 1:45; cf. Mal 4:5; *Ben Sira* 48:10).[14]

Frightened by this sight, Peter did the only thing that seemed appropriate. He offered to put up three *skēnas* ("shelters, tabernacles, tents, or booths"), one for each of them (Mark 9:5–6). Perhaps he is reminded of the glory that had once covered Israel's meeting tent (Exod 40:35) and did not understand that it was present in Jesus himself.

---

8. Rodney L. Cooper, *Mark*, Holman New Testament Commentary 2 (Nashville: B&H, 2000), 146–48.

9. R. Alan Cole, *Mark: An Introduction and Commentary*, Tyndale New Testament Commentaries 2 (Downers Grove, IL: InterVarsity Press, 1989), 212–18.

10. Craig A. Evans, *Mark 8:27–16:20*, Word Biblical Commentary 34 B(Nashville: Thomas Nelson, 2001), 35.

11. Craig S. Keener, *The IVP Bible Background Commentary: New Testament*, 2nd ed. (Downers Grove, IL: InterVarsity Press, 2014), 149.

12. Evans, *Mark 8:27–16:20*, 36.

13. Cole, *Mark: An Introduction and Commentary*, 212–18.

14. Cooper, *Mark*, 146–48.

Once again, Peter betrayed his lack of understanding by assuming that the three were the same. Granted, in Jewish tradition Moses, Elijah, and the Messiah were placed on the same level.[15] However, this event reveals that Jesus is greater than Moses and Elijah. Moses's transfiguration on Mount Sinai was a momentary occurrence that faded away (2 Cor 3:7, 13). Moreover, Jesus Christ's "glory on the mountain was his own: he was but reassuming that divine glory which was his with the Father before the world began (John 17:5)."[16] This scene therefore gives us a glimpse of Jesus's true and final glory and confirms that he is no mere prophet.

The readers have just noted Peter's shallow understanding of Jesus's identity (Mark 8:29), but Mark offers us a heavenly perspective. At that moment, a cloud appeared and covered them, and they heard God's voice saying the words, *"This is my Son, whom I love. Listen to him!"* (9:7; emphasis added). The cloud signals God's presence, as it did in Moses's experience on the mountain and the Israelites in the wilderness (Exod 13:21; 24:16; 40:38). This is the second time that God's public acknowledgement and approval of Jesus has occurred in this gospel (cf. Mark 1:11). The difference is that in the first occurrence, Jesus's baptism, God speaks to Jesus directly and it seems that no one else hears him. Here, God speaks of Jesus in the third person and the disciples hear his voice. At the very least, Mark indicates a progression in the narrative in terms of the inclusion of the disciples in the revelation of Jesus's identity. It also means that henceforth, the disciples were to listen to Jesus, not Moses or Elijah.[17] God's voice confirms that Jesus is greater than the Law and Prophets. They are to listen to him because he teaches with the authority of God, just as Moses had prophesied (Deut 18:15, 18).

As soon as these words were uttered, the disciples saw Jesus standing alone (Mark 9:8). Once again, the theme of the messianic secret emerges as Jesus orders them not to tell anyone wat they have seen until after his resurrection (9:9). Only after that could the implications of the transfiguration be fully understood. Not surprisingly, they do not comprehend what Jesus means (9:10). If they have not understood his teaching about his suffering

---

15. Cooper, *Mark*, 146–148.

16. Cole, *Mark: An Introduction and Commentary*, 212–18.

17. Evans, *Mark 8:27–16:20*, 38.

and death, how can they understand his resurrection? Clearly, the concept of resurrection or resuscitation was not foreign to them (cf. 2 Kgs 4:32–37; Dan 12:2; Heb 11:19). Their issue was not with his resurrection but with his suffering and dying, since this was not a part of their construct of the Messiah.[18] For the disciples, and indeed for Mark's readers, this event vividly demonstrates the paradox in his heavenly glory and his coming humiliation.

Most likely because the presence of Elijah was still fresh on their minds, the disciples asked about Elijah (Mark 9:11). The real question has to do with how Jesus can be the Messiah if Elijah has not yet appeared. Jews expected Elijah's return at the end to prepare the Lord's way (Mal 3:1; 4:5; *Sir* 48 1–10).[19] Jesus's answer affirms that, in John the Baptist, Elijah has already appeared as the promised forerunner and anticipated the rejection of the Messiah (cf. Isa 52:13–53:12; Dan 7). Jesus, then, is not just the fulfillment of the prophetic office anticipated in texts like Deuteronomy 18 and Mark 9. He is greater than Moses, greater than Elijah—indeed, he is greater than any prophet.

CHRIST IS PROPHET

MICHAEL S. HORTON

Jesus Christ is more than a prophet, of course, but he is a prophet indeed. Israel's prophets were witnesses to God's speech and acts in history.[20] Their words consist primarily of divinely revealed testimony to judgment and deliverance. Old Testament prophets even announced a "new thing" that God would do in the future, despite Israel's faithlessness. Moses and Aaron are both referred to as prophets in the exodus narrative (Exod 7:1–2): *nabi'*, the most frequently used term, along with *hozeh*. The New Testament comports entirely with this usage (*prophētēs* in Septuagint and New Testament), reiterating that the biblical prophets did not speak on their own authority but under divine inspiration (Acts 3:22–24; 2 Pet 1:21).

---

18. Cooper, *Mark*, 146–148.

19. Keener, *IVP Bible Background Commentary*, 150.

20. My portion of this introduction is indebted to my previous work in *Lord and Servant: A Covenant Christology* (Louisville: Westminster John Knox, 2005), 211–18.

Contrast with Gentile Prophets

In the ancient world, a prophet was possessed by a god, indicated by a suspension of the prophet's own faculties of reason, language, and observation. In fact, one was only regarded as inspired if he or she went into a frenzy or trance. In many contexts still today, "prophet" conjures the image of a wizard—a shaman, seer, or medicine man who uses spiritual technology to divine the future. In my context, there are two principal associations. On the one hand, self-proclaimed contemporary prophets claim to bring new revelations. In many cases such individuals are invested with tremendous authority, power, and even wealth. On the other hand, a prophet connotes a person who "speaks truth to power," as it is often said. In both cases, the danger is that people are invoking God's name for their own visions and agendas, whether for individual prosperity or social and political policies. In contrast, biblical prophets are God-centered, not human-centered; the message they bring is *for* us, not *about* us. The biblical prophets announce God's judgment and grace centering on the advent of the Messiah. In none of these alternative portraits is the distinctively biblical prophet to be found.

First, these popular notions are immanent rather than transcendent; that is, they are limited to natural possibilities. The prophet speaks whatever he or she feels, discovers, or experiences within or through natural portents (e.g., flight patterns of birds, reading entrails and livers, etc.), and the prophecy is concerned merely with individual or social well-being here and now. In contrast, the biblical prophet is not a religious specialist who possesses unique techniques of ecstasy but an ordinary person who is called away from an ordinary vocation to bring a message to God's people. In possession of his own wits, the biblical prophet communicates God's word in his terms drawn from his own cultural-linguistic milieu and personality. And the prophecy is something that the prophet could not have known apart from special communication from God: not merely foreknowledge of natural events but a revelation of God's miraculous acts of judgment and deliverance. Moreover, the prophet is sent with a word that not only threatens and promises but brings the reality into history.

Second, the God of the Bible accomplishes everything by speech. He is the archetypal preacher. "By the word of the LORD the heavens were made, and by the breath of his mouth all their host" (Ps 33:6).[21] Providence, judgment, redemption, and the consummation are all accomplished also by his powerful utterance. "So shall my word be that goes out from my mouth," says Yahweh. "It shall not return to me empty, but it shall accomplish that which I purpose, and shall succeed in the thing for which I sent it" (Isa 55:11). God's speech not only describes and explains timeless truths but creates, makes desolate, and makes fruitful; it judges and justifies, kills and makes alive, convicts and assures, terrifies and comforts. "Is not my word like fire, says the LORD, and like a hammer that breaks a rock in pieces?" (Jer 23:29). The idols are nothing. In contrast with Yahweh, they do not speak or hear, so they cannot announce future events, much less bring them to pass (Isa 44:6–8). The nations craft idols to behold their gods with their eyes, while Israel is called to listen and hear with the ears.

Third, if the Father is the archetypal preacher, the Son is the archetypal mediator of every word he speaks. Even before the world was made, the Son was the eternally begotten Word of the Father, and through him everything was made and holds together (John 1:1–5; Col 1:15–17). "For all the promises of God find their Yes in him. That is why it is through him that we utter our Amen to God for his glory" (2 Cor 1:20). And the Holy Spirit is the person of the Godhead who works within creatures to bring about the effect of this word. For example, "No one can say 'Jesus is Lord' except in the Holy Spirit" (1 Cor 12:3). Not only in salvation but in creation, providence, the miracles of the Old and New Testaments, and the inspiration of Scripture, the Son is the mediator. In that sense, he is the prophet *par excellence*, the substance in fact of the speech by which the Father creates, redeems, and glorifies.

Prophet as Attorney

If Christ is the original Word in his very essence, the human expression of the prophetic office is founded on his mediatorial office as a copy. Prophets are not merely teachers, but lawyers who speak for God and intercede for the people. The relationship God establishes with Israel draws from the field of international politics rather than religious superstition. The Bible is

---

21. Unless otherwise noted, this author quotes from the ESV translation of the Bible.

dominated by the language of covenant (*berit*), meaning a pledge or treaty, covering a wide range of arrangements. Some covenants are based on Israel's oath to keep God's law, as at Sinai when the people promised, "All this we will do," while the covenant of grace is based on God's unilateral oath, "All this I will do." We see the latter type of covenant in God's promise to Adam and Eve after the fall (Gen 3:15), the Abrahamic covenant (Gen 15), the Davidic covenant (2 Sam 7), and the new covenant (Jer 31). Inaugurating the Holy Supper, Jesus refers to the wine as "the blood of the new covenant" or "testament" (*diatheke*); thus, we call the apostolic writings the New Testament.

Pagan prophets turn to the things God has made rather than to God himself. They pretend to *see* the future through the flight pattern of birds, reading animal entrails, the falling out of sticks, and so on. Instead, biblical prophets *hear* the word of the Lord. There is no realm of gods made manifest in images; there is one God. Moreover, this God is not merely called upon as a witness to human treaties but is the great King who issues the treaty. Only in Israel is the deity also the head of state. And this great King accomplishes his will by speaking.

Within this royal context, prophets are Yahweh's lawyers and ambassadors. They have "stood in his council" (a familiar phrase in Israel's prophetic literature) and are sent from the throne of the great King to bring his sovereign warnings, judgments, promises, and salvation to the nation. As ambassadors, they do not create policy but convey the great King's royal decrees. "For the Lord GOD does nothing without revealing his secret to his servants the prophets" (Amos 3:7). But the false prophets dare to "'speak visions of their own minds, not from the mouth of the LORD, . . . filling you with vain hopes,'" Yahweh judges. "'They say continually to those who despise the word of the LORD, 'It shall be well with you'; and to everyone who stubbornly follows his own heart, they say, 'No disaster shall come upon you.'" (Jer 23:16–17).

> For who among them has stood in the council of the LORD
>> to see and to hear his word,
>>> or who has paid attention to his word and listened?
> Behold, the storm of the LORD! . . .

"I did not send the prophets,
　　yet they ran;
I did not speak to them,
　　yet they prophesied.
But if they had stood in my council,
　　then they would have proclaimed my words to my people,
and they would have turned them from their evil way,
　　and from the evil of their deeds." (vv. 18–22)

The so-called prophets of the nations pretend to be possessed within by a god, while Israel's prophets are addressed externally by God in ordinary language and sent from his throne to bring his message to the people. The prophets of the nations pretend to divine the future through superstitious rites of spiritual technology (Deut 18:14–15). According to God's law, it is a capital crime to practice such things, and yet the false prophets of Israel and Judah spread lies based on divination and pretended visions (Isa 2:6; Jer 27:9; 29:8; 50:36; Zech 10:2).

We normally associate mediation with priesthood, but in Israel, prophets (and kings, as we will see) were mediators as well. In the exodus narrative, Moses is made "like God to Pharaoh," as he, along with Aaron, brings God's word of judgment to the king. Even before we come to the priestly work of Aaron and the Levitical line, the prophet is treated as a mediator. The response of the people at Sinai to which Moses refers is recounted in Exodus 19 and 20, in the context of the giving of the Ten Words amid solemn signs: "'You speak to us, and we will listen, but do not let God speak to us, lest we die.' . . . Then the people stood at a distance, while Moses drew near to the thick darkness where God was" (20:19–21). Like Adam after his transgression, Israel's first instinct is to take flight from God's holy presence. A mediator was needed: not only a priest to intercede for violation, but a prophet to mediate the words that otherwise fill the people with fear. The people asked for a mediator at Sinai and the Lord answered, "They are right in what they have spoken. I will raise up for them a prophet like you from among their brothers And I will put my words in his mouth, and he shall speak to them all that I command him," and all that he speaks will come to pass (Deut 18:17–18; see vv. 15–22).

This prophetic mediation is more fully developed as the story unfolds. At the very moment that Moses descends the mountain with the marriage covenant he received from God, the bride is committing spiritual adultery on her wedding night. Moses intercedes and Yahweh restrains his wrath, giving the people a stay of execution (Exod 32–34). This is the dual function of the prophetic ministry: representing the covenant Lord as prosecutor and the covenant people as a defense attorney. A frequent charge is that the people have broken the covenant their forebears swore at Mount Sinai. Representing God's interests rather than their own agendas, the prophets press God's case. They have not loved God or their neighbor; instead, they commit idolatry and oppress the poor, the widow, and the alien. In the covenant lawsuit, God sides with victims of injustice. Yahweh's law establishes the basis for the proper relationships with God and each other that would render Israel an oasis of peace and prosperity in a sea of false worship and cruelty. The prophet's blessings and curses are God's blessings and curses. They bring announcements from God that in fact execute God's announced intentions (e.g., Gen 24:7; 1 Kgs 13:18).

This underscores the fact that the New Testament eschatology briefly summarized above is at work already in the Old Testament. The history of covenant-breaking by the people (which has led to exile in the first place) confirms this. We see this, for example, in Psalm 74:

> We do not see our emblems;
>> there is no longer any prophet,
>> and there is no one among us who knows how long.
> How long, O God, is the foe to scoff?
>> Is the enemy to revile your name forever?
> Why do you hold back your hand;
>> why do you keep your hand in your bosom?
>
> Yet God my King is from of old,
>> working salvation in the earth. . . .
>
> Have regard for your covenant,
>> for the dark places of the land are full of the haunts of violence.

Do not let the downtrodden be put to shame;
　　let the poor and needy praise your name.
　　Rise up, O God, plead your cause. (vv. 9–12, 21–22 NRSVue)

All hope for the future begins to focus on the unilateral promise to David and his seed. Wherever the prophet announces judgment, it is on the basis of the failure to live up to the terms of the covenant at Sinai (the past and present), but whenever the announcement turns to good news, it is always because of the seed promised to Abraham and David (the future). A hopeful future is established not on the covenant that the people made with God (at Sinai), "yet I will remember my covenant with you in the days of your youth, and I will establish with you an everlasting covenant . . . when I forgive you all that you have done, says the Lord GOD" (Ezek 16:60, 63).

Jesus calls himself a prophet (Luke 13:33), bringing his Father's message (especially in John). He proclaims future events (Matt 24, etc.), speaks with an authority that is unlike that of the scribes (Matt 7:29), authenticates his message with signs, and is thus recognized as a prophet by the people (21:11, 46; Luke 7:16; 24:19; John 3:2; 4:19; 6:14; 7:40; 9:17). Jesus sees himself as the fulfilment of the prophetic writings (Matt 5:17; cf. 1:22), and John the Baptist insists, concerning himself, that he was not "the prophet" but merely the forerunner (John 1:21–23). Jesus regularly attests, notably in the fourth gospel, that he not only has stood in the council of the Lord but literally comes from the Father. He comes to fulfill the Father's eternal decree, ushering into the present the Spirit's "future" for us.

More than a Prophet

A prophet like Moses, Jesus is nevertheless qualitatively greater. In fact, looking back across the great expanse of Israel's history from the vantage point of Christ's advent, Moses and all the other prophets are like him. He is the consummate advocate, judge, and justifier of the ungodly. In the New Testament, we learn that Christ's prophetic office was exercised even in the Old Testament (1 Pet 1:11) and afterward by his Word and Spirit. The prophets themselves share Moses's hope in the greater prophet to come, "one shepherd" who will gather his flock that has been scattered by the false shepherds (Ezek 34:11–31). While the false prophets bring their own word of false comfort, God himself will lead his people according to the truth (Jer 23). The difference between true and false prophets is that only the former have "stood in the council of the Lord" (v. 18). Yet in this prophetic literature (particularly Ezek 34 and Jer 23), the coming shepherd-prophet will be no less than Yahweh himself.

First, Jesus is greater than the angels (*angeloi*, "messengers"), God's most illustrious prophets. Angels brought announcements from the throne of God, both of blessing and of judgment, and even executed God's announced intentions in some instances (Gen 19:1; 24:7; 1 Kgs 13:18; Luke 1:11–38). Yet Jesus *is* the Word in essence, consubstantial with the Father and the Spirit. Through this Word, all of creation, including angels, were summoned into existence. Thus, the heavenly hosts are summoned to worship him. "Of the Son he said, 'Your throne, O God, is forever'" (Heb 1:8). Centuries of exegesis have identified some of the angelic appearances as Christophanies, especially where the angel is identified with Yahweh (Gen 18:1–33; 32:22–32; Exod 23:23; 32:34; 33:2; 2 Sam 13:20; 1 Chr 21:16; Isa 63:9; Zech 3:1–10, etc.). In fact, the messianic figure who "will suddenly come to his temple" is none other than "the angel [messenger] of the covenant" in Malachi 3:1. Zechariah 3 describes a vision of Joshua the high priest standing before "the angel of the LORD" with Satan standing at his right hand to accuse Joshua, who appears before God's throne in "filthy garments." In this courtroom scene, we read, "The LORD said to Satan, 'The LORD rebuke you, O Satan! The LORD who has chosen Jerusalem rebuke you! Is not this a brand plucked from the fire?'" (Zech 3:1–3). Once again, the angel's speaking is identified as God's speaking. Like Moses interceding for the Israelites in the wilderness, the angel of the Lord is the defense attorney for Israel as representatively embodied in Joshua the high priest (vv. 1–10).

Second, Jesus is greater than Moses and all the prophets of Israel. He has not only stood in the council of the LORD, but he is both the LORD who speaks and the servant who hears and obeys. He is the mediator in creation and providence as well as in redemption. "In the beginning was the Word, and the Word was with God, and the Word was God. He was in the beginning with God. All things were made through him, and without him was not any thing made that was made" (John 1:1–3; cf. Col 1:15–16). Throughout the Gospel of John, Jesus refers to his relationship with the Father before the world was made. The prophets promised salvation, but Jesus accomplished it. God's servants prophesied the outpouring of the Spirit, but Jesus, with the Father, sent the Spirit and gives the Spirit without measure to his people. The coming prophet whom Moses prefigured and prophesied will also bring about a new state of affairs through his words and deeds. "For the law was given through Moses; grace and truth came through Jesus Christ" (John 1:17).

At Jesus's baptism, the Father announces the presence of "my beloved Son with whom I am well pleased" (Matt 3:17). Some people speculated that Jesus might be a resurrected Elijah (Matt 16:14). Indeed, there were parallels between Jesus's ministry and those of the primordial prophets, Moses and Elijah.

> As Moses engaged in sea crossings and wilderness feedings, so did Jesus. As Elijah healed people and brought a virtually dead child back to life and multiplied food, so did Jesus. . . . With all these clear parallels to Moses and Elijah, it is no surprise at all when Mark relates that people generally believed Jesus was a prophetic figure—either John the Baptist raised from the dead or Elijah or "a prophet like one of the prophets of old" (6:14–16; 8:27–28)—and that Jesus refers to himself as a prophet (6:4).[22]

Yet in the transfiguration, attended by the most illustrious and foundational prophets, Moses and Elijah, we read, "[Jesus] was still speaking when, behold, a bright cloud overshadowed them, and a voice from the cloud said, 'This is my beloved Son, with whom I am well pleased; listen to him'" (Matt 17:5). He is the prophet greater than Moses (Deut 18:15; 34:12; see also 18:15 with Acts 3:18–24 and Heb 3:1–6). While Moses was a faithful servant in God's house, Jesus is God's Son (Heb 3:1–6; cf. 8:1–13). Jesus is both the

---

22. Richard A. Horsley, *Hearing the Whole Story: The Politics of Plot in Mark's Gospel* (Louisville: Westminster John Knox, 2001), 238.

Lord of the covenant who commands and the servant who obeys, the king and the ambassador.

Jesus is not simply another Moses. He not only acts as a mediator on behalf of Israel but offers forgiveness of sins in his person—which aroused the consternation of the religious leaders (Luke 7:48–49). Moreover, he assumes the authority to replace political laws of the Mosaic economy with commands for the new covenant: "You have heard that it was said, '. . . ,' but I say, '. . . .'" This formula Jesus gives on his Sermon on the Mount differs from Moses's commission at Mount Sinai. While Moses could only relate the commands God wrote with his finger, Jesus speaks *as* God (Matt 5:17–7:27). "When Jesus finished these sayings, the crowds were astonished at his teaching, for he was teaching them as one who had authority, and not as their scribes" (7:28–29).

Nor is Jesus simply another Elijah. True, Jesus announces Yahweh's covenant judgment on the faithless nation as Elijah did, but for the most part Jesus identifies this ministry of judgment and mourning with John the Baptist and his own ministry with a joyful wedding celebration (Matt 11:1–19; 17:10–13; cf. 3:1–13).

When Jesus enters Jerusalem triumphantly on a donkey, he executes the covenant curses on the Temple Mount itself (Matt 21). He drives out the money changers (vv. 12–17). Cursing the fig tree, he declares, "May no one eat of your fruit again" (vv. 18–22). The religious leaders challenge his authority for these actions, but Jesus replies by telling the parable of the wicked tenants (vv. 33–42). He is the Son sent by the Father who owns the vineyard (Israel: see Isaiah 5) and murdered by the tenants. He is the Israel vindicated by the Father and returning in judgment. The message of the prophets brought division in Israel. However, Jesus himself is the "rock of offense" who has become the cornerstone (Matt 21:33–42; cf. Isa 8:14 with 1 Pet 2:8 and Rom 9:33). The Rock of Israel is none other than Yahweh (e.g., Exod 17:6; 33:22; Isa 44:8; 1 Cor 10:4). Jesus is the new temple, redrawing the boundaries of Israel around himself. "'Therefore I tell you, the kingdom of God will be taken away from you and given to a people producing its fruits. And the one who falls on this stone will be broken to pieces; and when it falls on anyone, it will crush him'" (Matt 21:43–44). Jesus's parables not only describe what is happening but cause the events to unfold: "When the chief priests and the Pharisees heard his parables, they perceived that he was speaking about them. And although they were seeking to arrest him, they feared the crowds, because they held him to be a prophet" (vv. 45–46).

The prophets themselves share Moses's hope in the greater prophet to come, "one shepherd" who will gather his flock that has been scattered by the false shepherds (Jer 23; Ezek 34:11–31). While the false prophets bring their own word of false comfort, God himself will lead his people. Scattering is always a sign of judgment, from the expulsion of humans from the garden to the scattering of the nations at Babel to the exile itself, but the gospel announces a gathering to take place under the true and faithful Shepherd, the prophet greater than Moses. Indeed, in this prophetic literature (particularly Ezek 34 and Jer 23), the coming shepherd-prophet will be no less than Yahweh himself.

Third, Jesus is greater than the prophets because he is not only the messenger but the message, not only a prophet but the prophecy, not only a word spoken in time but the only begotten Word from all eternity, not only truth proclaimed but the Truth in the flesh. All the prophets spoke about him (Luke 24:25–27; John 5:39; 14:6). The apostles join the prophets in heralding Christ rather than themselves (2 Cor 4:5). Peter tells us that the Holy Spirit, speaking through the prophets, concentrated all attention on "the suffering of Christ" and "the good news" (1 Pet 1:10–12). The heart of the prophetic revelation is "the gospel of God, which he promised beforehand through his prophets in the holy Scriptures, concerning his Son" (Rom 1:1–3). In proclaiming the Father and his kingdom, Jesus proclaims himself. In doing so, he inaugurates the new world of which he speaks. And in the book of Acts, the apostles proclaimed "in Jesus the resurrection from the dead" (4:2). Paul was baptized "and immediately he proclaimed Jesus in the synagogues, saying, 'He is the Son of God'" (9:20). The preaching of Jesus as the climax and focus of God's saving revelation is the sum of all the sermons in Acts and the doctrinal instruction in the Epistles. From its opening verses, the book of Revelation centers on the incarnate Word:

> Grace to you and peace from him who is and who was and who is to come, and from the seven spirits who are before his throne, and from

Jesus Christ the faithful witness, the firstborn of the dead, and the ruler of kings on earth.

To him who loves us and has freed us from our sins by his blood and made us a kingdom, priests to his God and Father, to him be glory and dominion forever and ever. Amen. Behold, he is coming with the clouds, and every eye will see him, even those who pierced him, and all tribes of the earth will wail on account of him. Even so. Amen.

"I am the Alpha and the Omega," says the Lord God, "who is and who was and who is to come, the Almighty." (Rev 1:4–8)

Thus, Jesus is not only the prophet who speaks God's word but the human servant of the covenant who fulfills it and bears the curse for our transgressions. The proper atonement correlate for the prophetic office of Christ then is not the exemplarist or moral influence theory, but rather the active obedience of Christ and our union with him in that obedience. He has fulfilled perfectly the law that Adam, Israel, and we have all failed to keep.

Bearing our curse on the cross, Jesus "was raised for our justification" (Rom 4:25). He does not merely show us the way but is the way (John 14:6). As the new Adam, Jesus comes as the "faithful and true witness" (Rev. 3:14), the climactic and final Word from God (Heb 1:2). As the embodiment of God's command and promise, he not only judges and justifies but is himself "born of woman, born under the law, to redeem those who were under the law, so that we might receive adoption as sons" (Gal 4:4–5). In other words, even as prophet he takes his side with God in judgment and with us in listening to "'every word that comes from the mouth of God'" (Matt 4:4). He is therefore not only our vicarious sacrifice in his priestly office but in his prophetic office as well. The one who announces the covenant curses in the Gospels obeys the law in our place and bears them for us. He speaks both for God and for us, answering God's command (which is his own) representatively with a life consonant with our proper reply, "Here I am" (Isa 8:18 with Heb 2:13).

Still more, he is the Lord of the covenant in whose council the prophets stood and received their commission, just as the apostles received theirs as those who stood in his council as the incarnate Word. So when Jesus sends the apostles, only those who had been in his immediate presence were qualified to hold this office. Having committed his new covenant word to them by the Spirit as he promised in the upper room (John 14–16), Jesus speaks to us now through this word as it is proclaimed (Rom 10:1–17). And now he anoints us as prophets, sending us out to bring his word in the power of the Spirit (Matt 28:16–20; 1 John 1:1–4; 2:20–22).

Jesus was charged by the religious leaders not merely as a false prophet but as a blasphemer for making himself equal with God (Matt 26:64–66; Mark 2:7; John 5:15, 18; 10:33). Islam holds Jesus to be the greatest prophet until Muhammed. Indeed, Jesus is honored in many religions as a prophet, Bodhisattva, moralist, or enlightened teacher. Yet even if one rejects the claims Jesus made concerning himself in the Gospels, it is a fact attested by ancient Jewish and Roman sources that he was sentenced on the charge of blasphemy.

CHAPTER 1

THE CHURCH AS CHRIST'S PROPHETESS

WILSON JEREMIAH

I was raised in a conservative evangelical Chinese congregations in Indonesia, which included both the China-born *totok* and the accultur-ated *peranakan*.[1] Both of my parents are alumni and faculty of the seminary at which I currently teach, *Seminari Alkitab Asia Tenggara* (SAAT). It is an inter- or transdenominational seminary founded by Chinese missionaries and has since trained ministers to various church denominations, not just within evangelicalism but also in mainline churches.[2] While these churches

---

1. For more discussions on the history of my ecclesial tradition, see Jan Sihar Aritonang and Karel Steenbrink, "The Spectacular Growth of The Third Stream: The Evangelicals and Pentecostals," in *A History of Christianity in Indonesia*, ed. Jan Sihar Aritonang and Karel Steenbrink (Leiden: Brill, 2008), 867–902; Yusak Soleiman and Karel Steenbrink, "Chinese Christian Communities in Indonesia," in Aritonang and Steenbrink, *A History of Christianity in Indonesia*, 903–24; Albert R. Konaniah, "A Comparative Study on the Missionary Methodologies of the Evangelical and Ecumenical Churches in Indonesia" (DMiss diss., Reformed Theological Seminary, 1995); Susy Ong, "Ethnic Chinese Religions: Some Recent Developments," in *Ethnic Chinese in Contemporary Indonesia*, ed. Leo Suryadinata (Singapore: Chinese Heritage Centre and Institute of Southeast Asian Studies, 2008), 97–116; Chang-Yau Hoon, "'By Race, I am Chinese; and By Grace, I am Christian': Negotiating Chineseness and Christianity in Indonesia," in *Chinese Indonesians Reassessed: History, Religion and Belonging*, ed. Siew-Min Sai and Chang-Yau Hoon (London: Routledge, 2013), 159–77; Chang-Yau Hoon, "Between Evangelism and Multiculturalism: The Dynamics of Protestant Christianity in Indonesia," *Social Compass* 60, no. 4 (2013): 457–70; Chang-Yau Hoon, "Mapping Chineseness on the landscape of Christian Churches in Indonesia," *Asian Ethnicity* 17, no. 2 (2016): 228–47; Chang-Yau Hoon, "Reconceptualising Ethnic Chinese Identity in Post-Suharto Indonesia" (PhD thesis, University of Western Australia, 2006), 5.

2. To compare, one can say that this seminary (Seminari Alkitab Asia Tenggara, SAAT) is in many ways similar to Trinity Evangelical Divinity School (TEDS) in Deerfield, Illinois, where I took my doctoral studies, in that it is a broadly evangelical school with close affiliation to the Evangelical Free Church of America (EFCA), but it is not specifically managed by or under the same board with the EFCA. In SAAT's case, it is closely affiliated with the synod of *Gereja Kristen Kalam Kudus* (GKKK, Holy Word Christian Church). For more historical details, see Hoon, "Mapping Chineseness," 237–38.

tend to be conservative evangelical churches, doctrinal commonalities are generally less evident than social and cultural affinities. If an evangelical in North America can be described as "anyone who likes Billy Graham" (and perhaps others like Charles G. Finney, Dwight L. Moody, and Billy Sunday),[3] one can also say that a Chinese-Indonesian evangelical is anyone who likes John Sung, Andrew Gih, and Stephen Tong, among many others.[4] Chinese evangelical churches in Indonesia are primarily formed through a network of trust and other sociocultural properties and less through a common confessional standard, which is not usually regarded as an all-too-important qualification for membership.[5] Even in churches that belong to particular confessional traditions, it is often the case that such beliefs and practices are little known and passed down from generation to generation.[6] By and large, this posture of relegating doctrine to a minor position, whether consciously or unconsciously, is not uncommon among the evangelical Chinese traditional denominations.[7] In particular, ecclesiology is often marginalized as a distraction from the Christian life and mission.

---

3. Daniel Silliman, "An Evangelical Is Anyone Who Likes Billy Graham: Defining Evangelicalism with Carl Henry and Network of Trust," *Church History* 90, no. 3 (2021): 621–43.

4. Aritonang and Steenbrink tend to associate Indonesian "evangelicals" with the more conservative Christians, including fundamentalists, closely linked to American missionaries in the early twentieth century who founded many churches in Indonesia ("The Spectacular Growth," 869–79). However, that is not entirely accurate since many Indonesian evangelical churches were also founded by European missionaries and Chinese evangelists. The latter adhere more closely to the Pietistic and Revivalist traditions. See further Hoon, "Mapping Chineseness," 237. My point still stands, that Chinese evangelical churches in Indonesia are *Chinese* by following closely those esteemed pastors and evangelists whose names are mentioned above.

5. For example, Hoon tells us that many Chinese churches in early twentieth century Indonesia "became part of the *Bond Kristen Tionghoa* (BKT, or the Chinese Christian Union), which was formed in 1926," whose aim "was to unite all Chinese churches in Indonesia *regardless of their denominations, doctrines*, and *backgrounds* and to encourage them to break away from Western missions." Hoon, "Mapping Chineseness," 232, emphasis added.

6. As Hoon described, many of these Chinese churches cling more to their "Chineseness" that can be "traced within identity outlooks, *habitus*, and leadership and management styles of the individual churches" ("Mapping Chineseness," 231). To be fair, there must be quite a number of evangelical Chinese churches in Indonesia who care about doctrinal integrity and adherence to certain tradition. For example, one presbyterian church in Indonesia where I once served necessitates that their pastors subscribe to the Westminster Standards. However, in my experience of serving in one of their local churches, I could not see how the Standards are taught frequently to the congregation in catechetical classes nor discussed or even rethought by the pastoral team in terms of its contemporary relevance, and Sunday school classes typically follow the speaker's respective doctrinal positions that are either not Reformed or, at least, they are not self-consciously so.

7. Hoon, "Mapping Chineseness," 228–29, rightly mentions that Chinese-Indonesian Christianity has not received much scholarly attention partly due to the socio-political influences of the "New Order" by the Suharto administration in 1966–1998 whose assimilation policy suppressed

FROM ELIZABETH W. MBURU

Similarly, many churches in Africa are formed along sociocultural identity markers such as ethnicity rather than doctrinal commonalities. This can be traced back to the African worldview regarding people, which can best be described as "existence in relationship," also known as Ubuntu. It defines what it means to be human. However, despite this worldview of Ubuntu, negative ethnicity still rears its ugly head. This is because the concept of the ethnic group has both an objective and a subjective dimension. The subjective dimension is characterized by the presence of sociopsychological boundaries whose major characteristics are group inclusion and exclusion. Ethnic identity is so strong that the "other" is often regarded in dehumanizing terms. This results in negative ethnicity, which often finds expression in how churches are formed. Ethnic identity frequently overshadows Christian identity.

My goal in this essay is to highlight the relevance of the church's sharing in Christ's prophetic office, drawing especially on the insights of the Dutch theologian Herman Bavinck.[8] Especially in recent decades, the reflections of Herman Bavinck have received considerable interest as Asian churches seek to understand Christ's ministry in their own context.

---

and forced the Chinese minority to adopt a new identity. Cf. Soleiman and Steenbrink, "Chinese Christian Communities," 903. After Suharto's regime ended, however, the Chinese Christians of many Indonesian churches have started reclaiming their identities.

　　8. This chapter thus also contributes to this new wave of Bavinck scholarship that has yet to discuss his christological (*munus triplex*) ecclesiology in detail and in connection to Bavinck's whole dogmatic thinking. See, e.g., James Eglinton, *Trinity and Organism: Towards a New Reading of Herman Bavinck's Organic Motif* (London: T&T Clark, 2012); Cory C. Brock, *Orthodox yet Modern: Herman Bavinck's Use of Friedrich Schleiermacher* (Bellingham, WA: Lexham, 2020); Brian G. Mattson, *Restored to Our Destiny: Eschatology and the Image of God in Herman Bavinck's Reformed Dogmatics* (Leiden: Brill, 2011); N. Gray Sutanto, *God and Knowledge: Herman Bavinck's Theological Epistemology* (London: T&T Clark, 2020); Ximian Xu, *Theology As the Science of God: Herman Bavinck's* Wetenschappelijke *Theology for the Modern World* (Göttingen: Vandenhoeck & Ruprecht, 2022). Only Bruce R. Pass, as far as I know, has given some considerable space in tracing Bavinck's ecclesiology to his thinking on revelation, image of God, and Christology in his *The Heart of Dogmatics: Christology and Christocentrism in Herman Bavinck* (Göttingen: Vandenhoeck & Ruprecht, 2020), 144–55, though he did not discuss Bavinck's view on the church's spiritual *power* much. The recent and otherwise helpful introduction to neo-Calvinist theology also did not cover the Christology and the *munus triplex* in Bavinck's theology of the church and the world. See Cory C. Brock and N. Gray Sutanto, *Neo-Calvinism: A Theological Introduction* (Bellingham, WA: Lexham, 2023), chap. 9.

THE PROPHETHOOD OF ALL BELIEVERS

The Westminster Confession of Faith (WCF) 8.1 says this of our Lord Jesus Christ: "It pleased God, in his eternal purpose, to choose and ordain the Lord Jesus, his only begotten Son, to be the Mediator between God and man, the Prophet, Priest, and King, the Head and Savior of his church, the Heir of all things, and Judge of the world: unto whom he did from all eternity give a people, to be his seed, and to be by him in time redeemed, called, justified, sanctified, and glorified."[9] It has been customary in the Reformed tradition to extol Christ as the true prophet, priest, and king as he is *the* image of God, "the reflection of God's glory and the exact imprint of God's very being" (Heb 1:3; cf. 2 Cor 4:4; Col 1:15).[10] At the same time, believers are united to Christ and share in his anointing. Practical wisdom requires careful exegesis and doctrinal reflection here.[11] So how might Christians today bear witness to the world that Christ indeed is our prophet, priest, and king? Focusing on his prophetic office, I will explore how our participation in Christ affects the church's understanding of itself and its mission.

First, the Son was not invested in this office merely when he became incarnate. Throughout the Old Testament, he exercised his prophetic ministry by the Spirit through those he chose and called to bring his word. Christ has always had his church. As Louis Berkhof nicely summarizes,

> [Christ] exercised His prophetical office immediately, as the Angel of the Lord in the Old Testament period, and as the incarnate Lord by His teachings and also by His example. . . . And He exercised it mediately through the operation of the Holy Spirit, by means of the teachings of the Old Testament prophets, and of the New Testament apostles,

---

9. Taken from G. I. Williamson, *The Westminster Confession of Faith: For Study Classes*, 2nd ed. (Phillipsburg, NJ: P&R, 2003).

10. For a recent discussion of the Reformed use of the threefold office (*munus triplex*), see Ivor J. Davidson, "Christ," in *The Oxford Handbook of Reformed Theology*, ed. Michael Allen and Scott R. Swain (Oxford: Oxford University Press, 2020), 463–68. Unless otherwise noted, all biblical references are taken from the New Revised Standard Version, updated edition (NRSVue).

11. I am assuming Michael S. Horton's definition in his *Covenant and Eschatology: The Divine Drama* (Louisville: Westminster John Knox, 2002), 4: "Theology is the church's reflection on God's performative action in *word* and *deed* and its own participation in the drama of redemption" (emphasis added).

and exercises it even now through the indwelling Spirit in believers, and by the agency of the ministers of the gospel. This also means that He carries on His prophetical work both objectively and externally and subjectively and internally by the Spirit, which is described as the Spirit of Christ.[12]

In short, Christ's prophethood and its exercise have, more often than not, been done through the Spirit's agency in the lives of Israel in the Old Testament (Gen 12:1–3; Deut 18:15–22; Isa 30:18–26; Jer 23) and the church in the New (Gal 3:8; 6:16). Even when humanity failed to function as Christ's prophet, through Christ's atoning and redemptive act they are once again called to do so (1 Pet 2:1–10). Through the outpouring and inbreathing of the Holy Spirit, it is not just a few Christians who are enabled to become prophets but "all flesh" (Joel 2:28–32; John 20:22; Acts 2:17–21).[13]

How then should the church today exercise this prophetic embassy? In Reformed theology, as in others, this is answered by referring to the "marks" of the church. The prophetic office is executed by faithfully preaching and teaching the Word, the priestly office to the task of administering the sacraments, and the kingly office to the care and discipline of Christ's flock.[14] Thus, Christ himself is building, serving, and overseeing his church. The church not only witnesses to Christ and on his behalf, but Christ is addressing people through the ministry: "Therefore, we are ambassadors for Christ, God making his appeal through us. We implore you on behalf of Christ, be reconciled to God" (2 Cor 5:20 ESV). Thus, our ecclesiology should be more christological.[15] The church is first of all not active but acted upon; before it can bring the word of Christ to the world, it comes into being wherever this word is preached. These moves are basically structured around Craig Van

---

12. Louis Berkhof, *Systematic Theology: New Combined Edition* (Grand Rapids: Eerdmans, 1996), 301.

13. Robert Sherman, *Covenant, Community, and the Spirit: A Trinitarian Theology of the Church* (Grand Rapids: Baker Academic, 2015), 175.

14. Cf. the Belgic Confession, art. 29, in *Our Faith: Ecumenical Creeds, Reformed Confessions, and Other Resources* (Grand Rapids: Faith Alive, 2013).

15. For recent works that move toward demonstrating the need for a more christological ecclesiology, see Kimlyn J. Bender, *Karl Barth's Christological Ecclesiology* (Aldershot, UK: Ashgate, 2005); Michael S. Horton, *People and Place: A Covenant Ecclesiology* (Louisville: Westminster John Knox, 2008), chap. 6.

Gelder's thinking that a "full-orbed missiological ecclesiology" should be aware of these three interrelated aspects: "The church is. The church does what it is. The church organizes what it does."[16] It is impossible to do and organize a church well without a proper understanding of its nature and *telos*.

HERMAN BAVINCK'S CHRISTOLOGICAL ACCOUNT OF THE CHURCH'S SPIRITUAL POWER AND AUTHORITY

We sometimes assume that a high view of the church will push Jesus to the margins. There are many examples to substantiate this concern. However, as Craig Bartholomew says, "A big, biblical view of Christ will result in a big view of the church."[17] Besides being a theologian, Bavinck actually lived out his theology well in his vocation as a university professor, ordained minister, and public theologian and philosopher.[18] Bavinck emphatically stressed that "a church without a theology is a body without a head. A theology without the church dies. A church without theology languishes."[19] In other words, as Bavinck likes to put it, theology and the church are one organism. It is impossible to have one without the other: "[The church and theology] form one whole, an organism; they belong together closely. Both are the fruits of the activity of the Holy Spirit. Or more preferably, the Church, with everything that belongs to it, is wholly a creation of the Spirit. So is theology in it."[20]

---

16. Craig Van Gelder, *The Essence of the Church: A Community Created by the Spirit* (Grand Rapids: Baker, 2000), 37. On the importance of theological ecclesiology, see John Webster, "In the Society of God: Some Principles of Ecclesiology," in *God without Measure: Working Papers in Christian Theology*, vol. 1 (London: Bloomsbury, 2016), 177–94.

17. Craig G. Bartholomew, *Contours of the Kuyperian Tradition: A Systematic Introduction* (Downers Grove, IL: IVP Academic, 2017), 161.

18. Brock and Sutanto, *Neo-Calvinism*, 250; Cory C. Brock, "Bavinck as Public Theologian: Philosophy, Ethics, and Politics," *Unio Cum Christo* 6, no. 2 (2020): 115–31; and for more details, James Eglinton, *Bavinck: A Critical Biography* (Grand Rapids: Baker Academic, 2020).

19. Herman Bavinck, "De Wetenschappelijke Roeping Onzer Kerk," *De Vrije Kerk* 8, no. 2–3 (1882): 98, quoted and translated by Ximian Xu, "The Scientific Calling of the Church: Herman Bavinck's Exhortation for the Churches in Mainland China," *Studies in World Christianity* 27, no. 2 (2021): 149.

20. Bavinck, "De Wetenschappelijke Roeping Onzer Kerk," 100, in Xu, "The Scientific Calling of the Church," 150.

Thus perhaps if the church is the body of Christ, who has come into the world in an embodied form, its witness and effect should also be able to be heard, seen, looked at, and touched (1 John 1:1) so that the world might comprehend how great Christ is.

That is why Bavinck has a high regard for the visible church as an organism *and* institution. Bavinck recognizes that the church has always been understood as a gathered community *and* the mother of believers: "The two are given in conjunction and continually interact with and impact each other."[21] Hence, the people of God are simultaneously and paradoxically the product *and* the producer. The invisible church "is gathered and formed within the visible Church" and it "is inherent in and contained by the visible one."[22] Contrary to common misperceptions that Protestantism has a low view of the church, Bavinck and his Reformed predecessors at least think highly enough of the church that they could affirm Cyprian's dictum that there is no salvation outside the church ("*extra ecclesiam nulla salus*"). Again, the WCF 25.2 puts it well: "The visible church, which is also catholic or universal under the gospel (not confined to one nation, as before under the law), consists of all those throughout the world that profess the true religion; and of their children: and is the kingdom of the Lord Jesus Christ, the house and family of God, *out of which there is no ordinary possibility of salvation*."[23] Indeed, the visible church is the chosen instrument for the continuation of Christ's redemptive work, an indispensable means to bring about the kingdom of God on this side of eternity.

Such a high valuation of the visible church is indeed rooted in Bavinck's conception of the *munus triplex* as a significant part of the

---

21. Herman Bavinck, *Reformed Dogmatics*, ed. John Bolt, trans. John Vriend, 4 vols. (Grand Rapids: Baker Academic, 2003–2008), 4:332. Hereafter *RD* with corresponding volume and page number.

22. *Synopsis of Purer Theology* (1625), Latin Text and English Translation, vol. 2, ed. Henk van den Belt, trans. Riemer A. Faber (Leiden: Brill, 2016), disp. 40, thesis 34.

23. Emphasis added. Cf. Bavinck, *RD*, 4:289: "And it is really a Reformed doctrine that, though God *ordinarily* grants the benefits of Christ by means of Word and sacraments, he is not bound to this method and, be it very rarely, also grants salvation outside the institution of the church." From this, it should be clear that Bavinck and other Reformed theologians do not affirm the Cyprian dictum the same way the Roman Catholic Church does. See also the Belgic Confession, art. 28; Brock and Sutanto, *Neo-Calvinism*, 251; Dennis W. Jowers, "In What Sense Does Calvin Affirm 'Extra Ecclesiam Nulla Sallus,'" in *John Calvin's Ecclesiology: Ecumenical Perspectives*, eds. Gerard Mannion and Eduardus Van der Borght (London: T&T Clark, 2011), 50–68.

multifaceted work of Christ.[24] The church is "used by Christ as an instrument to bring others to his fold. By it Christ administers *his mediatorial office* in the midst of the world."[25] "Inasmuch as on earth the church is a church in process of *becoming*," says Bavinck, the institutional church exists along with its offices and government "by hypothetical necessity"—that is, according to the good pleasure and sovereignty of the triune God, as he decreed that the gospel of Jesus Christ be preached through his church.[26] Bavinck adds,

> Already designated mediator from eternity, Christ carried out his prophetic, priestly, and kingly office from the time of paradise, continued it in the days of the Old Testament and during his sojourn on earth, and now fulfills it in heaven, where he is seated at the Father's right hand. And this activity of Christ does not presuppose the existence of the church—except as conceived and willed in God's eternal counsel—but precedes and produces it. . . . But in still another sense as well the church is not conceivable without a government. Granted, Christ could have exercised his office without any service from humans. If it had so pleased him, he could have dispensed his spiritual and heavenly blessings without the help of institutions and persons. But this was not his pleasure; it was his pleasure, without in any way transferring his sovereignty to people, to nevertheless use their services in the exercise of his sovereignty and to preach the gospel through them to all creatures. And also in that sense the church was never without a government. It was always organized and institutionally arranged in some fashion.[27]

---

24. For a helpful exposition on Bavinck's view of the *munus triplex* in his Christology and anthropology, see Matthew Kaemingk, "Christology and Economic Ethics: Herman Bavinck's Prophet, Priest, and King in the Marketplace," *Journal of Biblical and Theological Studies* 6, no. 2 (2021): 383–400. Kaemingk did mention, albeit too briefly, how the *munus triplex* informs Bavinck's ecclesiology (394–95).

25. Bavinck, *RD*, 4:330, emphasis added.

26. Bavinck, *RD*, 4:329. The term *hypothetical necessity* can also be called a *conditional necessity* or *necessity of the consequence* that is usually contrasted with an *absolute necessity*. See further Richard A. Muller, *Dictionary of Latin and Greek Theological Terms: Drawn Principally from Protestant Scholastic Theology*, 2nd ed. (Grand Rapids: Baker Academic, 2017), s.v. *necessitas consequentiae*.

27. Bavinck, *RD*, 4:329.

Bavinck's christological ecclesiology thus motivates or, rather, necessitates the church—as the community of the elect and beloved of the triune God—to function and govern her people in the manner that Christ as her head exercises his mediatorial role as prophet, priest, and king (1 Pet 2:9).

Marks and Offices

A major reason for the institution of the church, according to Bavinck, is due to human sin and fallenness. Human beings fail to live according to the knowledge, righteousness, and holiness to reflect the image of Christ (cf. Rom 8:29; Eph 4:24; Col 3:10). Through Christ's incarnation and his atoning work, fallen humans are once again enabled and called to fulfill their original mandate to become prophets, priests, and kings.[28] In short, the *munus triplex* constitutes the functional aspect of what it means to be human, and so Christ's redemptive work provides the way back for humanity to live as the image of God:

> The truth is that the idea of humanness already encompasses within itself this threefold dignity and activity. Human beings have a head to know, a heart to give themselves, a hand to govern and to lead; correspondingly, they were in the beginning equipped by God with knowledge and understanding, with righteousness and holiness, with dominion and glory (blessedness). The sin that corrupted human beings infected all their capacities and consisted not only in ignorance, folly, error, lies, blindness, darkness but also in unrighteousness, guilt, moral degradation, and further in misery, death, and ruin. Therefore Christ, both as the Son and as the image of God, for himself and also as our mediator and savior, had to bear all three offices. He had to be a prophet to know and to disclose the truth of God; a priest, to devote himself to God and, in our place, to offer himself up to God; a king,

---

28. Bavinck speaks of Adam not only as a "micro-divine-being" but also as the image of God: "He is the prophet who explains God and proclaims his excellencies; he is the priest who consecrates himself with all that is created to God as a holy offering; he is the king who guides and governs all things in justice and rectitude. And in all this he points to One who in a still higher and richer sense is the revelation and image of God, to him who is the only begotten of the Father, and the firstborn of all creatures. Adam, the son of God, was a type of Christ." Bavinck, *RD*, 2:562.

to govern and protect us according to God's will. To teach, to reconcile, and to lead; to instruct, to acquire, and to apply salvation; wisdom, righteousness, and redemption; truth, love, and power—all three are essential to the completeness of our salvation.[29]

In other words, Christ's threefold office is not arbitrarily instituted to his humanity and human beings in general, but because sin corrupts the *whole* of human beings, the means to bring about the completeness of salvation must also be multilayered to solve a variety of human problems. It does not mean that all of Christ's redemptive work can be reduced only to the threefold office, but Bavinck's point is that this is a crucial aspect of it.[30]

Moreover, this important salvific scheme, Bavinck argues, provides the key to understanding the significance of the institution of the ecclesial offices, where each has its proper tasks and responsibilities that constitute the true marks of the church:

> The Reformed, by restoring the office of elder and that of deacon alongside that of the minister of the Word, have most accurately grasped the idea of Scripture and most firmly recognized the rights of

---

29. Bavinck, *RD*, 3:367–68. A question that might arise is whether Christ's threefold office is only "economic" and temporarily instituted for the salvation of fallen humans. Bavinck was aware of this and argued that the threefold office would remain even in the state of glory for it is essential to Christ's humanity, as he anticipated against those who would insist that it is only temporary: "The difference can be easily resolved by saying that the mediatorship of *reconciliation*, and to that extent also the prophetic, priestly, and royal office of Christ, ends. God will be king and [thus] all in all. But what remains is the mediatorship of *union*. Christ remains the prophet, priest, and king as this triple office is automatically given with his human nature, included in the image of God, and realized supremely and most magnificently in Christ as the Image of God. Christ is and remains the head of the church, from whom all life and blessedness flow to it throughout all eternity. Those who would deny this must also arrive at the doctrine that the Son will at some point in the future shed and destroy his human nature; and for this there is no scriptural ground whatever." *RD*, 3:482, emphasis added. If Bavinck is correct, this way of thinking demonstrates an even closer relation of the threefold office to what it means to be human (and the church), for Christ or humanity in general. However, this seems to bring to the surface a tension in Bavinck's own thinking, for he elsewhere rejects supralapsarian Christology, which is clearly presupposed here (cf. *RD*, 3:277–80; Pass, *The Heart of Dogmatics*, 155–65). Resolving this issue is beyond the scope of this chapter, but I simply refer interested readers to consider Oliver Crisp's way out of the same conundrum in Calvin's theology in his *Revisioning Christology: Theology in the Reformed Tradition* (Farnham, UK: Ashgate, 2011), chap. 2.

30. As rightly cautioned by Adam J. Johnson, "The Servant Lord: A Word of Caution Regarding the *Munus Triplex* in Karl Barth's Theology and the Church Today," *Scottish Journal of Theology* 65, no. 2 (2012): 159–73.

the local church. . . . From heaven he governs his church on earth by his Word and Spirit, by his prophetic as well as his priestly and royal activity. He continues the exercise of these three offices on earth, not exclusively yet also by means of the offices he has instituted. . . . These office-bearers are . . . the best, not in money and possessions but in spiritual gifts, whom he himself equips and allows the church to set apart for his service. By them he takes care of the spiritual and material interests of his church. By the teaching office he instructs, by the office of elder he leads, and by the diaconal office he takes care of his flock. And by all three of them in conjunction he proves himself to be our chief prophet, our eternal king, and our merciful high priest.[31]

Here again, the emphasis is clear: the ecclesial offices must work as one, just as the *munus triplex* can never be separated from one another. But another thing must also be underscored—that is, the nature and power of those offices, which are important to differentiate between regarding the role of the church and that of the state. For the former, after surveying the scriptural references that pertain to the ecclesial offices, Bavinck insists that all their power "is spiritual and moral in nature, essentially distinct from all other power that God has bestowed on persons over people or other creatures in the family, society, state, art, and science."[32] And his rationale is christological: "For Jesus acted in no way other than as the Christ—as prophet, priest, and king. He had no other office nor performed any other function."[33] This explains why the church's ministry as an *institution* should mainly focus on the spiritual, although Bavinck understands the gospel as a "leaven" that affects and redeems everything, including the natural or secular realm, and that the church as an organism indeed can become witness to Christ outside

---

31. Bavinck, *RD*, 4:388. Also Bavinck: "Accordingly, in connection with the offices of pastor, presbyter, and deacon and further in connection with the threefold office of Christ—the prophetic, the royal, and the priestly office—we must distinguish three kinds of power in Christ's church: the power to teach, the power to govern (of which the power to discipline is a part), and the power or rather the ministry of mercy" (ibid., 418).

32. Bavinck, *RD*, 4:395.

33. Bavinck, *RD*, 4:395.

the walls of the church.[34] Nevertheless, the institutional, ecclesial offices that represent Christ's continuing mediatorial offices in a unique way should therefore attend strictly to the spiritual need of the people in the church. In Bavinck's view, this spiritual power and authority of the church manifest most visibly in the teaching office that corresponds to the prophetic office.

The Church as Christ's Prophetess

Before getting into more specifics on the practical things that Bavinck suggested for any prophetic church, two caveats are in order. First, as Bavinck keeps reminding us, it is *Christ* who exercises his prophetic office by his word and spirit through the teaching office: "Christ never transferred it to any human being and never appointed any pope or bishop, pastor or teacher, to be his special deputy and surrogate, but he is still continually our chief prophet, who from his place in heaven teaches his church by Word and Spirit."[35] Thus, Bavinck is critical of the Roman Catholic view of his day that tended to put more premium on the sacraments above the administration of the word, especially during public services or other official meetings done in the church.[36] Second, when Bavinck states that the church is a "prophetess," he truly meant to say that "all Christians share in Christ's anointing and are called to confess his name" and are not just the "office bearers in the strict sense."[37] But still, Bavinck argues that scripture has set apart the name "teacher" as "the characteristic title of the minister of the Word" (e.g., Acts 20:27; Eph 4:11; 1 Tim 5:17). In short, the teaching pastors or elders in an

---

34. "There is a difference in nature, for the power of the church is spiritual, but the power of the political government is natural, earthly, secular. It extends to all subjects for no other reason than the fact that they are subjects and only regulates their earthly interests. They differ in purpose, for ecclesiastical power serves the upbuilding of the body of Christ, but political power is defined by its purpose in this life and strives for the natural and common good. They differ in the means employed, for the church only has spiritual weapons, but the government bears the sword, has power over life and death, and may exact obedience by coercion and violence." Bavinck, *RD*, 4:415; cf. Bavinck, "The Catholicity of Christianity and the Church," trans. John Bolt, *Calvin Theological Journal* 27, no. 2 (1992): 220–51; John Bolt, "Herman Bavinck on Natural Law and Two Kingdoms: Some Further Reflections," *The Bavinck Review* 4 (2013): 64–93.

35. Bavinck, *RD*, 4:418.

36. "According to Scripture, in any case, the Word has precedence, and the sacrament is added as an appendage and seal. There is no sacrament without the Word, but there is a Word without the sacrament. The sacrament follows the Word." Bavinck, *RD*, 4:418–19.

37. Bavinck, *RD*, 4:418.

institutional church are the ones primarily responsible for fulfilling their prophetic office in their public witness as part of the true church.

On this basis, Bavinck advised three concrete things for the church to function as a prophet.[38] First, the church should provide training and careful supervision for its future pastors by paying special attention to their skills in handling and delivering the word of God and the gospel either to believers or nonbelievers.[39] Second, the church should strive to preach the whole counsel of God in ways that attend to the specific needs of her congregation based on their nationality, age group, economic background, race, and culture. Moreover, Bavinck warns against understanding this second suggestion only in an "intellectualist" sense, meaning that pastors would exhort their people not only to understand Scripture thoroughly, but also to apply and embody it wisely in everyday living. Third, the church should continue to function as a "pillar and foundation of the truth" (1 Tim 3:15) by carefully translating and interpreting the word of God "according to the rule of faith and to defend it against all deceptive opposition."[40]

FROM NELSON MORALES FREDES

The need for biblically trained leaders is as urgent in Latin America as it is in Asia. Thousands of believers have come to Christ through the proclamation of his church. However, mainly due to the leaders' lack of training, those believers do not know even the ABCs of the Christian life or their role in society. I have been involved in theological education for more than twenty-six years and personally understand the urgent need for formal and nonformal training of those women and men who serve Jesus's flock. Jesus's call to prayer rings loudly in our ears: "The harvest is plentiful, but the laborers are few. Therefore pray earnestly to the Lord of the harvest to send out laborers into his harvest" (Luke 10:2 ESV).

---

38. Bavinck, *RD*, 4:419–21.

39. A major yet typically neglected part of such a training is honing the ability to preach not just with a firm knowledge of the Scriptures but also with "eloquence." Bavinck himself preached regularly and taught preachers to preach. For more on how Bavinck preached or what and how he thought about the act of preaching and the character of the preacher, see Herman Bavinck, *Herman Bavinck on Preaching and Preachers*, trans. and ed. James P. Eglinton (Peabody, MA: Hendrickson, 2017).

40. Bavinck, *RD*, 4:420.

In many cases, the problem is not apathy on the part of those who need training but lack of financial resources to access theological education. Latin America is a region with high rates of poverty. Many pastors and those whom they serve live under the poverty line, a line that is considerably lower in Latin America than in First World nations. As such, Latin American pastors can barely afford food, let alone the costs associated with studying, such as tuition, books, and travel. Even taking time off from work to study involves the loss of precious income and is exceedingly difficult for other reasons. If we are conscious of the importance of the formation of leaders around the world, we should look for concrete ways of supporting theological schools and training ministries that can come alongside leaders and instruct them such that their prophetic ministry will be better and stronger. In that way, we can contribute to the strengthening of the prophetic ministry of the church.

By "rule of faith," Bavinck does not strictly refer to the rule of faith that can be found in the writings of the church fathers like Irenaeus, Tertullian, or Origen, among others. He is referring to the pattern of authority and unity in some kind of rule of faith or catholic doctrine that "confessional churches" maintain and develop throughout the centuries against heresies or false religions. Bavinck even states that "in a world immersed in lies and deception, a church cannot exist without a rule of faith; it falls prey—as especially the history of the nineteenth century teaches—to all sorts of error and confusion without a fixed confession, and becomes subject to the tyranny of prevailing schools of thought and opinions."[41]

To be sure, Bavinck does not mean for any confessional statement to replace Scripture itself as the norming norm (*norma normans*), but confessions should be able to summarize and rearticulate what is contained and demanded by Scripture so that it becomes "a standard of doctrine received in a particular church."[42] Moreover, as much as it is important to confess our faith based on the authority of God's word, Bavinck warns us against turning a church confession into an absolute, magisterial document that forces a

---

41. Bavinck, *RD*, 4:420.
42. Bavinck, *RD*, 4:421.

particular congregation to submit to it at all costs and without questions. In Bavinck's words: "The church does not coerce anyone with this confession, nor does it fetter research, for it leaves everyone free to confess otherwise and to conceive the truth of God in some other sense. It listens attentively to the objections that may be advanced on the basis of God's Word against its confession and examines them as the confession itself requires."[43] Only the word of God in Scripture demands our absolute trust and has the highest authority over all traditions and confessions.

FROM WAGEEH MIKHAIL

The Church as a "prophetess" is a very important theme. Although the term itself is not explicitly found in the New Testament, we see this role clearly in Jesus's words: "You are the light of the world. A town built on a hill cannot be hidden. Neither do people light a lamp and put it under a bowl. Instead they put it on its stand, and it gives light to everyone in the house. In the same way, let your light shine before others, that they may see your good deeds and glorify your Father in heaven" (Matt 5:14–16). These words affirm the fundamental fact that the church has the mission of bringing light to the world. In practicing this role, the church will face the unavoidable task of exposing darkness in the world. Following the example of Old Testament prophets, the church is to speak against the evils of the day. She is expected to have a prophetic voice that is not always favored by those in political power. Of course, this is costly at times. We know from biblical history that many prophets lost their lives as a result of pointing out the evils of their days. The church has to be ready to pay a price as she practices her prophetic role. But we should not assume that the role of the church is to confront the world all the time. This is not true; the prophetic voice is the voice of conscience that ensures that things are done according to the principles of justice, truth, and beauty. It defends the marginalized and vulnerable while standing firmly against injustices. We cannot forget that an important part of the voice of the church is the blessing of everything that would elevate the status of justice and fraternity among people.

---

43. Bavinck, *RD*, 4:421.

So the prophetic voice is a voice *for* and *with* but sometimes *against* society and those who dominate it. This is what the light does to a dark room.

In a Muslim-majority country like Indonesia, many things are expected from the church. In Islam, the mosque addresses many societal issues, and I believe Muslims in Muslim-majority countries look at the church in anticipation to hear a message on certain issues. This is a delicate matter, given the limitations many churches face in Muslim societies. Yet if we go back to Jesus's words about the light, we realize that light exposes darkness, yet it is not a violent exposure, but it is done indirectly and peacefully. Thus, the church is called not for confrontation or militant opposition to darkness, but she is called to shine the light of Christ and to be ready to pay a price—even a costly one.

BECOMING A PROPHETIC CHURCH (IN AN INDONESIAN CONTEXT)

I believe that much, if not all, of what Bavinck has described and suggested above can benefit the church tradition of which I have been a part for most of my life. Craig Bartholomew aptly reminds us of the dangers of a "dysfunctional church," that is, a church that fails to function accordingly as the mother of believers, which tends to cause serious and often irreparable damages to her children.[44] Sadly, we have been reaping the consequences of such

---

44. Bartholomew, *Contours of the Kuyperian Tradition*, 186–87. Examples of such failures are legion and of different factors. Recent accounts or stories that tell of people's disappointments with the church or Christianity in general can be found in Jim Davis and Michael Graham, *The Great Dechurching: Who's Leaving, Why Are They Going, and What Will It Take to Bring Them Back?* (Grand Rapids: Zondervan, 2023); Ryan P. Burge, *The Nones: Where They Come From, Who They Are, and Where They Are Going*, 2nd ed. (Minneapolis: Fortress, 2021); Linda A. Mercadante, *Belief without Borders: Inside the Minds of the Spiritual but Not Religious* (Oxford: Oxford University Press, 2014). Those who choose to leave their evangelical-Protestant heritage and why they do so is rightly observed by Kenneth J. Stewart, *In Search of Ancient Roots: The Christian Past and the Evangelical Identity Crisis* (Downers Grove, IL: IVP Academic, 2017), esp. chap. 15. In my specific context, while there has not been any formal study yet, many younger Indonesian Christians are tired of trying to change the minds of church leaders and pastors who tend to be perceived as "old-styled" and "obsolete." Thus, they migrate to churches of a Pentecostal or charismatic background that are less rigid and open to accommodate their needs, including a more relational and communal approach to outreach through small groups, compared to the more traditional and conservative Chinese evangelical churches of various denominations.

a dysfunction everywhere in various parts of the globe. Thus, no church can "lord it over another." All churches have their blemishes, which is why there should be mutual admonition and correction.

With all these in mind, we can now explore how Bavinck's understanding of the institutional church as Christ's prophetess and its supposed functions could inspire evangelical Chinese churches in Indonesia.

First, churches in Indonesia should strive and continue to become a training ground for future pastors and a sending institution for missionaries to preach the gospel, teach the whole counsel of God, and become better theologians. As far as I have seen, although there have been many good pastors and preachers in the last few decades, there have only been a handful of theologians. In the Indonesian context, pastors and missionaries are assumed to be working in the field while theologians are supposed to be teaching at a seminary or theological faculty. Those who undergo further studies in theology are almost always recruited by the academy to become lecturers or professors, where there is also a great demand for theology professors, unlike what has been going on in the West with an ever-shrinking job market for the so-called theologians.[45] This is similar to the "great divorce" that Gerald Hiestand and Todd Wilson describe as the theological anemia of the church and the ecclesial anemia of the academy.[46] Hence, churches and seminaries should both reclaim the long-lost vision of the "pastor-theologian" and cooperate in producing more ministers who identify as such and who aim to alleviate the theological anemia in Indonesian churches at large. As Christ's prophetess, the church should not fail to see her role as the primary institution and the place where pastors and missionaries are mentored "to have the Word of God preached by their ministry both to believers and nonbelievers and thus to establish, expand, and propagate the church of God among humankind."[47]

---

45. As noted by Miroslav Volf and Matthew Croasmun, *For the Life of the World: Theology that Makes a Difference* (Grand Rapids: Brazos, 2019), esp. chap. 2.

46. Gerald Hiestand and Todd Wilson, *Pastor Theologian: Resurrecting an Ancient Vision* (Grand Rapids: Zondervan, 2015).

47. Bavinck, *RD*, 4:419.

FROM WAGEEH MIKHAIL

The belief that church ministry is done by practitioners while theological thinking is carried out by professionals who have spent many years in academic studies is destructive. We can never and should never choose between church ministry and theological education. A pastor who is not properly theologically educated cannot provide spiritual food for the edification of the church. Likewise, the theologian (albeit intellectually prolific) who is isolated from church life does not help the church grow. The pastor must be the theological thinker of the church he serves, and the theological thinker must always be concerned with the significance of what he writes for the local church. A theological thinker who is isolated from the life of the local church and from people's daily sufferings and problems is wasting time on intellectual theses written in an ivory tower that have nothing to do with people's realities. It is an intellectual luxury we cannot afford.

We can think of some concrete examples where churches in Indonesia can function more effectively in helping their congregations exercise their prophethood. For one, Indonesian churches, which are in the most-populated Muslim country, should constantly provide evangelistic training to help people better understand and reach their Muslim neighbors. Seminaries too should collaborate with churches by designing several courses to equip future pastors and missionaries to study Islam and other (folk) religions in Indonesia. Another good example is how some churches in Indonesia have specifically designed a one-year preparation class for those who are called to a full-time pastoral ministry before they enter a seminary or Bible school. Such classes can be expanded to train lay preachers and encourage them to be trained more extensively in cooperation with trusted seminaries.

FROM NELSON MORALES FREDES

There is a growing ignorance in congregations of basic Christian doctrine. The same problem is present in Latin America. Many churches have reduced the church gatherings to a "fiesta cristiana." Services revolve around music and good worship times. More and more frequently, preaching is reduced to short anecdotes or testimonies. I surmise that pragmatism is the main reason for this situation in Latin America. Preachers prefer to teach only what is "practical" for their congregations, things that believers can easily implement to live a moral life in society. As a result, after a few decades of growth in an evangelical church, the average believer is not able to explain the gospel or the Apostles' Creed. We must come up with creative ways of teaching the ABCs of Christian doctrine to the new generations of believers. Furthermore, new questions arise from the modern context. The church must ponder what God says in his word regarding these new challenges it is facing. This is not an either-or situation. To have a pertinent prophetic voice in current times, we must teach believers both the ancient consensus of doctrine and also answers to new challenges.

Second, part of being a pastor-theologian is to understand the real needs of people in the field according to the context of a particular church. Churches and seminaries in Indonesia, especially those who have the capacity to do so, should develop a more contextual, indigenized Indonesian theology.[48] This is something that Bavinck would definitely encourage, as Ximian Xu has helpfully shown in his own context in mainland China.[49] As Bavinck notes, "It is the calling of every Church to guard and preserve its individual character, and, instructed by the teachings of history, to labor for the Church and theology of the future."[50] If indeed the church without theology dies, and vice versa, there needs to be much more interaction between the two. One prominent Indonesian figure, the late Eka Darmaputera (1942–2005), who was awarded the Kuyper Prize for Excellence in Reformed Theology and Public Life in 1999, has been a role model for many Christians in Indonesia

---

48. I follow Andrew F. Walls's categorization of the *indigenizing* principle in contrast with the *pilgrim* principle in *The Missionary Movement in Christian History: Studies in the Transmission of Faith* (Maryknoll, NY: Orbis, 1996), 7–9.

49. Xu, "The Scientific Calling of the Church," 159–64. I believe much of Xu's discussion on how Bavinck's thought can benefit Chinese churches can also be applied to the Indonesian context.

50. Herman Bavinck, "The Future of Calvinism," trans. Geerhardus Vos, *The Presbyterian and Reformed Review* 5, no. 17 (1894): 23.

as he truly embodied the calling of becoming a "pastor as a public theologian."[51] Another great example is Gray Sutanto's option for how Indonesian churches can interact with its state Constitution's *Pancasila* ("five principles") while avoiding triumphalism in their engagement with religious pluralism and public life.[52] We could invoke other examples, but the point is clear: churches need to become more intentionally theological and contextual in order to function as Christ's prophetess.[53]

FROM ELIZABETH W. MBURU

This is precisely the situation of the church in Africa. There is the recognition that a church that is not self-theologizing, that depends on other contexts to provide a theological framework within which it should function, ultimately becomes irrelevant to the ordinary person in the pews. African worldviews tend to be holistic. Theology that is abstract and not functional, that does not address contextual realities, ultimately fails. For most people in Africa, the Bible is a sacred and powerful text. It is God's unchanging truth and norm for every believer. As such, the theological truths it provides address every area of life, both at the personal and at the communal level. However, theologizing also carries with it the very real danger of syncretism—the indiscriminate mixing of biblical truths with local customs, rituals, and religious ideologies. What results is a subversion

---

51. Kevin J. Vanhoozer and Owen Strachan, *The Pastor as Public Theologian: Reclaiming a Lost Vision* (Grand Rapids: Baker Academic, 2015). See, e.g., Eka Darmaputera, "Pancasila and the Search for Identity and Modernity in Indonesian Society: A Cultural and Ethical Analysis" (PhD diss., Boston College and Andover Newton Theological School, 1982), and his collected writings in Indonesian: Darmaputera, *Pergulatan Kehadiran Kristen di Indonesia: Teks-Teks Terpilih Eka Darmaputera* (Jakarta: BPK Gunung Mulia, 2001).

52. *Pancasila* consists of beliefs in (1) the one and only deity, (2) the just and civilized humanity, (3) the unity of Indonesia as a nation, (4) wise democracy among delegations or representatives, and (5) social justice for all people in Indonesia. See further N. Gray Sutanto, "Religious Pluralism in Indonesia: Reformed Reflections," in *Reformed Public Theology: A Global Vision for Life in the World*, ed. Matthew Kaemingk (Grand Rapids: Baker Academic, 2021), 71–81.

53. For example, Joas Adiprasetya, "Towards an Asian Multitextual Theology," *Exchange* 43 (2014): 119–31; Bernard Koh Ming Huat, "Constructing Chineseness in Ministry: A Contextualized (Re)thinking with Special Reference to Chinese Church in Indonesia and Singapore (Part 1)," *Asian Journal of Pentecostal Studies* 22, no. 1 (2019): 65–82; Chandra Wim, "Reconfiguring Asian Theology from the Ground Up: Watchman Nee and John Sung on Scriptural Interpretation" (ThD Thesis, Wycliffe College-University of Toronto, 2022).

and disintegration of a genuine Christian identity. Syncretism (which is not just an African problem) is attractive because it reinforces a sense of identity and ownership of faith. Finding the right balance between contextual relevance and biblical integrity is a challenge. Careful contextual theologizing is necessary if the rapidly growing church in Africa is to survive.

Finally, evangelical churches in Indonesia should practice more consistently what they believe through their affirmation of certain creeds and confessions of faith. In today's pluralistic and postmodern world, even more confusion and skepticism faces the institutional church—thus the need for churches to gain clarity regarding their beliefs about God and all things related to him. Churches should also strive to become more confessional to promote unity and catholicity within not just Protestantism but also Roman Catholic and Eastern Orthodox churches. It could also be another great opportunity for the Protestant evangelicals to retrieve another lost vision of the Reformers, that is, the constitutional principle called "conciliarism" in contrast with "monarchial Catholicism."[54] As Bavinck said earlier, "a church cannot exist without a rule of faith," which includes the responsibility to "confess the truth it believes and to maintain it as confession in its midst."[55] Becoming more confessional might help churches in Indonesia to minimize the ordinary Christians' reliance on their lead pastor, who acts as a celebrity pastor and/or prophet, as to not take his/her words as the only truth or the "word" of God.

FROM NELSON MORALES FREDES

Jesus prayed to the Father, "I do not ask that you take them out of the world, but that you keep them from the evil one" (John 17:15 ESV). In that sense, our prophetic ministry is not only limited to "spiritual affairs" inside the four walls of the

---

54. This conciliar spirit of the Reformers and beyond is described in detail by John T. McNeill, *Unitive Protestantism: The Ecumenical Spirit and Its Persistent Expression* (Richmond, VA: John Knox, 1964), 89–129.

55. Bavinck, *RD*, 4:420.

sanctuary. It is a call to be light in the world. Therefore, for an effective prophetic ministry, we should learn to read our surrounding world—namely, the people and society in which we live. In recent years, believers in Latin America have become more involved in the public arena, focusing on the important issues of abortion, marriage, and gender. However, they have neglected other important issues such as violence, migration, chronic malnutrition among children, corruption, and ecological sustainability. How can the church model God's will on these issues as the prophets of Israel did? Thankfully, some Latin American Christian nonprofit ministries and local churches with a more holistic understanding of the gospel have greatly contributed to their neighborhoods, regions, and countries. However, the challenge is still immense. Many churches continue to have a more limited view of their involvement in the world. As a result, their prophetic impact is less perceptible and, in many ways, limited to the believers inside their communities.

Jesus is still performing his prophetic ministry through his church. We, as his church, are still called to be his prophetesses in this world. The teaching ministry is incredibly important, but other aspects of the prophetic ministry are also urgently needed. We must train more leaders and lay people who are attentive to their surroundings. That way Jesus's prophetic voice will sound even louder in our world, a world that desperately needs his light of salvation.

It does not mean, however, that we continue to subscribe to past confessional documents rigidly without contextualization or development. For example, Xu observes two examples, the ordination of women and the administration of sacraments, that are not practiced consistently with the Reformed faith of many Chinese churches,[56] and I would say the same issues happen in Indonesian Chinese churches as well. Many churches not only allow women to preach in the main pulpit but also ordain them to the office of a reverend (*pendeta*).[57] Only those who are a reverend are allowed to lead and administer the sacraments of baptism and the Eucharist. In such cases,

---

56. Xu, "The Scientific Calling of the Church," 160–61.

57. In most Indonesian churches, a typical seminary graduate will receive the title "evangelist" (*guru Injil* or *penginjil*) or sometimes "vicar" (*vikaris*) when he or she joins a church, but only after several years of dedication and certain qualifications in ministry would he or she be offered to consider becoming a "reverend" (*pendeta*).

Xu aptly observes, "The church implicitly grants the visible word of God (sacraments) greater significance than the audible word of God (preaching)."[58] Situations like this may force the church to rethink its confession of faith, either to add or revise one or many statements to be implemented in the church life and organization. But that is the way it is, Bavinck would argue. The indigenization of the Christian faith always involves a dynamic of change and development in doctrinal standards.[59]

FROM WAGEEH MIKHAIL

One plight of the church in Muslim-majority countries is the absence of any creedal formula with Islam in mind. Most, if not all, the churches in Muslim-majority countries still hold on to the first ecclesiastical creeds. There are some other formulae of faith, most of which were produced after the advent of Islam, and it is discreditable that none of them address the Islamic faith. This absence of any creed or confession of faith with Islam in mind is not a healthy sign of the relevancy of the church in the Muslim world. Islam is a creedal religion; there is a *shahada*, which is repeated several times a day. One of the primary needs of the church in the Muslim world is to reflect on its context, to open its ears to the word of God, to open its eyes to the world of Islam, and to come up with a relevant creed or confession of faith that deals with the challenges of Islam.

One example of a church that emphasizes doctrine and confessional standards is *Gereja Reformed Injili Indonesia* (GRII; Reformed Evangelical Church of Indonesia) founded by Stephen Tong.[60] I am appreciative of what

---

58. Xu, "The Scientific Calling of the Church," 160.

59. Bavinck compares Reformed theology (Calvinism) with Lutheranism: "Another feature which serves to commend Calvinism consists in this—that it allows various minor shades, and in the application of its theological and ecclesiastical principles avoids all mechanical uniformity. Lutheranism, strictly speaking, has produced but a single Church and a single Confession. Calvinism on the other hand has found entrance into many nations and founded many and multiform Churches. It created not one but a number of Confessions.... To no individual man or individual Church has it been given to assimilate truth in all its fullness. Truth is too rich and manifold for this. Only in company with all the saints can we understand the breadth and length and depth and height of the love of Christ." Bavinck, "The Future of Calvinism," 22.

60. Tong's influence reaches far beyond Indonesia and some even named him "the Billy Graham of the East." See further, Hoon, "Mapping Chineseness," 240–41; Ong, "Ethnic Chinese Religions," 112.

GRII has done for evangelization and theological education in general.[61] Unfortunately, as Xu similarly writes of Tong's influence in mainland China, his theological movement tends to promote an anticatholic spirit toward other Protestant churches.[62] Such a posture is clearly out of bounds with what the Reformers have envisioned. Nevertheless, other churches can still learn from GRII through their intentionality toward developing an informed laity that is equipped to bear witness to Christ in a multicultural and multireligious society. Hopefully, in the end, the world will see churches today in ways that show how big Christ our Lord is.

---

61. My mother was called to ministry due to Tong's evangelistic crusade, and both my parents were taught by Tong during their time at SAAT. Tong himself not only was a graduate of SAAT, but even after he moved to Jakarta to start GRII, SAAT still has connections to GRII even until today, albeit in a limited way, especially through SAAT's alumni who serve at GRII. I am quite sure that there are lots of people directly or indirectly who have been influenced or even discipled through listening to Tong's sermons and lectures like I was.

62. "For many Chinese Reformed Christians, there are no Reformed *theologies*, but *the* Reformed theology, which is interchangeable with Westminster. . . . The Reformed movement exhibits the mindset of theological hegemony." Xu, "The Scientific Calling of the Church," 155–56, emphasis original. Thankfully, signs of openness and a catholic spirit within GRII, especially through some of their pastors, can already be identified.

CHAPTER 2

MORE THAN A PROPHET

Arab Christians and the Question of Christology

WAGEEH MIKHAIL

It seems fair to say that there is no way for a Muslim to maintain their belief in the prophethood of Muhammad alongside the supremacy of Christ as the eternal Word of God. The two beliefs are irreconcilable. While Christians believe that the Word of God became flesh, Muslims deny the eternity of Christ and his divine origin, reducing him to a dignified prophet who received a message from God to communicate to humans. His message is the *Injīl* (the gospel), while Scripture clearly informs us that Christ is the *Injīl* itself.

It is the "fate" of Christians in Muslim-majority countries to keep affirming that Christ is more than a prophet: he is the creator and the sender of all biblical prophets, who prepared the way for him (Mark 1:1–3; Heb 1:1–4). I suggest in this essay that, without weakening this essential belief in the slightest, we may draw profitably on a more indirect apologetic developed by our Arab forebears in the faith. Arab Christian theologians who flourished in the Middle Ages in the so-called *Dār al-Islam* (the World of Islam) left behind a treasure of theological materials in Arabic dealing with difficult issues in Christian-Muslim relations, such as the divinity of Christ. It is high time for contemporary Arab Christians and those who are interested in communicating the *Injīl* in Muslim-majority countries to discover these writings and learn from them new ways of speaking about Christ.

I focus here on Ibrāhīm al-Ṭabranī, an Arab Palestinian monk, who died in AD 820 and was earnest in his explanation of the doctrine of Christ: his transcendence, greatness, and uniqueness in comparison with other prophets and apostles. Although al-Ṭabranī certainly believed in the prophetic role played by Christ, he went further, emphasizing the supremacy of Christ above all prophets and apostles as the eternal Word of God.

This chapter will proceed to demonstrate this by providing a brief presentation of what Muslims say about Christ and an analysis of how Ibrāhīm al-Ṭabranī spoke of the uniqueness of Christ as more than a prophet with particular reference to his long disputation with ʿAbd al-Raḥmān ibn ʿAbd al-Malik ibn Ṣāliḥ al-Hāshimī, ruler of Damascus. I will provide some significant texts from the disputation in its original language, Arabic, followed by our English translation. Let us begin, then, by examining how Christ is seen in Islam.

CHRIST IN ISLAM: A PROPHET FROM GOD

Islam accords Jesus (ʿĪsa) special attention and high status, according to the text of the Qurʾān and the Hadith. The Qurʾān names one of its surahs after Mary (Maryam), who is the only woman named in the Qurʾān. The Qurʾān emphasizes her chastity, purity, and God's choice over the women of the worlds (3:42). The mother of Jesus (and Jesus himself) has a unique place in Islam. There were many female figures in early Islam, but only Mary is mentioned in the Qurʾān. The Qurʾān in a sense speaks of the uniqueness of Mary and, consequently, her Son.

According to Michel Hayek, the name of Christ is mentioned in fifteen surahs, in ninety-three verses.[1] The Qurʾān mentions the miracles of Jesus in detail in 3:49, and no fewer than six different miracles are attributed to him: speaking in the crib (19:30–33); creating a living bird from dirt (3:49); raising the dead (3:49); healing (3:49); disclosing the unknown (3:49); and providing the disciples with food from heaven (5:112–14).[2]

---

1. Michel Hayek, *al-Masīh fī l-Islām* (Beirut: Dar al-Nahār, 1960), 25.
2. See Beaumont Ivor Mark and David Emmanuel Singh, *Jesus in Muslim-Christian Conversation* (Eugene, OR: Cascade, 2018); cf. Deedat Ahmed, *Christ in Islam* (New Delhi: Adam, 2008); Khorchide

While Christ is the "Son" of God in Christian theology, God cannot have a son in Islamic theology. Having a son is only understood physically. God has no female partner, as the Qur'ān insists. No other way of understanding sonship is possible in Islam. Therefore, the Qur'ān is keen to speak of Christ as a mere prophet. He and Mary are fully human; Christ is likened to Adam as a human. As a prophet, Christ brings a message from God to humanity. His message is to call people to worship the one God who created heaven and earth. Christ, with permission from God, performed many miracles like the ones listed above in order to vindicate his message. The Qur'ān emphasizes Christ receiving or requesting divine support before performing miracles. The Qur'ān says, "A messenger to the Children of Israel: 'I have come to you with a sign from your Lord. I make for you out of clay the shape of a bird; then I breathe in it, and it becomes a bird by Allah's leave. And I heal the blind and the leprous, and I revive the dead, by Allah's leave. And I prophesy what you eat, and what you store in your homes. In this is a sign for you, if you are believers'" (3:49).

FROM NELSON MORALES FREDES

Wageeh Mikhail presents a good summary of how Jesus is described in the Qur'ān. In it, Jesus is no more than a prophet. Furthermore, Mikhail shows the early Christian responses to that depiction of our Savior. It is amazing to see how, so early in the history of Islam, Arab Christian theologians gave solid answers to the questions and objections about Jesus's divinity in the so-called *Dār al-Islam*. In contrast, the way that Jesus is often perceived in Latin America is significantly different. Due to more than five hundred years of Christian presence on the continent, people in general have a high concept of who Jesus is.

Mikhail presents the arguments of Ibrāhīm al-Ṭabranī regarding the Muslim challenges to Jesus's divinity. The first argument emphasizes that the miracles Jesus performed demonstrate his divine power. In Latin America, almost

---

Mouhanad et al., *The Other Prophet: Jesus in the Qur'an* (Chicago: Gingko, 2019); Robson James, *Christ in Islam* (Piscataway, NJ: Gorgias, 2010); Zahniser A. H. Mathias, *The Mission and Death of Jesus in Islam and Christianity* (Maryknoll, NY: Orbis, 2008).

everybody would agree with that assertion. Some evangelical and Catholic circles believe that those miracles simply confirmed his messianic-prophetic ministry but are not necessarily present in his church today.[3] Pentecostals, neo-Pentecostals, and charismatics, on the other hand, argue that signs follow the preaching of the gospel today through the activity of the Holy Spirit. In any case, it is good to return once more to the Gospels and, through preaching and teaching, reaffirm the significance of the miracles in Jesus's ministry for his church today, especially in the context of the growing agnosticism among the youth in Latin America.

This mix of views about miracles sometimes results in conflicts within churches or denominations. For example, sometimes those who attend churches that believe the spiritual gift of miracles is not necessarily present in the church today tend to view with suspicion those who perform the so-called miracles or experience the supernatural events. In other circles at the other extreme, miracle campaigns are celebrated and perhaps transmitted by television or social media, with a strong emphasis on the healer's or apostle's persona. Even though Jesus continues to do miracles through the work of the Holy Spirit in and beyond Christian communities, the issue of miracles is a cause for contention among Christians in Latin America.

In short, the Qur'ān emphasizes, "The Messiah, son of Mary, was no other than a messenger, messengers (the like of whom) had passed away before him. And his mother was a saintly woman. And they both used to eat (earthly) food. See how We make the revelations clear for them, and see how they are turned away!" (5:75). To avoid any confusion over his nature and message, Christ clearly says, "'I am the servant of God. He has given me the Scripture, and made me a prophet. And has made me blessed wherever I may be; and has enjoined on me prayer and charity, so long as I live. And kind to my mother, and He did not make me a disobedient rebel. So, Peace is upon me the day I was born, and the day I die, and the Day I get resurrected alive.'

---

3. Charles Ryrie is a classical and still influential thinker in some evangelical circles in Latin America. He presents the idea that the miracles of Jesus attest to "his glory" or "his being a true prophet," but are not part of the church's ministry today because the gift of miracles was temporary. See Charles Caldwell Ryrie, *Basic Theology: A Popular Systemic Guide to Understanding Biblical Truth* (Chicago: Moody, 1999), 214, 296, 429.

That is Jesus, son of Mary—the Word of truth about whom they doubt. It is not for God to have a child—glory be to Him. To have anything done, He says to it, 'Be,' and it becomes." (19:30–35). So Christ is no more than a prophet who received a message from God to pass along to humans—a message that was supported by divine answers to prayers and requests.

Consequently, the Qur'ān rejects the divinity of Christ and his sacrificial death on the cross, and it teaches that Christ was not crucified but rescued and taken to heaven. Ironically, the Qur'ān teaches that some prophets were killed by evil people who refused their message. Verse 2:87 reads, "Indeed, We gave Moses the Book and sent after him successive messengers. And We gave Jesus, son of Mary, clear proofs and supported him with the holy spirit. Why is it that every time a messenger comes to you [Israelites] with something you do not like, you become arrogant, rejecting some and killing others?"[4] Jesus, according to Islamic tradition, is alive now, living in the "second" heaven, worshiping God with other prophets and messengers. On the final day, Christ will return to earth as a ruler. In a hadith attributed to Muhammad, he says that the final hour will "not be established until the son of Mary descends amongst you as a just ruler, he will break the cross, kill the pigs, and abolish the *jizya* tax. Money will be in abundance so that nobody will accept it (as charitable gifts)."[5]

With this short background in mind, how did Arab Christian theologians and apologists speak of Christ?

FROM ELIZABETH W. MBURU

A similar situation arose when the missionaries that came with the modern missionary movement presented the gospel to ethnic groups in Africa that had a monotheistic religious framework. These groups also had a problem with Christ's divinity. They struggled to accept the notion of two Gods—God the Father and Jesus the Son. The problem of language complicated the issue further. Many preferred to hold on to their existing religious beliefs because it preserved their

---

4. Cf. 3:21.
5. *Sahih al-Bukhari*, 2476, vol. 3 (book 43, hadith 656).

understanding that there could only be one Supreme Being. Among Christians today, there is acceptance that Jesus is divine. However, many do not understand the relationship and consequently the distinctions between the Father and the Son.

CHRIST IN ARAB CHRISTIAN THEOLOGY

Arab Christians who first encountered Islam found themselves obligated to provide new proofs of the truth of Christianity in face of objections, especially regarding the Islamic claim that Christ was no more than a prophet sent from God with the *Injīl* (the gospel). Christian theologians defended their doctrines against objections raised by Greek intellectuals, but this time objections came from a very different quarter.

The problem is further complicated if we take into account the language of such objections. Not only did Islam direct its objections against the Christian faith and the divinity of Christ, but these objections came in a new language, Arabic, that was not necessarily the written language of most seventh-century Eastern Christian authors. Arabic was known before the advent of Islam. However, the written language is deeply connected to the spread of Islam, as the Qur'ān was the first complete Arabic book. Theological writings in the East before Islam were generally written in either Syriac, Coptic, or Greek. However, after the Umayyad Caliph 'Abd al-Malik Ibn Marwān (d. AD 705) led the movement of Arabization, most Eastern Christian centers such as Alexandria, Antioch, and Jerusalem adopted Arabic. Arab Christians found themselves forced to defend their faith in the *lingua franca*. Thus, as early as the eighth century, Arab Christian theologians started to compose theological works in Arabic. Their writings are a great treasure of the Arab Church—a treasure that ought to be shared with the rest of the world's Christians, especially with those who wish to establish an effective dialogue with Muslims.

Arab Christian theologians and apologists realized early on that Muslims confess many true things about Christ, such as his virgin birth and his divine teachings. However, they also knew that Islam regards Christ simply as a prophet. So it was necessary for Arab Christian theologians to emphasize that Christ is not merely a prophet but is, in fact, the incarnate Word of God. Similarly, he is the gospel of God, not merely someone who brought a "gospel" from God. While prophets sent by God in the Old Testament were given a certain message to communicate to people, starting their ministries proclaiming, "Thus says the Lord . . . ," Christ did not speak in this manner. He spoke with authority as God. Arab Christian theologians spoke repeatedly of the wonders performed by Christ with his free will and free decision. This is a clear opposition and rebuttal of the Qur'ānic claim that Christ performed wonderous miracles only after he prayed for God's permission (see Q. 3:49). Abū Qurra and 'Ammār al-Baṣrī are two prime examples of ninth-century apologists who spoke of Christ's miracles and wonders in the context of Islam.

Let us now turn to Ibrāhīm al-Ṭabranī and his arguments on the supremacy of Christ over all prophets.

IBRĀHĪM AL-ṬABRANĪ

Ibrāhīm al-Ṭabranī[6] was an Arab Chalcedon monk who died in AD 820. He is well known for his lengthy discussion in Jerusalem with the Muslim Amir 'Abd al-Raḥmān ibn 'Abd al-Malik ibn Ṣāliḥ al-Hāshimī, ruler of Damascus, under the Caliphate of Hārūn al-Rāshīd (d. AD 809). In his conversation with the Muslim Amir, he was known as al-Ṭabranī (from Tiberias, Palestine). When he was asked to defend the truth claims of Christianity, having been assured of his safety by the Amir, al-Ṭabranī prepared a text in which he refuted all Islamic objections against Christianity and read it aloud to the Amir. The Amir was angered and ordered three Muslim scholars to

---

6. See Giacinto Bulus Marcuzzo, *Le dialogue d'Abraham de Tibériade avec Abd al-Raḥman al-Hašimi à Jérusalem vers 820. Étude, edition critique et traduction annotée d'un texte théologique chrétien de la littérature arabe* (Rome: Pontificia Universitas Lateranensis, 1986); cf. Krisztina Szilágyi, "Mujādalat al-rāhib Ibrāhīm al-Ṭabarānī," in *The Orthodox Church in the Arab World, 700–1700*, ed. Samuel Noble and Alexander Treiger (DeKalb, IL: Northern Illinois UniversityPress, 2014), 90–111; Mark N. Swanson, "Mujādalat al-rāhib al-qiddīs Ibrāhīm al-Ṭabarānī ma'a l-amīr 'Abd al-Raḥmān ibn 'Abd al-Malik ibn Ṣāliḥ al-Hāshimī," in *Christian-Muslim Relations 600–1500*, ed. David Thomas and Barbara Roggema (Leiden: Brill, 2010), 1:876–81.

join the discussion to refute al-Ṭabranī's claims. But to the Amir's dismay, the monk (al-Ṭabranī) defeated all three interlocutors.[7] The Amir then tested al-Ṭabranī with fire and poison, but the sign of the cross secured al-Ṭabranī's safety. Moreover, some of those who listened to the dispute (Jews and former Christians) converted or reverted to Christianity. As a result, al-Ṭabranī was initially put in jail but was later released.[8] In this discussion, classic topics of Christian-Muslim theological conversations were discussed, such as the Trinity, the incarnation, the cross, and the identity of Christ. The text of this disputation is well known throughout the Arab Christian community, and "it ranks among the most popular Arab Christian writings."[9]

In his apology, al-Ṭabranī speaks of the supremacy of Christ and his free will in performing miracles, indicating:

أظهر المسيحُ الآياتِ بأمرٍ نافذٍ منه، لا يحتاجُ فيه إلى طلبٍ، ولا إلى تضرّعٍ، كمثل الأنبياءِ.[10]

He [Christ] has performed miracles by his firm order, not needing to request, or to supplicate, like other prophets.

Ibrāhīm al-Ṭabranī emphasizes Christ's free will in producing miracles. Christ was a prophet, but he did not follow the path of prophets who would pray and ask God for divine vindication for their message. In that sense, Christ's prophetic role is not identical to other prophets who need support for their message; he is the one who wills for miracles to happen because of his divine power.

---

7. Szilágyi, "Mujādalat al-rāhib Ibrāhīm al-Ṭabarānī," 90.

8. Al-Ṭabarānī "drank poison and survived after praying; a criminal was given the same drink and died. The monk healed the amīr's slave girl, who had been possessed by a jinni. The monk turned hot coals over with his bare hands. The amīr's servants who had converted from Christianity to Islam saw this, as did two Jews, and bowed before the monk and professed belief in Christianity and asked to be baptized. The monk replied that he couldn't, but that the patriarch and bishops in the audience could. The amīr asked the audience what to do. The audience argued that the Jews who convert should still pay the poll-tax, but the Christian-Muslim-Christian boys should be beheaded. The decisions were carried out. The monk was imprisoned, but the amīr freed him in the middle of the night. . . ." Jessica Sylvan Mutter, "By the Book: Conversion and Religious Identity in Early Islamic Bilād Al-Shām and Al-Jazīra." (PhD diss., The University of Chicago Division of the Humanities Department of Near Eastern Languages and Civilizations, 2018), 177.

9. Szilágyi, "Mujādalat al-rāhib Ibrāhīm al-Ṭabarānī," 92.

10. Marcuzzo, *Le dialogue d'Abraham de Tibériade*, 385.

Al-Ṭabranī points out that many aspects of Christ demonstrate his supe-riority over all other prophets. First, as the above quotation corroborates, he makes a distinction between the miracles of Christ and those performed by the prophets, asserting, "There is an enormous difference between Christ's miracles and miracles performed by other prophets. When want-ing to perform a miracle, a prophet would fast, pray, supplicate, pray again, and intercede afterwards. However, Jesus showed people signs by His firm command."[11] Clearly, we see here the emphasis on Christ's creative power as the eternal Word of God—a theme repeatedly used by Arabic-speaking Christians in showing the supremacy of Christ over all prophets. Second, the time of preforming miracles is indicative of Christ being the Word of God incarnate. He performed miracles whenever he willed. Unlike the other prophets, Christ opened the eyes of the blind, gave life to the dead, healed the sick, fed thousands of people—all because of his firm and free will.[12]

Third, Christ knew the unknown and what people have in their hearts and intentions, unlike other prophets. "Christ knew the depth of hearts of people and He knew the hidden things, He knew what was and what is to come."[13] Only God knows the unknown. Since Christ knew the unknown, he is more than human; he is the eternal Word of God. Conversely, other prophets' relationships to God are fundamentally different than Christ's. They proclaimed, "We are the servants of God." Christ proclaimed, "I am the Son of God."[14] This firm proclamation of Christ assured the hearers that the miracles they witnessed were not the result of a pious prophet who begged God for some sort of vindication; rather, they were signs that Christ is divine.

Fourth, in contrast with Muhammad, who is seen as the perfect human in Islam[15] and the one who is glorified and dignified with a highest rank among the offspring of Adam, al-Ṭabranī firmly insists that Christ is the one who holds supremacy in heaven and on earth:

---

11. Marcuzzo, *Le dialogue d'Abraham de Tibériade*, 387.
12. Marcuzzo, *Le dialogue d'Abraham de Tibériade*, 387.
13. Marcuzzo, *Le dialogue d'Abraham de Tibériade*, 398.
14. Marcuzzo, *Le dialogue d'Abraham de Tibériade*, 389.
15. See Cragg Kenneth, *Muhammad and the Christian: A Question of Response*, rev. ed. (London: Oneworld, 1999).

"فكيف يكون مَنْ تحت الثَّرى أكرم على الله على ممَّنْ هو في السّماء على كرسي العزّ"[16]

How can the one who is buried in dust be more dignified than the One who lives in heaven, seated in majesty?

Finally, al-Ṭabranī refutes the Qur'ānic claim that Christ should be likened to Adam and the other prophets. If this understanding is correct, then Christ should be where these individuals are: buried under dust. However, Christ is exalted over all. He is exalted in heaven, and they are buried. Therefore, he is greater than angels and all humans, by virtue of his heavenly status. Further, "If Christ is likened to Adam, he should have been where Adam is; if he is to be likened to Noah, he should have been where Noah is; if he is to be likened to Abraham, Moses, and the prophets and messengers of God, he should have been where they are."[17]

However, it is very important, according to al-Ṭabranī, to place the wondrous miracles Christ performed in their right place. They are not the reason Christians believe in the divine nature of Christ; rather, they are mere manifestations affirming Christ's supremacy. The ultimate reason for believing in Christ as the Son of God (the eternal Word) is what Christ taught after performing the miracles. Al-Ṭabranī explains,

"لسنا نتَّخذُ المسيحَ إلهًا، لأنّه أحيا الموتى فقط؛ لكنّه أحيا الموتى، وقال: "أنا ابنُ الله" ونورُ العالمِ، أنا الرّاعي الصّالحُ، أنا أميتُ، وأنا أُحيي، وأنا ديّانُ الدّين، "أنا أتوبُ على مَنْ أشاءُ، وأُعاقبُ مَنْ أشاءُ."[18]

We do not accept Christ as God because he raised people from among the dead only; rather he raised people from among the dead and said, "I am the Son of God," "I am the Light of the world," "I am the Good Shepherd," "I give life, I take life," "I am the Judge on the Day of Judgment," I accept the repentance of those I wish to cause to repent; and I punish those I wish to punish.

---

16. Marcuzzo, *Le dialogue d'Abraham de Tibériade*, 406–7.

17. Marcuzzo, *Le dialogue d'Abraham de Tibériade*, 495.

18. Marcuzzo, *Le dialogue d'Abraham de Tibériade*, 385.

Further, al-Ṭabranī refutes the allegation that Christians have elevated a prophet from God to the level of God and worshiped him. Al-Ṭabranī asserts:

"النّصارى لم يبتدعوا أنْ يقولوا إنّ المسيحَ ابنُ اللهِ الحيّ، لكنّ اللهَ هو الذي قال: "هذا هو
ابني الحبيبُ، الذي به سررتُ، له اسمعوا." فقلنَا: "يا ابنَ الله، سمعنَا، وأجبنَا." فقال لنا:
"أنا وأبي واحدٌ." بشّرتْ به الملائكةُ المقرّبون، وتنبّأت عليه الأنبياءُ المرسلون، وأخبرتْ به
الحواريّون المنذرون، واجتمعت عليه الأنبياءُ المكرّمون. ونحن لسنا مشركين."

Christians do not say Christ is the Son of the Living God, rather God [Himself] was the One who proclaimed: "This is my beloved Son, with whom I am pleased, listen to Him." Therefore, we responded, "Oh, Son of God, we give ear and accept you." He said, "I am One with my Father." Christians are those people who not only worship Christ as the Eternal Word of God, but they are the ones who obey God Himself in what He proclaimed about the nature of Christ, being His very Son. The denial of this is a clear and frightening objection to God.

To strengthen this point, Ibrāhīm al-Ṭabranī concludes:

"المسيحُ أكرمُ، وأعلى، وأشرفُ من لآدمَ""[19]
Christ is more honorable, more exalted, and higher than Adam.

Al-Ṭabranī's main point here is the supremacy of Christ, as a prophet over all other prophets. The miracles of Christ highlighted by al-Ṭabranī are deliberate. He has chosen miracles that are linked to the power of God over creation, such as walking on water and raising people from the dead. For him, these miracles correspond to the power of the triune God in creation, so Christ walked on the water *because he is the one who created it*. He raises people from the dead *because he is the author of life in the beginning*.

---

19. Marcuzzo, *Le dialogue d'Abraham de Tibériade*, 447.

FROM NELSON MORALES FREDES

Mikhail mentions another argument of al-Ṭabranī—namely, that Jesus is the Creator and a member of the Trinity. In Latin America in general and in Guatemala in particular, Jesus is easily recognized as the Son of God, the second person of the Trinity. However, in popular theology, Jesus is either the one who suffered on the cross or the exalted one at the right hand of God, but not necessarily the Creator. People tend to see God the Father as the Creator. In fact, in the Catholic world, the Apostles' Creed is repeated: "I believe in God, the Father . . . Creator of heaven and earth . . . and in Jesus . . . who suffered under Pontius Pilate." In the evangelical world, songs like "At the Foot of the Cross" by Don Moen or "Down at the Cross" by E. A. Hoffman frequently appear during worship services. Perhaps the continuous suffering experienced by the Latin American people, especially the poor, has led them to identify more with Jesus as the one who suffered for us and as such understands our sufferings. In evangelical liturgy, the idea of the exalted Christ is highlighted to such a degree that his humanity tends to disappear. Thus, we should imitate al-Ṭabranī and rescue a more Trinitarian and balanced depiction of Jesus in our teaching, preaching, and singing. We must bring a broader image of Jesus to new generations of believers.

Al-Ṭabranī makes a clear statement that God has not promised Ishmael that prophets or messengers will come out of him. This is a double use of Deuteronomy 18:15, in which al-Ṭabranī uses the text polemically to implicitly deny any Islamic claims that Muhammad was the prophet mentioned in Deuteronomy 18:15. By denying that Ishmael was a prophet and that from his descendants a prophet will come, al-Ṭabranī implicitly denies the prophethood of Muhammad—a point that could not have been made explicitly. This line of thinking is found verbatim in the apology of Būlus al-Būshī, bishop of Old Cairo in AD 1240, who indicates:

"مشى (المسيحُ) على البحر، كأنّه على اليبس، لِيُعْلَمَ أنّه ثبّتَ الأرضَ على المياه؛ صنع طينًا، وطلى بها عيني الأعمى المولودِ، فأبصرَ، لِيُعْلَمَ أنّه جَبَلَ الإنسان من ترابٍ؛ أشبع من خبزٍ يسيرٍ جمعًا كبيرًا، لِيُعْلَمَ أنّه يبارك على اليسير، فيصير كثيرًا، ويعطي غذاءً لكلّ ذي

جسدٍ؛ وأقام ألعازرَ بعدما نتن، وصحّح الجسدَ من نتانته، وأعادَ النَفسَ من حيث كانت، لِيُعْلَمَ
أنّه متسلّطٌ على النّفوس والأجسامِ، والباعثُ لها في اليومِ الأخير.''

He (Christ) walked on the water as if it was ground so that people
know that He established earth on water; He made mud and spread it
on the eyes of the blind man, and he saw, so that people would know
that He created Adam from dust; He fed many with little bread so that
people would know that He blesses little things and turn them great,
and that he gives food to all; He raised Lazarus from the dead after his
body smelled, and made his body whole again, and turned his soul back
to him so that people would know that He has power over souls and
bodies, and that He is the One who will cause them to resurrect.

To further assert the supremacy of Christ over all prophets, al-Ṭabranī
insists that not one of the prophets dared to identify himself with God; only
Christ spoke of himself as the eternal Word of God. Christ therefore was well-
aware of his divine identity, unlike the prophets who were sent with a divine
message. He knew himself and knew of his divine origin. Al-Ṭabranī asserts:

لو أنّ الأنبياءَ قالوا للنّاس: ''إنّا أبناءٌ لله،'' لحقّ النّاسُ أن يقبلوا قولهم، لما كانوا يظهرون
من الجرائح، ولكنّهم لم يكونوا يكذبون، ولا يدّعون ما ليس هو لهم. ولكنّهم قالوا: ''إنّا عبيدُ
اللهِ.'' وقال المسيح: ''أنا ابنُ اللهِ'' صَدَقَ المسيحُ، وصَدَقَ الأنبياءُ. [20]

If the prophets had said to the people, "We are 'sons' of God,"
people would have the right to accept their words, for they performed
marvelous things, but they were not lying, nor were they claiming what
was not theirs. But they said, "We are 'servants' of God." Jesus said,
"I am the 'Son' of God. He spoke the truth; they spoke the truth.

CHRIST IS THE WORD OF GOD

As early as the eighth century, Christians in the East found it attractive to
speak of the divinity of Christ in terms of him being the eternal Word of

---

20. Marcuzzo, *Le dialogue d'Abraham de Tibériade*, 400.

God. We can trace this line of argument to St. John of Damascus (c. 675–749), who introduces this argument in his *Dialogue between a Christian and a Saracen*.[21] In this short yet powerful work, John encourages his Muslim interlocutor to reflect on the Qur'ānic description of Christ as the Word of God.[22] He reasons that the Word of God is as eternal as God's essence is. The Qur'ān rightly describes Christ as the Word of God. Since God's Word is eternal, Christ must be eternal. If the Muslim refuses this conclusion, he is denying the eternity of God's Word, thus blaspheming by attributing "change" to God's essence. For denying the eternity of God's Word implies that God was "mute" and only later did he change and possess a Word. The Muslim is therefore left to acknowledging the eternity of the Word of God and thus the eternity of Christ. This line of thinking was sophisticatedly developed under the Mu'tazilah, the rationalist wing of Islamic theology that flourished in the ninth century—the context of al-Ṭabranī.

Al-Ṭabranī asserts the impossibility of separating between the light of the sun and the disk of the sun itself:

كما أنّه لا يُفرَّقُ بين الضَّوءِ وطبقةِ الشَّمسِ، كذلك لا يُفرَّقُ بين اللهِ وكلمتِه، وروحِه. لو عُزِلَ عن طبقةِ الشَّمسِ الضَّوءُ والحرارةُ لم يكن شمسًا؛ كذلك، لو فارق اللهُ كلمتَه، وروحَه، لعَدَم ولم يكنْ إلهًا، وكان غير حيٍّ، ولا ناطقٍ.

> So, as it is not the case that one cannot separate the light from the sun, so one cannot separate between God, His Word, and His Spirit. If it becomes possible to separate between the light of the sun or its heat from the dusk, then it becomes no sun. Similarly, if the Word of God or His Spirit depart God, then He will no longer become God. He will not be a Living God, nor will he be a Speaking God.

---

21. See Diego Sarrió Cucarella, review of *John of Damascus and Islam: Christian Heresiology and the Intellectual Background to Earliest Christian-Muslim Relations* by Peter Schadler, *MIDÉO*, 34 (2019), 390–94; cf. Janosik Daniel and Peter G Riddell, *John of Damascus, First Apologist to the Muslims, The Trinity and Christian Apologetics in the Early Islamic Period* (Eugene, OR: Pickwick, 2016); Peter Schadler, *John of Damascus and Islam: Christian Heresiology and the Intellectual Background to Earliest Christian-Muslim Relations* (Leiden: Brill, 2018); John W. Voorhis, "The Discussion of a Christian and a Saracen: John of Damascus," *The Muslim World* (1935): 266–73; Manolis Ulbricht, "John of Damascus, On Heresies, Chapter 100," in *Bloomsbury Reader in Christian-Muslim Relations 600–1500*, ed. Thomas David (London: Bloomsbury, 2022), 132–36.

22. "Behold! the angels said: "O Mary! Allah giveth thee glad tidings of a Word from Him: his name will be Christ Jesus, the son of Mary, held in honor in this world and the Hereafter and of (the company of) those nearest to Allah" (Q 3:45).

Al-Ṭabranī goes on to say,

كذلك الله وروحه وكلمته، بلا تفريق، ولا فصلٍ، ولا هو أقدمُ من كلمته وروحه، ولا
كلمته وروحه بأحدث منه، ولا نعرفُ الله إلّا بالكلمة والرّوح، ولو كان بين الله وبين كلمته
وروحه فصلٌ، لكان له ابتداءٌ وانتهاءٌ.

Likewise, God and His Spirit and His Word, are without distinction or separation, nor is He older than His Word and Spirit, nor is His
Word and Spirit newer than Him, and we do not know God except
by Word and Spirit, and if there was a separation between God and His
Word and His Spirit, then He would have had a beginning and an end.

The eternity of God's Word is very important for al-Ṭabranī's argument for
Christ's supremacy over all other prophets, who are created. But Christ is
eternal. Since he is the Word of God, he is worthy of all worship and honor.
Those who worship him are blessed as they obey God, unlike those who deny
him and rebel against God by doing so.

فلا شكّ بالذين يسمعون له ويتبعونه أنّهم حسنوا الحال عند الله، والخوف والخزي على من
أبى واستكبر. [23]

There is no doubt that those who listen to Him and follow
Him are well with God, and fear and shame for those who are proud
and arrogant.

CONCLUSION

The heritage explored in this chapter leads to a practical suggestion for recti-
fying the occlusion of Arabic Christianity even in Muslim-majority contexts.
Rarely, if ever, do seminary students find Islam interwoven or implemented
into the curriculum, although Islam addresses topics studied in Christian
theology explicitly. Furthermore, when the history of Christian doctrines
is taught, it is done in a manner that totally ignores Islam as a prevalent religion during the time and in the region where major Christian doctrines were

---

23. Marcuzzo, *Le dialogue de Abrahma de Tibériade*, 447.

formulated. Traditionally, seminarians are taught about the Jewish context of the early church, about persecutions and martyrdom. This is followed by introducing them to patristic literature, the ecumenical councils, Augustine and Pelagius, miraculously teleporting students to the Middle Ages, the Reformation and post-Reformation theology, and modern theology. Yet the Arabic-speaking church's response to Islam is given no place alongside these topics.[24] In a similar manner, classes on the history of doctrines at seminaries in Muslim settings are taught in isolation from Islamic theology and philosophy. But this is insufficient. Islam is not a topic among many that is to be taken as a course; it is a worldview. The curriculum as a whole must reflect this reality, as this has been the very reality of the church in the Arab world since the seventh century.

FROM NELSON MORALES FREDES

An important similarity between Mikhail's context and mine in Latin America is the absence of visible daily-life implications for Christians in society regarding their belief in Jesus as more than a prophet. It is understandable that in Muslim countries, people live their lives without taking into account Jesus's existence and presence. However, in Latin America, about 80 to 90 percent of the population identifies itself as Christian (between Catholic and Protestant), yet the recognition of the Lord Jesus as the Son of God is not reflected in the daily lives of the citizens. As in other parts of the Western world, Christians tend to make a marked division between their secular lives and their religious practices. In that way, the true challenge for Christians in these latitudes is to live their public lives as if Jesus is really their Lord, the Son of God, in every aspect of their lives.

Isn't this a summary of what most seminarians worldwide have learned about the Christian movement over two thousand years? This story is partial because the apostles went not only to the West but also to the East. Didn't the

---

24. The Second Council of Nicaea (787 AD), which was convened when Islam was in power, never gave attention to the reality of Islam, which was a major player in the political and religious life of the region, but rather discussed monothelitism and iconoclasm respectively.

members of the church of the East take the gospel to China and Central Asian countries in the seventh century? Didn't some people spread the good news to Arabia? How can we not hear about the Christians of Najrān, many of whom were martyred at the beginning of the sixth century AD by the Jewish King Dhū al-Nawās? How can we not appreciate the Christian presence among the Ghassānids and Manāthirs, those important Arab Christian kingdoms? How can we not study about the city of Ḥīra, or the kingdom of Kinda? Giving greater space to the story and sources of Arab Christianity is essential, not only in Muslim contexts but as a shared treasure of the global church.

CHAPTER 3

JESUS AND GOD'S PROPHETIC IMAGINATION

NELSON MORALES FREDES

Studies on Jesus's prophetic office have traditionally focused on Jesus as the mediator between God and human beings, as a messenger of God to them, and as Messiah. It is clear from a study of the gospels that Jesus is presented as a prophetic figure. He performs prophetic actions and his teachings are perceived with prophetic authority.[1] The evangelists present the person of Jesus and his deeds in connection with two key Old Testament passages that point toward a future prophet: Deuteronomy 18:15 and Malachi 4:5. During the Second Temple period, these two texts served as the foundation for the development of the hope for an eschatological prophet.[2] Thus, it would have been natural for the disciples to have understood Jesus as the fulfillment of those expectations as well. After all, they drank from the same contextual well.[3]

---

1. See the excellent summary by Scot McKnight, "Jesus and Prophetic Actions," *BBR* 10 (2000): 197–232. At the conclusion of his article, McKnight says: "In general, we can argue persuasively that Jesus' actions are more like the Jewish leadership prophets, particularly in their redemptive-liberation orientations, especially as they pick up themes connected with Moses and Joshua. They are even more like the actions of Moses. Jesus was indeed a prophet, but his prophetism is more like the Mosaic ideal than any one prophet of the preclassical and classical periods of Israel's prophets." Ibid., 231.

2. Dale C. Allison presents an exhaustive study on the development of figures like Moses during the Second Temple period in *The New Moses: A Matthean Typology* (Eugene, OR: Wipf & Stock, 2013), 11–95. For examples on Elijah in Second Temple literature, see Stanley E. Porter and Bryan R. Dyer, *Origins of New Testament Christology: An Introduction to the Traditions and Titles Applied to Jesus* (Grand Rapids: Baker Academic, 2023), 26–28.

3. Porter and Dyer present a good summary of how Jesus fulfills those expectations. Porter and Dyer, *Origins of New Testament Christology*, 36–44.

Given the well-attested nature of Jesus's prophetic ministry, it is intriguing that in evangelical circles in Latin America the topic is often overlooked and is relatively absent in the evangelical theological reflection. For example, Samuel Escobar, in his recent work *In Search for Christ in Latin America: From Colonial Image to Liberating Savior*, makes only one brief reference to the topic. In the chapter titled "Jesus Christ's New Time for Reflection and Dialogue," Escobar begins talking about CLADE II—the Second Latin American Congress of Evangelization, inaugurated on October 31, 1979. In that congress one of the founders of the Latin American Theological Fraternity (FTL), Emilio Antonio Núñez, presented the inaugural discourse on Christ. In one of his points about which Christ we preach, he mentions: "*Prophet Christ!* Herald of God the Father, interpreter of Deity, revealer of the divine will for his people and for all of humanity. His word lit on fire from heaven is consolation and hope for those of humble hearts, and an unavoidable warning of judgment for evildoers."[4] This is notably the only mention of Jesus's prophetic ministry in the book, whereas the prophetic ministry of the church is present in almost every chapter. Although one could suspect that Jesus's prophetic ministry is assumed as the basis for the prophetic ministry of the church, it is never explicitly stated—not only in that book but in almost all the christological discussion in evangelical circles.[5]

FROM ELIZABETH W. MBURU

The same is generally true in the church in Africa. Several christological studies identify Jesus as proto-ancestor, liberator, guest, revealer of the Father, ultimate curse remover, chief, master of initiation, and healer. Even though the notion of prophet still exists in many African communities, that label is generally attached to church leaders and, generally, in African Instituted Churches rather than

---

4. Samuel Escobar, *In Search of Christ in Latin America: From Colonial image to Liberating Savior* (Downers Grove, IL: IVP Academic, 2019), 264. Emilio Núñez's assertion reflects a similar approach to the depiction of the prophetic dimension of Jesus's ministry observed in the work of Jon Sobrino, mentioned below.

5. Only as a test case, the good work of the Honduran theologian Raúl Zaldívar, *Teología sistemática*, does not include the offices of Christ in its Christology section. Raúl Zaldívar, *Teología sistemática: Desde una perspectiva latinoamericana* (Villadecavalls: CLIE, 2006).

missionary founded ones. The role of Jesus as prophet is hardly explored. Indeed, the rubric of Christ as prophet, priest, and king is not one that many outside some academic circles are familiar with. This is an interesting gap given that prophets played a significant function in African traditional societies. Like priests, they often mediated between the divine and earthly spheres and had power to communicate with the spiritual world. They had foreknowledge of events in the community. For instance, Mugo wa Kibiru, a prophet in the Kikuyu community of Kenya, foretold the coming of pale-skinned colonialists, of the railway and airplanes (which he described as butterflies in the sky), and of guns (smoking sticks that spit out fire and kill instantly). He also predicted the eventual overturning of colonial rule. History proved him right.

Others have likewise perceived this omission. For example, David Suazo recognizes that Jesus's prophetic office is a neglected topic in the Latin American evangelical church: "It is interesting to observe that systematic theologians of the past would indeed speak of the 'prophetic office' of Jesus, but did not relate it to the prophetic voice nor did they describe it in these terms."[6] In Latin American Pentecostal circles, there have been discussions, using Ephesians 4:11, on the number of ministries functioning today.[7] It is argued that in this text, Jesus gives five gifts to believers. These gifts are persons who develop five specific ministries: apostles, prophets, evangelists, pastors, and teachers.[8] Even though this passage has a christological connection with prophetism, the correlation is rarely made in Latin American Pentecostal circles.[9] The text is usually used to justify the existence of apostleship today

---

6. "Es interesante observar que los teólogos sistemáticos del pasado sí hablaban del 'oficio profético' de Jesús, pero no lo relacionaban con lo que es la voz profética ni lo describían en esos términos." David Suazo Jiménez, *La función profética de la educación teológica evangélica en América Latina* (Barcelona: Clie, 2012), 74n6, my translation.

7. In other latitudes, the discussion around Ephesians 4 has been important, revolving around whether Paul is talking about offices, gifts to believers, or gifts of believers. For the sake of space, I only mention this text in connection with the Pentecostal discussion in Latin America. For more information, consult the relevant commentaries and systematic theologies.

8. See a good analysis of Ephesians 4:11 in Constantine R. Campbell, *The Letter to the Ephesians*, PNTC (Grand Rapids: Eerdmans, 2023), 177–80.

9. A good exception to the rule is José Reina, *Los cinco dones para el liderazgo: Manifestando la plenitud de Cristo en su iglesia* (Córdoba: Imagen, 2017). In particular, he presents a strong connection between Christ and the leadership gifts as an extension of his ministry in chapters 3 and 4.

or to explain the need for the five ministries in order to have a healthy church. Prophetism is always related to the gifts of the Holy Spirit, in particular against cessationist views.[10] Pentecostals do affirm a prophetic office but have not seen prophetism in the church as a continuation of Jesus's ministry but just as a gift of the Holy Spirit. Consequently, a paradox occurs in this context where the spiritual gift of prophecy is widely present and affirmed in the church, but the teaching of Jesus as prophet is almost absent.

FROM WILSON JEREMIAH

This is interesting, for although Indonesian Pentecostals do not have references to back this up, there is a similar understanding of prophethood as a gift from the Spirit, though typically manifested in the lead pastor in whom such a gift is manifested in its fullness. Not all Pentecostal (sometimes also with a charismatic blend) churches in Indonesia are led by a single lead pastor, but some megachurches are indeed led by *the* pastor, and just as Katelyn Beaty demonstrates in her book *Celebrities for Jesus*, the lead pastors looked very much like celebrities. Hence, I believe that the prophethood of Jesus, which is thus extended to the role of the church in receiving and constantly teaching the tradition (cf. Col 2:6–7; Jude 3), can serve as a safeguard against the subjective authority of celebrity pastors.

In contrast, liberation theologians have described Jesus's prophetic ministry as a foundational characteristic of his work.[11] However, they end up reducing his work to a political denunciation. The emphasis on Jesus's

---

10. Even though they are not Latin American thinkers, the discussion in *Are Miraculous Gifts for Today? Four Views* is a good example of what is observed in this region of the world. The cessationist position represented by Richard B. Gaffin Jr. is in the minority in Latin America. Pentecostals and neo-Pentecostals represent roughly 90 percent of evangelicals (in Guatemala, about 50 percent of Catholics are charismatics). Thus the perspectives of C. Samuel Storms and Douglas A. Oss are the most accepted views. Wayne A. Grudem, ed., *Are Miraculous Gifts for Today?: Four Views* (Grand Rapids: Zondervan, 1996). A good example of the way Pentecostals present the gift of prophecy is Siqueira Guterres Fernandes, *Revestidos de poder: Una Introdução à teologia pentecostal* (Rio de Janeiro: Assembleias de Deus, 2018), 75–98.

11. For a detailed bibliography of a Latin American liberationist Christology, see Jorge Costadoat, SJ, "Cristología latinoamericana: Bibliografía (1968–2000)," *Teología y Vida* 44 (2003): 18–61, https://www.scielo.cl/scielo.php?script=sci_arttext&pid=S0049-34492004000100002.

prophetic role is consistent with the liberationist emphasis on the humanity of Christ—his solidarity with the people. The Spanish-Salvadorian Jon Sobrino and the Uruguayan Juan Luis Segundo have been two of the most influential thinkers in the Christology of Latin American liberation theology. Their thoughts illustrate the contrast between liberationists and evangelicals in considering Jesus's role as a prophet.

Jon Sobrino developed his ministry and reflections on Jesus's prophetic ministry during the civil war in El Salvador.[12] In 1991, he reflected on Jesus's prophetic ministry in *Jesucristo Liberador: Lectura Histórico Teológica de Jesús de Nazaret*. He presents Jesus's prophetic praxis as a defense of the true God.[13] For Sobrino, Jesus expresses both a messianic and a prophetic praxis. By "messianic practice," he means the positive service to the coming kingdom, and by "prophetic praxis," he means the denunciation of the "antikingdom." The antikingdom is the manifestation of Satan as well as the people and structures whose actions, values, and words reflect opposition to what the kingdom of God represents. Consequently, according to Sobrino, in his prophetic praxis, Jesus is in the same prophetic line as the prophets of the Old Testament. That is, his proclamation had a "denouncing and unmasking dimension of real injustice and oppression."[14] Jesus's denunciations "address oppressive groups, collective rather than individual sinners, who produce the structural sin."[15] Among these groups are the rich, scribes and Pharisees, and priests. The governing political power is not directly addressed in the gospels; nevertheless, "this does not mean that his mission did not have a clear political dimension, and that he was not conscious of his popular political impact."[16] He concludes his chapter:

---

12. Jon Sobrino has done his ministry mainly in the Central American University José Simeón Cañas of El Salvador. In 1989, several of his colleagues were killed on the campus by the Salvadoran army. On that day he was also set to be killed, but he was providentially in another country. Later in 1991, he crystalized his thoughts in *Jesucristo liberador: Lectura histórico teológica de Jesús de Nazaret*, CTL 17 (El Salvador: UCA, 2000). This is the latest edition of that work.

13. Sobrino, *Jesucristo liberador*, 275–306.

14. Jesus is in the same line that the prophets of the Old Testament, in his "dimensión denunciadora y desenmascaradora de la injusticia y de la opresión reales." Sobrino, *Jesucristo liberador*, 277, my translation.

15. "Se dirigen a grupos opresores, a pecadores colectivos más que individuales, que producen el pecado estructural." Sobrino, *Jesucristo liberador*, 292, my translation.

16. "Esto no quiere decir que su misión no tuviera una clara dimensión política, y que no fuera consciente de su impacto político popular." Sobrino, *Jesucristo liberador*, 305, my translation.

Jesus not only announces the kingdom and proclaims God the Father, but also denounces the antikingdom and unmasks the idols. With this he goes to the roots of a society oppressed under all kinds of power: economic, political, ideological, and religious. Thus, the antikingdom exists and Jesus, objectively, gives an account of its roots. And he is not content with denouncing the Evil One, a transhistorical reality, but rather those responsible for him, very historical realities.[17]

Sobrino's approach to Jesus's prophetic ministry clearly focuses more on the political and social implications of his work.[18] However, the writings of Juan Luis Segundo are more emphatic in this aspect, to the point of almost neglecting that Jesus is more than a prophet and the Son of God. In the same year as Sobrino's publication, Segundo published *La Historia Perdida y Recuperada de Jesús de Nazaret: De los Sinópticos a Pablo.* Segundo presents Jesus as the prophet of the kingdom of God, who has a political focus that contrasts with John the Baptist's prophetic ministry.[19] To Segundo, Jesus's prophetic ministry shows that "not only does he not think of the end, but not even of a restructuring of the entire society of Israel destined to last, so that God's will be done on earth."[20] Segundo asserts here that Jesus's ministry never had an eschatological component and instead was meant to invite people to come alongside Jesus to build the kingdom of God with him.[21] Segundo argued that, given the fact that this kingdom was a political project that transforms the present society and gives freedom to the poor,[22] the best

---

17. "Jesús no solo anuncia el reino y proclama a un Dios Padre, sino que denuncia el antireino y desenmascara a los ídolos. Con ello va a las raíces de una sociedad oprimida bajo todo tipo de poder: económico, político, ideológico y religioso. Existe, pues, el antireino y Jesús, objetivamente, da cuenta de cuáles son sus raíces. Y no se contenta con denunciar al Maligno, realidad transhistórica, sino a sus responsables, realidades bien históricas." Sobrino, *Jesucristo liberador,* 305, my translation.

18. For an excellent evaluation of Sobrino's Christology, see Gerardo A. Alfaro, *Jesús para América Latina* (Fort Worth: El Faro, 2017).

19. Juan Luis Segundo, *La historia perdida y recuperada de Jesús de Nazaret: De los Sinópticos a Pablo,* PresTeo 65 (Santander: Sal Terrae, 1990), 149–86. This is an update of a former work, *El hombre de hoy ante Jesús de Nazaret* (1982), meant for secular and atheist readers. Juan Luis Segundo also ministered in the midst of a military dictatorship in Uruguay.

20. "No sólo no piensa en el fin, sino ni siquiera en una reestructuración de la sociedad entera de Israel destinada a durar, para que se haga en la tierra la voluntad de Dios." Segundo, *La historia perdida y recuperada,* 164–65, my translation.

21. Segundo, *La historia perdida y recuperada,* 165–75.

22. Segundo, *La historia perdida y recuperada,* 168–74.

way to read the Gospels in order to understand Jesus's prophetic actions is through a doggedly political lens.[23] Segundo would not exclude a religious understanding of Jesus's ministry.[24] Nevertheless, his emphasis on the historical Jesus brings him to describe Jesus as a merely human prophet.[25]

FROM WILSON JEREMIAH

Segundo offered an interesting yet ultimately reductionistic reading of what Jesus taught regarding the kingdom of heaven and the afterlife, if indeed he meant to steer his readers away from a kind of escapist mentality that commonly disregards life here and now. This is typical of the historicist, liberal social gospel movement *a la* Walter Rauschenbusch.[a]

_____
[a] For more examples and discussions, see Roger Olson's *Against Liberal Theology* (Grand Rapids: Zondervan, 2022), chaps. 5–6.

JESUS AS PROPHET,
AN EVANGELICAL PROPOSAL

At this point, it is clear that among Latin American perspectives, only liberation theology has an elaborate understanding of Jesus's prophetic office. This understanding has resulted in a key distinctive of Latin American theology. Nevertheless, it is not robust enough because the proposal tends to limit Jesus's prophetic ministry only to the political and social and leaves out other important aspects such as the spiritual and eschatological. In evangelical

_____
23. Segundo, *La historia perdida y recuperada*, 176.

24. Segundo, *La historia perdida y recuperada*, 177.

25. As a matter of fact, for Segundo, the resurrection of Jesus is not part of the historical Jesus but of the eyes of faith. He understands *historic* as verifiable through science. Segundo believes that Jesus's resurrection is only historic in the sense of his influence as verifiable in the church, *qua* influence in the creation of a community, the church. Segundo, *La Historia Perdida y Recuperada*, 313. For him, even though Jesus's resurrection is true, it is not historically verifiable. In an appendix, he answers different criticisms to his work, "Aclaraciones a lectores cristianos" ("Clarifications for Christian Readers"). Segundo, *La historia perdida y recuperada*, 347–67. Among these criticisms of his study is a lack of the redemptive sense of Jesus's passion. Sadly, he insists on his method of source criticism to support what texts he considers for his analysis and what texts he excludes. In that way, he attributes the belief in Jesus's resurrection to be a postpaschal retrojection into the text.

circles, this ministry has been assumed instead of explicitly studied prior to the derivation of implications for the prophetic ministry of the church.

However, an important Guatemalan theologian, David Suazo, recently presented an evangelical alternative that strengthens the Latin American understanding of Jesus's prophetic ministry. This understanding includes the political and economic, as well as the spiritual and eschatological. Suazo builds his proposal in dialogue with Walter Brueggeman's concept of prophetic imagination. He takes this concept, but instead of limiting it to the political and economic spheres as Brueggemann does, Suazo broadens the idea of prophetic function to include other areas of life. For Brueggemann, "The task of prophetic ministry is to nurture, nourish, and evoke a consciousness and perception of the dominant culture around us."[26] For Brueggemann, as David Suazo summarizes, prophetic imagination includes three fundamental characteristics:

> [1. It has a] clear vision of negative realities that politics and the economy can hide or mask as something good, when in reality they are something destructive.... [2.] Prophetic imagination is understood as that utopian construction of a new reality by the prophets, based on what God himself has revealed in his Word.... [3.] Prophetic imagination not only challenges the present, but it stimulates the hope of God's people and stretches their imagination as well.[27]

David Suazo connects this definition to Jesus's ministry. To Suazo, the prophetic imagination includes all the reality that is to be transformed by the kingdom of God. For that reason, he adds to the summary above: "It is Jesus who best embodies this imagination, by presenting the values of the Kingdom

---

26. Walter Brueggemann, *The Prophetic Imagination*, 40th anniversary ed. (Minneapolis: Fortress, 2018), 3.

27. "Esa visión clara de realidades negativas que la política y la economía pueden esconder o enmascarar como algo bueno, cuando en realidad son algo destructivo.... Se entiende por imaginación profética esa construcción utópica de una nueva realidad por parte de los profetas, basada en lo que Dios mismo ha revelado en su Palabra.... Esa imaginación profética no solo desafía el presente, sino que estimula la esperanza del pueblo de Dios y estira su imaginación también." Suazo Jiménez, *La función profética*, 14, my translation.

of God as something real and possible."[28] Suazo, in dialogue with N. T. Wright and Walter Brueggemann, proposes that the prophetic imagination helps us to understand better the prophetic ministry of Jesus. This understanding is important because Jesus is our model for the prophetic ministry of the church. Suazo mostly focuses on the implications of this model for theological education, but his conclusions are valid for other areas of the Christian life. He points out that Jesus, as the prophet per excellence, denounces and announces through his life (incarnation, crucifixion, resurrection), actions (miracles, for example), and teaching that a new world is possible, that the utopia of the Old Testament prophets has become a reality. Jesus's prophetic function is our paradigm. As his disciples we should reflect "the values of this new reality" that brought with it the inauguration of the kingdom of God.[29] In the next section I look through the lens of Suazo's reading to evaluate Jesus's life and work from the perspective of a broadened prophetic imagination.

FROM WAGEEH MIKHAIL

Regrettably, some conservative theologians put all their energy into emphasizing and defending orthodox theological positions against liberal views, while they do not give social issues appropriate attention. As a result, social engagement is often left to liberal theologians, secularists, or socialists, who advocate for the poor and the marginalized based on liberal convictions. Over the years, this has become the norm, although it has never been the Christian norm to neglect the social impact of the gospel. Our mission as theologians is to reflect the character of God to this suffering world. Our God is the God who redeems, but he is also the judge of this world. He judges all injustices, persecution, and evils. Therefore, we need to have a comprehensive biblical understanding of the gospel. In the New Testament, we see Jesus preaching, sharing the gospel, healing the sick, and feeding the poor and the needy. Jesus showed compassion and caring for the underprivileged. He spoke a lot about how important it is to share resources with others, love the underprivileged,

---

28. "Es Jesús quien mejor encarna esta imaginación, al presentar los valores del Reino de Dios como algo real y posible." Suazo Jiménez, *La función profética*, 14, my translation.

29. Suazo Jiménez, *La función profética*, 73–110.

and assist those in need. His comprehensive approach should be ours, and his way of addressing the whole of humanity ought to be our way. No sphere of life should be away from the light of the gospel. Conservative Christians are guilty of not giving this important aspect of Jesus's ministry the appropriate attention.

NEW TESTAMENT EXAMPLES

Time and space do not permit us to explore exhaustively the entire life and teachings of Jesus in the gospel. Nevertheless, the following examples are meant to illustrate Jesus's prophetic function. We focus on Jesus's birth, one of his teachings, one of his miracles, his crucifixion, and his resurrection.

As mentioned above, Deuteronomy 18:15 and 18 point toward a future prophet like Moses. Every true prophet of the Old Testament was "like him."[30] Willem VanGemeren summarizes the seven criteria that help to discern if a person was a true prophet: "1) He was an Israelite, 2) called by the Lord and 3) empowered by the Holy Spirit; 4) he served as God's spokesperson; 5) his authority lay in speaking in the name of the Lord; 6) he was a good shepherd over God's people; and 7) he vindicated his message by signs."[31] The gospels describe Jesus and his ministry in these terms. In one sense, his prophetic ministry is drawn with this Mosaic prophetic pattern.

The narratives of Jesus's birth in Matthew and Luke are both good examples of the prophetic dimension of Jesus's life that the evangelists present to their communities of readers/hearers. As Suazo says, the birth of Jesus is the prophetic sign, "the prophetic imagination of God which describes God himself breaking into human history to announce that the things will be different, that the utopia of the Old Testament prophets has become a reality."[32]

---

30. For the complexities behind the interpretation of Deuteronomy 18:15 and 18, see Ernest Nicholson, "Deuteronomy 18:9–22, the Prophets and Scripture," in *Prophecy and Prophets in Ancient Israel: Proceedings of the Oxford Old Testament Seminar*, ed. John Day, Claudia V. Camp, and Andrew Mein, LHBOTS 531 (New York: Bloomsbury, 2014), 151–71.

31. Willem VanGemeren, *Interpreting the Prophetic Word: An Introduction to the Prophetic Literature of the Old Testament* (Grand Rapids: Zondervan, 1990), 42–43.

32. The birth of Jesus is the prophetic sign, "la imaginación profética de Dios, que describe la irrupción de Dios mismo en la historia humana para anunciar que las cosas serán diferentes, que la utopía de los profetas del Antiguo Testamento ha venido a ser una realidad." Suazo Jiménez, *La función profética*, 76, my translation.

One of the most famous birth passages is the *Magnificat* (Luke 1:46–55), which Luke places near the beginning of the gospel. In it he presents some topics that he later develops in Luke-Acts. Echoing the Hannah and Samuel story in the Old Testament, Mary praises God for choosing her as the mother of the Messiah (1:46–48). Reflecting on what God will do through his son, her canticle is a prophetic window that permits the reader/hearer to see God breaking into human history to make "a great revolutionary reversal of the social order" by his mighty acts.[33] She says: "He has shown strength with his arm; he has scattered the proud in the thoughts of their hearts; he has brought down the mighty from their thrones and exalted those of humble estate; he has filled the hungry with good things, and the rich he has sent away empty" (Luke 1:51–53 ESV). As noted, this reversal has four spheres of action: social (1:50–51a), spiritual (1:51b), political (1:52), and economic (1:53).[34] Mary sees in Jesus that a new world is possible, that finally God will reverse the situation of the vulnerable and bring justice to this present world. Therefore, not only Jesus's birth, but his entire life is seen as a prophetic sign of God's mighty arm acting in this world. It is God's way of showing his covenantal love to those who fear him (1:50, 54).[35] Jesus began this reversal during his ministry through his actions, teachings, and miracles, but he will finish it at his parousia.[36]

---

33. Grant R. Osborne, *Luke: Verse by Verse*, ONTC (Bellingham, WA: Lexham, 2018), 48–49.

34. James Edwards admits that the *Magnificat* has diverse interpretations: "Feminist and liberation theologies tend to read the Magnificat largely in economic, political, and social terms, whereas traditional theology often spiritualizes it." James R. Edwards, *The Gospel according to Luke*, PNTC (Grand Rapids: Eerdmans, 2015), 56. However, one cannot avoid the reality of the sociopolitical tone of this canticle. As Paul John Isaak puts it, "The *Magnificat* is the great NT song of liberation, a revolutionary document of intense conflict and victory, produced by a woman who proclaims the virtues and values of peace, justice, humanness, compassion and the equality of humankind. It praises God's liberating actions on behalf of women and other exploited people whose rights are daily violated. In the transformed social and economic order, violence is overcome and food is provided for the hungry. In the spiritual realm, the focus is on the might, holiness and mercy of God, who has promised solidarity with those who suffer." Paul John Isaak, "Luke," in *Africa Bible Commentary*, ed. Tokunboh Adeyemo (Grand Rapids: Zondervan, 2006), 1234.

35. Darrell Bock correctly points out that "Ἔλεος (*eleos*, mercy) is used in the LXX to translate the Hebrew term חֶסֶד (*ḥesed*), which refers to the loyal, gracious, faithful love that God has in covenant for his people." Darrell L. Bock, *Luke*, vol. 1, 1:1–9:50, BECNT (Grand Rapids: Baker Academic, 1994), 152.

36. The five verbs in 1:51–53 are in the aorist indicative. The interpretation of the whole segment determines the understanding of the *Aktionsart* of these aorists. Bock presents four options: 1) past events, 2) gnomic aorists, 3) reflective of an iterative perfect in Hebrew, and 4) prophetic aorists. He considers this last option to be the best. Bock, *Luke*, 1:155. However, Osborne adds another possibility: the ingressive aorist. He considers that "Mary is celebrating the new stage of God's redemptive work with the gift of the Christ child." Osborne, *Luke*, 48. I agree with Osborne. This prophetic action inaugurates the emergence of God's kingdom. It is not just that someday God will do these mighty deeds, but he has begun to do them through Jesus's life and works.

Not only do the birth and life of Jesus give account of prophetic actions, but his teachings also have the same prophetic tone.[37] Throughout his teachings, Jesus challenges the different spheres of life and the world-views of his time and ours. The Sermon on the Mount is one of the most emblematic teachings of Jesus. Like Moses, but also as the prophet greater than Moses, Jesus presents an authoritative teaching from the mountain (Matt 5:1–7:29). In the section from 5:21 to 5:48, Jesus, with prophetic authority, denounces six adages that seem to be misinterpretations of the law. The six situations are introduced by the phrase "You have heard that it was said to those of old . . ." (5:21, 27, 31, 33, 38, 43 ESV) and countered with his own perspective by the phrase "But I say to you . . ." (5:22, 28, 32, 34, 39, 44 ESV).[38]

In the second (5:27–30) and third (5:31–32) antitheses, Jesus deals with lust and divorce. Through these contrasts, he challenges the standards of a patriarchal society that marginalizes and penalizes women and attributes to them the causes of lust and divorce, topics the Mishnah later sheds light on in m. Našim in general and m. Giṭṭin in particular.[39] Jesus reverts the situation of women by protecting them and giving them back their dignity. In Matthew 5:27–30, he points out that the person's own heart is the locus of lust, not the woman being lusted after.[40] In Matthew 5:31–32, he limits the

---

37. In line with the message of the Old Testament postexilic prophets, Willem VanGemeren comments insightfully: "The messages of the postexilic prophets have much in common with the preaching of our Lord and his disciples. First, they preached the reality of *judgment* on the Day of the Lord. Second, they made an offer of *grace, salvation,* and *full participation* in the righteous kingdom of Yahweh and of his Messiah. Third, they called for a lifestyle of *discipleship, purification,* and *preparation* for the kingdom-to-come. Fourth, they announced the *presence* of Yahweh, the covenant, and his kingdom. Fifth, they also called for *perseverance* to live godly lives and to hasten the day of the establishment of the kingdom." VanGemeren, *Interpreting the Prophetic Word*, 68, emphasis original.

38. Sidney De Moraes Sanches points out that in this section, "The words of Jesus are a rereading with a new interpretive focus on the ten commandments . . . different from the rabbinic tradition, especially in terms of the social conduct of the people with whom God had made an alliance" ("Las palabras de Jesús son una relectura con un nuevo enfoque interpretativo de los diez mandamientos . . . distinto a la tradición rabínica, especialmente en cuanto a la conducta social del pueblo con el que Dios había hecho una alianza"). Sidney De Moraes Sanchez, "Mateo," in *Comentario bíblico contemporáneo: Estudio de toda la Biblia desde América Latina,* ed. C. René Padilla, Milton Acosta Benítez, and Rosalee Veloso Ewell (Lima: Puma, 2019), 1204, my translation.

39. See for example m. Naš Yebam. 2:6–10, 3:1–10, 4:1–13, 5:1–6, 10:6, 15:7; Ketub. 4:9; Giṭ. 1–9.

40. Craig Keener says: "Jewish writers often warned of women as dangerous because they could invite lust (e.g., Sir. 25:21; 26:9; Ps. Sol. 16:7–8; Test. Reub. 3.11–12; 5.1–5; 6:1; Jos. *War* 2.121; *Ant.* 7.130; b. Taʿan. 24a), but Jesus placed the responsibility for lust on the person doing the lusting." Craig S. Keener, *A Commentary on the Gospel of Matthew* (Grand Rapids: Eerdmans, 1999), 187.

reasons that permit divorce in order to protect women.[41] Matthew expounds on Jesus's teaching on this issue later in his book (19:3–12). With this teaching, Jesus is challenging the status quo of a society that marginalized women. His prophetic act of dignification teaches the community of believers that the standards of the kingdom are different and that a new world is possible. As Juan José Barreda highlights in the case of Matthew 19:1–12: "Jesus proposes for them to leave the paradigm of masculinity that was based on dominance over the wife, which limited the bond with women to an erotic relationship, and assume a full life bonding with them in friendship and fellowship of equals, as a testimony and for the proclamation of the kingdom."[42] The same could be said of Jesus's teaching in Matthew 5:27–32.

His teachings and miracles share this prophetic quality. Jesus's miracles signal him to be the Messiah, the Son of God, serving to authenticate his ministry as the signs of a true prophet.[43] Furthermore, as Suazo insightfully says: "Jesus's miracles [are] prophetic actions that speak of the power of God that gives life and of the person of Jesus that brings salvation and the Kingdom of God." Additionally, they are "a form of protest against the religious world . . . protesting against a society that is extremely religious and insensitive to the needs of others."[44] One of those miracles that makes this prophetic confrontation apparent is the healing of the man with a withered hand (Matt 12:9–14; Mark 3:1–6; Luke 6:6–11).

---

41. As Craig Keener rightly points out, "Jesus' central point, which the hyperbolic image is meant to evoke, is the sanctity of marriage. . . . Addressing the hardness of legal interpreters' hearts (19:8), Jesus opposed divorce to protect marriage and family, thereby seeking to prevent the betrayal of innocent spouses." Keener, *A Commentary on the Gospel of Matthew*, 192.

42. "Jesús les propone dejar el paradigma de masculinidad que se fundamentaba en el dominio sobre la esposa, que limitaba el vínculo con las mujeres a una relación erótica, y que asuman la vida plena vinculándose con ellas en la amistad y el compañerismo de pares como testimonio y para la proclamación del reino." Juan José Barreda, "Leer la Biblia 'Naturalmente,'" in *Buenas nuevas desde América Latina: Reflexiones en honor a John Stott*, ed. Nelson Morales Fredes (Lima: Puma, 2021), 84, my translation.

43. The written material about the significance of Jesus's miracles in his ministry is legion. I just mention the wise words of John Meier: "Thus, in both word and deed, Jesus made God's future kingdom a present experience, at least in some partial or proleptic sense. Jesus was not just another prophet uttering more prophecies about the future. He was the prophet who was accomplishing what the prophets had foretold (Matt 13:16–17; Luke 10:23–24)." John P. Meier, *A Marginal Jew: Rethinking the Historical Jesus*, vol. 2, *Mentor, Message, and Miracles* (London: Yale University Press, 1994), 1043.

44. "Los milagros de Jesús [son] acciones proféticas que hablan del poder de Dios que da vida y de la persona de Jesús que trae salvación y el Reino de Dios." Additionally, they are "una forma de protesta contra el mundo religioso . . . que protestan en contra de una sociedad extremadamente religiosa e insensible a las necesidades de los demás." Suazo Jiménez, *La función profética*, 142, my translation.

The synoptic gospels present the healing of the man with a withered hand as a dispute between the Pharisees and Jesus after a similar confrontation involving the Sabbath (Matt 12:1–8; Mark 2:23–28; Luke 6:1–5). In the narrative Jesus has established that he is Lord of the Sabbath and therefore "not merely human life but human need in general takes precedence over regulations."[45] The three evangelists each describe Jesus entering a synagogue and finding a man with this health problem. In addition, a group of Pharisees were looking attentively at what Jesus would do on the Sabbath "so that they might find a reason to accuse him" (Luke 6:7 ESV). Mark highlights the hardness of their hearts. Jesus looks around at them "with anger, grieved at their hardness of heart" (Mark 3:5 ESV). Even though Jesus did not touch the man and only asked him to raise his hand, the Pharisees reacted in anger and fury against him, looking to destroy him.[46] In this case, as N. T. Wright points out, Jesus is threatening "a major symbol of national identity and aspiration."[47] Jesus's miracle as a prophetic action highlights the insensibility of the leaders and how Jesus challenges the religious status quo. This narrative teaches the community of believers that the standards of the kingdom are different, that a new world is possible, where people and their needs take priority over regulations and religious laws and procedures.

Two of the most transcendental events in Jesus's life are his crucifixion and resurrection, and both events are fundamental for our faith and have been studied extensively. Not only do both events reflect Jesus's offices of priest and king, they are also tremendous examples of Jesus as prophet. Colossians 2:15 says that "having disarmed the powers and authorities, [God] made a public spectacle of them, triumphing over them by the cross."[48] Thus, Jesus's death is a prophetic symbol of God's triumph over evil. In that sense,

---

45. Keener, *Matthew*, 357.

46. The contrast of words is illuminating. Jesus experiences *orgē* ("anger") while the Pharisees were filled with *anoia* ("a state of such extreme anger as to suggest an incapacity to use one's mind"). J. P. Louw and Eugene A. Nida, *Greek-English Lexicon of the New Testament: Based on Semantic Domains* (Minneapolis: Fortress, 1999), 88.183. The situation is so disturbing for them that they lose their mind.

47. N. T. Wright, *The Resurrection of the Son of God* (London: SPCK, 2003), 393.

48. The pronoun *autō* at the end of this verse could have Jesus as referent or the cross. In any case, the meaning is not affected. Jesus died on the cross. His death and the cross are not symbols of a defeat. On the contrary, they are signals of God's triumph.

"The cross of Christ is prophetic because it offers a different way to face the powers of the world, a different way to win the battles, a way radically opposed to the way the world uses."[49]

The cross is central in Christianity, but it lacks meaning without the empty tomb. Jesus's resurrection is crucial in many ways and, like his crucifixion, is a prophetic act. Through the resurrection, Jesus demonstrated that the future is here: "That future that the prophets dreamed of, which seemed utopian, now, by virtue of the resurrection, has become present and brings hope that surprises, but encourages."[50] As Suazo correctly points out, it is prophetic in several ways: "The resurrection, understood as a prophetic event, contains the elements of every prophetic message: a denunciation of evil when it exposes the wickedness of the system (Matt 28:11–15), a call to repentance . . . when the disciples are confronted with the resurrection and the proclamation of repentance (Luke 24:45–47) and the announcement of the new reality with the presence and power of the Holy Spirit (Luke 24:48–49; Acts 1:8)."[51]

Jesus's crucifixion and resurrection as prophetic actions teach the community to face life and adversity with hope. Believers celebrate the resurrection, "but they also [have to] proclaim it as a prophetic act that denounces, announces and dreams of an 'other' world and, furthermore, [that] it must be lived through concrete acts that reflect that future already present in the world."[52]

---

49. "La cruz de Cristo es profética porque ofrece una manera distinta de enfrentar los poderes del mundo, una manera distinta de ganar las batallas, una manera radicalmente opuesta a la manera que el mundo usa." Suazo Jiménez, *La función profética*, 89, my translation.

50. "Ese futuro que soñaron los profetas, que parecía utópico, ahora, en virtud de la resurrección, se ha hecho presente y trae esperanza que sorprende, pero que alienta." Suazo Jiménez, *La función profética*, 90, my translation.

51. "La resurrección entendida como un acontecimiento profético, contiene los elementos de todo mensaje profético: una denuncia del mal cuando pone al descubierto la maldad del sistema (Mt 28:11–15), un llamado al arrepentimiento . . . cuando los discípulos son confrontados con la resurrección y la proclamación del arrepentimiento (Lc 24:45–47) y el anuncio de la nueva realidad con la presencia y el poder del Espíritu Santo (Lc 24:48–49; Hch 1:8)." Suazo Jiménez, *La función profética*, 91, my translation.

52. Believers celebrate resurrection, "pero también [tienen que] proclamarla como un acto profético que denuncia, anuncia y sueña con un mundo 'otro' y además, [que] hay que vivirla por medio de actos concretos que reflejen ese futuro ya presente en el mundo." Suazo Jiménez, *La función profética*, 95, my translation.

FROM WAGEEH MIKHAIL

The cross of Christ, being a prophetic event with eternal effects, is followed by the glorious resurrection. This redemptive work of Christ, the prophet, assures us that our prophetic work in the world will succeed and that societies can be "resurrected" to follow the gospel and walk in light. This hope is what differentiates the Christian engagement with societal issues from secular engagements, which often overlook the communal effects of sin on societies. However, the Christian gospel has the power to change. It can change societies drastically because it starts with the change of the heart. If we keep this fact in mind, we will not hesitate to engage the society because we know that we will succeed and that change will happen. We need not neglect our social commitment to the world. As we seek to articulate orthodox doctrines, we ought to help people live "orthodoxly."

CONCLUSION

The prophetic ministry of Jesus challenges his church today. We are also called to continue his prophetic ministry until his coming. We live in the hope of Jesus's second coming, and this hope helps us to live according to the standards of his kingdom.

FROM WILSON JEREMIAH

Carl Henry in his somewhat neglected *God, Revelation and Authority* says: "By instilling a Christian view of vocation the church has, in fact, already provided some leadership in social, political, economic and other realms and has thereby contributed to educational enlightenment and to better legislation."[a] This is a great example of how the church can practically contribute to the betterment of both the mind of her people, as well as their daily witness as "prophets." An influential book by Robert Bellah et al., *Habits of the Heart*, contends that one remedy to cure the expressive individualism of the American people is as follows: "To make a real difference . . . [there would have to be] a reappropriation of the idea of vocation or calling, a return in a new way to the idea of work as a contribution to the good of all and not merely as a means to one's own advancement."[b] In other words, if the doctrine of vocation as taught in Scripture makes its way from the church to her people, it would certainly contribute something to the betterment of society and justice in the workplace.

[a] Carl F. H. Henry, *God, Revelation and Authority*, 2nd ed. (Wheaton, IL: Crossway, 1999), 4:548.

[b] Robert Bellah, Richard Madsen, William M. Sullivan, Ann Swidler, and Steven M. Tipton, *Habits of the Heart: Individualism and Commitment in American Life* (Berkeley: University of California Press, 2007), 287–88.

From Suazo's use of prophetic imagination, we see that Jesus's prophetic ministry challenges us on several fronts. As Mary expressed in the *Magnificat*, we are in the midst of a reversal that Jesus began with his ministry; therefore, we should be attentive to and focus on his work and not on the temptation of power, wealth, and pride of this world. As mentioned above, Jesus denounced a marginalizing world, one that limited women. In this way, we are called to embrace his perspective and live according to his standards. Jesus's sensitivity to the needs of people over and against religious regulations is a permanent call to us to open our prophetic eyes to the needs of the people of our world. Through his crucifixion, Jesus identified himself with the crucified of our world, with our pain, not as a sign of defeat but as a sign of victory over evil. Finally, through his resurrection, as the one greater than a prophet, he opened the future and brought us hope. Another world is possible. He is the prophet, priest, and king who makes this possible. We should live in the light of this new reality until he makes all things new.

PART II

CHRIST AS
PRIEST

INTRODUCTION: CHRIST AS PRIEST

THE PRIEST GREATER THAN MELCHIZEDEK AND AARON

ELIZABETH W. MBURU

Old Testament: Psalm 110

The Old Testament text that best captures the office of Jesus as priest is Psalm 110. This is a prophetic psalm of David that looks forward to the Messiah, who is priest and king. It is a beautifully styled poetic couplet that reflects a balance/parallel between the two halves. Each is introduced by a brief prophecy (110:1, 4) that finds its ultimate fulfilment in Christ. Like Psalm 2, its style is that of a coronation psalm. Such psalms were composed to celebrate the enthronement of a new Davidic king. Whether David was being deliberately prophetic, or whether he intended this psalm for his son Solomon, or even himself, is not clear.

Psalm 110 is probably the most directly prophetic of all the psalms. It was quoted by Christ himself, to show that the Messiah would be so much more than just David's descendant (Mark 12:36; cf. Matt 22:44; Luke 20:42), as well as by Peter (Acts 2:34–36) and the author of Hebrews (Heb 1:13; 5:6–10; 7:11–28). The first half of this psalm begins with the words "The Lord says." The word *ne'um* ("says") is used frequently in the Old Testament for a formal divine announcement through a prophet. This first half thus begins by expounding on a king that is greater than David, one that sits at God's right hand in the place of honour and authority.

The second half (110:4–7) begins with a prophecy in God's voice concerning the priesthood. This in itself is unusual given that religious and civil offices were never combined in the Old Testament (Ps 99:6). However, in the ancient world, it was not unusual for a king to also hold the highest priestly office in the land.[1] The role of the priesthood was to mediate God's presence to the people, to offer sacrifices, and to reveal God's will.

In addition to keeping his covenant with David regarding the royal line, God promises an eternal and irrevocable priesthood "in the order of Melchizedek" (110:4; cf. Gen 14:18–20; Heb 5:5–10; 6:19–7:28). The name Melchizedek means "king of righteousness." He was the king of Salem (Jerusalem) in Abraham's time as well as a priest of the Most High God (Gen 14:18). In him, as in Christ after him, both offices of king and priest were combined. The words *nishba' yahweh* ("Yahweh has sworn") has the sense of "to promise" or "to pledge." In this context, it is an unbreakable, divine oath. This understanding is indicated by the negated Niphal imperfect of נֶחָם *nakham* ("will relent"), which is a way of marking an announcement as an irrevocable decree (cf. 1 Sam 15:29; Ezek 24:14).[2]

While it was not the norm, this combined office can also be seen in Israel's history (2 Sam 6:12–19; 8:18; 1 Kgs 8).[3] It was also prophesied with regard to Christ (Zech 6:12–13). Melchizedek, as a type of Christ, pointed forward to the eternal priest-king, who would supersede him in every way. In the New Testament, Hebrews speaks about the eternal nature of his office and 7:4–9 in particular reveals that in his giving gifts and receiving tithes (Gen 14:18–20), he had priority not only over the Abrahamic people, but also over the Aaronic priesthood, which he preceded. As Allen Ross notes, "That ancient unity of priest and king in one person will be reunited in the Messiah, a fact which necessitates the end of the line of Aaron's priesthood."[4]

---

1. Victor Harold Matthews, Mark W. Chavalas, and John H. Walton, *The IVP Bible Background Commentary: Old Testament*, electronic ed. (Downers Grove, IL: InterVarsity Press, 2000), Ps 110:1–7.

2. *The NET Bible First Edition Notes* (Biblical Studies Press, 2006), Ps 109:31–110:7.

3. Matthews, Chavalas, and Walton, *The IVP Bible Background Commentary: Old Testament*, Ps 110:1–7.

4. Allen P. Ross, "Psalms," in *The Bible Knowledge Commentary: An Exposition of the Scriptures*, ed. J. F. Walvoord and R. B. Zuck, vol. 1 (Wheaton, IL: Victor, 1985), 873–874.

The rest of the psalm continues in the voice of the psalmist, with the imagery of warfare culminating in the victory of the Lord's anointed. The priest-king, who sits at God's right hand (110:1), is now described with the Lord siting at his right hand (110:5). God himself energizes him. Thus, he is also a victorious warrior who acts in unity with the Lord.

The already-but-not-yet eschatology of this psalm is evident. While the inauguration of this victory was clearly seen in Christ, its final fulfilment, while certain, is still to come. Unlike the Aaronic priests, "*This* priest will never abuse his office, and this priesthood is both older and more perfect (as the New Testament will show) than that of the whole house of Levi."[5]

New Testament: Hebrews 8:1–6

The backdrop for the understanding of Jesus as priest in the New Testament is primarily found in Hebrews. Although we refer to Hebrews as a letter, it is more sermonic in style, with numerous admonitions and exhortations. It was written by an unnamed author, although it is likely that the recipients knew him. The readers were Jewish converts familiar with the Old Testament and the temple, whose activities were more than likely still going on, given that the author speaks of them in the present tense. Its contents indicate that the readers were being tempted to abandon Christ and return to Jewish practices or perhaps even to follow a syncretized form of it. Hebrews thus points to the sufficiency and supremacy of Christ.

Therefore, it is only fitting that in Hebrews the superiority of Christ's priesthood is fully unveiled and the title of high priest for him made explicit (Heb 2:17; 4:14–5:10; 8:1–6; cf. Gen 14:18–20; Ps 110:4). Paul Ellingworth notes that "these texts in fact speak of a priest, but are interpreted by the writer of Hebrews as referring to the supreme priesthood realized in Jesus."[6] The writer of Hebrews thus applies a hermeneutic that reinterprets these texts as speaking about Jesus's higher and better priesthood. As we noted above, the prophecy in Psalm 110 speaks of one who would be not only the

---

5. Derek Kidner, *Psalms 73–150: An Introduction and Commentary*, vol. 16, Tyndale Old Testament Commentaries (Downers Grove, IL: InterVarsity Press, 1975), 426–431.

6. Paul Ellingworth, "Priests," in *New Dictionary of Biblical Theology* (Downers Grove, IL: InterVarsity Press, 2000), 700.

promised Davidic king but also a priest in the order of Melchizedek. Several texts in Hebrews confirm that the offices of king and priest are combined in the person of Christ (Heb 4:14–7:28).

Hebrews 8:1–6 provides us with a snapshot of this superior high priest. It is found in the larger section that ends at 10:18. This larger section presents an argument developed from Jeremiah 31:31–34, which speaks of the New Covenant. In 8:1–6, the author of Hebrews emphasizes the superiority of Christ's priesthood and his relationship to the new covenant by making several comparisons.

The immediate context reveals that Christ preceded the Aaronic priesthood and was therefore not in Aaron's line but in the superior one of Melchizedek (Heb 7:11–18; cf. Ps 110:4). The initial words *kephalaion de* ("now the sum" or, better yet, "now the main point") shows that the author is making an inference from the previous section (8:1). Christ's superior status is also shown by his position, seated at the right hand of God's heavenly throne, where he exercises his priesthood (1:3; 10:2; 12:2; cf. Ps 110:1). In contrast, Old Testament priests could stand in God's presence, but their task was never finally completed.[7] And when they did stand before God in the holy of holies, it was only once a year on the Day of Atonement (Lev 16) and even then only briefly.[8] However, this high priest has fully completed the task that Levitical priests anticipated and is in God's presence eternally. This position shows that Christ shares in God's heavenly rule.[9]

Moreover, his superiority is reflected in the sphere in which he serves— the true tabernacle set up by the Lord (Heb 8:2, 5). The author of Hebrews draws a parallel between the Levitical cultus and Jesus's spiritual service. The earthly tabernacle was also divinely instructed (*kechrēmatistai*) and had a specific function of providing access to God. However, it was a mere shadow, an imperfect and impermanent copy of the heavenly one (Exod 25:40). David Peterson points out,

---

7. Thomas D. Lea, *Hebrews, James*, vol. 10, Holman New Testament Commentary (Nashville: B&H, 1999), 152–54.

8. Robert Jamieson, A. R. Fausset, and David Brown, *Commentary Critical and Explanatory on the Whole Bible*, vol. 2 (Oak Harbor, WA: Logos, 1997), 458–59.

9. David G. Peterson, "Hebrews," in *New Bible Commentary: 21st Century Edition*, ed. D. A. Carson et al., 4th ed. (Downers Grove, IL: InterVarsity Press, 1994), 1338.

Some readers with a Jewish background may have considered that there was something lacking in Christianity because it offered no elaborate ceremony in an earthly sanctuary. Hebrews makes the opposite point. Christ introduces the ultimate, spiritual realities to which the old covenant ritual pointed, fulfilling and replacing the whole system prescribed in the law of Moses.[10]

The superiority of Christ is also reflected in how he fulfills the function of the priestly office. Priests were expected to offer up gifts and sacrifice (8:3, 4). Christ did so but with a crucial difference. Christ's priestly activity on earth pointed to the cross rather than a physical temple in heaven.[11] The surrounding context shows that as a high priest, he not only offered an eternal sacrifice but was himself the sacrifice that would atone for the sins of all humankind (Heb 5:9; Heb 7:27–28; 10:10). In this context, the word *anankaion* ("necessary") shows that this was a divine necessity.[12] This verse reveals "that Christ's priestly office is exercised in heaven, not in earth; in the power of His resurrection life, not of His earthly life."[13]

Moreover, he is the mediator of the new covenant (8:6). There is a close connection between priesthood and covenant, and as Peterson points out, "the theme of Jesus' high-priestly ministry is closely linked with the fulfilment of the promises of Je. 31:31–34 in chs. 9–10."[14] Consequently, not only is his priesthood eternal, but it is also superior to the Levitical priesthood (cf. Heb 7:11–12, 21–26, 28; 8:13; 9:15). The author points out that Christ's ministry is as superior to the Levitical priesthood as the new covenant is to the now obsolete old covenant. The word used to describe this is *diaphorōteras* (more excellent; cf. 1:4). This is because it is established on better promises (8:10–12). This does not mean that some of God's promises are qualitatively better than others. What the author underscores is that "the Old Testament promises were mainly of earthly, the New Testament promises, of heavenly

---

10. Peterson, "Hebrews," 1338.

11. Lea, *Hebrews, James*, 152–54.

12. Donald Guthrie, *Hebrews: An Introduction and Commentary*, vol. 15, Tyndale New Testament Commentaries (Downers Grove, IL: InterVarsity Press, 1983), 172–77.

13. Jamieson, Fausset, and Brown, *Commentary Critical and Explanatory on the Whole Bible*, 458.

14. Peterson, "Hebrews," 1338.

blessings: the exact fulfilment of the earthly promises was a pledge of the fulfilment of the heavenly."[15]

"CHRIST IS PRIEST"

MICHAEL S. HORTON

The writer to the Hebrews belabors the point that Jesus is not only the prophet greater than Moses but the priest greater than Aaron and the Levitical priesthood. It is necessary to delve into that typological system in order to understand what Christ fulfills and transcends. Yet as we also see in this section, our own contexts influence how we hear that Christ is our high priest.

In most cultures, from ancient times to the present, priests form a special class. The chapters in this section display the various ways in which Christ's mediatorial priesthood is conditioned by cultural assumptions.

My context is relatively unique in that regard. Until the middle of the twentieth century, an interdenominational Protestantism, fused with civil religion, was the dominant religious influence. Priests were seen as part of an Old World from which humanity had been emancipated. Shaped especially by the revivalism of the First and Second Great Awakenings, American piety was more individualistic, suspicious of external authority and mediation. Anything that stood in between the soul and God was considered alienating. Rituals, including baptism and the Lord's Supper, along with formal liturgies recited communally, were seen as stifling to a personal relationship with God. Priests are associated with hearing confessions and giving absolution, but the priesthood of all believers has come to mean for many American evangelicals that there is no divinely ordained ministry or means of grace. Instead, ministers are seen increasingly in secular terms as charismatic leaders, CEOs, entertaining personalities, life coaches, and therapists. Indeed, therapists have considerably greater prestige in American society than pastors. No doubt,

---

15. Jamieson, Fausset, and Brown, *Commentary Critical and Explanatory on the Whole Bible*, 458–59.

this is due largely to the loss of a Godward relationship. Not sin but dysfunction, not redemption but recovery become the dominant categories.

But if priesthood and mediation are pushed into the background, it becomes increasingly difficult to understand the central role of Christ. To introduce this section, I summarize briefly the priestly activity of Jesus as part of his messianic anointing.

Lamb on a Throne

We have a paradoxical image of the glorified king in heaven as a slain lamb upon a throne (Rev 5:6; 7:10). This is not the usual portrait of a powerful ruler on earth. The threefold office is integrative of aspects that are often separated into false choices—or at least emphases that marginalize other essential unbalanced emphases. In particular, it integrates Christ's person and work as well as his priestly ministry with prophetic and royal offices. Moreover, as a threefold office rather than "three offices," this rubric encourages us to view the offices dialectically: Christ's royal conquest, ascension, and session are not merely exclamation points to his sacrificial death but are further achievements in our redemption. Similarly, Christ's royal majesty is revealed precisely where it is hidden to the world (and often to us): at the cross where he was "lifted up" in order "to draw all people to myself" (John 12:32 ESV). Consequently, the threefold office integrates Christ's victory over the powers with his substitutionary sacrifice.

For this reason, I am wary of atonement theories as encountered in modern systematic theologies. The moral influence theory sees Christ's mediatorial work as exemplary: just as Jesus laid down his life for others, we should live sacrificially. Christ's death shows us how much God loves us, so we should love him and others in the same way. The chief question is: What would Jesus do? The governmental theory teaches that God's moral government is at stake in human rebellion and Christ's death shows us how seriously God takes sin, making it possible for him to offer forgiveness on easier terms than fulfilling the whole law. These are basically subjective theories of atonement in that the effect of Christ's work provides an example or offers terms that human beings fulfill in order to be reconciled to God. What is missing is the propitiation of God's wrath, based on his righteous judgment.

A more objective theory is "Christus Victor"—or the victory of Christ over Satan and demonic powers. According to this view, Christ actually accomplishes liberation of those oppressed by evil forces. Another objective theory is penal substitution; in other words, Christ's taking the place of sinners in bearing the full sentence that God's righteous law imposes.

Christ's work cannot be divided into theories but is a seamless garment that answers the complex problem of sin. First, we are born in original sin. Created good—indeed, in the image of God—we fell with Adam, our first mediator, into ruin and condemnation. Adam's sin is imputed to us and his corruption becomes our pollution. We are not sinners because we sin; we sin because we are sinners. Christ's work addresses this tragedy by imputing our sins to Christ, the last Adam, and by the imputation of his obedience to us. In this way, Jesus recapitulates (re-headships) the church. His new humanity, the body of Christ, is justified—declared not only "not guilty" but "perfectly just" in Jesus Christ. Yet he is also the answer to our corruption—the bondage of sin. This is where the emphasis on Christ as victor comes into view.

Yet it becomes clear that each theory by itself falls short of the whole biblical teaching. Only if Christ is the vicarious sacrifice is he actually an example of self-sacrifice (Phil 2:5). If Jesus is *only* an example, he does not save helpless sinners but only redirects them. And he cannot restore God's moral government if he does not actually satisfy the whole law on our behalf. Only if Christ is "the Lamb of God who takes away the sin of the world" (John 1:29) is it possible for God to be "just and the justifier of the one who has faith in Jesus" (Rom 3:26). And according to the Scriptures, Christ is the victor over Satan and the evil powers, including death, because he satisfied the legal requirements of God's righteousness. Satan holds us in his power and prosecutes a legitimate case against us, requiring our excommunication to his dungeon of death. But if Christ has fulfilled the law's demands and born the death-sentence for us, he loses his title to us:

> And you, who were dead in your trespasses and the uncircumcision
> of your flesh, God made alive together with him, having forgiven us
> all our trespasses, by canceling the record of debt that stood against

us with its legal demands. This he set aside, nailing it to the cross. He disarmed the rulers and authorities and put them to open shame, by triumphing over them in him. (Col 2:13–15 ESV)

Jesus conquers death itself by bearing the *sentence* that requires it according to the law: "The sting of death is sin, and the power of sin is the law. But thanks be to God, who gives us the victory through our Lord Jesus Christ" (1 Cor 15:56–57 ESV). In other words, Christ is only victor over death, hell, Satan, and demons because he has taken our place in fulfilling the law and bearing our transgressions (see also Isa 53). He is only an example of loving self-sacrifice for others if he indeed offered himself as a sacrifice for sin. He only ensures God's moral government if he fulfills every command of God and bears its sanction in our place. Vicarious substitution is not the whole of Christ's mediatorial priesthood, but apart from it all of the other effects are suspended in midair.

Presuppositions of an Adequate Doctrine of Christ's Priesthood

The first presupposition is the God revealed in Christ's priestly ministry. The triune God is absolutely free from the world he created; there is no necessity in his act of deliverance, whether imposed from without or required by his nature. The economic missions of the persons of the Trinity are "fitting" exhibitions of the immanent processions but must be distinguished. The Father sent his Son merely out of the freedom of his love (John 3:16), and the Son freely gave his life in love through the Spirit (John 10:18). The Father freely chose a bride for his Son from all eternity (John 17:9; Eph 1:4–5). In joyful anticipation of the union, the Son freely accepted the role of her as mediator, already knowing that it would include his humiliation and sacrifice. This intra-Trinitarian pact serves as the absolute and unconditional basis of gracious redemption and its application. "He was foreknown before the foundation of the world but was made manifest in the last times for the sake of you" (1 Pet 1:20). Consequently, God's very heart is revealed in Christ's priestly ministry.

A second presupposition of Christ's priestly office is the teaching of Scripture concerning the plight from which he came to save us.

The threefold office lies at the heart of humanity's creation in God's image and likeness, male and female. Although Adam is the representative head of the race, Eve shared equally in this image with its threefold office. This status was not something added; it belongs intrinsically to human nature. Their personhood discloses the work they had to accomplish, and their work discloses their identity as God's creaturely analogies. Imitating the triune God's pattern of work and rest, they were to interpret reality by relying on every word from God as true prophets, to bring a sacrifice of obedient thanksgiving as priests and, as subordinate monarchs, to rule God's kingdom and subdue all his enemies. Fulfilling this task, they and their posterity would be confirmed in righteousness, qualified to eat the immortalizing fruit of the Tree of Life (which returns at the end of the story). Tragically, the covenant head of the human race chose instead to seek life from himself. After the fall, Adam and Eve needed not only to bring a tribute-offering to Yahweh as the source of their biological life but a sacrificial offering for guilt.

The complexity of our fallen condition is the presupposition of Christ's multifaceted work. On the one hand, there has always been a Pelagian temptation to reduce the human problem to sinful actions that render people sinful. In this perspective, one downplays or even denies the reality of inherited guilt and corruption. To become righteous, one merely has to heed God's commands and refuse to commit sinful acts. If Adam serves merely as a bad example, Christ is viewed merely as a good example: a prophet and king, perhaps, but his priestly work seems to be hardly necessary. Correspondingly, salvation may be seen only as a fresh opportunity to repent and conquer individual sins in our life, but this leads inevitably to alternating between self-righteousness and despair.

If, however, we are conceived "in Adam" (1 Cor 15:22), in a condition of guilt and corruption, bound by and even "dead in trespasses and sins" (Eph 2:1), then a moral teacher and example will not help us. "For by works of the law no human being will be justified in his sight, since through the law comes knowledge of sin" (Rom 3:20). Often, especially in our day, this assumption leads many to downplay the reality of the fallen condition that extends to the whole person, body and soul, and to the whole world, human and nonhuman. We are sinners and those sinned-against, perpetrators and victims. We are responsible agents and sufferers from mental illnesses, genetic mutations, chemical imbalances, and systemic injustices. Only if the curse is so extensive can we rejoice in a redemption that is greater than our sin: "Where sin increased, grace increased all the more" (Rom 5:20)—or as the hymn "Joy to the World" puts it, "far as the curse is found." Athanasius and Anselm are remembered for a similar formulation of Christ's person from his work based on the sinful condition in which God finds humanity. The savior must be identical with our nature to be our representative head, recapitulating what was lost in Adam. However, only God can save us.

Third, any satisfactory account of Christ's priesthood must be a fulfillment of the types and shadows of the Aaronic/Levitical priesthood. By themselves, exemplary and moral government theories evade the seriousness of sin and the righteous judgment of God, rendering the sacrificial system of the Old Testament quite beside the point. Christ is the scapegoat, the sacrificial lamb, the high priest, and the victim: hence the startling portrait of the conquering Lamb who was slain in Revelation 5. Yet his priesthood transcends this typological order since he belongs to the "order of Melchizedek." Hebrews 7 delineates the superiority of Christ's Melchizedekian priesthood to that of Aaron and the Levites.

Fourth, Christ's priestly ministry cannot be separated from his royal office. In Adam, we all cast off God's sovereignty for the mirage of autonomy, leading only to tragic consequences not only for ourselves but for others. Yet even Israel rejected Yahweh as king, preferring to have a powerful warrior-king they could see and boast in before the nations. But united hypostatically in Christ's person is the Lord who commands and the servant who fulfills the covenant. In our name and nature, a human son finally has submitted himself to "every word" (Matt 4:4) and deed commanded by his Father. At the same time, as God he has reassumed his throne in the historical economy, not only in Israel but universally. God is king but now and forever is one of us, bone of our bone. Usually, rulers demand the blood of their subjects to protect the kingdom. Nowhere can we see the redefinition of lordship more than in the King of Heaven hanging on a cross to secure his realm.

Priestly Mediation of the Ascended Christ

Christ's current reign as king is priestly in a variety of ways: (1) interceding for us; (2) creating and sustaining the church through the gospel of forgiveness in him; (3) granting us his Spirit who convicts and assures us of this forgiveness through the gospel in preaching, baptism, and the Lord's Supper; (4) the priestly identity and mission of the church as "a kingdom of priests" (Rev 1:6) sharing in his anointing. In Christ, who is the last Adam, the children of the first Adam have been restored in their threefold office at last. As hearers, heralds, and doers of God's word rather than of Satan's lies, they are made faithful prophets. They exhibit their priesthood by intercessions and absolution and by their sacrifice of praise. Seated with Christ in heavenly places, his anointed are restored to a proper function of ruling by serving and, one day, by participating with Christ in his final judgment.

In the following three essays, we hear from Chinese, Indian, and Korean theologians, each of whom considers what it means for Christ to fulfill this priestly office and its significance in their particular contexts. What emerges is a varied yet consistent affirmation that, like his prophetic office, Christ's priesthood is greater.

CHAPTER 4

CHRIST'S PRIESTLY OFFICE IN CONFUCIAN CONTEXTS

SHAO KAI TSENG

This chapter explores the significance of a Chalcedonian understanding of Christ's priesthood in a Chinese context informed by historic developments and contemporary receptions of Confucianism. In the first section, I will offer a historical analysis of how the conglomeration of the high-priestly and imperial offices in Confucianism came to inform modern and contemporary Chinese national consciousness.

In the second section, I will offer an analysis of how Chinese churches have come under the influence of Confucian understandings of priesthood. In particular, I will give examples of this phenomenon from my experience as a member of a loosely held confessional Reformed Presbyterian movement that has been taking place in China and in ethnically Chinese regions and communities worldwide for about two decades.

The purpose of this chapter is to demonstrate the significance of a Chalcedonian understanding of priesthood in a Chinese cultural context informed by Confucianism(s). I will argue that many Confucians in Chinese history, in diverse manners, aspired to a universal priesthood of all enlightened individuals under heaven and yet were unable to fulfil such aspirations because they lacked the qualitative notion of transcendence as the pretext of the priestly office. My thesis is that the Chalcedonian understanding of Christ's priestly office, predicated upon strong notions of transcendence defined in terms of the Creator-creature distinction and of the gulf of sin between God and humanity as a result of the fall, allows for the truly universal priesthood of all believers that many Confucians longed for: all believers, not just the supreme political ruler on earth or high-ranking officials elected by the ruler, come before the ever-transcendent and holy God, once hidden in the Most Holy Place, to offer ourselves as sacrifices in, through, and with Christ, who is at once our high priest, our sacrifice of satisfaction and expiation, the temple, the Most Holy Place, and the way to God through the curtain torn (see Heb 10:1–23).

CULTURAL UNDERSTANDINGS OF THE PRIESTLY OFFICE IN CHINESE HISTORY

The philosopher Immanuel Kant (1724–1804) aptly observed that the problem of atonement is "the greatest difficulty" of philosophy and rational religion.[1] He states the problem: "Whatever may have happened in [a human being's] case with the adoption of a good attitude, and indeed, however persistently he continues in this attitude in a way of life conforming to it, he yet started from evil, and his indebtedness will never be possible for him to erase."[2] This impossibility lies in the fact that "moral evil carries with it an infinity of violations of the law and hence an infinity of guilt," and finite human beings are utterly unable to erase this guilt by their own efforts.[3]

---

1. Immanuel Kant, *Religion within the Bounds of Bare Reason*, trans. Werner Pluhar (Indianapolis: Hackett, 2009), 80.

2. Kant, *Religion*, 80.

3. Kant, *Religion*, 70. See John Hare, *The Moral Gap: Kantian Ethics, Human Limits, and God's Assistance* (Oxford: Oxford University Press, 1996), 35. Twentieth-century Anglo-American philosophers and theologians popularly understood Kant to be taking on the mission impossible, so to speak, of solving the problem of the atonement with a moral and civic religion developed *by reason alone*, a view that has come to be challenged and even discarded among many leading Anglophone Kant scholars today. See Chris Firestone and Stephen Palmquist, eds., *Kant and the New Philosophy of Religion* (Bloomington: University of Indiana Press, 2006). Kant himself states in *The Metaphysics of Morals* (1797) that pure religion "is not . . . derived from reason alone but is also based on the teachings of history and revelation, and considers only the harmony of pure practical reason with these." Immanuel Kant, *The Metaphysics of Morals*, ed., trans. Mary Gregor (Cambridge: Cambridge University Press, 1991), 276. For an authoritative comment on this quote, see Hare, *The Moral Gap*, 40n4.

Confucians, generally speaking, are humble enough to claim educated ignorance on the problem of the atonement. Confucianism is sharply aware of the problem of sin as moral guilt but refrains from trying to answer it. Instead, Confucianism, apart from special revelation, wisely focuses on what human beings *ought to do* by inquiring into the cosmic moral order reflected in the structures of human reason and society. That is, instead of speculating on the possibility of atonement for sin, Confucianism typically places the emphasis of philosophical reflections on sanctification.

FROM ELIZABETH W. MBURU

Many African societies, even today, hold to a retribution theology—what Kenyatta calls "the law of give and take." In the Kikuyu culture of Kenya, angering God or the ancestors by doing or saying things that would cause a rift in the family or community fellowship was bound to invoke their wrath and swift judgment in the form of disease and other natural catastrophes. The only recourse was the priestly activity of sacrifice, which had the propitiatory function of appeasing the wrath of the beings to whom offense had been caused.

It pertains to another discussion of whether sanctification is possible apart from the work of the Holy Spirit in Christ. What interests us at this juncture is the development in historic Confucianism(s) of the notion of *moral* priesthood. In this regard Confucianism differs sharply from religious practices in which priestly activities, such as those found in Shamanism as discussed in Tom Park's chapter, are intended for bribing the gods or appeasing their tantrums, so to speak.

FROM THOMAS PARK

Numerous studies have been conducted on the leadership styles of the Korean pastors, especially in American contexts.[a] It is not uncommon to hear about fractures happening in Korean American churches due to negative pastoral leadership.

Some studies have investigated further regarding the reasons for these problems in Korean and Korean American churches and have found a link to unhealthy shamanistic elements. "Thus, in the midst of rapid modernization, shamanism remains an underground value system that easily blends with Confucianism, Buddhism, and even with Christianity."[b]

Too often Korean American pastors negatively wield their authority in churches. Rather than pastors serving their congregants and ministry partners, they become like despots and secular politicians: ruthless and vindictive. The senior pastor of a Korean-language ministry might exercise authority over the English-speaking Korean ministry simply because the senior pastor is older. Then the Korean-speaking pastor and members treat their English-speaking pastors and members like second-class citizens by rarely placing assistant pastors and English-ministry members in the leadership positions or as decision makers.[c]

Many scholars have pointed out that shamanism might be responsible for contributing to this phenomenon. In the world of shamans, whoever can predict the future and fix their clients' problems becomes the popular and influential shaman. Anthropologist Andrew Kim explained shamanism this way: "The fundamental purpose of Shamanism is to fulfill practical needs: People solicit the service of a shaman in hopes of realizing their material wishes, such as longevity, health, male births, and wealth."[d] The Machiavellian dictum "the end justifies the means" fits the psyche of the Korean-shaman world and some unhealthy Christian congregations.

---

[a] Moo Yong Lim, "Leadership and Culture: A Phenomenological Study of the Impact of Cultural Dimensions on the Leadership Behavior of Pastors in the Korean Evangelical Church of America" (PhD diss., Concordia Theological Seminary, 2011); Sehwan Kim, "A Study of Intergenerational Conflict between Pastors in Korean American Immigrant Churches" (PhD diss., Concordia Theological Seminary, 2014).

[b] Gyeongchun Choi, "A Theology of Missional Leadership in the Book of Revelation" (PhD diss., St. Andrews Seminary, 2016), 18; Byong-suh Kim, Robert E. Buswell Jr. and Timothy S. Lee, *Modernization and Korean Protestant Religiosity in Christianity in Korea* (Honolulu: University of Hawaii Press, 2006), 324; Andrew Eungi Kim, "Christianity, Shamanism, and Modernization in South Korea," *Cross Current* 50, no. 1/2 (Spring/Summer) (2000): 116; Nam-hyuck Jang, *Shamanism in Korean Christianity* (Edison, NJ: Jimoondang International, 2004).

[c] Tom, "Has the Second-Generation Korean-American Church Failed Us?," *Tom Talks* (blog), January 31, 2018, http://www.tom-talks.org/blog/2018/1/26/has-the-second-generation-korean -american-church-failed-us; Terence Kim, *A Letter to the Korean American Church: Reconciling the Gap Between First and Second Generation Koreans* (Afton, VA: ANM, 2019).

[d] Andrew Kim, "Korean Religious Culture and Its Affinity to Christianity: The Rise of Protestant Christianity in South Korea," *Sociology of Religion* 61, no. 2 (2000): 119.

Gaozi (告子, 420–350 BC) propagated the view that human nature at birth is like a blank slate without natural inclinations. Propensities toward moral good or evil are all acquired through social influences. Disagreeing with Gaozi, Mencius (孟子, 372–289 BC) taught that human beings are naturally inclined toward the good, though he acknowledged that human beings easily become wicked through social influences.

Among historic schools of Confucianism, the views of Xunzi (荀子, 316–237 BC), who envisions heaven as corporeal and entirely immanent to nature, come closest to the Christian doctrine of human fallenness. In line with Confucian norms, Xunzi posited the reality of a higher cosmic order to which ethical conventions in society ought to conform. Human nature, however, is naturally inclined toward evil. Followers of Xunzi thus tend to be more compassionate toward those who behave in morally bad ways. They dedicate themselves to the ritual cultivation (禮儀教化) of sinful individuals, believing that enlightenment or learning as such would enable human beings to discover the moral laws of heaven with the use of reason and be trained through ritual exercises to behave habitually in accordance with these laws. Such ritual exercises would include, for example, acts of filial piety (孝) toward one's parents and ancestors.

The Confucian notion of rituals does not necessarily involve rites. Some rituals are performed through ways of living. For example, Confucians take it as a ritual principle that a son should never travel afar when his parents are alive, unless there is an absolute necessity (父母在, 不遠遊, 遊必有方). Other rituals are performed through formal aspects of everyday behaviors. For instance, in order to honor the ethical hierarchy in a family, a father and son should never dine at the same table, and an uncle and nephew should never drink together (父子不同桌, 叔侄不對飲). Rituals involving rites would include burning incense and offering up meat cut in the shape of perfect cubes as acts of remembrance in ancestral tributes (in mainline Confucianism) or veneration and even worship (in folk Confucianism).

The ultimate object of ritual piety is heaven (天), and this piety is manifested through one's devotion to the supreme political ruler as Son of Heaven (天子). This is not just the view of Xunzi; rather, it has been a consensus among Confucians through the ages until the rise of New Confucianism (新儒家) in the twentieth century.

In the Confucian tradition that originated from the Eastern Zhou Dynasty (東周, ca. 770–256 BC), the priesthood is composed of high-ranking government officials closely related to the imperial court. The supreme ruler of the Zhou (周, c. 1046–256 BC) was given the title of the Son of Heaven (天子). A longstanding tradition in Catholic sinology, handed down from the time of Matteo Ricci (1552–1610) to contemporary scholars like Fu Pei-Jung (傅佩榮), has forcefully argued that before the Qin Period (秦, 221–207 BC), in which the first emperor in Chinese history adopted the divine title of *Di* (帝), the notion of heaven, also called the Supreme *Di* (上帝), was largely understood to be a personal and qualitatively transcendent being.[4]

The title Son of Heaven, then, was first and foremost that of a high-priestly office playing an ethically and relationally mediatorial role between transcendent heaven and earthly humanity on earth, representing heaven to his subjects and his subjects to heaven. When the wrath of heaven against sinful behaviors on earth is revealed through natural disasters, the Son of Heaven is responsible for performing rites of repentance to heaven on behalf of the people.

FROM HAVILAH DHARAMRAJ

In the royal courts of ancient India, the task of mediation between "earth and heaven" belonged to a specialist. This was the astrologer. From the Hindu sages in the early centuries AD comes this advice: "As the night without a light, as the sky without the sun, so is the king without an astrologer; he is like the blind man who wanders on the road. If there were no astrologer, the hours, lunar days, stars, seasons, and half-years would all be confused. Therefore a wise and eminent astrologer should be consulted by a king who desires victory, fame, good fortune, pleasures, and health."[a] The king was supported by a priest and an astrologer, but even the priest appears to have been subject to the favor of the astrologer: a king

---

4. See Pei-Jung Fu, "The Concept of 'T'ien' in Ancient China: With Special Emphasis on Confucianism" (PhD diss., Yale University, 1984).

should abandon a priest who is opposed to the astrologer. This is because it was the astrologer who linked the worlds. He studied and interpreted the planets, he could predict how they influenced the fate of the king, and he knew the ways to appease unfavorable celestial dispositions. In Jesus, we have the "wise" ultimate "astrologer." He does not need to study the planets and stars. He made them. His work is far greater than that of the Chinese Emperor-priest and the Indian court astrologer. His wisdom allows him to mediate between God and humankind and to save the latter from the wrath of the former, not by deflection or dissipation but by sacrificially letting that wrath fall upon himself.

[a] Varahamihira, *Brihat Samhita*, 2.6; 8–10.

When the First Emperor of Qin (秦始皇, 259–210 BC) adopted the title of *Di*, from the word for "oracle" (諦), the status of the Son of Heaven was elevated to that of a demigod in whom supreme priesthood, prophethood, and kingship converge.[5] This was partly responsible for the immanentization of the notion of heaven in subsequent Chinese history and Confucian schools of thought. Throughout the history of imperial China, the emperor retained the office of a high priest mediating between heaven and humanity, while humanity and divinity in the person of the emperor had been significantly confused.

Neo-Confucianism of the Song Dynasty (宋, 960–1279) gave rise to the Scholastic School (理學) that continues to inform Chinese culture to our day. Incorporating certain insights of Daoism into its system, neo-Confucianism of the Song consistently holds to a quantitatively rather than qualitatively transcendent notion of heaven.

The neo-Confucian School of the Heart (心學), which culminated in Wang Yangming (王陽明, 1472–1529) of the Ming Dynasty (明, 1368–1644), further posited an identity between heaven and humanity. This movement led to the deification of the common folk. It taught that the process of learning is to discover the divine nature and cosmic order that dwell within every

---

5. According to the *Kanxi Dictionary* (康熙字典, 1716), "The reason why *Di* is named *Di* is that it is one name of Heaven. The word *Di* [帝] refers to *Di* [諦] or divine Word" (帝者, 天之一名, 所以名帝。帝者, 諦也).

human heart. New Confucians of the twentieth century like Mou Zongsan (牟宗三, 1909–95), drawing on both the Scholastic School and the School of the Heart while borrowing the terminology of Western philosophy and theology, describe the Christian notion of transcendence as an "objective" (客觀) one, insisting that Confucianism holds to the dogma of an "inner transcendence" (內在超越).[6] That is to say, the infinite *Dao* that transcends all finite human individuals inheres within the human mind such that the finite and the infinite are simply two poles of the same entity.

These immanentistic developments from medieval to recent Confucianisms significantly weakened the exclusivity of the mediatorial role of the supreme political ruler. Still, the notion that China is the heavenly realm (天朝) with a supreme political ruler as the union of the physical embodiment of heaven and the representative of the subjects of the heavenly realm in a single person remains deeply ingrained in Chinese culture even to this day. That is, although the common folk can communicate with heaven through their hearts, the nation as a whole would be saved from the plight of evil (including moral evil and sufferings) and blessed by heaven only if the supreme ruler as the representative of the people behaves in accordance with the moral will of heaven.

This cultural understanding of the union of divine and human natures in the person of the supreme political ruler in a high-priestly capacity partly explains why contemporary China continues to hold to Marxism as the official state religion even after the dissolution of the former USSR. Marxist materialism, which Soviet philosophers came to describe as "dialectical materialism," is in fact pantheistic. It does not simply view the material universe as a "heap of rubbish poured out at random" (Heraclitus).

Marxism, following Left Hegelians like Ludwig Feuerbach (1804–72), sees matter as inherently "divine" and purposive. This divinity, of course, is an immanentized version of the Christian notion of the transcendent God and is to be strictly differentiated from the God of Scripture. Feuerbach contends that "the divine being is nothing else than the human being, or rather,

---

6. See Mou Zongsan [牟宗三], *Topics and Developments in Song-Ming Confucianism* [宋明儒學的問題與發展] (Taipei: Linking, 2003).

the human nature purified, freed from the limits of the individual man.... All attributes of the divine nature are ... attributes of the human nature."[7]

The Taiwanese sinologist Chao-Ying Chen has demonstrated striking parallels between Xunzi's theory of heaven and Feuerbach's immanentization and universalization of the union of divine and human natures: both deny the qualitative transcendence of the divine nature and attribute it to the human "species-being."[8] This Confucian notion of the immanent union of heaven and humanity, as we saw, is not peculiar to Xunzi, though amongst the Confucian masters Xunzi comes closest to the Feuerbachian view.

Marxism relies on Feuerbach's criticism of religion and further argues that religion lies with absolutist regimes rather than with the church as Christ's body and God's invisible kingdom, to actualize the divine potentiality within human nature. The twentieth-century German jurist Carl Schmitt (1888–1985) incisively observes that "all significant concepts of the modern theory of the state" after Hegel, including and perhaps especially that of Marx, "are secularized theological concepts" because, as far as their "historical development" is concerned, "they were transferred from theology to the theory of the state."[9] The Jewish Christian philosopher Karl Löwith (1897–1973), student of Martin Heidegger (1889–1976) and intellectual mentor of Wolfhart Pannenberg (1928–2014) no less, has also pointed out that Marxism is essentially a secularized version of Christianity.[10]

Marxism, on this view, drew all its key ideas from Christianity, but it desacralized the sacred and leveled the qualitatively transcendent to the dust in order to elevate the mundane to a sacred and quantitatively transcendent status. In many ways, then, the religious tenets of Marxism cater to the religious sensibility that contemporary Chinese society inherited from imperial

---

7. Ludwig Feuerbach, *The Essence of Christianity*, trans. George Eliot (New York: Prometheus, 1989), 14.

8. See Chen Chao-Ying [陳昭瑛], "Humankind as Species-Being: Xunzi's Humanistic Spirit Revisited [人作為「類的存有」：荀子人文精神重探]," in Hong-Hsin Lin [林鴻信], ed., *Humanistic Spirit from Intercultural Perspectives: Confucianism, Buddhism, Christianity, and Judaism in Dialogue* [跨文化視野中的人文精神——儒、佛、耶、猶的觀點與對話芻議] (Taipei: National Taiwan University Press, 2011), 40–43.

9. Carl Schmitt, *Political Theology: Four Chapters on the Concept of Sovereignty*, trans. George Schwab (Chicago: Chicago University Press, 2005), 36.

10. See Karl Löwith, *Meaning in History: The Theological Implications of the Philosophy of History* (Chicago: University of Chicago Press, 1957).

China. Marxism, like the older Confucian religion, attributes to the reigning political regime or supreme political ruler a high-priestly office in the patterns of Christ the God-man. This partly explains why the People's Republic of China as a purportedly atheistic state constitutionally describes itself as "*shénshèng*" (神圣), variously rendered as "sacred" and "inviolable" in the official English translation but literally meaning "divine and holy."

FROM THOMAS PARK

Some Christians and non-Christians view Christian pastors as possessing the same responsibilities as shamans, invoking the name of Jesus to bring health, wealth, and success. The prosperity gospel became the focus of many congregations, pastors, and members who do not clearly understand the essence of Christianity and Christ. The word 기복신앙 (*Gibok Shinahng*)[a] is loosely translated to "faith in blessings." Just the way that nonbelievers tried to coax ancestors and household deities to bless them, some Christians use similar tactics to force God to bless them. Therefore, there are tendencies to look at health issues, poverty, demotion, job loss, and children not being able to attend four-year colleges as the sign of divine displeasure. Rather than comforting other Christians who face difficulties with words of God's love and grace, those who subconsciously embrace the shamanistic understanding of the world would condemn those brothers and sisters for committing sins or lack of faith. Connecting disasters and misfortunes to specific sins and seeing these as the evidence of the divine judgment has been common at least since Job's friends accused Job for his sins.

In my Christian faith tradition, Lutheranism, we discuss the theology of the glory and theology of the cross. The theology of the glory is the worldview promoted by shamans, which sought success and prosperity. If disasters strike, the theologians of the glory blame others for sinning and not being dedicated to God. They view setbacks in life as God's judgment. On the other hand, the theology of the cross teaches that if we believe in Christ, we will face persecution and difficulties from the forces of evil. Our lives will be like Jesus's life on earth.

---

[a] Rhonda Garrison Haynes, "Korean Christianity and Influence of Shamanism," paper, Trinity Evangelical Divinity School, 2018, 14.

CONFUCIAN PRIESTHOOD IN CHINESE REFORMED CHRISTIANITY

The Confucian notion of priesthood, broadly understood, continues to inform not only Chinese societies but also Sinophone churches today. Of all major brands of Christianity in China, the Reformed tradition to which I belong is exceedingly emphatic on God's qualitative transcendence to creation. But even this tradition of Sinophone theology has come under the influence of Confucian understandings of priesthood.

One highly influential view that runs through Chinese Reformed theologians from Jia Yuming (賈玉銘, 1880–1964) and Charles Chao (趙中輝, 1916–2010) to Stephen Tong (唐崇榮, 1940–) is the description of Christ's human nature as an eternal and uncreated part of his divine person. This view, condemned with other Origenist doctrines at the Fifth Ecumenical Council (553), not only contradicts the theological axioms undergirding the Symbol of Chalcedon but is also at odds with the explicit teaching of the Belgic Confession: "Christ's human nature has not lost its properties but continues to have those of a creature—it has a beginning of days; it is of a finite nature and retains all that belongs to a real body" (art. 19).

The application of the axiom "the finite cannot contain the infinite" (*finitum non capax infiniti*) to Christ's human nature, of course, was not the invention of Calvin or later Reformed theologians.[11] It goes all the way back to the Church Fathers like Athanasius and is clearly stated in Thomas Aquinas.[12] Yet Reformed theology's concerted emphasis on this Chalcedonian formula is grounded in the Creator-creature distinction. The fact that the aforementioned Chinese Reformed theologians would develop such an un-Reformed view, then, is highly intriguing to historians of doctrine like myself.

My belief is that what these theologians found in Reformed theology is

---

11. *Extra-Calvinisticum*: the Reformed application of the theological axiom of the Latin West, "the finite cannot contain the infinite" (*finitum non capax infiniti*), to the abiding distinction between Christ's two natures. The doctrine says that Christ, according to the finite creatureliness of his human nature, never came to and can never come to possess any of God's incommunicable attributes such as omniscience and omnipresence.

12. Aquinas, *Summa Theologae* 3, q. 9, a. 2.

a doctrine of God with high promises to restore qualitative notions of divine transcendence (and sovereignty) in the Chinese context. What this unilateral emphasis on divine transcendence misses is the way Reformed theology applies the Creator-creature distinction to Christology in general and to Christ's priestly office in particular.

Stephen Tong, for instance, has set forth the syllogism that (1) if the uncreated God alone is to be worshiped, and that (2) Christ is to be worshiped, then (3) no "part" of Christ can be of a creaturely nature. This means, for Tong, that the human "part" of Christ has to be uncreated along with the whole Christ and the whole *of* Christ.[13]

This line of argument is doctrinally problematic in at least two aspects. First, the Reformed Orthodox unanimously affirmed that Christ as the incarnate God-man, the Creator who became a creature without ceasing to be uncreated, is to be the object of divine honor and worship.[14] John Owen states that "all divine honour is due to the Son of God incarnate—that is, the person of Christ," not because he is uncreated according to his human nature but because the "infinite condescension, in the assumption of our nature, did no way divest him of his divine essential excellencies."[15]

Second, Tong's argument departs from Chalcedonian Christianity in the first instance in thinking of Christ's human nature as a "part" of his person: the Symbol of Chalcedon is abundantly clear that Christ's person is *fully* divine and *fully* human. Traditionally, the divine and the human are defined as predicates of the entire person of Christ, rather than different parts of the person.

What is especially pertinent to our discussion of Christ's priesthood is that this syllogism overlooks the patristic argument that Christ can be a priest—a worshiper—*only if* he is a creature. To deny the creatureliness of Christ in his human nature while concurring that Christ is our high priest is tantamount to asserting a subordinationism according to which the Son is a

---

13. See Stephen Tong [唐崇榮], *Christology* [基督論] (Taipei: CMI, 1994), 161–62.

14. For example, Francis Turretin, *Institutes of Elenctic Theology*, 3 vols., ed. James Dennison, trans. George Giger (Phillipsburg: P&R, 1992–97), 2:496.

15. John Owen, *A Declaration of the Glorious Mystery of the Person of Christ*, in *The Works of John Owen*, ed. William Goold, 23 vols. (Edinburg: Banner of Truth, 1956), 1:105.

lesser deity owing worship to the Father. The famed Athanasian formula that runs through the writings of Cyril and undergirds Chalcedonian Christology makes this point clear: only in "Jesus Christ our Lord, through whom and with whom, to the Father with the Son himself in the Holy Spirit" can we offer ourselves as sacrifices pleasing to God.

This Patristic teaching was retained by Reformed Orthodoxy. Owen explains that in view of the unity of Christ's person, he "as God and man . . . is the object of all divine honour and worship. His person, and both his natures in that person, is so the object of religious worship."[16] In view of the abiding distinction between the two natures, however, "it is as he is God, equal with the Father, and not as Mediator," that honor and worship are due to him, while he honors and worships the Father *as* a creature in the priestly office "in which respect he [Christ] is inferior unto him [the Father]."[17]

In his priestly office, furthermore, Christ acts not only as the high priest but also as the sacrifice of atonement. That is to say, Christ "was made man" in order to die "for us and for our salvation" (Chalcedon). The Creator is immutably immortal—he cannot die. So unless Christ was made a creature, his death on the cross would not have been real. It would have been the death of a fleeting shadow that was not his true being. Yet this was precisely the heresy of docetism. Chalcedonian Christianity has consistently emphasized that he who died at the cross—though he *is* the Creator—did not die *as* the Creator but rather *as* a creature.

Still, he who died *as* a creature at the cross *is* God. This statement goes hand in hand with Chalcedon's recognition of Mary as the "mother of God" (*theotokos*). To say that Mary is only the "mother of Christ" yet not the "mother of God" is tantamount to saying that Christ is not God— that the man Jesus Christ and God the Son are two separate persons. But because the man Jesus *is* God the Son, the mother of this man has to be regarded as the mother of God: not only the "mother of God the Son" but also the "mother of God." Christ is "fully" God—he is the fulness of the Godhead—rather than one third of the triune God.

---

16. Owen, *A Declaration of the Glorious Mystery*, 1:119.
17. Owen, *A Declaration of the Glorious Mystery*, 1:119.

FROM THOMAS PARK

When it comes to understanding the divine and human natures of Jesus, the Reformed and Lutherans have some differences. The Reformed described Christ's two natures by using the axiom "the finite cannot contain the infinite" (*finitum non capax infiniti*). Interestingly, this understanding of Christology also influences the Reformed view of the Lord's Supper. The resurrected and ascended Jesus is sitting at the right hand of God in heaven. The orthodox understanding of Christ is that even in his glorified state he is fully God and fully human. Therefore, whenever the Lord's Supper is celebrated, the human nature of Jesus cannot be omnipresent. Thus, the Reformed uphold Christ's spiritual presence in the Lord's Supper rather than the bodily presence, or Real Presence as the Lutheran Church believes, confesses, and teaches. Luther's Small Catechism defines the Lord's Supper this way: "It is the true body and blood of our Lord Jesus Christ, under the bread and wine, for us Christians to eat and drink, instituted by Christ Himself."[a]

Lutheran theology spells out that Christ's divine nature and human nature communicate and cooperate in the work of salvation. There are three genuses, but in order to address Dr. Tseng's points, I will provide definitions of *Genus Maiestateticum* and *Genus Aposlesticum*. As indicated previously, one's christological views affect other aspects of theology, especially the understanding of the Lord's Supper.

Genus Maiesteticum states that "the divine attributes are ascribed to the Person of Christ also according to His human nature, not indeed as essential to it, but as imparted in time, or as communicated attributes, since the divine nature with its attributes dwells in the human nature as in its own body and functions through it. . . . [This genus] expresses the fact that Christ, according to His human nature, possesses not merely extraordinary finite gifts, but divine majesty, or infinite divine attributes, by virtue of the personal union."[b]

The Formula of Concord defines *Genus Apolestiscum* this way: "As to the execution of the office of Christ, the person does not act and work in, with, and through, or according to only one nature, but in according to, with, and through both natures, or, as the Council of Chalcedon expresses it, one nature operates in communion with other what is the property of each. Therefore,

Christ is our Mediator, Redeemer, King, High Priest, Head, Shepherd, etc., not according to one nature only, whether it be the divine or the human, but according to both natures."[c]

―――――――

[a] Edward Engelbrecht, *The Lutheran Difference* (St. Louis: Concordia, 2014), 426.
[b] Francis Pieper, *Christian Dogmatics* (St. Louis: Concordia, 1951), 220.
[c] Pieper, *Christian Dogmatics*, 247.

There is an influential view among Chinese Reformed theologians that the Chalcedonian title of Mary is a Roman Catholic tradition that ought to be rejected by Protestants. Those who hold to this view include Stephen Tong and Luke Lu (呂沛淵).[18] Lu in particular contends that it is a doctrinal error to speak of the death of the Son of God at the cross, for God is immortal, and the agent that died at the cross was Christ's human nature.

One initial problem with this line of argument is that "human nature" cannot die. Human individuals die. God never created a universal "thing" called human nature. God created Adam and Eve as particular human individuals in accordance with his universal idea of humanity.

This is a consensus within the broad Christian tradition, but Reformed theology is especially emphatic on this point. Herman Bavinck reports that according to the Reformed faith, "universals . . . do not exist in reality. The tree, the human being, the science, the language, the religion, the theology are nowhere to be found. Only particular trees, human beings, sciences, languages, and religions exist."[19] This means that teachers of Reformed theology are supposed to have a clear understanding that Christ's human nature could not have been the subject of the death. It was Christ's person that died according to the human nature.

―――――――

18. Lu writes: "On the surface it would appear that the [Nestorian] controversy was about the biblical veracity of the term *Theotokos*. In fact, however, this was not the real point of contention. Indeed, as Christians who hold to orthodox faith, we would not choose to give to Mary this title (Lk. 8:20–21; 11:27–28), because the wording easily invites misunderstanding and enhances the heresy of the cult of Mary" (表面看來, theotokos 用詞是否合乎聖經真理, 是爭論的焦點。其 實, 問題癥結並不在此。我們正統信仰的基督徒, 的確不會選擇以此名稱稱呼馬利亞 (《路》8:20–21, 11:27–28), 因為字面意義容易引起誤會, 也會助長崇拜聖母的異端). Luke Lu [呂沛淵], "Church History 32: Foundation of the Righteous [教會史話32:義人的根基]," *Behold* [舉目] 38 (2009): https://behold.oc.org/?p=4347.

19. Herman Bavinck, *Reformed Dogmatics*, ed. John Bolt, trans. John Vriend, 4 vols. (Grand Rapids: Baker Academic, 2003–2008), 1:85.

Moreover, Christ's person is none other than the person of God the Son, and so we have to acknowledge Christ's death as the death of God just as we ought to recognize Mary as the mother of God. This is of utmost importance to our salvation. Anselm of Canterbury (1033/34–1109), in his celebrated *Cur Deus Homo*, offered a scholastic set of arguments for a position that the Nicene-Chalcedonian fathers already taught: only the death of him who is fully and truly God can be of infinite value as a sacrifice of atonement pleasing to God.

Building on this tradition, the Canons of Dort teaches: "God . . . has been pleased of His infinite mercy to give His only begotten Son for our Surety, who was made sin, and became a curse for us and in our stead, that He might make satisfaction to divine justice on our behalf" (second head, art. 2). And more: "The death of the Son of God is the only and most perfect sacrifice and satisfaction for sin, and is of infinite worth and value, abundantly sufficient to expiate the sins of the whole world" (second head, art. 3).

To refuse to acknowledge that he who died at the cross *is* very and fully God is to commit the error of a heresy known as Nestorianism. This refusal compromises the Reformed doctrine of Christ's priestly office by practically downplaying the efficacy of Christ's work of satisfaction as stated in the Canons of Dort.

This very un-Reformed reception of Reformed Christology again reflects the cultural context in which Sinophone theologians are situated. On one hand, they are eager to restore strong, qualitative notions of divine transcendence in this cultural context where so many other denominations and schools of theology try to reformulate the Christian doctrine of God in terms of a Confucian or Daoist understanding of the "union of heaven and humanity" (天人合一). The often unilateral emphasis on transcendence in Chinese Reformed traditions is partly responsible for compromises of the qualitative immanence (read: creatureliness) of Christ's human nature.

On the other hand, their departure from the *extra-Calvinisticum* is reflective of the immanentistic patterns of thinking characteristic of major Chinese traditions like Daoism, later (neo-)Confucianisms, and the various schools of mysticism (玄學). That is, their understandings of the union of Christ's two natures are closer to traditional Chinese understandings of the "union of Heaven and humanity" as the union of two qualitatively identical entities rather than the union of two natures distinguished by an infinite qualitative difference.

One result of the denial of the creatureliness of Christ's human nature in his priestly office is that it effectively expels him from the creaturely world. One would then need to establish a priestly mediator between Christ and believers in a way akin to the Confucian tradition of imperial priesthood handed down from the Zhou Period, when Heaven was still considered to be a qualitatively transcendent entity.

This partly explains why many churches in the older Chinese Reformed denominations have adopted patriarchal or paternalistic forms of church governance akin to authoritarian institutions in traditional Confucian society. This particular cultural background has been a significant hindrance to the universal priesthood of all believers and Presbyterian church governance in culturally Chinese contexts worldwide.

FROM HAVILAH DHARAMRAJ

The Indian Church has similarly accommodated patriarchy in its governance structures, influenced, perhaps, by Hinduism. In a temple, the deity—as represented by the idol—is the confluence of transcendence and immanence. When a new idol is to be installed in a newly built temple, the pupils of the eyes remain uncarved till the time of installation. At that point, an elaborate procedure called the "eye opening" takes place. The sculptor completes the pupils. A paste of collyrium may be applied as makeup. A consecrated mixture of ghee and honey is daubed on the eyes using a diamond-tipped gold stick.

It is thought that the ceremony, conducted by priests away from the public gaze, opens the channels through which the god can look through into the earthly realm. Before that is allowed, the deity is presented with ten auspicious items to view in succession, including an elephant, a cow with young, a saint, a king, a virgin, and a married woman. After these, the idol is considered ready to receive devotees and is open for the public to pay homage. The image itself is considered energized and powerful, but it only represents the deity rather than being the deity itself. Its purpose is as a focal point for veneration. As such, the transcendence of the deity remains intact and yet channels down into the idol, allowing a meeting point between deity and devotee. Even then, transcendence is maintained by the requirement of a priest to mediate between the idol and the worshiper. That priest is traditionally male.

In Christianity the idea that a merely human priest is a necessary go-between dissolves. In contrast to this role of a priest, whether in Hinduism or in the worship of YHWH, Jesus's person and work segues transcendence into immanence. He is Immanuel, "God with us." He is both God and priest, the door through which a devotee may directly access the Godhead.

Strange then, in the Indian church, is the continued idea that the priest or pastor functions as an exclusive and (only) proper channel between God and the lay Christian. This is not only true in liturgical traditions but also in congregational churches. The clergy, instead of viewing their role in terms of caring for the congregation, often see themselves as a hotline to God. This, of course, allows them the desired power to manipulate the laity. Authoritarianism and corruption result. All this, when Jesus, as God-priest, has established himself as the go-between for perpetuity.

Confessional Reformed Theology in Chinese Christianity: Promises and Caveats

In recent decades, Reformed Christians in China have launched an *ad fontes* movement to return to the confessional roots of the Reformed tradition. Their discoveries hold significant promises for the future of Chinese Christianity. I will conclude this chapter by outlining some of these promises while issuing certain caveats on the topic of Christ's priestly office.

Reformed Christians in China are increasingly aware of the catholic heritage of their tradition. The significance of Christ's priestly office, understood ecumenically, is evident in the Chinese context on at least the following points.

First, Christ was also born into a royal bloodline, but his priestly office and kingly office remain abidingly distinct though inseparably united. This serves as a reminder for Christians not to look for high-priestly figures in political or ecclesiastical rulers on earth.

Second, Christ who died at the cross *is* God, but he did not die *as* God. This means that although Christ's mediatorship consists in both his divine and human natures, in his priestly office he has acted and continues to act in accordance with his human nature, which remains abidingly distinct from yet inseparably united to his divine nature in one unabridged person. This speaks powerfully to the Chinese context in which the priestly notion of the "union of heaven and humanity" presupposes some qualitative identity between the two natures.

Third, on a particularly Protestant understanding, this view of Christ's priestly office allows for a truly universal priesthood of all believers to which Song-Ming neo-Confucians aspired: all believers, not just the emperor or high-ranking officials elected by the emperor, come before the ever-transcendent and holy God, once hidden in the Most Holy Place, to offer ourselves as sacrifices in, through, and with Christ, who is at once our high priest (Heb 9:11), our sacrifice (9:26–28), the temple (9:8–11, Jn. 2:19–21), the Most Holy Place (Heb 9:1–11), and the way—the only way—to God through the curtain torn (10:20).

FROM HAVILAH DHARAMRAJ

In the seventh and eighth centuries AD, a religious movement began in South India and became established in North India in the centuries that followed. This was the bhakti tradition. Its peculiarity was that it reduced the mediation of the Brahminical priesthood in the devotee's relationship with deity. All castes were thought to have unrestricted access to deity through personal devotion. This democratization of access allowed women into what was hitherto a male domain—the domain of saints and composers of hymns.

One such is Andal, a grand example of the poet-saint of bhakti tradition and a female. Dated to the eighth or ninth century AD, her story is that a priest found the supposedly abandoned infant in the temple precincts under a *tulsi*, or holy basil shrub, and fostered her. She lived out her short life of sixteen years in complete dedication to the deity Vishnu. At his temple in Madurai, she vowed: "O Lord . . . if you accept me, I will offer you a hundred pots of sweet rice-pudding and a hundred pots of pure white butter." The story goes that she took to wearing the garlands she wove each day before handing them to her priest father for the worship of Vishnu. Discovering a strand of long black hair in a garland one day, her father berated the young Andal for what he thought was her arrogance. That night, Vishnu appeared to him in a dream, assuring him that he was unperturbed by Andal's seeming audacity and explaining that Andal wore Vishnu's garland only out of her deep love for him. Sometime after this, Andal was on a visit to Vishnu's Srirangam temple. Approaching the idol of Vishnu, she touched his feet in homage, raised herself to sit on his feet, and promptly disappeared. An alternate version of the legend is that she persuaded her foster father to present her to the idol of Vishnu at Srirangam, clothed in full wedding dress. At the shrine, the idol stretched out his hands to embrace her, and she disappeared. Her devotion had caused her apotheosis—her crossing over into divinity by merger with Vishnu.

It is thought that the bhakti tradition influenced Islam in the Indian subcontinent, giving rise to a similar strand of personal devotion with no need for the clergy as intermediary. This was the mystical and deeply intimate practice that came to be called sufism. Jesus, in his execution of the role of high priest, reminds us of the longing of the bhakti and sufi traditions. He leveled for all time and for all people—Jew and gentile, male and female, slave and free, forward and oppressed castes—equal access to God. India has a cynical saying: what God grants, the priest sometimes withholds. With Jesus, the free access he grants none can challenge, because he is both priest and God.

The more specifically Reformed application of the axiom *finitum non capax infiniti* to the doctrine of Christ's priestly office, in my view, does not hold promise apart from the more ecumenical stipulations outlined above. However, I would contend that it does so more emphatically and with greater force and clarity than other theological traditions familiar to Christians in Chinese contexts.

I would, however, issue some caveats for confessional Reformed Christians in Chinese contexts. The general caveat is against treating the sixteenth and seventeenth centuries as the penultimate source of divine truths next to Scripture as the ultimate source. Failure to appreciate the patristic and medieval-scholastic heritage of Reformed Orthodoxy has led some of the finest Reformed theologians (e.g., Robert Reymond) to depart from the tradition of ectypal theology under the influences of the radical intellectualism and Enlightenment rationalism.[20] One reason why someone like Carl Henry is so popular among contemporary Chinese Reformed believers, in my view, is that his intellectualistic and rationalistic formulation of biblical authority appeals to the Confucian-trained appetite for putative God's-eye views of everything that is or is not God.[21]

On a related note, Chinese Reformed believers have shown a strong tendency to embrace theonomy of various forms, especially distorted, triumphalist forms of Kuyperianism. Henry's proposal for social reform is often cast in that light in Chinese Reformed communities worldwide.[22] There is, again, something deeply Confucian about this tendency. An enlightened person, according to Confucianism, is endowed with the responsibility to "rule over the state and subdue everything under heaven" (治國、平天下).

In this regard, I am convinced that Chinese Reformed Christians would find dialogues with Lutherans to be highly rewarding. Taking the two-kingdom doctrine of Lutheran theology seriously and engaging with it concretely is often a fruitful way for Reformed believers to reflect on their possible departures from some of the core principles that Reformed theology

---

20. *Ectypal theology*: Reformed theology normatively teaches that God's knowledge of himself is archetypal and original, while true human knowledge of God is like an ectype or mirror image of God's self-knowledge. Archetypal and ectypal theology are distinguished by the infinite difference between the Creator and the creature; because God has revealed himself through creaturely means, creatures are enabled to think God's thoughts after God in an ectypal manner.

21. For explanations of my uses of the terms *intellectualism* and *rationalism* in relation to Carl Henry, see my *Karl Barth* (Phillipsburg: P&R, 2021), 101–25. Also see Michael S. Horton, "A Stony Jar: The Legacy of Karl Barth for Evangelical Theology," in *Engaging with Barth: Contemporary Evangelical Critiques*, ed. David Gibson and Daniel Strange (Nottingham: Apollos, 2008), 377.

22. I offer an analysis of this phenomenon in the appendix to the Chinese translation of Carl Henry, *The Uneasy Conscience of Modern Fundamentalism* [現代基要主義不安的良心], trans. Jia Lu [陸迦] (Shanghai: Shanghai Sanlian, 2018).

inherited from the great ecumenical tradition, including those principles underlying the normative Reformed formulation of Christ's threefold offices.

On the other hand, engaging with Roman Catholic traditions, including more recent schools such as *nouvelle* theology,[23] can be a good way for Protestant believers to be cautioned against going down the path of radical nominalism. When the universal priesthood of all believers as an ecclesiological notion is detached from the catholic understanding of Christ's priestly office, what often ensues is the secularization of worship and church governance that decentralize the role of Christ. Such decentralization caters to the deformalizing impulse of the neo-Confucian School of the Heart that has enjoyed great popularity in China in the recent decade.

Intercontextual ecumenical witness to Christ, as attested by the authors of the present volume, is of utmost importance in the globalized *world* today, a world that is at once Christ's own and one that refuses to receive him (John 1:11). "The way of the world"—as the Christian sociologist Craig Gay so aptly puts it—is delimited by the "will-to-self-definition."[24] The Confucian way is no exception. The body of Christ is called to testify against this Adamic way of self-definition by either domineering collectivity (as seen in Confucian societies and Marxist communities) or selfish individuality (as manifested in the American libertarian, nay, libertine ideal of "the pursuit of happiness"). The Catholic theologian J.-M. R. Tillard is perfectly agreeable to a neo-Calvinist like myself when he comments that the church bears witness to Christ through *communion*: "The church is neither abolition nor addition but communion of 'differences.'"[25] He explains that "communion demands that a *common reality*, a *unique value* be present in all members and that all have part in it, albeit in very diverse ways. There is a radical unity on

---

23. *Nouvelle théologie* was a mid-twentieth-century Catholic theological movement reacting against what its proponents deemed to be the dogmatic over-systematization of the neo-scholasticism that dominated Catholic theology in the aftermath of the First Vatican Council (1869–70). The first generation of theologians associated with this movement include Henri de Lubac (1896–1991), Yves Congar (1904–1995), Karl Rahner (1904–1984), Jean Daniélou (1905–1974), Hans Urs von Balthasar (1905–1988), Henri Bouillard (1908–1981), and others. Joseph Ratzinger (Pope Benedict XVI, 1927–2022) and Hans Küng (1928–2021) pertain to the second generation.

24. Craig Gay, *The Way of the (Modern) World: Or, Why It's Tempting to Live As If God Doesn't Exist* (Grand Rapids: Eerdmans, 1998), 184.

25. J.-M. R. Tillard, *Flesh of the Church, Flesh of Christ: At the Source of the Ecclesiology of Communion*, trans. Madeleine Beaumont (Collegeville, MN: Liturgical Press, 2001), 9.

which their difference flourishes."[26] Speaking as a Reformed theologian from a Chinese context, I hope to join the other authors of this book in a choir of worship to Christ, who is our prophet, priest, and king.

CONCLUSION

This chapter has offered an analysis of royal priesthood in the history of Chinese thought and culture—particularly that of Confucianism—from a Christian perspective. The case of China reflects the broader historical reality that ancient societies operated on the basis of three dominant powers, namely, the royal (or chiefly, in the case of tribal societies), the priestly, and the prophetic offices. Chieftain-priests are most common in tribal societies, while convergences of royalty and priesthood are not at all uncommon in the history of human civilizations. The Brahmin royalty of the Gupta Empire (fourth century to early sixth century BC) in Indian history serves as a classic example of royal priesthood in ancient society.

FROM HAVILAH DHARAMRAJ

In the Old Testament, the relationship between the institutions of monarchy and priesthood may have been fuzzy in the early days but soon came to be clearly demarcated. Jeroboam of the Northern Kingdom offers sacrifices without priestly help (1 Kgs 12:33). Saul, the first king of all Israel is commanded to wait for Samuel, the prophet-priest, to come perform the prewar sacrifice and is reprimanded for not doing so (1 Sam 13:7–14). Uzziah, the Judahite king, catches leprosy for attempting the priestly duty of offering incense (2 Chr 26:16–21).

In the Greek period, when from 198 BC onwards Judea was annexed by the Seleucids to the north, the office of the high priest was more or less up for sale. The appointment was made by the Seleucid incumbent. Those aspiring to the position would bribe their way into it, with one even using gold vessels from

---

26. Tillard, *Flesh of the Church, Flesh of Christ*, 9, emphasis added.

the temple for the purpose. Under the Seleucids, the high priest also was the civil ruler of Judea. Once the Seleucids were overthrown, the family that took power—the Hasmoneans—gradually combined into one the offices of civil head, commander of the military forces, and the high priesthood. When the succession to the throne was disputed, one Hasmonean prince, Antigonus, cut off the ears of his rival Hyrcanus II in the knowledge that a person with physical defects could not hold the office of high priest (Lev 21).

When with the favor of the Romans Herod the Great cunningly unseated the house of Hasmon to take over the rulership of Palestine, he could not lay claim to the high priesthood. He was an Idumean. He managed, however, to have the high priesthood under his control. It is significant, given the separation of these offices during the monarchy and given the highly fraught fusion of these offices in the decades before the birth of Christ, that Jesus lays claim to both kingship and priesthood.

Convergences of the three offices in a single person were not peculiar to post-Qin China either. The Sumerian king Lugalzagesi (r. c. 2358–2334 BC) is described at the beginning of the famed *Nippur Inscription of Lugalzagesi* as "Lugalzagesi, king of Uruk, king of the nation, incantation-priest of An, lumah-priest of Nisaba."[27]

While these different civilizations historically developed in divergent ways, I would venture to say—without writing another chapter to solidify my case—that consolidations of priestly, prophetic, and royal/chiefly offices in general reflect two fundamental aspects of being human in the state of fallenness.

The first is the original sin of desiring to be "like God" (Gen 3:1–5). Christ alone, who is God, is worthy of consolidating these three offices in one person. In the community of God's elect before Christ, the priestly office was restricted to the tribe of Levi and the kingly office to the tribe of Judah. Royal priesthood was strictly forbidden among God's people and was reserved for the Son of God, who was to come. While kings sometimes

---

27. "Lugalzagesi Translation," translating the inscriptions on a bowl, CDLI (431232), Sumerian Shakespeare, http://sumerianshakespeare.com/70701/81701.html.

took on prophetic roles, as seen most prominently in the cases of David and Solomon, the power of the royal office was still kept in check by prophets like Nathan, Elijah, Isaiah, Jeremiah, and other major and minor prophets. Defying this principle of separation of powers, both in the history of Israel and those of other civilizations, is symptomatic of the original sin of desiring to replace God.

The second is fallen humanity's longing for a king who rules through servanthood (Phil 2:7) and a prophetic master calling us to obey his will while calling us friends and dying for us (John 15:13–15), both in the person of a mediator who is not just a shadow of God or a shadowy ("docetic") human being. The name of Jesus Christ alone satisfies this longing. Were it not out of this ultimate longing, it would be difficult to imagine why innumerable people in history flocked to the rulers of imperial China, the Caesars of Rome, and the royal Brahmins of the Gupta Empire, surrendering to these manmade gods their dignity, freedoms, and rights as human beings.

The interesting case of the historic developments of Confucianism as discussed in this chapter is demonstrative of these two aspects of being fallen humans. As a philosophical tradition respected even among some of the greatest thinkers in the modern West—G. W. Leibniz and Christian Wolff, to name but two—its historic representatives have exhausted their wits to try out every possible formula permissible on its fundamental terms to create the ideal of a perfect combination of priest, prophet, and king. This ideal, as we saw, ranged from that of an enlightened Son of Heaven to that of the common folk cultivated with inner transcendence.

What the historic developments of Confucianism also demonstrate, as we saw, is a concomitant longing for the democratization, so to speak, of the priestly office (as well as the royal and prophetic offices, for that matter). Fallen human beings estranged from God cannot escape the desire to approach God or be approached by God. This longing is so profound that the Confucian literati eventually came to realize that having a high priestly figure in the person of the Son of Heaven is insufficient. They came to recognize that every person longs to be in the presence of heaven through some universal priesthood. This longing also, as we saw, can never be fulfilled apart from Jesus Christ.

FROM HAVILAH DHARAMRAJ

India's Nobel laureate for literature (1913), Rabindranath Tagore (1861–1941), expresses in many a poem the human desire to meet God or to be met with by God. This poem is titled "Waiting":

> The song I came to sing
> remains unsung to this day.
> I have spent my days in stringing
> and in unstringing my instrument.
> The time has not come true,
> the words have not been rightly set;
> only there is the agony
> of wishing in my heart.
> I have not seen his face,
> nor have I listened to his voice;
> only I have heard his gentle footsteps
> from the road before my house.
> But the lamp has not been lit
> and I cannot ask him into my house;
> I live in the hope of meeting with him;
> but this meeting is not yet.

In this chapter I have disclosed some of the devastating consequences of Confucianism's "idolatrous" (in both a biblical sense and a Feuerbachian one) answers to these longings while applauding Confucianism's common-sense wisdom that reflects God's common grace to a very remarkable extent. It is not sufficient for followers of Jesus to stop short at this disclosure and critical appreciation, however.

We are called to testify to the hope that we have in Christ through our godly ways of living, honoring Christ the Lord as holy in our hearts. But more than that, the apostle adjures us: be "prepared to make a defense to anyone who asks you for a reason for the hope that is in you" (1 Pet 3:15 ESV).

It was to this very end that I gave in this chapter an exposition of the church's historic and normative understanding of the biblical doctrine of the priestly office of Christ, as understood and inherited by the Reformed tradition. I did so in a concrete context, namely, that of Sinophone Reformed communities informed to various extents by Confucian values and worldview presuppositions.

My reflections in this chapter may not be immediately applicable for readers outside of this context. The theology—as an intellectual explication of our faith—to which I resorted, however, is not so personal to the extent that I speak only for myself and in my own context. I have sought to align my theological reflections with the Reformed tradition and the catholic norms of the church, for we were "called to one hope when [we] were called," not as individuals but as individual members of the body of Christ (Eph 4:4). To that extent, I believe, not out of self-confidence but rather confidence in the dogmatic wisdom that God has given to the church through the work of the Holy Spirit, that this chapter would provide some edification to the reader, regardless of the cultural or denominational background. Finally, and in that connection, it has been of tremendous joy and comfort to me that the exercise of theology-in-context in this chapter, the exercise of explaining the reason for the hope that we have in Jesus Christ as priest, prophet, and king, is joined by such a blessed choir of contributors called to "one Lord, one faith, one baptism; one God and Father of all, who is over all and through all and in all" (Eph 4:5–6).

CHAPTER 5

JESUS THE HIGH PRIEST

A South Asian Reading

HAVILAH DHARAMRAJ

The job description of ancient Israel's high priest had a single item: providing the people with access to God. Access, as the garden narrative of Genesis 2–3 tells us, had been lost when the first humans sinned. Death entered the precincts of the tree of life, and sinful humans came to share space with a holy God. This intolerable juxtaposition of polarities was resolved with the expulsion of the man and woman from Eden. Glowing cherubim with whirling swords ensured that the two would remain separate.

The priesthood was instituted as an antithesis to the cherubim. The high priest mediates between holiness and sinfulness, between life and every reminder of death. Holiness and life are inextricably bound together in the category of purity. Sinfulness and death pair together as pollution or impurity, of which there are two kinds: moral and ritual. The popular tendency is to match sin with moral impurity and death with ritual impurity. But in ancient Israelite understanding, as in South Asian Hinduism, the moral and the ritual are enmeshed. And so the priest's defining function is to prevent, through the medium of ritual-moral purity, the pollution of the sanctuary, so that he can channel the favor of the deity to devotees. This priestly function is the lens through which I, as a South Asian, will explore Jesus's office of high priest.

FROM ELIZABETH W. MBURU

Sin in traditional African contexts was understood in different terms. It was relational and involved a breakdown of relationships. The only solution was to present a sacrifice that would enable the restoration of vertical and horizontal relationships. John Mbiti, who charted the path for modern African theology, explains that the purpose of sacrifice can be understood in terms of the maintenance of the ontological balance between God and man, the spirits and man, the departed and the living.

Our discussion uses the method of comparative religions and traverses the following path: first, we define the concept of impurity/pollution in Israelite religion and in Hinduism to arrive at commonalities and differences. Based on this, we examine how purity laws apply to the priesthood in the two religions, watching for shared motifs. Next, we will track these motifs into the priesthood of the time of the Second Temple and the New Testament. This is to prepare the ground for understanding Jesus as high priest in his historical context. In our final and most significant section, we investigate Jesus's engagement with purity/pollution as set out in the Gospels. We will find, to our amazement, that in the process of becoming established as the high priest *par excellence*, Jesus overturns, and even reverses, defining distinctives of priesthood common to Hinduism and Judaism. This appreciation of Jesus from a South Asian perspective, I believe, adds a fresh trajectory to the existing conversation on his office as high priest.

THE CONCEPT OF IMPURITY

While we might think of pure and impure as antonyms, Milgrom sets out a more sophisticated schema that ancient Israel appears to have held:[1]

---

1. Jacob Milgom, *Leviticus 1–16*, Anchor Bible (Garden City, NY: Doubleday, 1991), 732.

holy	pure	common/profane	impure/polluted
qadosh	*tahor*	*hol*	*tame*

The third pair—pure and common—are states of being. A cooking pan in a kitchen would be common while its counterpart pan used in the temple cultus would be pure; a layperson would be common while a priest would be labeled pure.

The outer pair—holy and impure—are not states of being but sources of contagion. That is, they can attach themselves to items in the middle pair, rendering them contaminated either by holiness or impurity. So, for example, a common man or a pure priest is temporarily contaminated by the impure in the process of burying a parent. Similarly, through "sacred contagion,"[2] the priestly vestments of Aaron and his sons contract holiness by being sprinkled with a holy item, blood from the altar (Exod 29:21). Sacred contagion can be lethal, as when an unauthorized person from either the pure or common category comes into contact with that which is holy. The common Uzzah dies on the spot for unthinkingly reaching out to steady the ark tottering on its oxcart (2 Sam 6:3–8).[3]

Jewish society was constructed along the purity gradient. The stratification of persons would be: gentile < female Jew < male Jew < priests. Within the priestly tribe of Levi, a further hierarchy of purity existed: Levites < priests < high priest.

In South Asia, a parallel purity hierarchy has existed in Hinduism for some three thousand years, but it is based on kinship communities within the caste system.[4] Painting with a broad brush we get a classification that appears to have arisen out of a distribution of labor: outcaste or untouchable (those who perform menial jobs) < shudra (peasants, servants) < vaishya (landowners, merchants) < kshatriya (warriors) < brahmin (priests).

---

2. Timothy H. Lim, "The Defilement of Hands as a Principle Determining the Holiness of Scriptures," *Journal of Theological Studies*, New Series 61, no. 2 (2010): 511.

3. Josephus clarifies this: "Now because he was not a priest and yet touched the ark, God struck him dead" (*Ant* 7.81).

4. For a quick survey, see Donald Johnson and Jean Johnson, "Jati: The Caste System in India," *Asia Society*, https://asiasociety.org/education/jati-caste-system-india.

FROM ALEX SHAO KAI TSENG

The author's observation that in both Jewish and Hindu societies social hierarchies are historically determined by some priestly order is remarkable. The same may be said of premodern China, though one's social status in this case would depend on one's distance from heaven (see discussions of Confucian priesthood in my chapter).

Hierarchy conceptually implies inequality. Inequality (Gen 3:6), death (Gen 2:17), painful toil (Gen 3:17), and the thorns and thistles that grew out of the earth (Gen 3:18) were all curses that ensued from the fall. In this sense inequality is an "unnatural relation" just as Paul calls homosexual behaviors "unnatural relations" (Rom 1:26–27).

That social hierarchy and inequality became the first curse on humanity after the promise of salvation in Christ (Gen 3:14–15), however, carries a redemptive-historical significance that modern advocates of equality tend to neglect. The truth that all humans are created equal and thus the equality of all in society *ought to be* established does not translate to the factual claim that equality *can be* established. The Christian Kant scholar John Hare has commented that the enlightenment principle *"ought* implies *can"* (OIC) has created a "moral gap" in Kant's philosophy of religion, where atonement for sin ultimately becomes impossible without significant amendments to the system.[a] Hare may well have misunderstood Kant with regard to the role of OIC in Kant's philosophy, but at least Hare rightly demonstrates the inevitable failure of this enlightenment principle.

Henry J. S. Maine (1822–88), celebrated jurist who contributed significantly to the modernization of Anglophone law, set forth the epoch-changing thesis that premodern society and law consider human communities to be determined by hierarchical and unequal social statuses, while modern society and law consider human communities to be formed by contracts between autonomous agents as equal individuals.[b] I do not see any reason for Christians to object to such changes in our jurisprudence, but if we think that human dignity and equality can be based on a libertarian notion of autonomy—rather than autonomy as voluntary determination to submit to the revealed will of God despite our inabilities in radical sinfulness (which is in fact Kant's view, incidentally)—then our society will never attain genuine equality. In our own day, especially in the West, we have come to witness how the dignity-as-(libertarian)-autonomy paradigm, with its maximalist enlightenment individualism, has created legally endorsed inequalities in the name of *choice*, such as those between mothers and unborn children in their wombs.

The fact that social hierarchies were determined by priestly orders in so many ancient societies serves to show that the core problem underlying inequality is one that the priesthood is aimed at solving. In the case of India, the problem is primarily unholiness and ritual impurity. In premodern China, the priestly is chiefly concerned with the plight of estrangement from heaven.

The Old Testament cultus deals with both and points to Christ as the only high priest who *can* save us from these plights. Where *ought* does not imply *can* for communities of totally depraved sinners, Christ has come as our head to accomplish for us what we cannot accomplish. Of course, on one hand there can be no equality between God and man, and so we worship the whole Christ because he is God.

On the other hand, he who is God has, as a man, in his high priestly speech called us friends in a cultural context where friendship entails equal social status (John 15:13–15). Where inequality between husband and wife ensued from the fall of our ancestors, Christ has come to his bride in self-sacrificial love. The church as the body of Christ is the only human community that diminishes social hierarchy, which was inevitable even in the Old Testament cultus because it was only a shadow of the things to come (Heb 10:1). Christians might give the best of their efforts to bring about the equality of all in society, but when all efforts fail—remember that this world hates the Lord (John 15:18)—the church will always stand as a priestly community on earth to witness to the unity and coequality given to us in Christ in the image of the triune God (1 Cor 12:13; Gal 3:28).

---

[a] John Hare, *The Moral Gap: Kantian Ethics, Human Limits, and God's Assistance* (Oxford: Oxford University Press, 1996).
[b] See Henry Maine, *Ancient Law* (London: Routledge, 2001).

There is one critical difference between the Jewish and Hindu social constructions *re* purity that is significant to the South Asian reading of Jesus as high priest. The association between castes and labor allows the higher castes to maintain their degree of inherent purity. It is the outcaste who handles animal carcasses to make the leather, considered highly polluting, for the sandals of the upper castes; who maintains the cremation grounds for the upper castes to perform the last rites for their dead; who attends to blocked latrines so that the upper castes can defecate without worrying about having to contract impurity by doing the job themselves. On the other hand, through a logical symbiosis, the brahmin mediates purity to the lower castes. An example[5] is the preparation of food at a mixed-caste event, which is traditionally the domain of a brahmin cook. Purity passes through the food cooked by his intrinsically pure hands to the partakers of the feast, allowing the brahmin guests to keep their purity intact and the lower caste guests to contract purity. In sum, the priesthood, which is the most vulnerable to impurity on account of its dizzyingly high status on the purity ladder, depends daily on the lower castes to draw impurity toward themselves and away from them. This makes "the impurity of the Untouchable," as Dumont so succinctly puts it, "conceptually inseparable from the purity of the Brahman."[6]

To conclude, both Hinduism and Judaism have a hierarchy of persons as concerns purity/pollution. At the top of each hierarchy is the priesthood. With this as background, we will look at the details of the demand for purity as concerns the priest in Hinduism and in ancient Israel. This will provide a starting point for a South Asian reading of Jesus as high priest.

PURITY AND THE PRIEST: HINDUISM AND ANCIENT ISRAEL

In the temple town of Madurai in South India stand the twin sanctuaries of the goddess Meenakshi and her husband Sundareshwara. The daily worship of these gods, performed by priests, includes bathing the idols, dressing them with clothes and jewelry, making offerings of food, waving lighted camphor

---

5. Diana Mickeviciene, "Concept of Purity in the Studies of the Indian Caste System," *Orient Alia Vilnensia* 4 (2003): 242.

6. Louis Dumont, *Homo Hierarchicus: The Caste System and Its Implications* (Chicago: University of Chicago Press, 1980), 143.

before them, and, at the end of the day, ceremonially transporting them to their bedchamber. Besides these routine tasks there are myriad rituals, such as those for the private worship of the deities, their public procession, and high days.

The understanding is that the purity of the environment of the idol is directly proportional to the power that the deity can manifest through their idol. Efforts to maintain this purity cover the treatment of all sacred paraphernalia, but most critical is the priest himself. The priest performs his daily purification rituals of bathing accompanied by the recitation of sacred verses at set times. But before rituals that require the highest standards of purity, he not only cleanses his physical body but also his "subtle body" and his soul. This requirement for inward purity is achieved through a ritual using set chants and purifying substances—usually water and a mixture of the five products of the "holy" cow: milk, curds, ghee, dung, and urine. Such inward sanctification is mandatory for a priest seeking to engage directly with deity.[7]

Enabled by his inherent purity (which the lower castes make possible) and by his self-purification (both outward and inward), the priest is able to serve the deity on behalf of the people and so channel the deity's favor to the devotees. Should there be any breach of the purity perimeters around the gods, the gods are liable to anger—and the equivalent of the biblical divine punishment falls upon the culpable, whether the priest or the larger community. The proper process in the event of a breach of purity is a ritual of reparation, called *prayaschitta*.[8] Interesting to us is that the word falls in the semantic range of the Christian terms atonement, penance, and expiation.

FROM THOMAS PARK

Dr. Havilah Dharamraj insightfully points out the similarities between the Old Testament priesthood and the priesthood in Hinduism. To carry out certain rituals, these priests could not deviate from the prescribed directions—for the Old

---

7. C. J. Fuller, "Gods, Priests and Purity: On the Relation between Hinduism and the Caste System," *Man* (new series) 14, no. 3 (1979): 466–67.

8. Fuller, "Gods, Priests and Purity," 469.

Testament tradition, the Lᴏʀᴅ specified what he wanted. In Hinduism, the priestly class speaks on behalf of various deities. In both traditions, the priests recognized the concept of profane and pure, clean and unclean. They created measures to minimize contamination and to deal with the aftermath of failures to reach the prescribed statutes. Surprisingly, these concepts are also present in the Hmong and Korean shamanistic rituals. Just like the Lᴏʀᴅ in the Old Testament prescribed how sacrifices were offered and how priests were to behave, Hmong and Korean shamanistic rituals have strict mandates describing how to offer sacrifices.

When Hmong people arrange their homes, they have different items placed according to tradition. However, the problem is that these mandates were handed down orally from generation to generation. There are debates among the Hmong scholars concerning the written scripts. However, as far as we could tell, the ancient Hmong scripts did not survive. Until Christian missionaries from France and the United States manufactured the Hmong writing, utilizing the Roman scripts, before the "invention" of the Romanized Popular Alphabet (RPA), Hmong documents were minuscule.

During the aftermath of the Vietnam War and the conflict in Laos, the Hmong became collateral damage to the struggles of the world powers and ideological conflicts. Survival became the foremost goal for many Hmong when communists took over Laos. Many Hmong people ended up as refugees in Thailand and were later dispersed to various countries—Australia, Germany, France, French Guyana, Canada, and the United States.

Once again, surviving in their new homes became the goal for many Hmong.

However, they wanted to retain their traditions and rituals, but their surroundings did not provide the optimal conditions to worship and continue their old ways. I remember seeing a photograph from the 1980s, taken in France after the United Nations had resettled the Hmong. In that picture, several Hmong men were pondering how to build a chicken coop on an apartment balcony. Back in China and Laos, the Hmong had ample space to raise their sacrificial victims like chickens or pigs. The new surroundings made it challenging to obtain the necessary items to conduct their traditional rituals. Could some items be substituted with the things from the host countries? Will the ancestors and house gods accept their offerings?

Let us turn to the priest in ancient Israel to consider how the concept of purity/pollution regulated the cultus of YHWH, the manual for this being, of course, the book of Leviticus. The starting point for the cultus is the installation of Aaron as the high priest (Lev 8–9) and his sons as priests. The ritual, as any in Hinduism, requires materials: water; a bull, two rams, and their blood; unleavened bread; oil; and vestments made according to detailed specifications (Exod 28). Again, as in Hinduism, the materials are employed in a series of maneuvers: a purification offering,[9] a burnt offering, and an ordination offering.

What is achieved at the end of it is the atonement (Lev 8:34) of the candidates, who now meet the purity requirements for intimate service in YHWH's sanctuary. YHWH floods the sanctuary with his presence (Lev 9:23–24), but the holiness of YHWH sits dangerously alongside the impurity of Israel. The person and work of the high priest stands in between, keeping them from (explosive!) collision. The purity of the high priest, it would appear from Leviticus 8–9, includes both the ritual and the moral. Leviticus's atonement processes encompass five objects—the Most Holy Place, the Tent of Meeting, the altar, the priests, and the people—and not all of them have the capacity for moral impurity. And so we understand that contrary to the common (Western?) reading[10] Leviticus, as seen in the preparation of the high priest for his crucial function, holds together both moral and ritual impurity, that is, both sin and the material reminders of death.

We have shown in this section the scope of the demands of priestly purity in Hinduism and ancient Israel. In both, the purity of the priest encompasses the inseparable ritual-moral dimension. Any breach is preempted by, or repaired by, rituals of atonement. In both, the priest, because he ensures upon himself the highest possible degree of purity, mediates between deity and devotees. Is this the way it works for Jesus as high priest? Before we discuss that, we must lay out what the expectations were of priesthood in Jesus's time, in the Second Temple period. We will see that the bar for priestly purity was raised even higher.

---

9. To follow the literal translation for the Hebrew *khatta'ah* would render this as a "sin" offering, leading to a misconception that the other sacrifices have no atoning function. See Gordon Wenham, *Leviticus*, New International Commentary on the Old Testament (Grand Rapids: Eerdmans, 1979), 88.

10. See, e.g., Wenham, *Leviticus*, 93–96. He rightly refutes the reading of the purification offering as Israel's principal expiatory offering and engages with the puzzle of why sacred objects receive purification. But he still concludes that "pollution and defilement" are those "caused by sin."

FROM ELIZABETH W. MBURU

The idea of mediation is similar to traditional African contexts. Although people could approach God directly, it was a general belief among African peoples that they could not. This reflected the hierarchical social and political life of African societies. This is where the mediatory role of priests came in. The role had several religious aspects. Priests acted as mediators between God and the people; offered sacrifices, offerings, and prayers on behalf of their communities; officiated at religious rites and ceremonies; performed rituals of cleansing and healing; offered prayers of petition, repentance, and thanksgiving to God; contacted the spiritual world; were the repositories of national customs, knowledge, taboos, theology, and oral history; made intercession for the people; performed judicial or political functions; and cared for the temples and shrines where these existed.

PURITY AND THE PRIEST:
THE SECOND TEMPLE PERIOD

Dissatisfaction against the priesthood runs through the prophetic books (e.g., Jer 6:13; Hos 6:9; Mic 3:11; Zeph 3:4; Mal 1:6). In the Second Temple period, under the Greek Seleucid rule, it reached a peak. The Greeks added to high priesthood the role of civil head of state and reserved the prerogative to appoint the high priest. With that, Zadokite descent became irrelevant[11] and the position could be gained and kept through bribery, murder of opponent candidates, or dividing the Jerusalem public into factions and inciting riots. Moral purity was clearly nonexistent; any zeal for ritual purity disappeared.

All this invited comment from the conservatives. *Aramaic Levi*, datable to either the third or early second century BC,[12] adds to the Torah regulations on ablutions, aromatic trees that should be used to combust offerings, avoiding sacrificial blood on priestly garments, the ordering of the various

---

11. H. W. Basser, "Priests and Priesthood, Jewish," in *Dictionary of New Testament Background*, ed. Craig A. Evans and Stanley E. Porter (Downers Grove, IL: InterVarsity Press, 2000), 826.

12. George W. E. Nickelsburg and Michael E. Stone, *Early Judaism: Texts and Documents of Piety*, rev. ed. (Minneapolis: Fortress, 2009), 165.

actions in a sacrifice, and the laying out of the parts of the sacrificed animal.[13] *Jubilees*, similarly, echoes *Aramaic Levi* in going into detail where the Torah is brief.[14]

Does this mean that in the Second Temple period the scope of purity is largely reduced to ritual? No. It appears that the priesthood engaged in profiteering and sexual offences, both moral lapses with grim consequences (cf. 1 Sam 2:12–17; Lev 18).[15] These sins are picked up by the *Testament of Levi*, a Christian reworking of the earlier *Aramaic Levi* clearly intended to delegitimize the Jerusalem priestly establishment:

> The offerings of the Lord you will rob; and from his portions you will steal, and before you sacrifice to the Lord you will take the choice portions, eating contemptuously with harlots. In greediness you will teach the commandments of the Lord. Married women you will pollute, and the virgins of Jerusalem you will defile, and with harlots and adulteresses you will have intercourse. . . . And you will be puffed up because of the priesthood, raising yourselves up against men. (14:5–8)[16]

With this indictment, the *Testament of Levi* clears the stage for the entry of a high priest who consummately supersedes Jerusalem's religious mafia: "When Jerusalem's priesthood has failed, then the Lord will raise up a new priest, to whom all the words of the Lord will be revealed. . . . With his priesthood all sin will vanish, and the lawless will cease to do evil" (18:1–11).[17]

The epistle to the Hebrews steps in to give *Levi*'s "new priest" a name: Jesus is the perfect high priest, immeasurably out of reach of the reproaches slung against the priesthood of his time. Where the priesthood might not even meet the purity requirements that allow access to the Second Temple, here is "a great high priest who has ascended into heaven," into that heavenly original of the YHWH's temple in Jerusalem. In Jesus, we have—declares the writer to

---

13. Hannah K. Harrington, *Holiness: Rabbinic Judaism in the Graeco-Roman World* (New York: Routledge, 2001), 64–67.

14. Harrington, *Holiness*, 72–76.

15. Nickelsburg and Stone, *Early Judaism*, 73–74.

16. Nickelsburg and Stone, *Early Judaism*, 83–84.

17. Nickelsburg and Stone, *Early Judaism*, 190.

the Hebrews—"one who has been tempted in every way, just as we are," just as any Second Temple high priest was. "Yet," in contrast with the morally compromised and ritually inconsistent priesthood, "he did not sin" (Heb 4:15).

How exactly did Jesus the high priest fulfil the expectations of *Levi* and the claims of *Hebrews*? For this, we must turn to the Gospels, and here, we are in for a surprise. Jesus fulfils the demand for purity, in part by acting in direct contradiction to the norm.

FROM THOMAS PARK

The Old Testament and the New Testament spell out what constitutes sin: breaking God's commandments. According to the Scriptures, people are born with consciences; the apostle Paul describes this as "the law . . .written on their hearts" (Rom 2:15).

Koreans and the Hmong view sin differently. In Korea, the confluences of shamanism, Confucianism, and Buddhism shaped the psyche of the people. These three belief systems not only stand on their own but have influenced one another. The concept of the Hegelian dialectical materialism is powerful in the Korean religious scene. Instead of two opposing forces contending with one another, at least three religious worldviews exist and interact, creating religious environments unique to the Korean context.

Shamanism has no concept of sin that is comparable to the Christian understanding; its concept centers on committing crimes against other human beings and not treating the spirits and ancestors properly. In Confucianism, if an individual does not carry out that person's responsibility as a child, spouse, ruler, and citizen, that infraction is deemed to be negative. In the Korean context, 綱常罪 (*Gang Chang Zui*, 강상죄) described individuals not fulfilling their responsibility in their stations of life.

There are continuing debates determining whether Confucianism is a religion. Max Weber held the opinion that "Confucianism was indifferent to religion. . . . Completely absent in Confucian ethic was any tension between nature and deity, between ethical demand and human shortcoming, consciousness of sin and need for salvation."[a]

For Buddhism, sin is going against the Eightfold Path: correct view, correct intention/thought, correct speech, correct action, correct livelihood, correct effort, correct mindfulness, and correct concentration. Since the concept of sin differs from one teaching to the other, practitioners of these religions obtain the state of "sinlessness," perfection, and paradise differently.

Even within a religion, there are variations due to regional differences. One region in Korea has the practice of having two sets of offerings for ancestral worship services. The descendants offer one set of offerings to the ancestors. The second set of offerings is for the family to sell to others who desire to eat 제사밥 (*Jaesa Bop*).

Since there is no universal set of laws or rules, practitioners of shamanism, Confucianism, and Buddhism are often unsure how to carry out rituals properly, and they do not know whether their deities accept their sacrifices and rituals.

---

[a] Xinzhong Yao, An Introduction to Confucianism (Cambridge: Cambridge University Press, 2002), 40; Max Weber, The Religion of China: Confucianism and Taoism (New York: Free Press, 1968), 146, 235.

PURITY AND JESUS THE HIGH PRIEST

The evangelists regularly narrate Jesus's encounters with the purity laws of his time. Scholars are divided about Jesus's approach to purity protocols: Did he respect them or dismiss them?[18] Whatever the answer, the agreement is that Jesus was pushing his audiences, especially the ritual-purity-obsessing religious establishment, toward the superior of the two aspects of purity—the inward (Mark 7:1–23). Given this, the rest of this section discusses Jesus in interaction with ritual impurity.

Of the evangelists, Mark shows Jesus in engagement with the full range of what the Judaisms of the first century considered the most dire of pollutants. These are situations that are most closely related to death. From Leviticus, we understand that the defining logic of impurity is its association with death. Thus, the ejaculating male or menstruating female losing

---

18. See brief overview on the Jewishness of Jesus and his attitude toward purity laws in Cecilia Wassen, "The Jewishness of Jesus and Ritual Purity," *Jewish Studies in the Nordic Countries Today* 27 (2016): 11–17, 22–24.

life-giving fluids, namely, semen and blood respectively, become impure. A second example is that in the dietary laws, the restricted birds and beasts are those that feed on carrion. Third, there is the impurity of the one afflicted with *lepra*, any of the various kinds of skin disorders, in whom death is already at work through the putrefaction of flesh.[19] And, ultimately, there is the corpse itself. In rabbinic teaching, the impurity caught from worshiping other gods is explained with the same death-logic: "The gods of the idolaters are lifeless things. Shall we then forsake him who lives and worship dead objects?"[20] A South Asian finds parallels here in Hinduism's category of things that pollute since they all have to do with human waste: excreted body fluids like semen and blood; hair and nail clippings; excreta; and the epitome of human "waste," the corpse. As in Judaism, pollutants are associations with or reminders of death. Later rabbinic hierarchies of impurities listed the three most polluting objects in this ascending order: the woman with an irregular genital discharge; the person with *lepra*; and "a bone the size of a barley corn," which means that the "impurity of the corpse is stronger than all of them."[21]

Before we treat death-related impurity, there is one other—powerful—form of impurity that demands attention. This impurity, as Thiessen explains, is not part of the Leviticus spectrum: the "impure spirit," or demon. In Zechariah 13:2, YHWH declares his intention to cleanse the land of impurity. The list of items removed includes the "spirit of impurity/uncleanness" (*ruah hattum'ah*). In later Judaism, this text is sometimes understood to refer to demons, with this phrase and similar ones used to describe demons.[22] Demon impurity is one motif that the gospel writers regularly feature. In Mark, Jesus is freshly baptized and has just recruited his first disciples when he performs his first miracle, an exorcism, placing him in contact with demon impurity. "Impure spirits" (Mark 1:27) feature regularly thereafter, even multiplying in number as we go. From the "impure spirit" that inhabits a man (1:23–27) to "many demons" (1:34) to a collective that calls itself Legion

---

19. Harrington, *Holiness*, 38.

20. *Lev. R.* 6.6, cited in Harrington, *Holiness*, 40.

21. See Matthew Thiessen, *Jesus and the Forces of Death: The Gospels' Portrayal of Ritual Impurity within First-Century Judaism* (Grand Rapids: Baker Academic, 2020), 201–2.

22. Thiessen, *Jesus and the Forces of Death*, 30. See also 146–68.

(5:9), which has the capacity to overwhelm a herd two thousand pigs strong (5:13), exorcisms become so controversial a feature of Jesus's ministry that the religious establishment concludes that he can do this only because he himself is possessed by a higher order of demon, Beelzebul, the prince of demons (3:22–30). In South Asia, this conclusion would be logical, since exorcisms are the remit of the *mantrawadi*, the occultic specialist. In Mark, impure spirits are unable to resist Jesus even in the unclean places in which they should be able to hold their own, graveyards (5:3) and areas outside the boundaries of holy space, Tyre (7:24–25). Relevant to our interest is that the demons confess Jesus to be "the Holy One of God" (1:24). This is where Jesus supersedes your regular high priest. The best the high priest could do was to keep the holy and the impure from encroaching on each other's boundaries. He was the vigilant watchman against outbreaks of either holiness or impurity. Jesus, in healing the demoniacs, bursts into impure territory, his holiness evacuating it of that which made it impure. Demons tear their way out of their host in their haste to exit. They "shriek" (9:26), convulse (9:20, 26), and fall down before Jesus, whimpering, "You are the Son of God" (3:11). As holiness aggressively invades their space, they beg Jesus repeatedly to be allowed access out, even making recommendations for where they can be sent (5:2–13)!

Similarly, Jesus's encounters with the trio of the most serious sources of pollution are instructive of the uniqueness of his office as high priest. All the Gospels present Jesus voluntarily engaging with situations of contagion, but perhaps Mark most labors to showcase this. When the man infected with *lepra* falls on his knees beseeching deliverance from a health situation that renders him chronically impure, Jesus is "indignant" (Mark 1:41). Since Jesus cannot be indignant at the man's approach or at the request, which he will immediately attend to, we may infer that it was the pathetic situation of the man that moved him to indignation. The South Asian reader thinks of a parallel case that is cause for outrage. Like the biblical *lepra*-inflicted man, the outcaste too lives at the outer edges of the village (Lev 13:46). Should he enter the village, he is to cry out to identify himself, much like the one with a defiling skin disease calling out "Unclean! Unclean!" (Lev 13:45). Jesus's anger at the exigencies of a world drowning in impurity moves him to act, and what he does goes astonishingly beyond the profile of Leviticus's priest.

Jesus is not simply immune to impurity as he "reached out his hand and touched the man" (Mark 1:41). At the advance of holiness, the *lepra* flees and the impurity vanishes: "Immediately the leprosy left him and he was *cleansed*" (Mark 1:42, italics added). Thiessen rightly understands that what has happened here is the case described in Leviticus 14:2: the man has been "healed" of his "defiling skin disease."[23] Not naturally and gradually, as envisaged in Leviticus, but instantaneously, as in Markan language: "immediately." Holiness has expelled the pollutant. Jesus's instructions to the man are to see a priest and make sacrifices, as in line with the Torah regulations (Lev 14:4–31), so that the man can be officially proclaimed fit to return into community. Again, Jesus has superseded the regular high priest. Where the high priest can only certify healing, Jesus the high priest can effect healing. While the high priest examines the skin disease (Lev 14:3), Jesus the high priest expels it.

So it is with the hemorrhaging woman of Mark 5, a chapter bristling with persons and places and, even, animals unclean: the gentile-dominant regions of the Gerasenes and the Decapolis (5:1, 20); a demoniac; pigs; a bleeding woman; a twelve-year old corpse. As if to clear all doubt that the woman is ritually impure, Mark gives details on her condition. She has been bleeding for twelve years, and if she is getting worse under the attention of physicians, it means the flow has been getting heavier. She fits the case described in Leviticus 15 to the extreme. She is unclean, anything she lies on or sits on is unclean, and anyone who comes into contact with the objects she lies on or sits on becomes unclean and must cleanse their bodies and clothes. She may not live outside the city walls, but she is just as isolated. The situation is not unfamiliar in South Asia, especially in rural Hindu communities, where menstruation is believed to be polluting.[24] Menstruating women are not to enter the kitchen because their bodily pollution is caught by the food they handle and passed on to those who eat that food. Should they touch the (holy) cow, the animal may be rendered infertile; seeds they sow will not sprout. With such strong overtones of death impurity, menstruating women

---

23. Thiessen, *Jesus and the Forces of Death*, 83.

24. Suneela Garg and Tanu Anand, "Menstruation-Related Myths in India: Strategies for Combating It," *Journal of Family Medicine and Primary Care* 4, no. 2 (2015): 184–86.

in rural India may even be isolated in an outhouse for the length of their period and are reincorporated into the household after purification rites, which include bathing.

Understandably, the hemorrhaging woman would not ask publicly for healing. "If I just touch his clothes, I will be healed," she tells herself (Mark 5:28). The logic of secondary pollution is inverted. Her (bed)clothes are a source of contagion. She thinks Jesus's clothes will be a source of sacred contagion. His holiness, she thinks, will overwhelm and obliterate her state of impurity. Thiessen puts it well: "The story of the hemorrhaging woman gives readers the impression that Jesus is innately, one could say ontologically, opposed to ritual impurity and that his body, like a force of nature, inevitably will destroy impurity's sources."[25] See how Jesus again supersedes the priest. When a woman is healed from irregular genital discharge, it takes seven days to establish privately that she is clean, after which a priest makes offerings on her behalf "to make atonement for her before the LORD for the uncleanness of her discharge" (Lev 15:30). The priest merely mediates purity. Jesus the high priest is purity itself.

This brings us to what Judaism—as also Hinduism—considers the most extreme of the sources of contagion: corpse impurity. In Numbers 19, several markers set it apart as uniquely polluting. First, unlike *lepra* impurity or impurity from genital discharge, regulations for corpse impurity open with a prologue. The prologue sets out a procedure to reduce a red heifer to ashes for making the "water of cleansing," which is to be sprinkled on the corpse-impure person (Num 19). Clearly, corpse impurity cannot be neutralized with just ordinary water.

Second, unlike in the case of a woman with genital discharge who pollutes her bed, a corpse can infect from a distance. It corrupts the air in a dwelling into a miasma of impurity; therefore, food in an open container is contaminated by being within the tent; persons are rendered impure simply by being in the same space as the body. After burial, impurity ripples outward from the dead body, rendering the grave's surface a pool of infection; just touching the grave pollutes a person. That is why the tent

---

25. Thiessen, *Jesus and the Forces of Death*, 114.

and its furnishings require sprinkling with the red heifer water. In Judaism, impurity could be transmitted simply by sight of the corpse![26] In parallel, the Hindu understanding is that a person's death causes ripples of pollution outward through degrees of kinship—a relative locationally distant from the corpse is contaminated from the day he heard of the death.[27]

Third, while the prescribed purification for those coming into contact with persons with *lepra* or genital discharge is a single ablution (Lev 15), the corpse-impure person must bathe twice, on the third and seventh days of their period of uncleanness (Num 19:12). And fourth, a unique law restricts the priesthood from corpse impurity. Ordinary priests may participate only in funerals of a tight circle of immediate biological family—parents and children, brothers and unwed sisters (Lev 21:1–3). As for the high priest, the restriction on him is astonishing: "He must not enter a place where there is a dead body. He must not make himself unclean, even for his father or mother" (21:11). His priority is the sanctuary, and he cannot be absent from it for the weeklong period required for purification of corpse impurity (Lev 21:12). We now understand better the actions of the priest and the Levite in Jesus's parable of the good Samaritan (Luke 10:31–32). There lay a motionless body on the road to Jerusalem, and these religious functionaries, perhaps on their way to the temple, could not risk corpse impurity. In their reasoning, the risk overrode the responsibility to save a life. So they crossed over to the other side of the road. Indeed, a later rabbinic term for the corpse was "father of fathers of impurity," in relation to a person with *lepra* infection or genital flow, who is a "father of impurity."[28]

This background prepares us for understanding Jesus's interactions with the dead. The three resurrection miracles can be arranged into an ascending series, as Thiessen does. First, there is Jairus's daughter. She has either recently died (Mark 5:35; Luke 8:49) or has been dead a while (Matt 9:18), but the body has not yet left the house for burial. Jesus takes the body "by the hand" (Matt 9:25) to speak words of life to it. According to the injunctions in Numbers 19, just entering the house of the dead child

---

26. Harrington, *Holiness*, 60.
27. Mickeviciene, "Concept of Purity," 244.
28. Harrington, *Holiness*, 41.

was polluting, but Jesus thinks nothing of intentionally putting himself into contact with the little corpse. At the city gate in Nain, Jesus meets the funeral procession of a young man, presumably on the way to burial outside the town's perimeters. Here, Jesus touches the bier, and the "dead man sat up and began to talk" (Luke 7:15). The time lapse since death is greater, and the reviving touch is less intimate. These two feature dramatically in the last of the resurrection miracles. Lazarus is dead four days (John 11:39), and the body Jesus raises has been laid to rest in a tomb in a cave. From miracle to miracle, the demonstration of the irresistibility of Jesus as the source of holiness intensifies. It is as if the corpse's capacity to pollute even from a distance has met its match.[29] Jesus's holiness surges corpse-ward to reverse the effect of the "father of the father of impurities." This is the death of death, the first cause of impurity, which underlies all manifest sources of pollution.

Beyond these resurrection miracles that Jesus performs intentionally, Thiessen points out a final one. In Matthew's telling of the Jesus story, there is a resurrection simultaneous with Jesus's crucifixion: "The tombs broke open. The bodies of many holy people who had died were raised to life" (Matt 27:52). In the most Jewish of gospels, with its concern for priestly matters, how significant that at the "moment when the forces of impurity appeared to overwhelm Jesus himself," there is a liberation of holy persons who have been made "irreversibly impure in death."[30] The separation between Jesus and these corpses is even further exaggerated in temporal and spatial distance. Nevertheless, so complete is their purification that they enter the holy city of Jerusalem (albeit after an unexplained waiting period of three days) to intermingle with its people, needing neither sprinkling nor sacrifices.

In this lies the unsurpassable superiority of Christ in his office as high priest, that he is himself a source of holiness. Where the priest is a sort of medical practitioner, peering at lesions and scabs of *lepra* to pronounce the afflicted one pure or impure, at the touch of Jesus the priest the *lepra* instantaneously removes itself. Where the priest's assistance to the one with

---

29. Thiessen, *Jesus and the Forces of Death*, 141.
30. Thiessen, *Jesus and the Forces of Death*, 130, 141.

irregular genital discharge comes after the corrupting irregularity has somehow ended, the holy body of Jesus spontaneously neutralizes the unclean ailment. Where the high priest must be carefully protected against corpse impurity to the extent that he is forbidden to bury even his parents, Jesus the high priest returns corpses from death into life, delivering them from an inexorable pollution that swallows up even a high priest. As for demon-impurity that seeks to maim and destroy life—this appears to be beyond the scope and service of any priest. But in the presence of Jesus the high priest, demons evacuate their hosts in fearful haste.

FROM THOMAS PARK

I frequently hear Korean and Hmong Christians and non-Christians mention that some view pastors as shamans. They treat Christian leaders the way that they would treat shamans. They compare shamans with different spirits inhabiting them to pastors having the Holy Spirit in their hearts. Some people look at shamans and pastors to provide earthly comfort and solutions rather than focusing on heaven or paradise. The Parable of the Good Soil comes to mind. The faith of specific individuals grew rapidly, but the care and concerns of the world choked their faith.

Some Christians who cannot shake shamanistic views see tithing and Sunday offerings like payments to shamans: the more they give, the more God will bless them. One Christian pastor preached a sermon, and it went like this: "People are going to heaven because they have faith in Christ. However, the ones that gave more will be closer to Jesus' throne than those who gave less."

In the Old Testament, we encounter many believers of the Lord who are afraid of him because they recognize that they are sinful while God is holy and perfect. The Scriptures clearly state that God does not tolerate sin. Individuals wanted to follow God's law and the ritual prescriptions, but they failed because of their sinfulness. Whenever the high priest, the one set apart by God, approached the holy of holies, he was unsure whether he would come out alive. He was afraid that the Lord might strike him dead for his sins. Even the chosen people and the servants of God were afraid of God.

Viewing God as the wrathful judge has continued. We might encounter Christians still cowering under this misconception. Yes, God is the righteous judge, but he is also merciful and forgiving. Martin Luther's (1483–1546) father, Hans, was a miner, a self-made man. To please his father, the young Luther was studying to be a lawyer. Because of his religious upbringing, he considered God a wrathful judge. During his time, many people attempted to placate the vengeful God by buying indulgences, making pilgrimages, viewing relics, and so on.

Once, Luther and his friend were lost in a thunderstorm. A lightning bolt struck a tree not too far from where Luther stood. He was afraid and cried out, "Help me, St. Anne, I will become a monk."[a] After this, the weather cleared, but Luther kept his promise. He gave away his belongings and books related to studying the law to others. This change in the direction of his life dampened his relationship with his father.

Luther struggled with sin as a monk and tried to appease an angry God. Burdened with guilt, he confessed his sins and sought the counsel of his superior in the monastery, Johann von Staupitz (1460–1524). After hearing Luther's confessions and noticing his intellect, the head monk encouraged Luther to pursue the position of theology professor. To prepare to teach his students, the new professor immersed himself in studying the Bible. As he was reading Romans, he started to understand that by faith in Christ God forgives sinners. This is often described as his "tower experience." After understanding the gospel, Luther protested the Roman Catholic Church's malpractices, especially selling and buying indulgences. Initially, this problem was a local issue and not connected to the hierarchy of the church. He soon found out that the pope and the leadership of the Roman Catholic Church were intimately connected to the practices of indulgences.

Luther wanted to reform the church and rectify aberrations. However, the Roman Catholic Church excommunicated him in 1520. After exiting the church, he struggled to understand gospel-driven worship. To help create such worship, Luther composed numerous hymns and wrote the German Mass (*Deutsche Messe*). The Lutheran Confessions state Christian worship in this way, "The Mass is retained among us, and celebrated with the highest reverence. Nearly all the usual ceremonies are also preserved, save that the parts sung in Latin are interspersed here and there with German hymns, which have been added to teach the people. For ceremonies are needed to this end alone that the unlearned be taught [what they need to know of Christ]."[b]

Those that observe Lutheran worship superficially often comment that the Lutheran services look like the Roman Catholic Mass. The crucial difference is that people have the freedom to worship God rather than forcing them to do so. Luther encouraged liturgical worship, but vestments and outward adornments were adiaphora. Freedom from sin through faith in Christ is the central idea for worship in Lutheran churches, and this crucial point is repeatedly proclaimed in the divine services. According to the Book of Concord, "Concerning ceremonies and church rites which are neither commanded nor forbidden in God's Word, but are introduced into the Church with a good intention, for the sake of good order and propriety, or otherwise to maintain Christian discipline, a dissension has likewise arisen among some theologians of the Augsburg Confession."[c]

Many are uncertain of their salvation and wonder whether their deities and ancestors accept their offerings and sacrifices. Unfortunately, even Christians have often been unclear about their salvation. Regarding Christianity, the high priest is perfect but died on the cross to redeem us from our sins. Although the perfect high priest was innocent, he became the sacrifice to take our sins on himself and grant us his righteousness.

There are many similarities between the Old Testament and Hinduism. Both belief systems have priestly offices and address problems like clean and unclean, pure and profane. However, the author of the book of Hebrews juxtaposed the high priestly office with Christ.

Authentic and orthodox Christianity is built on the foundation of the sinless Christ, who is both God and man. Because of his identity and actions, he is superior to sinful people. Although our earthly religious leaders might fail us, our high priest will never abandon or disappoint us.

---

[a] Martin Brecht, *Martin Luther: His Road to Reformation 1483–1521* (Minneapolis: Fortress, 1993), 48.

[b] Augsburg Confession 24, https://bookofconcord.org/augsburg-confession/of-the-mass/#ac-xxiv-0001.

[c] Formula of Concord Solid Declaration 10, https://bookofconcord.org/solid-declaration/church-rites-adiaphora/.

The evangelists wish their readers to note this: Jesus is the embodiment of divine holiness. That is why they tell us that Jesus takes his ministry into places Jews classified as sources of contagion: Samaria, the region of the Gerasenes, the Decapolis. They record stories of the healing of *lepra*, of the raising of the dead. They move their narrative toward the crucifixion. Though death is impure, the impurity surrounding Jesus's death was compounded by being an execution, which required the expulsion of the condemned outside the walls of the holy city. A South Asian reader is reminded that in Hinduism, while all corpses are sources of impurity, those dying by execution for crimes committed come up for special mention. The corpse of the executed person is considered "severely and . . . irremediably polluted."[31] Jesus's manner of execution is not even at Jewish hands. He is handled by Romans. Not one of the evangelists omits to mark Jesus's final day as a Friday (Matt 27:62; Mark 15:42; Luke 23:54; John 19:42). In the synoptics, this Friday is Passover day, so that Jesus eats the Passover meal the night previous, the last supper (Matt 26:17–29; Mark 14:12–25; Luke 22:7–23). In John, this Friday is the day of preparation for a doubly sacred Passover falling on the Sabbath (John 19:31). Whether on a holy high day or holy day of the week, this is the day Jesus is taken into an unclean space, the Praetorium, the palace of the Roman governor (Matt 27:27; Mark 15:16). John adds in the detail that the Jewish religious elite "did not [want to] enter" so that they would remain ritually qualified and "be able to eat the Passover" that evening (John 18:28). In that unclean place, Jesus is struck and scourged—his bleeding leading to a further state of impurity. Had Jesus been a priest, his condition would have barred him from any priestly service at Herod's glorious temple not far away—a temple that had been built by priests in priestly vestments—some trained as stonemasons and carpenters—to maintain the highest possible protection from contamination.[32] When Jesus dies on the Roman cross, he is not only impure but also, as Paul presents him, far worse: he is under curse (Gal 3:13; cf. Deut 21:23).

---

31. Henry Orenstein, "Death and Kinship in Hinduism: Structural and Functional Interpretations," *American Anthropologist* 72 (1970): 1362.

32. Josephus, *Antiquities of the Jews*, 15.11.2–3.

CONCLUSION

The contagion of impurity, whether ritual or moral, flees Jesus as darkness flees light (John 1:5). Read alongside the Hindu priest, Jesus has no need for washing his body in the temple pond and cleansing his inner self. More significantly, he does not depend on another social category to draw impurity off him. In contrast to the Levitical high priest, Jesus does not protect himself from the dire impurity of the corpse. Evaluated against the high priest of his day, Jesus can refute any moral charge the religious elite level at him.

The starkest comparison between Jesus and any human priest comes with his death. Jesus dies on a cursed instrument of death. In the hours before his death, he is contaminated by gentile spaces. His death is located outside the holy city and (according to John) outside a doubly sacred day. At his death, his body is thick with the pollution of bloody lacerations. Beyond all these accretions of ritual impurity is the moral: "in his body on the cross" he "bore our sins (1 Pet 2:24; cf. Isa 53:4–6).

And yet—and this is the wonder of it!—he has access into "the greater and more perfect tabernacle that is not made with human hands" (Heb 9:11), the impeccable heavenly copy of YHWH's earthly sanctuary, as a "high priest . . . who is holy, blameless, pure" (Heb 7:26). During his life there had been demonstrations of the irresistibility of his holiness, but it is in his death that we best understand his all-surpassing incomparability to any human high priest.

CHAPTER 6

CHRIST AS THE HIGH PRIEST
AND ASIAN SHAMANISM

THOMAS PARK

Exalting the incomparable priesthood of Christ, the letter to the Hebrews assumes some familiarity with the Jerusalem temple and its cult. Not long after the destruction in AD 70, the generation would pass that possessed direct memory of the sacrifices, washings, and other rituals at the heart of Israel's identity. Moreover, as the balance shifted to the gentile world, the letter to the Hebrews formed a crucial link between old and new covenants, promise and fulfillment. Some did not appreciate this connection. Instead of recognizing Christ's ministry as surpassing the priestly cult by fulfilling its types and shadows, Marcion of Sinope (AD 85–160) rejected the Hebrew Scriptures as the revelation of a different deity, a God of wrath who requires a propitiatory sacrifice.

However, Christ is revealed clearly in the gospels and the epistles as the "Lamb of God who takes away the sin of the world" (John 1:29) and as the temple and high priest. Consequently, Marcion found that he had to pare down much of the New Testament as well if he were to separate his image of God from God's self-revelation in the history of Israel.[1] After he dissected the Scriptures, only one of the Gospels and an edited version of Paul's epistles survived. Marcion's favorite book in the New Testament was Galatians because Paul attacked Judaizers. Unlike other heresies, Marcionism affected

---

1. John Arendzen, "Marcionites," in *The Catholic Encyclopedia*, vol. 9 (New York: Appleton, 1910).

both the Eastern and Western churches. The church fathers from East and West deemed Marcionism as heresy. Nevertheless, a neo-Marcionite bias has plagued modern scholarship, especially in Germany, since the nineteenth century. Only after World War II was there a deliberate effort to recognize the integral connection of Christianity to the Hebrew Bible. Yet more recently a host of theological programs, especially in the West, return to Marcion's approach. More generally, Marcionism is taken for granted by many today who have little knowledge of the Old Testament.

Working in Asia has brought additional challenges to Christians seeking to communicate the concept of Christ as the high priest due to issues unique to living and working in that continent. The pervasive challenge in sharing Christ's high priestly office is that Christianity is perceived as a Western religion not pertinent to Asians. Confucianism influenced many Asian countries, spreading the idea of honoring parents and ancestors as a filial obligation. Therefore, many individuals viewed Christianity as subversive and antitraditional, especially when Protestant missionaries and Christians prohibited ancestor worship.

Although no Old Testament priesthood or modern-day counterpart exists today, one might consider using what many Asian people encounter daily to discuss Christ as a high priest. Shamans and their activity in helping others can help introduce one aspect of Christ as the high priest. Many start with something concrete to understand abstract ideas regardless of where people are from. To communicate the foreign concept of the Old Testament priesthood, one must begin with what is familiar.

ASIAN SHAMANISM

The Old Testament high priest was chosen from among the priests. All priests had to be male, without physical defect (Levi 21:21), and from Aaron's lineage. However, Christ was different because he was not from the priestly tribe in a traditional sense: Christ is from "the order of Melchizedek" (Heb 7:11). We will discuss in-depth differences and similarities between the Old Testament high priest and the Korean shaman.

FROM HAVILAH DHARAMRAJ

In ancient West Asia, one of the fundamental requirements for a priest was that he should be free of any physical defect. Those with disabilities were either not priests or belonged to a lower order of priests. Israelite law (Lev 21) does not seem to follow this practice. Priests—those of the house of Aaron—enjoyed their hereditary prerogative irrespective of disabilities. The restrictions, it appears, applied only to the cultic duties for sacrifices, not to regular priestly duties. In terms of sacred space, the area in front of the tabernacle, where the altar for sacrifices and tabernacle were, was off limits for priests with disabilities. The underlying cultic rationale in ancient West Asia was possibly that disability was equated with ritual imperfection, and since only that which was whole or perfect could be offered to the deity (Mal 1:6–14), the one mediating the offering had to similarly be whole or perfect. Given these specifications, it is remarkable that Jesus, as the perpetual high priest, continues to wear on his resurrected body the scars of the crucifixion. His sinless perfection "perfects" what would, in any other case, be a blemish.

South Korea is ranked tenth in economic power. Imposing high-rise buildings tower over the country's landscapes, and many cutting-edge cellphones and home appliances come from the Land of the Morning Calm. Surprisingly, some Koreans recognize that if illness or other life issues are not resolved through "ordinary" means, they could seek "extraordinary" or "supernatural" ways. In Korea, some individuals go to a 무당 (*mudang*)[2] to assist in resolving conflicts and predicaments. Health problems, a successful outcome on the university entrance examination, infertility, infidelity, and job prospects call for the shaman's assistance. Depending on the problem, the *mudang* might write out amulets[3] like a medical doctor

---

2. Dirk Schlottmann, "Dealing with Uncertainty: 'Hell Joseon' and the Korean Shaman Rituals for Happiness and against Misfortune," *Shaman* 27, no. 1–2 (2019): 12. The term 무당(*mudang*) comes from the Chinese word 巫堂. It refers to a shaman. The *mudang* performs a 굿 (*gutt*, a shaman ritual) to dispel evil spirits.

3. "부적(符籍)," Encykorea.aks.ac.kr, https://encykorea.aks.ac.kr/Article/E0024533. There are two types of amulets. One type is believed to ward off malicious spirits from wreaking havoc. The other kind is to increase blessings and fulfill wishes.

giving out prescriptions. It is interesting to see Western medicine doctors in Korea donning amulets in their offices where they examine and consult their patients. It is not uncommon to see a makeshift altar built with a pig's head before the filming of a movie. The director, the cast, and the staff bow down before the altar and offer drink offerings to the spirits for a safe filming.[4]

FROM HAVILAH DHARAMRAJ

In India, the equivalent of the shaman would be, variously, the *mantrawadi* (the sorcerer) or the astrologer. Usually, the sorcerer would be consulted for ongoing problems. These are often a case of failing health, an illness that seems to have neither cause nor cure, or a business that is doing badly. Typically, the astrologer would be consulted for predictions about the future. These would be, for example, for advice on who one should marry or whether one should start a new venture. While the sorcerer's methods verge on the occult and involve consulting the spirits of the dead, the astrologer's methods are a pseudoscience by which he draws inferences from planetary configurations. Common to both, and in common with shamanism, is that the person being consulted is thought to possess extraordinary capabilities. With these, they can control what is normally beyond human control. Therein lies their enormous attraction. Jesus, as high priest, takes control over that which is inevitable to all humans, including shamans, sorcerers, and astrologers: death. Because he overthrew death, death has lost its sting, and the grave has lost its victory.

The Hmong people among whom I have ministered are indigenous to East and Southeast Asia. In the Hmong context, *Txiv neeb* (shamans) perform *hu plig* (soul-calling) to bring back lost souls. It is commonly believed that if a person is sick, one of that individual's spirits has departed or been kidnapped by an evil spirit. Hmong typically believe that humans possess multiple

---

4. Yong Shin Ryu, "'불꽃속으로' 대박 기원 고사," 부산일보, https://www.busan.com/view/busan/view.php?code=20140305000178; Geum Seok Park, "군산시, 영화촬영 명소 만들기 총력," 光州日報, http://www.kwangju.co.kr/read.php3?aid=1516028400621949168.

souls.[5] "Souls may be lost, separated, trapped, or confined to a particular location for many reasons. They may wander and leave the body for a period of time out of curiosity or as a result of a fall or physical trauma."[6] Hmong view illnesses as connected to souls. This concept of Hmong spirituality was made more commonly known through the book *The Spirit Catches You and You Fall Down* by Anne Fadiman.[7] In this book, the author chronicled a girl's health woes. In this process, the book lays down the conflicts between non-Hmong medical staff and the Hmong parents who believed that the spirit caused their daughter's epilepsy. Shamans will conduct a diagnostic ritual to assess the problem; then, depending on other issues, animals will be slaughtered as sacrifices. Sometimes, shamans go into a trance to venture into the spirit world to rescue lost souls. Since ordinary people cannot transport themselves to the netherworld, clients need someone who can connect the physical and spiritual realms. Trying to use physical means to appease spirits and ancestors is common.

FROM ALEX SHAO KAI TSENG

The revival of supernaturalism in our day has often been described as a postmodern phenomenon, as if modernization were all about naturalistic disenchantment. There is in fact a common ground between the superstitious supernaturalism of our day and the naturalism that began to emerge in the seventeenth century and dominated much of the intellectual scene in Europe by around 1740. The theologian Karl Barth (1886–1968) offers an intriguing analysis of how medieval nominalism gave rise to the modern process of disenchantment. In addition (though not entirely in opposition) to the more familiar theory, represented in Barth's time by his erstwhile colleague in Göttingen, Emanuel Hirsch (1888–1972), that nominalism detaches our understandings of the world from higher realities and undermines religious authorities, Barth points out that nominalism also gave

5. St. Olaf College, "Shamanism," https://pages.stolaf.edu/hmg/shamanism/.

6. Austin Virathone, "Illness and the 'Neeb' Shaman: A Review of the Spiritual Antecedents of the Illness in the Hmong Community," unpublished paper, 3 .

7. Anne Fadiman, *The Spirit Catches You and You Fall Down: A Hmong Child, Her American Doctors, and the Collision of Two Cultures* (New York: Farrar, Straus and Giroux, 2012).

rise to a highly enchanted view of the world according to which the apparent laws of nature have no permanent or ordinate grounding in the works of an immutable God who does not contradict himself. In particular, the notion of *potentia Dei absoluta* (absolute power of God) in relation to creation, as formulated in a voluntaristic framework by the otherwise realist theologian Duns Scotus, practically rendered God as the prototypical shaman, so to speak. "The *potentia divina absoluta* was understood by the Nominalists of the later Middle Ages in such a way as to retransfer the *potentia extraordinaria* into the essence of God."[a] In opposition to Thomas Aquinas and mainline Protestant theologians of the sixteenth and seventeenth centuries who insisted on the stability of the physical and moral laws of nature on the basis of strict distinctions between God's *potentia absoluta* and *potentia ordinata* (ordained power), nominalism introduced the idea that God's powers in relation to creation are as unconstrained and unconditioned as his absolute power prior to and apart from creation. On one hand, then, nominalism noetically detached our natural world and the ethical order of human society from a higher cosmic order and brought about what might be called the "disenchantment" of the world. On the other hand, nominalism also enchanted the world by undermining the stability of the physical and moral orders of creation. Evangelicals can well agree with Barth's observation that, according to biblical Christianity, "*potentia extraordinaria*" and "*potentia ordinaria* . . . are mutually inclusive."[b] Grace is supernatural but not magical. The power of the shaman is antinatural rather than supernatural. Magic destroys nature; grace restores nature.

---

[a] Karl Barth, *Church Dogmatics*, ed. Geoffrey Bromiley and Thomas Torrance, trans. Geoffrey Bromiley, 4 vols. (Edinburgh: T&T Clark, 1936–75), II/1, 538.
[b] Barth, *Church Dogmatics*, II/1, 537.

Hmong and other ethnic groups make use of ghost money.[8] Burning joss money is a regular event; one can witness it twice monthly in Taiwan.

---

8. "Joss Paper: Chinese Customs," www.nationsonline.org, https://www.nationsonline.org/oneworld/Chinese_Customs/joss_paper.htm. To appease ancestors and spirits, many residents from Asian countries burn ghost money or hell money, also known as joss paper. The descendants are responsible for providing money for their deceased on their journey after death. Shopkeepers burn ghost money to help ancestors and spirits in order to help the business prosper. The common understanding is that dissatisfied ancestors roam the physical world and negatively affect their surviving family members. The ghost money provides the means for the souls to spend fewer days in punishment, leading them to their ancestral land for the Hmong and heaven in Korean and Chinese contexts.

The shopkeepers regularly do this to dispel disasters and usher prosperity into their stores. No one wants to offend a spirit or ancestor because unsatisfied entities bring misfortune. Hmong in the United States often burn the ghost money to give to the ancestors as they travel to the netherworld.[9] Having a shaman visit Hmong patients in hospitals in metropolitan Minneapolis is common. One medical doctor in California is also a shaman who can "cure" his patients "holistically." Some medical facilities in the United States allow shamans to be part of the medical team to help patients and their families. Western medicine practitioners in Korea sometimes listen to patients who want to use traditional remedies. For example, if someone has indigestion, the folk remedy is to prick the tip of the index finger to let out the "bad" blood. Sometimes, medical experts want to ease patients' minds and shield themselves from potential malpractice lawsuits. Since traditional healing and Western medicine occupy many places in Asia, it is important to examine what traditional recovery entails, especially the shamans who exercise these conventional ways.

FROM HAVILAH DHARAMRAJ

For many Indian Christians, the local sorcerer has continued to be a reasonable last resort. My mother, a second-generation Christian with a deep and mature understanding of Jesus, is an example. As a child, I suffered a mysterious stomachache that no "English" medicines could cure. She eventually took me to see a sorcerer, located in a dingy alleyway in an unfamiliar part of our city. I recall I was made to drink a copious amount of a tepid liquid that caused me to throw up. He fished out of the vomit a small indeterminate solid and pronounced it to have been lurking in my stomach causing problems. According to him, it was a magic item that someone had tricked me into ingesting, intending to cause me ill health and thus inconvenience my family. My mother worked out that this person was probably a relative with whom we were then having inheritance disputes.

---

9. "A Reflection on Hmong Funeral Rituals," *Hmong Daily News*, October 9, 2021, https://hmongdailynews.com/a-reflection-on-hmong-funeral-rituals-p295-95.htm.

> Nowadays, in the Indian church, pastors have taken over this role, especially those who ascribe to themselves the gift of healing. Their healing is in demand, and they charge large sums of money for their services, with some regularly featuring in "healing crusades."
>
> The healing of physical and nonphysical illnesses locates best within Jesus's office as high priest. Healing involved a priest, not a king or a prophet. But while the best the Israelite priest could do was to pronounce a person either infected or cured (Lev 13–14), Jesus is the priest who himself performs the cure (Luke 5:12–14).

Who becomes a shaman? Many Hmong and Korean shamans trace their ancestry back to find a shaman. It is believed that shamanic spirits come down to choose certain individuals to be the next shaman. According to Brenda Johns and David Strecker, "Heaven will send the clan of shamanic spirits to take possession of him [the person whom the spirits identified as the new shaman]. . . . First, when a person is going to know how to perform shamanic ceremonies, heaven and Grandfather Shau sends Shi Yi [who is the head of the shamanic spirits] to lead the shamanic spirits to take possession of that person. If his faint voice fits and joins in, Shi Yi will give him a pair of shamanic spirits."[10]

Sometimes the new shamans, who have been chosen by the shamanic spirits, become severely ill, and modern physicians are unable to diagnose the illness. There are stories about frustrated and desperate individuals going to shamans for help with mysterious sicknesses. Most often, shamans tell them to accept the shamanic spirits to become shamans. Several Hmong people I know have had similar experiences but refused to become shamans. For them, some of their Christian friends, neighbors, and family members prayed, and they received Christ. After becoming a Christian, the mysterious illness suddenly left them.

The primary duty of a shaman is to be the bridge to the spirit realm. They attempt to help people and deliver them from malicious spirits.

---

10. Brenda Johns and David Strecker, "Shi Yi: the First Hmong Shaman," unpublished paper, 2.

Shamans from various locations have different responsibilities. Hmong and Taiwanese identified some as the "hungry ghosts" or "cave demons." To assess the situation of the illnesses and disasters, shamans will hold diagnosis rituals to determine whether the problems have spiritual roots. When diseases and disasters are tied to unsatisfied evil spirits, shamans enter the spirit world to act as hostage negotiators. The evil spirits' fee is paid by offering an animal (a rooster or an ox) as sacrifice. Unfortunately, shamans can become the prey of evil spirits too. Jean Mottin states the unsuccessful outcome of shamanic endeavors: "Shamans perform nine or ten healing ceremonies at the altar, but succeed only once."[11] Spirits and ancestors often exhibit humanlike behaviors. If they feel neglected and no one is giving them food, they often bring calamity to others. In the case of ancestors, they cause problems in their descendants' lives. Therefore, people in Asia, especially the Hmong, Korean, and Taiwanese contexts, offer sacrifices to placate spirits and ancestors.

FROM ELIZABETH W. MBURU

Similarly, in traditional Africa, the priest (in the technical sense of the word) functioned as the chief intermediary or mediator between the divine and human. He was the religious symbol of God and the religious head in much the same way that the king or chief was the political symbol of God's presence. However, even this religiopolitical distinction is artificial given the African holistic worldview. In some cases (e.g., the Baganda), one person combined both offices.

SHAMANS AND HIGH PRIESTS

The similarity between the shamans and the Old Testament priesthood is that these two groups become the bridge between the spiritual and physical realms. Shamans use their unique skills to help people in their time of need. The Old Testament priesthood helped Israelites offer various

---

11. Johns and Strecker, "Shi Yi," 1.

sacrifices to Yahweh. Just as the people became shamans by the mandate of the higher power, the Old Testament priests were chosen by the LORD through the Levitical laws. To be a priest, one must be a male without any physical ailment (Lev 21:21) from the tribe of Aaron. Lessing and Stenmann encapsulate the essence of the Old Testament priests' responsibilities, often muddled by various rites: "Yahweh directs his holy nation to set apart some of its members to be priests to administer his forgiving presence so that the nation, in turn, could be the channel and conduit of his grace for the world."[12] Henshaw describes the duties of the Old Testament priest as "the guardian of the holy place (Numbers 18:5)."[13] Priests offered "whole burnt offerings, sin offerings, guilt offerings, and peace offerings, as animal sacrifices and grain offerings."[14]

FROM ALEX SHAO KAI TSENG

In addition to the spiritual and the physical, shamans also seek to bridge the gap between the natural and the nonnatural. In the Old Testament, the former is ascribed primarily to the priestly office that began with Aaron, as the author mentions below. The task of mediating between the natural and the supernatural belongs primarily to prophetic figures like Moses and Elijah through the performance of miracles.

Two points may be observed here. First, the Bible strictly forbids the conglomeration of the three offices in human communities. Christ alone is prophet, priest, and king in one person. The shaman takes on both prophetic and priestly tasks. This is worsened by the fact that in tribal societies shamans often serve as chieftan-priests. Second, shamans perform magic, while prophets perform miracles. Miracles differ fundamentally from magic (German: *Zauber*, to use the phrase with reference to Max Weber's famous but deeply flawed thesis of disenchantment or *Entzauberung*). Magic is antinatural; miracles are supernatural.

---

12. R. Reed Lessing and Andrew Steinmann, *Prepare the Way of thE Lord: An Introduction to the Old Testament* (Saint Louis: Concordia, 2009), 105–6.

13. Richard A. Henshaw, "Priesthood, Israelite," *Eerdmans Dictionary of the Bible*, ed. David Noel Freeman, Allen C. Myers, and Astrid B. Beck (Grand Rapids: Eerdmans, 2000), 1083.

14. Lessing and Steinmann, *Prepare the Way of thE Lord*, 106.

That is, shamanism posits an opposition between the natural and what is falsely deemed supernatural and resorts to putatively supernatural powers to defy the laws of nature. The shamans of Pharaoh perform magic against the Creator.

Moses, by contrast, performs miracles in the name of the Creator, whose *potentia ordinata* contradicts neither itself nor God's immutable essence. The providential works of God in Exodus are supernatural; the powers that Pharaoh's shamans invoke are not above nature but against nature. The Old Testament scholar V. Philips Long has pointed out that miracles are God's supernatural ways of working through nature without breaking the laws of nature with which God created the world.[a] This is well in line with the doctrine of *concursus Dei*, based on medieval scholasticism and developed by Lutheran and Reformed orthodox theologians in the seventeenth century as a response to the rise of modern naturalism.

Shamanism and naturalism may seem to be polar opposites, but they are in fact two sides of the same coin: both posit a fundamental opposition between the natural and that which is beyond nature. The supernaturalism of Scripture is "disenchanting" in the sense that it dispels magic and reveals to us the creator God who works providentially through nature—not apart from or in opposition to nature—without ever becoming identical with anything in nature.

---

[a] V. Philips Long, *The Art of Biblical History* (Grand Rapids: Zondervan, 1994).

The priests accepted the animals brought by the Jewish people and presented them on Yahweh's altar according to the directives the Lord provided through Moses and his brother Aaron. The priests slaughtered and separated parts of the animals: some parts were burned for the Lord, the priests consumed some parts, and others belonged to the givers of the sacrifice. Unlike the burnt offering, only a portion of the grain offering was burned on the altar (Lev 2:2, 9, 16), with the rest consumed by the priest (2:3, 10). The portion of grain offered on the altar was to have the aromatic incense frankincense burned with it (2:16).

The Old Testament high priest carried out tasks similar to the other priests. However, he was chosen on a rotating basis from among the Aaronic priests. The high priest wore the special garment, and his requirements were more restrictive. Unfortunately, the high priest was also sinful, and he had to shed the animal's blood for his sins and the sins of others. The high priest alone could enter the holy of holies once each year on the Day of Atonement. There, he was in the presence of God, which was manifested in the ark of the covenant. *The Dictionary of New Testament Background* explains, "The high priest was the foremost priest and had special rites on the Day of Atonement."[15] Kleinig succinctly describes what the high priest did on that day, "The high priest enters into the second tent (the inner shrine) and the holy places annually alone. On that special day, he sacrifices goats and bulls for his own sins and the people's sins of ignorance. The blood of the sacrifices are shed for himself and others."[16]

When the Old Testament priests offered sacrifices to the LORD, they not only did so for the people but for their own sins as well. But Jesus was different. The book of Hebrews is explicit on this point. Jesus, our high priest, does not offer a sacrifice for himself because he is sinless (Heb 4:15). The book of Hebrews calls Jesus a high priest in the order of Melchizedek (Heb 7:17). When Abram defeated his enemies and rescued his nephew Lot, Melchizedek appeared from nowhere (Gen 14). Abraham gave an offering to the priest. The exciting fact about Melchizedek was that he was both a priest and the king of Salem. His name means "king of righteousness." Melchizedek's priestly office was instituted before the priesthood of Aaron.

FROM HAVILAH DHARAMRAJ

We know Melchizedek largely from Hebrews 7, where he is a type of Christ. Here, Abram returns from a war that has changed the power equations in the region and as the leader of a successful coalition (Gen 14:13). Understandably, other local rulers are keen to make friends with him. The kings of the city-states of Salem (Jerusalem; Ps 76:2) and of Sodom are on such a diplomatic exercise.

Two points are of relevance here. First, Melchizedek ("king of righteousness") is both a king and a priest. In the ancient world it was not uncommon for these two roles

---

15. H. W. Basser, "Priests and Priesthood, Jewish," in *Dictionary of New Testament Background*, ed. Craig A. Evans and Stanley E. Porter (Downers Grove, IL: InterVarsity Press, 2000), 825.

16. John W. Kleinig, *Hebrews* (Saint Louis: Concordia, 2017), 428.

to be merged into one. He worshiped El-Elyon, the "God of gods." El was the chief of Canaanite gods, but "El" was used generically as well, just like we use *parameshwar* ("almighty god") to refer to either the supreme Hindu deity or to the Christian God. So we cannot say with certainty who Melchizedek worships (Gen 14:18) or who he is referring to in his blessing over Abram (14:19–20). It could be a Canaanite deity, or it could be YHWH. It is in Abram's response to the king of Sodom (14:22) that he specifies his god as YHWH, El-Elyon ("God of gods" or "God Most High").

Second, goods are exchanged. Melchizedek comes bringing food and drink—bread and wine, the basics of a Mediterranean meal—as a demonstration of his political friendship. The food is probably for the battle-weary troops, not just for Abram, just as Barzillai will provision David and his army in a later story (2 Sam 17:27–29). Even the king of Sodom seems to have brought provisions for Abram's army (Gen 14:24). In the ancient world, a meal, usually involving the slaughter and consumption of an animal, was part of the sealing of an agreement (Exod 18:12; 24:1–11). Gifts would also be exchanged as a sign of goodwill. Here, Abram offers the king of Salem a tenth of the booty from the war. In a story to come, he will offer another Canaanite ruler, Abimelek, a gift of livestock (Gen 21:27–30). It is known that in this period, individuals paid a tenth of their income to the temple, in goods. Similarly, there is archaeological evidence that villages paid a tenth of the community's grain harvest to the royal storehouses. Perhaps Abram's goodwill gift to Melchizedek is made according to that commonly used measurement.

The priest-king Melchizedek becomes a convenient referent in Psalm 110:4. Here a priestly title is conferred on the house of David, bringing this royal line on par with other Canaanite royalty, even though the priestly roles and responsibilities still belong to the tribe of Levi. In the centuries between the Old and New Testaments, Judaism picks up Melchizedek and uses him variously. In the second century BC, the royal house of the Hasmoneans sees in him a validation for establishing a line of priest-kings, which conveniently concentrates both religious and political power in the king. Religious sects, such as the one that produced the Dead Sea Scrolls, create a heavenly messianic figure called Melchizedek, who brings the world to an apocalyptic end. Hebrew 7 draws on all these traditions in its interpretation of the person and work of Christ. As the ultimate son of David, he is the perfect priest-king Melchizedek. As the cosmic Messiah, he ushers in salvation to humankind.

When did Christ's high priestly office begin? Jody Barnard quotes David Moffitt on this matter, "Although his earthly service prepared and commended him for the priesthood, it is only after he has risen and ascended into heaven that his official consecration to the priesthood takes place."[17] According to David Schrock, the motif of the high priestly office began in Eden. The LORD gave Adam the responsibility to serve his "garden-temple."[18] This idea fits well with the notion of Adam being the prototype of the priest-hood, even expanding upon it. Jesus created the perfect priestly office by being the *sine pari* high priest.

FROM HAVILAH DHARAMRAJ

Inserted into the second account of creation (Gen 2:4–25) is what appears to be an excursus: a delightful description of the garden of Eden (2:10–14). An ancient reader would have spotted the sanctuary symbolism running through the text. In the middle of the garden is a significant tree, just as in the Holy Place one of the sacred objects is a stylized tree, the seven-branched candlestick. Trees were a symbol of fertility in the ancient world. A river flows out of Eden, a symbol of life, like the figurative rivers connected to the sanctuary (Ps 46:4; Ezek 47:1–12). Associated with Eden is good gold, reminding us of the overlay of gold and pure gold that will adorn the walls of the Holy Place and Most Holy Place, respectively. Precious stones and aromatic resin in the land of Havilah resonate with the stones on the high priest's ephod and incense that rises from the altar in the Holy Place. The gateway of the garden, like the temple, faces east (Gen 3:24; Ezek 47:1). The guardians of the gates are cherubim, heavenly figures who feature prominently in the Most Holy Place, their outstretched wings covering the ark of the covenant (Gen 3:24; Exod 25:18–22).

All of this sanctuary symbolism would have communicated to the ancient reader that this was the earthly residence of God, and indeed God would meet

---

17. Jody A. Barnard, *The Mystical Origin of Christ's Heavenly High Priesthood* (2011), 6; David M. Moffitt, *Atonement and the Logic of Resurrection in the Epistle to the Hebrews* (Leiden: Brill, 2011), 145–296.

18. David S. Schrock used Genesis 2:15 and Numbers 3:8 to support his claims in *The Royal Priesthood and the Glory of God* (Wheaton, IL: Crossway, 2022).

daily with the first-created humans in this garden. The man is placed in the garden to serve it (Gen 2:15; Exod 28:1), a verb used of the priestly service rendered in the sanctuary. This first priest is indeed superseded by the second Adam. So complete is his work that it removes the need for a temple. The Lamb of God himself becomes the temple of the New Jerusalem. In language reminiscent of Eden and the temple of Solomon, the city's foundations are made of precious stones, its streets are as transparent gold, and from his throne springs a life-giving river (Rev 21:1–22:5).

Christ is the true God, as John indicates: "In the beginning was the Word, and the Word was with God, and the Word was God. He was with God in the beginning. Through him all things were made; without him nothing was made that has been made. In him was life, and that life was the light of all mankind" (John 1:1–4). As God, his sacrifice on the cross was sufficient to pay for all sinners, and his righteousness was given in exchange for the sins of the entire world. In the Lutheran tradition, we believe and confess that Christ atoned for the sin of the world.[19]

Jesus is truly human (Matt 4:2; Luke 2:7, 40, 52; John 1:14). Thus, he can sympathize with us. He felt hunger, sorrow, pain, and joy. However, he was without sin. According to authentic Christianity, he was not born with original sin. Thus, he did not have a proclivity to sin. It is clear from the Scriptures that he did not sin (Heb 4:15).

WHAT HAPPENED TO THE OLD TESTAMENT PRIESTHOOD?

We are told in Hebrews (10:8–10) that Christ became the ultimate sacrifice. There the inspired writer tells us that the animal sacrifices of the Aaronic priesthood were only a foreshadowing of Christ's once-for-all sacrifice. Jesus the high priest offered himself to be the ultimate sacrifice. The human high

---

19. Johann Gerhard, *On Christ* (St. Louis: Concordia, 2009), 320.

priests and priests offer animal sacrifices continually because those animals themselves could not take away sins. In the case of Jesus the high priest, his sacrifice was accepted by his Father in heaven because Jesus did not commit any sin. As God, his work transcended the linguistic differences, generations, and geographical challenges. The writer of the book of Hebrews continues in verses 11–23 to tell us that Jesus has cleared the way for all of us to go boldly into the presence of God. We can go to the Father with all of our needs, being assured that our consciences are clean, and our confident faith will be rewarded due to the all-sufficient work of Jesus.

What aspects of the priesthood continue with Christ?

First, Christ intercedes for us at the Father's right hand. When his disciples asked Jesus to teach them how to pray, he willingly taught them to pray to his Father as "Our Father." He also taught them to seek first the kingdom of God and his righteousness. So Jesus taught them to pray, "Our Father in heaven, hallowed be your name, your kingdom come, your will be done, on earth as it is in heaven" (Matt 6:9–10). Believers are also to ask God, who is the giver of all good things, for what they need. So Jesus taught them to pray, "Give us today our daily bread. And forgive us our debts, as we also have forgiven our debtors. And lead us not into temptation, but deliver us from the evil one" (6:11–13). Whereas the shaman intercedes as a mere human for temporal prosperity, Christ pours out the Holy Spirit and his gifts leading to salvation and empowering believers for bold witness to the ends of the earth.

Second, Christ gives his church pastors and the means of grace. Intercessory prayer is one of the things that priests did that the Lord commanded his disciples to continue. "Therefore confess your sins to each other and pray for each other so that you may be healed. The prayer of a righteous person is powerful and effective" (Jas 5:16). And in Philippians 4:6, "Do not be anxious about anything, but in every situation, by prayer and petition, with thanksgiving, present your requests to God." The Lutheran divine services include the Prayer of the Church. The presiding pastor prays for the people of God. A Simple Explanation of the Church Service states, "In the Prayer of the Church, we pray for the needs of the world, the Church, the congregation, and local and special concerns. All those in the congregation are invited to add their voices to each petition by responding with 'Hear our prayer' or with the words from the Kyrie, 'Lord, have mercy.'"[20]

The Old Testament priests offered forgiveness, and many churches practice confession and absolution as an opening to their worship services, acknowledging that we are sinners coming into the presence of a Holy God. In the Lutheran context, forgiveness of sins is a crucial part of the worship service. Pastors speak the absolution this way: "Almighty God in his mercy has given his Son to die for you, and his sake forgives you all your sins. As a called and ordained servant of Christ, and by His authority, I therefore forgive you all your sins in the name of the Father, and of the Son and of the Holy Spirit."[21] The Augsburg Confession speaks about the confession and absolution this way: "It is not the voice or word of the man who speaks it, but it is the Word of God, who forgives sin, for it is spoken in God's stead and by God's command."[22]

Just before Jesus went to the cross, Jesus also taught his disciples to break bread and share wine in remembrance of his body and blood offered for the forgiveness of sin. In what we call the Lord's Supper, Jesus commanded his disciples to continually "do this in remembrance of me" (Luke 22:19). So his church continues this practice as we await his return. The Augsburg Confession states concerning the Lord's Supper this way: "Our churches teach that the body and blood of Christ are truly present and distributed to those who eat the Lord's Supper [1 Corinthians 10:16]."[23] As part of the Lutheran communion liturgy, we sing the "Agnus Dei" (Lamb of God) to signify what happens during the Eucharist. Lutherans believe that the forgiveness of sins is offered through the Lord's Supper. "These words, 'Given for you' and 'shed for you for the forgiveness of sins.' This means that in the Sacrament forgiveness of sins, life, and salvation are given [to] us

20. *A Simple Explanation of the Church Service* (St. Louis: Concordia, 2018), 17.

21. *Lutheran Service Book*. Prepared by the Commission on Worship of the Lutheran Church—Missouri Synod (St. Louis: Concordia, 2006).

22. Augsburg Confession 25.3, in *Concordia: The Lutheran Confessions; A Reader's Edition of the Book of Concord*, ed. Paul Timothy McCain et al., 2nd ed. (St. Louis, MO: Concordia, 2006), 58. The Augsburg Confession was written by Philipp Melancthon in 1530 to confess that Lutherans were not teaching new things, but their belief was biblical and in line with what the Christian Church believed. Confessional Lutherans subscribe to the Book of Concord. The Augsburg Confession is one of the books from the Lutheran Confessions.

23. Augsburg Confession 10, in McCain et al., *Concordia*, 39.

through these words. For where there is forgiveness of sins, there is also life and salvation."[24]

Many church services conclude with a benediction, which means "blessing." Jesus continued in the practice of blessing people. Jesus often said, "Peace." *Shalom* carried the concept of total well-being: mental, physical, and spiritual. At the conclusion of worship services, many Christians use the Aaronic benediction, "The LORD bless you and keep you; The LORD make his face shine on you and be gracious to you; the LORD turn his face toward you and give you peace" (Num 6:24–26).

Third, Jesus continues his high priestly ministry in and through the whole baptized community. Jesus's disciple Peter wrote, "But you are a chosen people, a royal priesthood, a holy nation, God's special possession, that you may declare the praises of him who called you out of darkness into his wonderful light. Once you were not a people, but now you are the people of God; once you had not received mercy, but now you have received mercy" (1 Pet 2:9–10). Martin Luther emphasized that Christians are a "priesthood of all believers." All Christians, not just clergy, are able to share the good news of Jesus with all the world. When we know and understand that Christ's sacrifice is for me, we are given hope and a new life of forgiveness to share with those around us.

COMMUNICATING CHRIST'S PRIESTHOOD TO PEOPLE OF OTHER RELIGIONS

Because of globalization and international immigration, people from different linguistic and geographical backgrounds live next to each other. Regions once known as homogenous locations are becoming multiethnic. With that, many places are becoming diverse in creed and religion. In this pluralistic society, how can we share with others about Christ, the high priest who takes away the sins of the world? When one looks at the places where the

---

24. Smaller Catechism 6, in McCain et al., *Concordia*, 343; Edward A. Engelbrecht et al., eds., *The Lutheran Difference: An Explanation and Comparison of Christian Beliefs* (St. Louis: Concordia, 2014), 430.

apostle Paul did his preaching and teaching ministry, those places were highly diverse with a very pluralistic religious milieu. Examining what happened at Areopagus will help us to communicate with people of other religions.

The Lord called a blasphemer and persecutor of the church to be the apostle to the gentiles. In the case of Paul, Jesus had to intervene without the means to call and mold Saul.[25] Christ appeared to him on the road to Damascus, and the Lord called the enemy of the church to be his servant (Acts 9). Although the apostle Paul had every justification for being forceful in his mission work because of his immediate apostolic calling and credentials, he was respectful and thoughtful. With the Judaizers, he was vocal in confessing that Christ alone can offer salvation. Although Paul had an outstanding resume, he set everything aside to proclaim Christ crucified. The following was Paul's resume: "circumcised on the eighth day, of the people of Israel, of the tribe of Benjamin, a Hebrew of Hebrews; in regard to the law, a Pharisee" (Phil 3:5).

Paul, with all these qualifications, did not become pompous. One can encounter his winsome mission approach on Mars Hill, engaging with the highly educated yet spiritual (Acts 17:22–31). Paul utilized his education and knowledge. What type of resume did he have? He not only grew up as a Jew in Tarsus, knowing all things Jewish (Phil 3:4–6), but also was exceptionally well-versed in Greek and Roman cultures and customs. One example is Paul quoting a poet while engaging with Athenians. His nonnaturalized Roman citizenship was the envy of those who obtained it with money (Acts 22:28).

While having all these qualifications, how did Paul start his conversation? He began by observing numerous statues, altars, and other religious memorabilia. The apostle primarily focused on the altar dedicated to the unknown god. To cover all the bases, Athenians erected this altar not to offend any deities. "I see that in every way you are very religious" (Acts 17:22). The apostle quoted the following statement, probably well-known to Athenians, "'In him we live and move and have our being. As some of your

---

25. My denominational tradition, Lutheran, emphasizes the "means of grace." We believe that God is powerful to reveal and accomplish His will in any way possible. However, His preferred method is to use the "means." Lutherans traditionally confessed and taught that God uses the Word and Sacrament to create, sustain, and strengthen faith. Saul is another name for Paul.

own poets have said, 'We are his offspring'" (Acts 17:28). Paul was creating common ground to talk to these Athenians about Christ.

Paul wanted to clarify that this unknown god he professed was personal and powerful. The Athenians erecting this monument to the unknown god shows people's feelings about deities. From the caricatures of Greek gods and goddesses, Greeks believed these deities were immoral and fickle, much like humans. Another aspect one can learn from the altar dedicated to the unknown god is that they had no clue how to explain this god. Athenians were agnostic in that they could observe the power and evidence of this deity but did not have the knowledge to fashion its image and tell others who this god was. Having this plot of land dedicated to the unknown god in the Areopagus meant people wanted blessings from this god and not harm. Van der Horst captures this sentiment: the Athenians had a "sense of fear or anxiety that by naming one god instead of another their acts of worship would not yield the results desired. To be on the safe side, a Greek could use the formula, 'unknown god.'"[26] One can observe the transactional nature of Athenian worship. Worshipers and their deities were in "reciprocal relationships."

However, Paul did not stop his conversation by simply acknowledging what he saw; he provided what he believed. The apostle indicated whom his faith relies on for salvation. "In the past God overlooked such ignorance, but now he commands all people everywhere to repent. For he has set a day when he will judge the world with justice by the man he has appointed. He has given proof of this to everyone by raising him from the dead" (Acts 17:30–31). The resurrection of Christ sets Christianity apart because the promises of God were fulfilled, and Christians believe in the living God. Witnessing the risen Jesus changed the timid and doubtful apostles into witnesses and martyrs. The message of the resurrection of the "man whom he has appointed" brought mixed reactions. Some mocked Paul, but some believed: "We want to hear you again on this subject.... Some of the people became

---

26. Pieter Willem van der Horst, "The Altar of the 'Unknown God' in Athens (Acts 17:23) and the Cult of 'Unknown Gods' in the Hellenistic and Roman Periods," in *Band 18/2: Teilband Religion (Heidentum: Die religiösen Verhältnisse in den Provinzen [Forts.])*, ed. Wolfgang Haase (Boston: De Gruyter, 1989), 1426–56.

followers of Paul and believed. Among them was Dionysius, a member of the Areopagus, also a woman named Damaris, and a number of others" (Acts 17:32–34).

Benno van den Toren's "Why Inter-religious Dialogue Needs Apologetics" laments the fact that many interreligious dialogues are based on relativism, looking at Christianity as one of many ways to live a good life.[27] However, it is necessary to discuss deep-seated epistemology. Van den Toren emphasizes that apologetics must be an essential part of interreligious dialogues and posits that these talks need to be done with individuals with strong religious convictions: "In your hearts honor Christ the Lord as holy, always being prepared to make a defense to anyone who asks you for a reason for the hope that is in you; yet do it with gentleness and respect" (1 Pet 3:15 ESV).

CONCLUSION

As in any interreligious conversation, we must seek analogies while respecting differences. Jesus's priestly ministry does not correspond to the work of a shaman at any point. And yet I have shown that there are analogies that may help people to understand the Scriptures, similar to Paul's approach in Athens. Specifically, I have argued that there are analogies between the Korean shaman and the Old Testament high priests. The latter examined people and determined whether they were clean. For example, people who were healed of leprosy had to see the priest first before returning to their families. And shamans diagnose problems. These human helpers confirmed or denied or proclaimed the message from the higher being, but they could not cure people. The Old Testament priesthood was the shadow of the things to come.

But Jesus the high priest can diagnose and successfully heal people, restoring them to be in the family of God: "He has done everything well"

---

27. Benno van den Toren, "Why Inter-religious Dialogue Needs Apologetics: Intrinsic to Bearing Witness to Christ Is Making Truth Claims," *Word and World*, November 8, 2017, https://ifesworld.org /en/journal/why-inter-religious-dialogue-needs-apologetics-benno-van-den-toren/.

(Mark 7:37). His heavenly Father anointed Jesus the high priest. His tenure is from eternity to eternity (Heb 7:24). Even after his Day of Atonement, he still carries out his responsibility as the high priest. Listening to our prayers and interceding for us, he is the perfect and sinless mediator who offered himself as the final sacrifice that reconciled the whole world to him and God the Father, granting eternal life and peace to all who believe.

PART III

CHRIST AS KING

INTRODUCTION: CHRIST AS KING

THE KING GREATER THAN DAVID

ELIZABETH W. MBURU

Old Testament: 2 Samuel 7:5–16

One of the clearest indications in the Old Testament that God would establish a king greater than David is found in 2 Samuel 7:5–16. The book of 2 Samuel presents David, although imperfect, as a type of the true theocratic king. In David's time, the united kingdom extended from Egypt to the Euphrates, evidence of God's fulfillment of his promise to Abraham (Gen 15:18). The narrator begins by setting the scene (2 Sam 7:1–4). The kingdom was at peace, and David felt that the ark deserved a better resting place. Its current residence fared unfavorably with David's living situation. Although the prophet Nathan endorsed his idea, God declined his request. A likely reason is that the Israelites might focus more on the external structure than on God's majesty.[1] Instead, he sent Nathan back with a message to pass on to David (7:5–8).

What is known as the messenger formula appears in 2 Samuel 7:8.[2] The divine title *yhwh tseba'ot* ("Lord Almighty" or "Lord of Hosts") is used here.

---

1. J. Robert Vannoy, *1–2 Samuel*, Cornerstone Biblical Commentary 4 (Carol Stream, IL: Tyndale, 2009), 306–8.

2. Craig E. Morrison, *2 Samuel*, ed. Jerome T. Walsh, Berit Olam Studies in Hebrew Narrative and Poetry (Collegeville, MN: Liturgical Press, 2013), 99–101.

This divine title, coupled with the messenger formula, underscores the solemnity of this discourse.[3] Another feature is that God refers to David as "servant" even though he was king over Israel. This is also David's self-reference. In the ancient world, this was how a person of lower status addressed a superior.[4] David thus showed God honor in this way. Moreover, as Baldwin points out, "It is worth pondering that it was by 'servant' imagery that the role of Jesus was most profoundly foreshadowed in the Old Testament."[5]

The Davidic covenant is set within the context of what God himself has done for David and Israel (2 Sam 7:8–11). This is signaled by first-person singular verbs. From 7:9–11, there is a shift from past to future tense, focusing on what God would do in the future. He promised to make David's name great (cf. Gen 12:2). This promise extends beyond David's lifetime and gives new significance to David's kingship.[6] God also promised to establish the Israelites in the land and to give them rest from their enemies (Exod 15).

In the verses that follow (2 Sam 7:11–16), new terminology such as *kingdom, throne, establish,* and *forever* is introduced.[7] As a way of signaling the formal nature of God's dynastic promise to David, the form of the verb changes from first person to third person in 7:11 (*yhwh*; the Lord). Rather than have David build him a house, God promises to establish a house for David. This is a play on the word *bayit*, which is used several times in this section to refer to different things. When David used it earlier it referred to a temple; here it refers to a dynasty. J. Robert Vannoy notes, "In this beautiful wordplay on the term 'house' . . . is a promise that lays the groundwork for messianic expectation in Israel and is often referred to as the Davidic covenant."[8]

From 7:12, there is a shift back to first-person verbs. God would also raise up his offspring to succeed him. It would be David's son who would build a temple for God (7:13; cf. 1 Kgs 5–6; 1 Chr 22:2–5; 28:2–3, 6). Like the tabernacle, it would provide access to God.[9] God would be his father,

---

3. Morrison, *2 Samuel*, 99–101.

4. Morrison, *2 Samuel*, 99–101.

5. Joyce G. Baldwin, *1 and 2 Samuel: An Introduction and Commentary*, vol. 8, Tyndale Old Testament Commentaries (Downers Grove, IL: InterVarsity Press, 1988), 229–32.

6. Baldwin, *1 and 2 Samuel*, 229–32.

7. Morrison, *2 Samuel*, 99–101.

8. Vannoy, *1–2 Samuel*, 306–8.

9. Baldwin, *1 and 2 Samuel*, 229–32.

and he would be God's son. The explicit use of the first-person personal pronoun *'ani* ("I") in 7:14 "underscores God's personal relationship to the king who will succeed David."[10] However, the kingdom would experience several crises and God would discipline David's successors (7:14). Nevertheless, through David's son, God would establish an eternal kingdom, and he would never take his love away (7:13, 15). The oracle ends at 7:17 with the narrator's insertion that Nathan reported all the words of the divine message.

Accounts in the Old Testament show that David's kingdom was not eternal. It is evident that this promise extends beyond David's lifetime and thus "provides the basis for the subsequent development of the messianic hope in the writings of the prophets and psalmists and finds its ultimate fulfillment in 'Jesus the Messiah, a descendant of David and of Abraham' (Matt 1:1)."[11]

New Testament: Matthew 21:1–11

The gospel of Matthew is probably best placed to demonstrate that Jesus is the promised eternal king. This is because it is both retrospective as well as prospective. It looks back to present Jesus's messianic reign as a fulfillment of Old Testament hopes. It also looks forward to provide readers with a foretaste of the consummated kingdom. Matthew is pivotal in introducing the Messiah and relating him to the Old Testament. He is concerned to show how Jesus in his life and ministry fulfilled Old Testament prophecies.

The text that shows the most explicit description of Jesus as the promised Davidic king is Matthew 21:1–11, generally known as "the triumphal entry." This text reflects the two concepts of king and prophet. R. T. France notes with regard to the implications of this event that "among this crowd, and with their vocal support, Jesus' arrival is a deliberately staged 'demonstration', a sequence of symbolic actions designed to have an unmistakable impact on the already suspicious Jerusalem authorities (see on 15:1)."[12] The setting is Bethphage on the Mount of Olives, a city about three kilometers east of Jerusalem (21:1). It was the time of Passover, the greatest of the annual festivals in Jerusalem.

---

10. Morrison, *2 Samuel*, 99–101.

11. Vannoy, *1–2 Samuel*, 306–8.

12. R. T. France, *Matthew: An Introduction and Commentary*, Tyndale New Testament Commentaries 1 (Downers Grove, IL: InterVarsity Press, 1985), 299–303.

Matthew writes that Jesus sent two of his disciples to a village ahead of them to bring him a donkey and colt that had been tied up there. Given their close proximity to Jerusalem, it is unlikely that Jesus needed to ride the donkey. Perhaps it was intended as a reminder of David's triumphant return after Absalom's rebellion. He too probably rode a donkey (2 Sam 16:1–2).[13] It was also "an acted allusion to Zechariah's prophecy (Zech 9:9–10) of the coming of the Messianic King."[14] Commentators suggest that Jesus had made prior arrangements for this or perhaps even demanded the animals for his temporary use. However, it is more likely that he had divine foresight and knew the animals would be there. Jesus's use of the title *kyrios* (Lord) to refer to himself is unusual here. In this context it does not have divine implications. Rather, it means "master."

As is characteristic of the retrospective and prospective nature of this gospel, Matthew explains the need for these two animals as a fulfillment of Old Testament prophecy (21:4). Although not identified explicitly, this is a messianic prophecy from Zechariah 9:9 with the initial clause coming from Isaiah 62:11. In Zechariah, the prophecy points forward to Jesus's entry into Jerusalem as king. Matthew 21:4–5 draws out messianic implications and shows that Jesus presents himself as king of the Jews.[15] This aligns with Mathew's particular theological emphases.

During the major festivals in Jerusalem, nationalistic hopes for freedom or redemption from Roman occupation ran high. Given that messianic fervor was high, the entrance into Jerusalem of a prophet from Galilee (21:11) who was already linked to messianic claims and deeds (e.g., 14:19–21) would naturally fuel expectations that political independence was near. Once the disciples had brought the donkey and the colt, they placed their cloaks on them for Jesus to sit on (21:6–7). Both Mark and Luke indicate that he rode the colt (Mark 11:7; Luke 19:35). The Passover festival inevitably attracted great crowds as Jews from all over congregated to celebrate together. Some of the people from the numbers who had gathered spread their cloaks on

---

13. France, *Matthew*, 299–303.

14. Richard T. France, "Matthew," in *New Bible Commentary: 21st Century Edition*, ed. D. A. Carson et al., 4th ed. (Downers Grove, IL: InterVarsity Press, 1994), 931.

15. France, *Matthew*, 299–303.

the road while others used branches (Matt 21:8). Only in John are these identified as palm branches (John 12:13). This was an act of homage paid to conquerors and great princes and was also a sign of particular honor and respect to those who deserved it in some way or other (cf. 2 Kgs 9:13).[16]

A colt is an unusual animal for a king to ride on, and the crowds would probably have preferred the Messiah to be on a warhorse as befits a conqueror. However, this fulfills Zechariah's prophecy while at the same time reflecting that the kingdom requires a paradigm shift. It is about servanthood (Matt 20:28). As France points out, "Matthew thus emphasizes what surely Jesus' symbolic act was designed to show, that he is Messiah indeed, but a Messiah whose triumphal route leads to suffering and humiliation, not to a show of force."[17]

The word *hosanna* that the crowds were shouting is literally a cry for divine help that means "save us." Applied to this context, it was a cry for help from an oppressed people to their king. It may have a twofold meaning because by this time it was also an expression of praise.[18] The other gospels (Mark 11:10; Luke 19:38; John 12:13) include an explicit reference to kingship. In addition to *hosanna*, they also sang words from Psalm 118, a psalm of ascent that was composed to celebrate a national deliverance. In this quote is an acknowledgement that Jesus Christ has come from God. The messianic title "son of David" reveals that although the crowds did not recognize the significance of this event, they believed that this was the promised Davidic king (Matt 21:9) who would deliver them from Roman bondage. They focused on deliverance from physical oppression, not recognizing that the kingship of Jesus Christ entailed spiritual deliverance. As Weber points out,

> For a short time, the people would acknowledge Jesus' true identity as the sovereign Son of David, but they would fail to identify him also as the sacrificial Son of Abraham. They knew he had come to restore his

---

16. James M. Freeman and Harold J. Chadwick, *Manners and Customs of the Bible* (North Brunswick, NJ: Bridge-Logos, 1998), 450.

17. France, *Matthew*, 299–303.

18. Stuart K. Weber, *Matthew*, Holman New Testament Commentary 1 (Nashville: B&H, 2000), 337–39.

kingdom, but they missed the fact that he was also here to redeem his people. They anticipated the sovereignty but overlooked the sacrifice. Jesus would not exercise the rule without the redemption.[19]

The stir caused by the celebrating crowds led others to ask who Jesus was. The word *eseisthē* ("was stirred") is also translated "was moved" or "was shaken." It is not clear if this event caused consternation or enthusiasm to those in Jerusalem. France suggests it was concern.[20] Such a negative reaction is likely, given that the religious authorities were already suspicious. The answer is surprising given the intensity of the entire event. Rather than the "Messiah" or the long awaited "Davidic king," the crowds point to his prophetic identity (21:11). France suggests that "as well as identifying the stranger to the people of Jerusalem, the phrase alludes to the hope of the coming of 'the prophet', based on Deuteronomy 18:15–18, which was a significant factor in the eschatological expectation of many Jews (cf. John 6:14)."[21] This triumphal entry thus unveils Jesus as the anticipated prophet-king to whom the Old Testament pointed.

CHRIST IS KING

MICHAEL S. HORTON

A turning point occurred in civilizations across Asia, from India to the Mediterranean and from the Aegean to Egypt, around the sixth century BC. The Achaemenid (Persian) empire under Cyrus and Darius encompassed these regions. People had discovered that they were "individuals" who could organize into political units. Previously, they had seen themselves as *subjects*, embedded in family, society, and the city-state or kingdom embodied in the sacred monarch.

"The king-god, the embodiment of the cosmic and earthly order,

---

19. Weber, *Matthew*, 337–39.
20. France, "Matthew," in Carson, *New Bible Commentary*, 931.
21. France, *Matthew*, 299–303.

disappeared," says Shmuel N. Eisenstadt, "and the model of the secular ruler appeared, who could still embody sacral attributes, but who was in principle accountable to a higher order or authority, to God and divine law."[22] Francis Oakley explains, "Kingship . . . emerged from an 'archaic' mentality that appears to have been thoroughly monistic, to have perceived no impermeable barrier between the human and divine, to have intuited the divine as immanent in the cyclic rhythms of the natural world and civil society as somehow enmeshed in these natural processes, and to have viewed its primary function, therefore, as a fundamentally religious one, involving the preservation of the cosmic order and the 'harmonious integration' of human beings with the natural world."[23] The individual's identity is found in the family; the family's in the clan, the clan's in the polis, the polis's in the ruler, and the ruler's in the cosmos. One was not even conscious of being embedded *in* society and the cosmos, much less disposed to taking a "step back" to evaluate it. Gods and spirits had an ambivalent and often capricious attitude toward humans. "Feeding them" rendered a favorable disposition more likely. Glory and honor in this world was the goal, not escape from this world into another one. The monarch embodied the values of the heroic age and its myths.

My context reflects the extreme outworking of self-discovery in modernity. Indeed, it is widely assumed that every individual possesses a divine spirit within—an autonomous inner light, voice, or reason—that trumps all external authorities. "We serve no king here." "Don't tread on me." "Give me liberty or give me death." These slogans make sense in the context of the American colonies seeking independence from the British monarch. However, this attitude bleeds into religious faith and practice. The passion of the Second Great Awakening (1790–1840) for enshrining the free will of the individual not only challenged traditional authorities in the church but

22. Shmuel N. Eisenstadt, "The Axial Conundrum between Transcendental Visions and Vicissitudes of Their Institutionalizations: Constructive and Destructive Possibilities," in *The Axial Age and Its Consequences*, ed. Robert N. Bellah and Hans Joas (Cambridge, MA: Harvard University Press, 2012), 280. But isn't this what *Enuma Elis*, the *Rigveda*, and other pre-Axial claimed—namely, that earthly kingship depended on the Mandate from Heaven? This is an example of where I think the thesis goes too far in its contrasts between pre-Axial and post-Axial.

23. Francis Oakley, *Kingship* (Oxford: Blackwell, 2006), 7. Robert N. Bellah: "Both tribal and archaic religions are 'cosmological,' in that supernature, nature and society were all fused in a single cosmos" (Bellah, "What Is Axial about the Axial Age?," *Europeain Journal of Sociology* 46, no. 1 (2005): 70.

traditional views of God and humanity. In any event, studies show that today Christ is viewed mainly as friend, guide, example, and co-sufferer, but not as king. Whatever we say about Christ as king in any highly modernized democracy (including those with titular monarchs) is often heard as law rather than gospel, as oppression rather than liberation.

At the same time that the surrounding nations were feeding their gods, the Hebrew prophets were proclaiming the sovereignty of Yahweh. Israel rejected God as king, wanting a king like the nations (1 Sam 8). God acceded to their request. They meant it for evil, but God meant it for good: to unite the royal bloodline of the human mediator to his eternal sovereignty. The messianic Son of David would be both the mediatorial king of Israel and universal monarch as the eternal Son of God. God would be acknowledged as king once more. Instead, his subjects rejected him again, as Jesus alluded to in a parable: "His citizens hated him and sent a delegation after him, saying, 'We do not want this man to reign over us'" (Luke 19:14 ESV). His parable was fulfilled on Good Friday: "They cried out, 'Away with him, away with him, crucify him!' Pilate said to them, 'Shall I crucify your King?' The chief priests answered, 'We have no king but Caesar'" (John 19:15 ESV). However, once again, what humans intended for evil, God intended for good, as Peter proclaimed: "Men of Israel . . . this Jesus, delivered up according to the definite plan and foreknowledge of God, you crucified and killed by the hands of lawless men. God raised him up, loosing the pangs of death, because it was not possible for him to be held by it" (Acts 2:22–24 ESV). Because of his death and resurrection, Christ has purchased a kingdom consisting of people from every people and nation on earth (Rev 5:9). Exalted to the right hand of the Father, he rules to save and saves to rule.

With the arrival of the King at the Temple Mount, we have Jesus hailed as both the Son of Man (Dan 7) and the Son of David (1 Sam 7). Thus, Jesus's action on the Temple Mount is the revelation of the kingship of Yahweh over his people. It was believed widely in Second Temple Judaism that the Messiah would be the Davidic king, but this is precisely why the idea of him dying—much less being crucified—was unimaginable. Jesus redefined kingship. When the mother of the sons of Zebedee asked if her sons could sit at Jesus's right and left in his kingdom, Jesus replied, "You don't know what you are asking" (Matt 20:22). After all, her plea was tantamount to asking for her sons to be crucified on Jesus's left and right. As the disciples quarreled over power,

> Jesus called them to him and said, "You know that the rulers of the Gentiles lord it over them, and their great ones exercise authority over them. It shall not be so among you. But whoever would be great among you must be your servant, and whoever would be first among you must be your slave, even as the Son of Man came not to be served but to serve, and to give his life as a ransom for many." (Matt 20:25–28 ESV)

Jesus repeatedly foretold his death and resurrection but was rebuffed, especially by Peter. The disciples were expecting a kingdom of glory in Jerusalem, installing Jesus as King and Messiah, but Jesus assumed his throne on a cross: "I, when I am lifted up from the earth, will draw all people to myself" (John 12:32).

In Mark 10, it becomes especially clear that the King must die:

> And James and John, the sons of Zebedee, came up to him and said to him, "Teacher, we want you to do for us whatever we ask of you." And he said to them, "What do you want me to do for you?" And they said to him, "Grant us to sit, one at your right hand and one at your left, in your glory." Jesus said to them, "You do not know what you are asking. Are you able to drink the cup that I drink, or to be baptized with the baptism with which I am baptized?" And they said to him, "We are able." And Jesus said to them, "The cup that I drink you will drink, and with the baptism with which I am baptized, you will be baptized, but to sit at my right hand or at my left is not mine to grant, but it is for those for whom it has been prepared." And when the ten heard it, they began to be indignant at James and John. And Jesus called them to him and said to them, "You know that those who are considered rulers of the Gentiles lord it over them, and their great ones exercise authority over them. But it shall not be so among you. But whoever would be great among you must be your servant, and whoever would

be first among you must be slave of all. For even the Son of Man came
not to be served but to serve, and to give his life as a ransom for many."
(Mark 10:35–45 ESV)

As in the washing of the disciples' feet in John 13, Jesus counters the jock-
eying of disciples for power by representing the true nature of kingship:
offering oneself for one's people. A theology of glory will always fall from
its utopianism into despair, which is the condition in which Jesus found two
disciples on the way to Emmaus. "And he said to them, 'O foolish ones, and
slow of heart to believe all that the prophets have spoken! Was it not necessary that the Christ should suffer these things and enter into his glory?' And
beginning with Moses and all the Prophets, he interpreted to them in all the
Scriptures the things concerning himself" (Luke 24:25–27 ESV).

Two Ages, Two Installments

I am a gentile, a Western gentile, in fact. Historically, that means that my
default setting is to imagine some sort of airy "afterlife." However, biblical
eschatology anticipates the resurrection of the body and restoration of the
whole cosmos.[24] It does not speak of two worlds but of two ages: "this age"
and "the age to come."[25] The old gospel song "When the Roll Is Called Up
Yonder" anticipates "when time shall be no more." However, Jesus did not
think in terms of an "end of history" but "the end of the age" (Matt 28:20).
The exiles in Babylon were buoyed ultimately not by an "afterlife" some-
where else but a this-worldly promise of resurrection, vindication, and everlasting rest from violence, sin, death, war, and injustice:

On this mountain the LORD of hosts will make for all peoples a feast
of rich food, a feast of well-aged wine, of rich food full of marrow,
of aged wine well refined. And he will swallow up on this mountain

---

24. See D. S. Russell, *The Method and Message of Jewish Apocalyptic, 200 BC–AD 100* (London:
SCM, 1964), especially 269; cf. C. Rowlands, *The Open Heaven: A Study of Apocalyptic in Judaism and
Early Christianity* (Eugene, OR: Wipf & Stock, 2002), especially 355.

25. Jesus appeals to the distinction in the Gospels (Matt 12:32; 13:49; 19:28; 24:3; Mark 4:19;
8:38; 10:30; Luke 18:30; 20:35) and it is found frequently in the Pauline Epistles (1 Cor 2:6; 10:11; Gal
1:4; Eph 1:21; 1 Tim 6:19) as well as Hebrews 6:5.

the covering that is cast over all peoples, the vail that is spread over all nations; He will swallow up death forever. The Lord GOD will wipe away tears from all faces, and the reproach of his people he will take away from the whole earth. (Isa 25:6–8 ESV)

These are not different worlds but different epochs marked by different regimes. The present age lies under sin and death, blinded by "the god of this age" (2 Cor 4:4), with the whole creation subjected to corruption because of man's sin (Rom 8:12). However, the age to come is marked by immortality, incorruption, righteousness, peace, joy, and fellowship with God and each other.

So where are we located in time right now? The prophets spoke of the "last days" when the Lord's mountain would rise above all others and the nations would stream into it (Isa 2:2); a new covenant of forgiveness and new birth by grace alone (Jer 31:31–37), when the Spirit would be poured out on all flesh (Joel 2:28–32). Are we living in the last days yet? We do not need to speculate, since we are told that we have been living in "these last days" since Jesus rose from the dead (Heb 1:2; cf. Acts 2:17; 1 Tim 4:1; 2 Tim 3:1; 2 Pet 3:3, etc.). His resurrection started the clock. Time is running out for "the present evil age" (Gal 1:4). Jesus's return in glory marks the transition between the two ages. So how much of the age to come can we expect in these last days of this present age?

According to Hebrews 6:4–5, the age to come is breaking into this present evil age through the preaching of the word, baptism, and the Lord's Supper: we are "enlightened," the term used in the early church for baptism, and "have tasted the heavenly gift, and have shared in the Holy Spirit, and have tasted the goodness of the word of God and the powers of the age to come" (ESV). United to Christ through faith, we already possess "every spiritual blessing in the heavenly places," including election, redemption, and regeneration (see Eph 1:3–11 ESV). In this declaration of the gospel here and now I hear God's final verdict on judgment day. Thus, the future judgment is realized fully for me now in justification. "Therefore, since we *have been* justified by faith, we *have* peace with God through our Lord Jesus Christ" (Rom 5:1 ESV, emphasis added). "So we do not lose heart. Though our outer self is wasting away, our inner self is being renewed day by day" (2 Cor 4:16 ESV). Our bodies are not getting better. Nor is the world at large. Following in the train of our King, we embrace the cross now and glory in the end.

> For I consider that the sufferings of this present time are not worth comparing with the glory that is to be revealed to us. For the creation waits with eager longing for the revealing of the sons of God. For the creation was subjected to futility, not willingly, but because of him who subjected it, in hope that the creation itself will be set free from its bondage to corruption and obtain the freedom of the glory of the children of God. For we know that the whole creation has been groaning together in the pains of childbirth until now. And not only the creation, but we ourselves, who have the firstfruits of the Spirit, groan inwardly as we wait eagerly for adoption as sons, the redemption of our bodies. For in this hope we were saved. Now hope that is seen is not hope. For who hopes for what he sees? But if we hope for what we do not see, we wait for it with patience. (Rom 8:18–25 ESV)

Christ is king, and he is drawing people from every tribe to himself. Each local church is an embassy of grace, sending out ambassadors of reconciliation. One day he will return, raise the dead, judge the world in righteousness, and usher us into his eternal Sabbath glory. In Matthew's gospel, Jesus says he has come to "restore all things" (Matt 17:11). The word he uses becomes, with the definite article, a distinct event: *tē palingenesia*. It is like *the* Fourth of July. In fact, "the new birthday" would be a fair translation. (Reference is made in Matthew 14:6 to Herod's birthday, *genesiois*.) "Jesus said to them, 'Truly I tell you, at the renewal of all things [*tē palingenesia*], when the Son of Man sits on his glorious throne, you who have followed me will also sit on twelve thrones, judging the twelve tribes of Israel'" (Matt 19:28).[26] Peter proclaimed that "heaven must receive [Jesus] until the time for restoring all the things about which God spoke by the mouth of his holy prophets long ago" (Acts 3:21 ESV). Thus, the restoration is seen as an event

---

26. Strangely, the ESV renders *palingenesia* "new world." The NIV is more accurate here.

that will occur when Jesus returns. It will be all-encompassing, "far as the curse is found."

> And being found in human form, he humbled himself by becoming obedient to the point of death, even death on a cross. Therefore God has highly exalted him and bestowed on him the name that is above every name, so that at the name of Jesus every knee should bow, in heaven and on earth and under the earth, and every tongue confess that Jesus Christ is Lord, to the glory of God the Father. (Phil 2:8–11 ESV)

In the following essays, we hear from Indian, Brazilian, and Ethiopian scholars about the kingly office of Christ and what it means to declare that he is Lord.

CHAPTER 7

CHRIST'S SOVEREIGNTY AND HIS PRESENT KINGDOM

ARUTHUCKAL VARUGHESE JOHN

The term *kingdom* often invokes notions of a specific territory or a geographical domain, and for today's audience, both *kingdom* and *reign* can evoke unfavorable associations tied to the historical baggage of colonialism and human empires. In the New Testament, these terms serve as a means to address and rectify the human excesses through God's kingship and his sovereignty.

This chapter delves into the significance of the kingdom of God, emphasizing its current manifestation, which carries profound implications for our responsibility to remain faithful to our generation. It will contend that the kingdom inaugurated through Christ's arrival signifies the liberation of individuals from the clutches of Satan. Furthermore, as citizens of the kingdom of God residing in the transitional period between the "already" and the "not yet," believers are called to emulate Christ in bringing about the fuller dominion of God upon earthly matters.

FROM HEBER CARLOS DE CAMPOS JR.

How do we emulate Christ as citizens of the kingdom? This is not a question with an easy answer. As evangelical churches fragment into several strands with falsified gospels, we see some reducing the atonement to an example of sacrifice, others speaking of the church's incarnational ministry, and still more accept the message

that we should bring New Heavens and New Earth to this world. All these emphases stress what we do as we follow in Christ's footsteps over what Christ has done
for us. These versions of the gospel undermine the singularity of Christ's work:
we should emulate Christ's willingness to suffer (1 Pet 2:21), but the atonement is
unmatched; we should imitate Christ's willingness to step down from his glorious
position in order to serve others (Phil 2:3–8), but the incarnation is unparalleled;
we should live as the new creatures that we are (2 Cor 5:17), but New Heavens
and New Earth are the work that only the Creator can accomplish (Isa 65:17). Thus,
we should always be very thoughtful about what we are in fact called to emulate.

I would start with two ideas of where our emulation of Christ honors the
gospel. First, we mimic the language of power and authority that Christ portrayed
in his earthly ministry. Just as Christ was sent by the Father, we are authorized
by him as ambassadors with a message of reconciliation (2 Cor 5:20), announcing
what he alone accomplished for our salvation (2 Cor 5:21). As authorized announc-
ers, we are taught to do everything in Christ's name (Col 3:17), like the kingdom
advanced as the apostles healed (Acts 3:6), witnessed (4:12; 9:15), and baptized
(8:16) in Christ's name. Second, we emulate Christ's trajectory of humiliation
prior to exaltation. Stories of rulers like Joseph in Egypt and David in Israel have
a similar plot: a servant starts to stand out in service and is soon despised before
he is finally exalted to glory. This plot foreshadows the path of our Savior, but
it also reminds us that we first go through a path of humiliation in our kingdom
lane before we reach exaltation (1 Pet 2:21–23; 4:12–14). Our hearts should be
prepared to serve the kingdom, knowing that it advances through our humiliation.

CHRIST AND HIS KINGDOM:
THE ALREADY AND THE NOT YET

There is a tendency for some Christians to focus too much on the future
aspect of God's kingdom and fail to recognize that divine sovereignty is
already active in the present. The Bible preempts the notion that God's kingdom is only to be hoped for in the distant future and far away from earth.[1]

---

1. In *The Quest for the Historical Jesus* (1906), Albert Schweitzer examined the concept of God's
kingdom as existing solely within the future apocalyptic and supernatural realm.

The New Testament presents the kingdom of God in a theological tension,[2] where it is at once "already" present and "not yet" in fullness. Although a believer has indeed experienced adoption (Rom 8:15), redemption (Eph 1:7), and sanctification (1 Cor 1:2), these experiences have not reached their complete realization in their lives. This is because there is an awaiting of full adoption (Rom 8:23), redemption (Eph 4:30), and sanctification (1 Thess 5:23–24). While Jesus proclaimed that the kingdom is already manifested and exists in the present moment (Luke 17:20–21), the New Testament also portrays the expectation of the restoration of all of creation along with humanity (Rom 8:18–25).

Jesus declared the fulfillment of prophesy of Isaiah 61:1 as he read from the scroll and declared, "Today this scripture is fulfilled in your hearing" (Luke 4:21). Jesus's assertion of fulfilling the Scripture is evident through the realization of specific elements of the messianic prophecy found in the book of Isaiah. This prophecy pertains to the anointed one upon whom the Spirit of the Lord has descended "to proclaim good news to the poor" and "to proclaim freedom for the prisoners and recovery of sight for the blind, to set the oppressed free" (Luke 4:18). In the fulfillment of this specific prophecy in the ministry of Jesus, the arrival of the king and his kingdom is manifested. Although Jesus is anointed at Simon the Leper's house in Bethany (Matt 26:6–13), this anointing primarily symbolizes the presence of the Holy Spirit upon Jesus. The Spirit comes upon Mary and "overshadows" her at his conception (Luke 1:35). Furthermore, at the beginning of his earthly ministry, John the Baptist bears witness to his baptism by the Spirit (John 1:32), and Jesus is referred to as the "Spirit baptizer" (John 1:33).

The arrival of the king not only marks the beginning of the kingdom but also grants Christian believers both citizenship and a new identity within the kingdom. This newfound identity in Christ transforms the believer, bestowing upon them a "new self, created after the likeness of God in true righteousness and holiness" (Eph 4:24). The apostle Paul also characterizes this new identity in Christ as a state of being a "new creation; the old has passed

---

2. During the 1950s, G. E. Ladd emphasized two interpretations of the term *kingdom of God*: (a) God's authority and legitimate rule, and (b) the domain where God exercises his royal authority.

away, behold, the new has come" (2 Cor 5:17 ESV). Since this transformative reality experienced by the believer is rooted in the completed work of Christ, it is recognized as the "already" present dimension of the kingdom. The new creation begins in the kingdom of God here and now where Christ proclaims, "All authority in heaven and on earth has been given to me" (Matt 28:18). The authority of Christ extends not merely over our souls but over everything there is. "The earth is the LORD's and the fullness thereof, the world and those who dwell therein" (Ps 24:1 ESV).

Nevertheless, even as believers undergo numerous changes in their lives, there remain aspects where the struggle between the flesh and the spirit is evident, as described in Romans 7. Furthermore, the world appears to persist in adhering to principles that are contrary to the values of the kingdom of God. This is understood as the "not yet" dimension of the kingdom, which will find its fulfillment upon the second coming of Christ.

FROM HEBER CARLOS DE CAMPOS JR.

Evangelical theology has long been criticized for a spiritualized understanding of heaven, allegedly having an otherworldly focus that forgets one's place in this world. Those making such criticisms often become prey to an overrealized eschatology, a triumphalist portrayal of the kingdom. They speak of the church as "agents of transformation of this earth" here and now, almost as if there were no barriers to this transformation. They sound like postmillennialism of the past or social theologies of the present, but they don't identify with either of them in their entirety. However, the similarity in eschatology is because they overemphasize the "already" and undermine the "not yet" of life in between Christ's two comings. Their optimistic stance on civil changes seem to come from a simplistic view of sin in their hearts; it is arguable that most passionate claims for justice in the world (justice outside) come from an understanding of self-righteousness that belittles the deceit of sin that goes on in the heart (injustice inside). That is why Varughese's application of Romans 7 to the eschatological kingdom is so helpful as we are reminded that the beauty of the freedom provided by Christ should not annul the still pervasive effects of the indwelling sin of believers.

I believe the apostle Peter learned such a lesson, because he used to be someone less aware of changes still to happen on the inside (Mark 14:29–31) but prone to establish the kingdom on the outside (John 18:10–11). However, in his letters he talks about a war inside our soul (1 Pet 2:11) but a peaceful witness in this world (1 Pet 2:12–14) that will occasionally silence the wicked (1 Pet 2:15), and other times it will not change the attitude of those around us (1 Pet 2:20). Because changes in this world are not always effective, he awaits the coming of his Lord to transform this world (2 Pet 3:10–13). Peter learned how to wage war with the "already" in mind, being fully cognizant that we hope for permanent changes in the "not yet" of redemptive history.

Jesus uses the parable of weeds among the wheat (Matt 13:24–43) to illustrate how Christians may think about the present state of affairs—tangled and messy. It also illustrates the importance of patiently awaiting the "not yet." During this period, even the weeds sown by the "enemy" (Matt 13:28) are allowed to "grow together until the harvest" (Matt 13:30). The wise householder notes that ultimately, the harvesters will "first collect the weeds and tie them in bundles to be burned; then gather the wheat . . . into my barn" (Matt 13:30).

FROM SOFANIT T. ABEBE

The Andemta tradition, a seventeenth-century Amharic collection of biblical commentaries, originated in Gondar, the Ethiopian capital at the time. It includes older material from the Ge'ez Tergwame and is a significant part of the Ethiopian Orthodox Church's literary heritage. The Andemta commentary on Matthew 13:24-43 reflects a similar outlook on the present state of affairs—tangled and messy—and an invitation to patiently await Christ's return. The authors first consider the possibility of weeds as a representation of heretical teaching that Satan planted in the harvest of Christ's true gospel. They imagine angels conversing with the Lord. The weeds are the fourth-century heresies of Arianism (that declared Christ as created), Macedonianism (that denied the divinity and personhood of the Holy Spirit), and Nestorianism (which bifurcated the divine and human natures of Christ). Then the angels ask Christ if he would like them to destroy the heretics, to which he replies, "Leave them be. In trying to destroy the weed you will destroy the wheat. When the right time comes, I will order the angels to separate the weeds and the wheat. . . . It is not possible for you to do it now, this has been demonstrated in the case of Noah and Lot, for there will be those who will be born of the weeds who will return through repentance."[a] Those entangled in these teachings are imagined to be inseparable from believers that uphold the true gospel, perhaps hinting at the authors' subtle critique that doctrinal literacy in seventeenth-century Ethiopia is not where it ought to be. However, the authors hold the possibility of a "return"—repentance—the possibility of grace untangling the wheat from the weeds before the time comes for the harvest to be gathered.

Typical to the style of the Andemta commentary tradition, the Matthean commentators then offer a second interpretation of the same passage. In this case the harvest represents the human heart. Again angels are imagined as wondering about how humanity has an evil conscience when God created men and women in goodness. The Lord explains to them that humanity's evil conscience originates from Satan, and he refuses to let them destroy people's evil conscience, saying, "You will destroy the good in trying to destroy evil. Leave them, let it grow together. I direct Fathers [i.e., clergy] who work in teaching to identify evil conscience and to work at it through correct doctrine. Regarding good conscience I tell them to have it entrusted to the Holy Spirit."[b] In this portrayal of the evil/good conscience, the authors approach the issue of moral conscience—the inner capacity of alienation from evil or the failure to do so and therefore get entangled in doing evil. In both this and the earlier interpretation of Matthew 13:24–34, Christ is portrayed as the embodiment of hope. In patiently awaiting the "not yet" of Christ's Kingdom inaugural, believers are to imitate him—holding out the hope and faithfully working toward the vision that, in this period of transition, Christ the King will continue to liberate people from the entanglement of the weed through his word.

---

[a] Ethiopian Orthodox Theological College, *Andemta Commentary of the Gospels* (Addis Ababa: Birhan ena Selam, 2002), 180.

[b] *Andemta Commentary of the Gospels*, 181.

It is this theological tension that inspired Augustine and Luther. In *The City of God*, Augustine influentially argued that the world is a mix of both the temporal city (or kingdom) of man and the eternal city (or kingdom) of God. Luther built on this idea of two kingdoms, each with distinct and visible principles of law and grace: "God has therefore ordained two regiment(s): the spiritual which by the Holy Spirit produces Christians and pious folk under Christ, and the secular which restrains un-Christian and evil folk, so that they are obliged to keep outward peace, albeit by no merit of their own."[3]

Although our focus is not Augustine or Luther, their distinction between two cities or kingdoms provides a framework to understand the warring forces at play in the "already" of the present age. One should not mistake it, however, for the modern, secular separation of church and state. Often, an approach to this separation, which removes the church's presence or influence from the public sphere, runs counter to the very essence of what Jesus had in mind when he responded to the Pharisees' trick question about paying taxes to Caesar. Rather, in addition to "personal salvation," the gospel will, as Ladd argues, "also transform all of the relationships of life here and now and thus cause the Kingdom of God to prevail in all the world," including "the social, economic and political orders."[4]

FROM HEBER CARLOS DE CAMPOS JR.

Whether you think of Augustine's two cities or Luther's two kingdoms, there seems to be a Christian tradition on the eschatological tension of living for the kingdom in a worldly environment. And the fact that pagan Rome in Augustine's day and Luther's medieval Germany are two very different contexts should teach us that both have room for this eschatological posture. So before we overstress context to say that cultural exegesis is crucial to be socially relevant, we should echo the chorus of the ages that we live in between the first and the second

---

3. *Luther's Works*, WA, 11.251, 15–18.
4. George Eldon Ladd, *The Gospel of the Kingdom: Scriptural Studies in the Kingdom of God* (Grand Rapids: Eerdmans, 1995), 16.

coming. We do not separate ourselves from the public sphere (a monastic asceticism), and we do not claim that culture's best aspirations are synonymous with the gospel (a liberal message), for both have missed on the eschatology of the kingdom. Whether it is David in the kingdom of Israel or Daniel in the kingdom of Babylon, two very different contexts, the believer has always lived boldly based on God's past accomplishments while waiting for the fulfillment of divine promises. Thus, we are the people of hope, recognizing the tension of having experienced the power of our King but hoping to see it consummated. The "tension" is eschatological, not civil nor political. The issue is not how much space we have in the public sphere, but if our public standing takes into consideration the eschatological tension.

Even though people of faith in the Old Testament are counted as part of God's kingdom (Luke 13:28), the arrival of Jesus, the awaited Messiah, ushers in the kingdom of God in a distinctive and unprecedented manner. Jesus as king is especially apparent during his birth, as affirmed by the wise men who declare him as king (Matt 2:2), and also during his trial and crucifixion (Mark 15:2). Interestingly, the inscription "Jesus of Nazareth, the King of the Jews," originally intended as a mockery, becomes an ironic twist as the Jews, trapped in their own irony, later request the removal of the inscription (John 19:20–21).

Right from the start of his earthly ministry, Jesus sought to turn his disciples' attention away from the temple as the exclusive place to encounter God and receive blessings, healing, and forgiveness. Instead, he encouraged his followers to turn to him as the living embodiment of God, the one to whom his people should gather. The overturning of the tables in the temple premises as he entered Jerusalem (Matt 21:12–17), the prediction about the destruction of the temple where "not one stone will be left on another" (Luke 21:6), and the prediction about his own resurrection (Matt 17:23; Mark 9:31) all testify powerfully to this shift from finding God's presence in the temple to finding it in the person of Jesus.

Christians must watch out for the temptation to compartmentalize church and state, which can obscure the political and social import of this shift of the kingdom's location from the temple to Jesus. The temple was not merely the religious arena; rather, it was the religious fulcrum upon which Israel's social, political, and economic policies also turned. The shift from the temple to Jesus meant that all the spheres of life overseen by the God of Israel—and are any left out?—would now come under the oversight of the Lord Jesus. This redefinition asserts the kingship of Jesus as more than just personal salvation; it takes up a political angle to challenge the oppressive structures by subverting the cult of Caesar. Paul's Christian communities, established later, persist in subverting the hierarchical power structures of the Roman Empire in the subsequent years.

MARKERS OF THE KINGDOM AND THE CALL TO CHRISTIAN SOCIAL ENGAGEMENT

An essential aspect of the inverted kingdom is Jesus's alignment with those on the fringes of society. The earthly ministry of Jesus involved teaching, preaching, healing the sick, and delivering those in the clutches of evil spirits—a ministry Luke succinctly describes as "he went around doing good" (Acts 10:38). Each aspect of Jesus's ministry is part of the establishment of his kingdom. In response to John's (the Baptist) question if he was the one to come (Matt 11:3), Jesus goes back to the markers of the Messiah in Isaiah 61:1. He asks the disciples of John to report what they saw: "The blind receive their sight and the lame walk, lepers are cleansed and the deaf hear, and the dead are raised up, and the poor have good news preached to them" (Matt 11:5 ESV).

The new kingdom's values stand in stark contrast to the earthly kingdom's. This contrast becomes evident in God's identification with the oppressed and marginalized within society, with Jesus himself often found in the margins (cf. Matt 25:35–40; Luke 1:47–55). The circumstances of Jesus's birth in a humble manger (Luke 2:1–7), rather than the palace the wise men anticipated (Matt 2:1–12), serve as a testament to the inverted nature of his kingdom. Simeon's prophecy foreshadows a shifting of fortunes in Israel, where some will decline while others will ascend (Luke 2:34). This prophecy plays out in the disgrace of the privileged and the exaltation of the humble and poor. Herod's insecurities led Jesus's family to migrate to Egypt (Matt 2:13,16), a foreign country. Luke particularly highlights that Jesus's ministry is dedicated to addressing the most vulnerable members of the society. He liberates those possessed and under Satan's bondage (Luke 4:31–37, 41; 8:26–39; 9:37–42), heals lepers who were shunned as untouchable and impure by society (Luke 5:12–16), and restores sight to the blind (Luke 4:18; 7:21; 18:35–43). Jesus placed particular emphasis on addressing the inequalities faced by women, shedding light on the challenges widows encountered (Luke 4:25; 18:1–8; 20:46–47). He also highlighted the commendable generosity of the poor widow (Luke 21:1–4) and the remarkable faith and perseverance of the widow deprived of justice (Luke 18:1–8). Additionally, Jesus accepted the anointing at Bethany (Matt 26:6–13), underscoring his support for women and their plight.

FROM SOFANIT T. ABEBE

The early Jewish apocalyptic framework presents the suffering and evil that mark this life in terms of cosmic evil forces and their human counterparts. Despite the suffering and persecution this entails for God's elect, life in the here and now is but a time of reprieve for evil doers: the end will come, and there will be a final judgment. On the day of the Lord, God will execute final judgement on the wicked, and it will be cosmic and universal (1 Enoch 100:3). Following this cosmic-scale divine judgement, the righteous will rest under God's lordship (Isa 24:18-19, 23; 1 Enoch 10:21, 98:2-11; 105:1-2). Furthermore, the final judgement also entails both reversal and retribution (cf. 1 Enoch 95:7; 96:8; 99:11-16; 100:9; 102:9; 103:9-15). Within this framework, the New Testament makes the radical claim that in and through Jesus Christ, the cycle of evil and oppression has been finally broken. The anticipation of salvation from evil is fulfilled in Jesus Christ. For the downtrodden and the disenfranchised, there is the hope of future glory and living hope for the present: in Christ, believers are God's elect, chosen and precious members of the household of God (1 Pet 1:2; 2:4-10).

The inverted kingdom of Christ is the hope that sustains the persecuted and the disenfranchised. This hope of status reversal and future judgement helps to mitigate the arbitrary evil and persecution of the weak and powerless that has marked the sociopolitical life of Ethiopians in the past fifty years. The majority of Ethiopians are Christians, predominantly Orthodox, for whom all of the Bible, as well as the book of Enoch and other Jewish apocalyptic texts like 4 Ezra, hold a deuterocanonical status. This impacts the way people imagine their social existence. In Ethiopia, the lamentation of the meek encapsuled in the Amharic adage *daha tabadala feteh taguadada* ("the poor are oppressed, and justice is trampled upon") is a particularly significant slogan that has been used to describe the yearning for social justice during the student uprisings of the 1970s.

Power imbalances and hegemonic subjugations are expressed with the notion of *gef* (oppression/exploitation). *Gef* is an action that is necessarily committed by people in positions of power and privilege or those in positions of strength, even momentarily. It also describes an attitude of self-reliance or extravagance on the part of abusers. Committing *gef* (i.e., oppressing or exploiting) is thought to bring down the wrath of God, while administrating justice has salvific significance. Enabling things and events in general and suffering in particular to appear meaningful, the notion of *gef* embodies the notion of retribution even when state laws and religious orders are broken. Even if the public sphere is under the hegemonic control of *ye zemenu Sew* (that is, "man of privilege") or the *bale gize* (that is, "man of the hour" or "strong man"), the idea of *gef* and the notion of divine punishment it entails for wrongdoers sustains a social imagination that is built upon the belief that good will ultimately triumph over evil. Shared evil that befalls all humanity but to which the poor are particularly susceptible is thus understood and managed better. How comforting is it then to proclaim that the kingdom over which Christ reigns is in stark contrast to earthly kingdoms. The humble and poor are exalted, those against whom *gef* has been committed from generation to generation can finally rest, there is no *bale gize* who will lord it over them. In Christ's kingdom, those who belong to him are restored to glory.

Another crucial aspect of the inverted kingdom is represented by the cross itself. Christ's kingdom takes a cruciform nature as he willingly submits to "[obedience] to death, even death on a cross" (Phil 2:8 NAB). The "supreme penalty" of crucifixion was the most brutal method of execution reserved for traitors of the Roman Empire and aimed to serve as a deterrent against potential acts of rebellion.[5] Throughout Jesus's ministry, he experienced suffering, ridicule, and constant threat of violence and death from those in positions of power. This emptying of Christ leads to his exaltation, and he is given "the name that is above every name, that at the name of Jesus every knee should bow, in heaven and on earth and under the earth, and every tongue acknowledge that Jesus Christ is Lord, to the glory of God the Father" (Phil 2:9–11).

FROM SOFANIT T. ABEBE

Ethiopian paintings from the twelfth and thirteenth centuries affirm the royal character of the cross. The motif of the triumphant Christ is a dominant feature of Christian art from this period and depicts Christ's victory over death on the cross. In fact, none of the surviving pre-fifteenth-century Ethiopian crucifixion art types display a suffering Christ, affirming the association between the kingdom of God's motif of status reversal and the cross in the book of Revelation's Andemta commentary. The commentators note that the cross is a symbol of the glory of Christ that represents his victory over mortality and the redemption and glorification of humanity it heralds. According to the Andemta commentators, John is saying (in Rev 5:9–10):

> "With your blood you purchased for God persons from every tribe and language and people and nation." Again he repeats this saying, "those that are tribes and a people." When he says (v. 10), "You have made them," he is saying, "You have installed them as kings and priests." On the one hand, he is saying, "You have made them to be a kingdom and priests to serve our God." And when it says, "They will reign on the earth," it is that they will be called angels of grace as it says in Revelation 1:6; 20:6; and 22:5.

5. Tom Holland, *Dominion: The Making of the Western Mind* (London: Little, Brown, 2019), xiv–xvi.

In its call to participate in the kingdom work, Scripture summons Christians to imitate Jesus in accomplishing the task given to them by "looking to Jesus, the pioneer and perfecter of our faith, who for the sake of the joy that was set before him endured the cross, disregarding the shame, and has taken his seat at the right hand of the throne of God" (Heb 12:2 NRSVue). The kingdom of God is "righteousness, peace and joy in the Holy Spirit" (Rom 14:17). Christians are urged to imitate the righteous conduct of their suffering master, Christ, who left them "an example" to "follow in his steps" (1 Pet 2:21). As God's children, Christians are likewise called to emulate their Creator and walk in love, imitating the love of Christ (Eph 5:1–2).

The call to imitate Christ is also an invitation to align with the agenda of his kingdom and its principles, particularly the special attention given to the poor and the marginalized as seen in Jesus's ministry. Where his will is enacted, the kingdom is present. Jesus intends that those who pray, "Your kingdom come. Your will be done on earth as it is in heaven" (Matt 6:9–10), by expressing this desire and offering this prayer, become active participants in kingdom work, thereby hastening its complete realization (2 Pet 3:12).

Spheres in Which Christ's Rule Can be Evident

Christ's Supremacy in Believers' Hearts

As you land at the Bangalore airport, it is almost impossible to miss the impressive 108-foot, 220-ton statue of Kempe Gowda, who was a chieftain under the Vijayanagar Empire in early modern India and the founder of the city of Bangalore. It is common practice for kings to place their images within the territory of their reign as a reminder to the people. Yet Scripture testifies that the battleground for supremacy remains the human heart. A heart that reveres Christ's reign and anticipates its full glory may pray with Tennyson, "Our wills are ours, to make them thine!"

Jesus reasoned with the Pharisees that the coin bearing the embossed image of Caesar belonged to Caesar; therefore, whatever belonged to Caesar should be devoted to Caesar, and whatever belonged to God, devoted to God (Matt 22:15–22). If we bear God's image, we belong to God. The greatest form of devotion is to offer one's heart to one's king. According to the Westminster Shorter Catechism, our ultimate purpose is to glorify God through hearts and lives devoted to him. The finished work of Christ inaugurates the redemption of the hearts of individual men and women, illustrating the perfect form of allegiance deserved by the perfect king.

The moment of faith in Christ may be understood as the inauguration of Christ's rule in one's heart or God's kingdom into one's life. "In the incarnation," Mark C. Taylor remarks, "the Eternal becomes temporal but remains eternal; in the moment of faith, the sinner realizes the possibility of eternal blessedness (immortality), but remains temporal."[6] The moment of faith can be regarded as the personal unveiling of the king, mirroring the moment of incarnation, which is the external and historical revelation of the king. The New Testament reclaims for God the authority and lordship often vested in human demigods—emperors and kings—by proclaiming Christ as the only Lord and Savior.

We who believe still await what we will be (1 John 3:2). Our identity within the kingdom as "new creation" (2 Cor 5:17), accomplished by Christ's completed redemptive work, is predicated on human incapacity to earn our salvation. The Spirit's sanctifying presence in us, likewise, is predicated on human incapacity to live according to the kingdom's values. Yet Christ's finished work and the Spirit's coming at Pentecost establish the reality of new life. The heart of stone has been changed into a heart of flesh and the coming of the Holy Spirit is the seal of the kingdom of God that we already possess (Eph 1:13–14).

The assurance of the inheritance in God's kingdom that Christians possess empowers them to maintain a posture of confidence in the world, even in the face of persecution, rather than adopting a passive approach to stay out of trouble. A heart truly dedicated to the supreme King does not adopt a stance of passivity and indifference. Instead, Peter urges, "Have no fear of them, nor be troubled, but *in your hearts reverence Christ as Lord*. Always be prepared to make a defense to anyone who calls you to account for the hope that is in you, yet do it with gentleness and reverence" (1 Pet 3:14–15 RSV, emphasis added).

---

6. Mark C. Taylor, *Kierkegaard's Pseudonymous Authorship: A Study of Time and the Self* (Princeton, NJ: Princeton University Press, 1975), 10.

Christ's Supremacy in the Church

The church reflects the present reality of Christ's supremacy by ordering the gathered lives of the saints by a new set of values and principles, a kingdom calculus. The kingdom that Christ inaugurates on earth is what N. T. Wright calls a "cruciform theocracy."[7] The human tendency to use even the cross as though it were a sword has often plagued Christians. God's means of saving the world, however, is quite antithetical to the world's means of bringing about change. The cross, in this sense, demonstrates how the kingship of Christ works: it shows that the king reigns in the hearts and through the lives of those he saves into loving fellowship with himself and one another.

Redemption through his sacrificial death on the cross is thus a central paradigm for Christ's rule. How unlike the calculus of the world, where "the rulers of the Gentiles lord it over them, and their high officials exercise authority over them" (Matt 20:25)! The mother of the sons of Zebedee came with a request for key positions in King Jesus's cabinet, generating a fair amount of jealousy among the other disciples. He warns them that the world's thinking had crept into their own: "It shall not be so among you. But whoever would be great among you must be your servant, and whoever would be first among you must be your slave; even as the Son of man came not to be served but to serve, and to give his life as a ransom for many" (Matt 20:26–28 ESV).

If Jesus had overthrown the Roman Empire and reestablished a Jewish kingdom as his fellow Jews had anticipated, he would have been better appreciated. However, Jesus's upside-down kingdom overturns expectations, turning the heart into his battleground more so than the geopolitical stage. Each of his soldiers is required to put our swords back in their sheaths (John 18:11), turn the other cheek (Matt 5:39), love our enemies, and pray for those who persecute us (Matt 5:44).

In Ephesians 3, Paul argues that even though this new order was kept a mystery until Christ's coming, the Old Testament prophets understood that salvation through the covenant God established with Israel was foreordained to include the gentiles also. Previously, those who did not belong to Israel had

---

7. Andy Walton, "Theocracy: Did a Leading Theologian Call for a Christian Caliphate?," in *Christian Today* October 23, 2015, https://www.christiantoday.com/article/theocracy.did.a.leading.theologian.call.for.a.christian.caliphate/68523.htm.

to come to Jerusalem to meet God, and the gentiles had to follow the law of Moses. But now they had together become partakers of the promise in Christ (Eph 3:6). God's kingdom is where his Word and Spirit are at work bringing his saving reign, and this is not limited to Israel but now extends to all nations of the world and the whole of creation.

The church, therefore, is the sphere in which the kingdom of God is publicly established and the supremacy of Christ is openly evident. The church is where believers unite in the name of Jesus, guided by the Holy Spirit, to foster fellowship and dismantle all barriers that divide humanity, whether it be the caste system in South Asia, racism in the West, or any other human wall of separation. Our redeemed unity in Christ displays "the mystery of his will, according to his purpose, which he set forth in Christ as a plan for the fullness of time, to unite all things in him, things in heaven and things on earth." (Eph 1:9–10 ESV).

This way of being in the world marks Christians out from the world as kingdom people. Yet this impetus toward being marked out cannot confine the church's work within her own walls; it should purposefully encompass engagement with the world, attending to both the great commission as well as the great commandment of her King. The world, however, may be the sphere where the present reality of Christ's supremacy as king is most difficult for us to recognize.

Christ's Supremacy in the World
Christ's Kingdom: Enchanted Garden and Spirit Theology

Until the advent of modern education, South Asia (and much of the Global South) remained as what Max Weber called "the great enchanted garden."[8] To a great extent, it continues to be so. The enchanted garden is a porous cosmos with continuity between the natural and the supernatural, the immanent and the transcendent, the sacred and the secular. Physical and spiritual beings coexist on a continuum, where a suprarational sense transcends the limits of the empirical world. Among certain tribes in South Asia, the words "come tomorrow" often appear on the outer walls of houses.

---

8. Max Weber, *The Sociology of Religion* (1922; repr., Boston: Beacon, 1969), 270.

The words are written with the intention of politely warding off malevolent spirits that might visit. Of course, when the spirits return, the words that still remain on the walls will, at the very least, ensure that the spirits remain outside of their homes indefinitely.

The modern world's attempt to expel the transcendental and the supernatural calls to mind the cynical Lord Farquaad banishing all fairy-tale creatures from his kingdom of Duloc in the 2001 animated movie *Shrek*. He was not successful for long. The Western Enlightenment project presents its own secular version of the Christian story of growth and progress, into which the claims of Christ's ever-expanding rule does not comfortably fit. Even though the secularization theory that predicted the demise of religion has been proven false,[9] tendencies to undermine religious beliefs continue to characterize public discourse in Western societies. If left unchallenged, the secularist disenchanting of the world entails an expulsion of the Spirit, turning Christians into practical deists who subscribe to a belief system that retains nothing of its robust communion with God or its robust witness to the supremacy of Christ.[10]

Christians who are called to live as faithful citizens of the kingdom of God are not to leave their identity at the door when they enter "secular" spaces. Instead, Christians are called to reenchant the world because the Holy Spirit, whom the world cannot see, is with us and in us (John 14:17). A deistic notion of Christianity, which merely acknowledges God as a metaphysical reality rather than embraces the full import of the meaning of "Immanuel, God with us," is antithetical to a theology shaped by the present realities of incarnation and Pentecost. "The wind blows wherever it pleases. You hear its sound, but you cannot tell where it comes from or where it is going. So it is with everyone born of the Spirit" (John 3:8). Whether in ways obvious or hidden, the Spirit-empowered church bringing good news of the reigning King remains the most powerful instrument in the hands of God for the transformation of the world.

---

9. See, Peter L. Berger, "Secularization Falsified," in *First Things*, Feb 2008.

10. For further elaboration, see my "Third Article Theology and Apologetics," in *Holy Spirit and Christian Mission in a Pluralistic Context*, ed. Roji T. George (Bangalore: SAIACS, 2017), 202–22. See also my "Holy Spirit, Sanctification, and South Asia" in *Modern Reformation* 30, no. 5 (2021): 10–17.

FROM HEBER CARLOS DE CAMPOS JR.

There is no doubt that the good news of the reigning King is the power placed in our mouths to announce salvation to the whole world (Rom 1:16). This is not to say the obvious since many Christian versions of the social agenda have arisen in the West and have affected their view of the gospel. Whenever the gospel is reduced to a horizontal concern to feed the poor and fight against oppression (concerns that are not different from secular moral agendas), we have emptied it of its power to impact a country like Norway, a place where poverty and social dissatisfaction is not a major issue. On the other hand, if we understand the power of the gospel of the reigning King, there will be no context where it won't have its social impact. Paul's epistle to Philemon is a great example of how the gospel transcends the complexities of the social fabric. Paul did not condemn Philemon for having slaves, as many of us who live after slavery would hope to read. However, he teaches his disciple to receive Onesimus not as a slave but as "a beloved brother" (Philem 15–16 ESV). Paul is announcing to us that the gospel transforms social relations even when the social fabric is marred by less-than-ideal structures. That is why the gospel has its effect in all parts of the world, despite its contextual challenges.

In contrast to the Western world, the Global South continues to witness significant church growth. One of the reasons for this growth is the sense of continuity provided by Pentecostal and charismatic Christianity to animistic and tribal communities, which previously practiced ancestral spirit worship. Despite the stark contrast between the Christian understanding of the Holy Spirit and animistic spirit worship, Pentecostal Christianity nevertheless assumes something of an enchanted cosmos. Throughout most of human history, as noted by Weber, the world was perceived as a "the great enchanted garden," with the exception of ascetic Protestantism, which "completely eliminated magic and the supernatural quest for salvation, of which the highest form was intellectualist, contemplative illumination."[11]

While the reenchantment of secular space poses a challenge for Christian

---

11. See Weber, *The Sociology of Religion*, 269–70.

missions in the West, Christian mission efforts in the Global South often involve a reorientation of their earlier beliefs toward a focus on empowerment by the Holy Spirit alongside strong biblical teaching.

Christ's Kingdom and Social Transformation

The idea of the kingdom of God on earth is not unique to Christianity. In fact, several other religious and cultural traditions conceive of a perfect world somehow intertwined into their theological thinking. As a theologian in the Indian subcontinent, I immediately think of the popular Hindu legend of Ram-Rajya ("the kingdom of Rama"), which is infused with utopian visions of life under the reign of the god Rama, one of the avatars of Vishnu. His kingdom is imagined as "ideal in all respects, where all living beings have been endowed with auspicious qualities; where people would be completely satisfied and full of bliss; where there would be no trace of greed and lust in anyone; where no one would have to bear any kind of suffering of this material world."[12]

Another legend of Ram and Mahabali captures the many virtues of their rule on earth. Srimad Valmiki's Ramayana illustrates the ideals of Ram-Rajya, where "there were no widows to lament, nor was there fear of wild animals or diseases" (6.128.99); "the world was bereft of thieves and robbers" (6.128.100); "every creature lived happily and did not kill other creatures" (6.128.101); "people survived for thousands of years, with thousands of their progeny, all free of illness and grief" (6.128.102); "the trees bore flowers and fruits in season, without injury from pests and insects" (6.128.104).

An ideal world of this kind does sound familiar to a Christian. Yet there is something crucial missing: Ram's utopia always existed in some unspecified past. The search for Ram's kingdom is one that looks back to what things might have been because it does not possess a future hope for what will be. It is no wonder that religious and cultural nostalgia is the prominent disposition in the Hindu social psyche rather than hope for a real future grounded in reliable promises. Apart from the promise of New Jerusalem, we are left with only the longing for Eden.

---

12. See "Sri Rama-Rajyam (Kingship of Sri Rama)," Lord Rama, https://lordrama.co.in/rama -rajya.html.

The stark difference between Ram-Rajya and the (biblical) kingdom of God is not that South Asian religions have no imagination of, or longing for, an ideal world where God rules with fairness and justice and evil is banished. The difference is that, unlike Ram-Rajya, the coming of Christ's kingdom is one that is already established in Christ's finished work of atonement and the outpouring of his Spirit. This kingdom alters the present lived reality and points to a future fulfillment. This infuses Christians with a hope that reshapes their perspective on the world and propels their commitment to a "faithful presence" in the world.[13]

FROM HEBER CARLOS DE CAMPOS JR.

Ever since H. Richard Niebuhr argued that the relationship John Calvin articulated between Christ and culture was one of transformation, it became pervasive to say that we should transform society or redeem culture, to avoid both separation from society or embracing culture rather indistinctly. I would argue a different stance, where Christians should make every effort to redirect culture in a benevolent route that will freeze as much as possible the decaying effects of sin (common grace). But this does not mean that we *transform* or *redeem* the world around us—these two optimistic words do not represent the language of Scripture.

Redemption is always a divine act. The only time Scripture connects our actions with redemption is the Pauline expression that some translations have rendered "redeeming the time" (*exagorazomenoi ton kairon*; Eph 5:16; Col 4:5). Still, no one would argue for a control of the hours as if we could change time (most translations prefer the idea of make good use of time). This is because redemption is divine business, out of our league.

Redemption never recedes. You could perform social changes where moral values are preserved for a while, but these changes are never permanent, but always subject to be undone by later contamination. Redemption is always portrayed as progressively certain (Rom 8:28–30; Phil 1:6). In the history of

---

13. James Davison Hunter advocates "faithful presence" as a noncoercive form of Christian influence in the world. See *To Change the World: The Irony, Tragedy and Possibility of Christianity in the Late Modern World* (New York: Oxford University Press, 2010).

redemption, we are led in triumphal procession (2 Cor 2:14) and transformed from one degree of glory to another (3:18).

Considering these Scriptural reflections, I would argue for the language of reformation rather than redemption. Reformation is a continuous need since things in this fallen world are still prone to decay and chaos. When we argue that the way the businessperson uses the company's profit with good stewardship or the politician shapes laws and policies that convey public justice as "redemption," we present a secularized version of redemption that atheists could also perform; the gospel is thus reduced to the best humanist ideals in this world. True redemption, on the other hand, does have its impact in the public sphere. It exceeds good actions in the public square because it transforms people from the inside out, produces fruit that truly conveys gospel ideals, and eventually renews the living place where new creatures will dwell. Before culture is permanently transformed, we undertake the task of articulating a "faithful presence," as Varughese so helpfully articulates in this section. And the social impact is always significant because faithful witness doesn't always lead to redemption, but it always elicits a reaction. That is what it means to be salt of the earth and light of the world.

The faithful presence of conversionary protestant missionaries played a pivotal role in reshaping numerous cultures. Contrary to the prevailing notion that "social transformations traditionally associated with 'modernity' developed primarily as the result of secular rationality," Robert Woodberry persuasively contends that "Western modernity, in its current form, is profoundly shaped by religious factors."[14] Through a comparative analysis of social changes in neighboring societies, Woodberry highlights the impact of conversionary Protestants in regions that initiated and propagated numerous reforms. Beyond advocating for religious liberty, he asserts that the core areas of focus for conversionary Protestant endeavors encompassed "mass education, mass printing, new papers, voluntary organizations, most major colonial reforms, and the codification of legal protections."[15]

---

14. Robert D. Woodberry, "The Missionary Roots of Liberal Democracy," in *American Political Science Review* 106, no. 2. (May 2012): 244.

15. Woodberry, "The Missionary Roots of Liberal Democracy," 244–45.

Achieving a harmonious social life cannot be realized through mere wishes; it demands both conceptual imagination and practical tools. Among these essential tools are theological and cultural beliefs, especially the correlation between the idea of God's reign/kingdom within a culture and its sociopolitical constitution. Even if we avoid a strong causal relationship, a form of "reciprocal influence and conditioning"[16] can be drawn between religious and cultural imaginations of the kingdom of God and the earthly kingdoms or states that societies construct. That is, our social anthropology reflects our theology. As political derivatives of a Unitarian theology, monarchies tend to function as "extensions of God's kingdom," often as direct divine agents on earth—and expectedly autocratic and authoritarian. Likewise, a polytheistic imagination may entail a society without a unifying principle, often exhibited in the lack of epistemic and moral absolutes with societies functioning with shifting and opportunistic centers of power. This social role-play grounded in religiocultural imaginations of God's kingdom not only influence nations and societies but also human families and communities.

Similarly, it may be argued that sociocultural and religious beliefs exert substantial influence on the path of economic development. According to the Argentinean sociologist and historian Mariano Grondona, "The paradox of economic development is that economic values are not enough to ensure it. . . . The values accepted or neglected by a nation fall within the cultural field. We may thus say that economic development is a cultural process."[17] Building on this perspective, he suggests that cultures can be categorized as either "resiliently progress-prone" or "persistently progress-resistant."

Christ's Kingdom, Cultural Reimagination, and Bridge Building

A well-known *Upaniṣadic* prayer states: *"Asato mā sad gamaya; tamaso mā jyotir gamaya; mṛtyor mā amṛtam gamaya,"* which means, "lead me from delusion to truth; lead me from darkness to light; lead me from mortality to

---

16. Jürgen Moltmann, *The Trinity and the Kingdom: The Doctrine of God* (San Francisco: Harper & Row, 1981), 193.

17. Mariano Grondona, "A Cultural Typology of Economic Development," in *Culture Matters: How Values Shape Human Progress*, ed. Lawrence E. Harrison and Samuel P. Huntington (New York: Basic Books, 2000), 46.

eternal life."[18] It is hard not to contemplate whether this *sloka*[19] was specifically spoken in reference to Jesus Christ. Three passages from the gospel of John unmistakably associate truth (14:6), light (8:12), and eternal life (11:25) self-referentially in the person of Jesus Christ.

Forging connections between the depictions of truth in the *Upaniṣad* and the figure of Jesus serves not only to fulfill particular spiritual yearnings but also elevate what is considered desirable within the culture. In this regard, the cultural adoption of the gospel is a two-way process: it establishes links between Christ and the culture for identification while also subjecting the culture to Christ's influence for sanctification.[20]

Likewise, the South Asian legend of Mahābali—also known as Balirāja, the sacrificial king (*Bali* meaning "sacrifice"; *Raja* meaning "king") is a story of the Asura king that speaks of his benevolence and generosity. After being tricked into consuming the eternal nectar of *amritham*, he becomes immortal. Egged on by other envious gods, Vishnu decides to trick Mahābali and appears before him as Vāmana, a dwarf Brahmin. Vāmana asks for alms of three steps of land for himself, which Mahābali obliges. At this point, Vāmana morphs into a giant Trivikrama, and with the first step he covers the whole earth, and with the second the whole heaven and waits to be given the next. Mahābali offers his own head as the place where Vishnu can place his third step, leading to him being pushed into the netherworld of *Pātāla*.

Before he recedes to the underworld, he requests Vāmana to grant his wish to return to visit his people once a year. The noble sacrifice of Mahābali is celebrated each year as the Onam festival when he returns to his former kingdom. It is this story to which Jyotirao Govindrao Phule (1827–90), the great Indian social reformer, alludes the person of Christ. Drawn to the person of Christ who accepted the downtrodden and influenced by the holistic work of the missionaries, Phule identifies Jesus as the second Balirāja and speaks of the kingdom of God.[21] These and other legends in South Asia

---

18. *Bṛhadāraṇyaka Upaniṣad* 1.3.28. Author's translation.

19. A *Sloka* is a Sanskrit verse, usually in a couplet form.

20. For further discussion, see Aruthuckal Varughese John, "The Gospel and Truth Predicates in a Hindu Context," in *One Gospel, Many Cultures: Doing Theology in Context*, ed. Arren Bennet Lawrence (Minneapolis: Fortress, 2022), 161–88.

21. See Rosalind O'Hanlon, *Caste, Conflict and Ideology: Mahatma Jotirao Phule and Low Caste*

serve as bridges for cultural reimagining of an ideal to appropriate the kingdom of God.

Christ's Kingdom Establishes the Meaning and Goal of History

According to Karl Löwith, the early Greeks, in the absence of special revelation, derived their conception of time from observable repetitive phenomena "like the eternal recurrence of sunrise and sunset, of summer and winter, of generation and corruption."[22] This is very much like the polytheistic Hindu conception and very much unlike the Judeo-Christian, in which history is moving toward a specific eschatological *telos* (an end or goal). It therefore reflects what he calls "the formal structure of the meaning of history." Löwith's point is not that the Greeks failed to attach significant meaning to historical events but that "they were not meaningful in the sense of being directed toward an ultimate end in a transcendent purpose that comprehends the whole course of events"—especially the events of salvation.[23] Christ reigns supreme over all things in part because he alone is able to give them ultimate meaning: "For by him all things were created, in heaven and on earth, visible and invisible, whether thrones or dominions or rulers or authorities—all things were created through him and for him. And he is before all things, and in him all things hold together" (Col 1:16–17 ESV).

In the present reality of the supremacy of Christ—his incarnation, life, death, resurrection, and rule—that Christian hope becomes more than wishful thinking. It is a hope where the future is visible in the present, even if only in part. At his ascension, Jesus promised that he will return to seal his authority and reign on earth as king when he, along with his forces, battles the evil kingdoms of the world at the end of the age. While Christian believers still await that great battle, we ought not lose sight of the reality that his authority is already established, especially as we look around at the problems we face in this world.

Protest in Nineteenth-Century Western India, Cambridge South Asian Studies (Cambridge: Cambridge University Press 2002).

22. Karl Löwith, *Meaning in History: The Theological Implications of the Philosophy of History* (Chicago: University of Chicago Press, 1946), 4.

23. Löwith, *Meaning in History*, 6.

FROM SOFANIT T. ABEBE

In Ethiopia, the hope of future judgement against powerful persecutors imparts present hope through the possibility for vindication and the restoration of honor to the persecuted. This hope is further conceptualized through the notion of *tur*, which describes the idea that, in addition to the final judgement at the eschaton, God metes out judgement in the form of misfortunes that people invite into their lives whenever they wrong those who do not have the power to redress it. Though it might not be immediate, the ubiquitous belief in *tur* among vast groups across the country indicates how powerfully immediate its usefulness is to people who suffer under social injustice or extreme suffering. Knowing that ill fate awaits those deemed as oppressors empowers sufferers to negotiate everyday life in the face of injustice without falling into hopelessness, succumbing to retaliation, or living under the illusion that evil will be completely eradicated in this life. While this is one way of addressing arbitrary evil and suffering, it is important to not lose sight of the Bible's clarity on what our attitude toward others should be. Our abhorrence should never be directed at fellow human beings; our attitude toward hostile others should be directed at the underlying evil and demonic systems of oppression at work behind the scenes. Our critique should be systematic enough to encompass all worldly systems—like the materialism and economic persecution that stand in sharp opposition to the Christocentric reign of God. Therefore, to be a Christian is to participate in the collision between God's rule and that of all worldly systems through love and bearing witness to God's redemptive plans in Christ.

There are multiple stories in the history of war about how news of the enemy's defeat or surrender in major arenas of the conflict inspired soldiers to persevere in their own smaller battles on the periphery. Even though in certain regions of Christ's kingdom battles may seem like a lost cause, Christians possess essential intel: the war is already won. This positive message continues to inspire Christians to stay on the front lines, even if it entails sacrificing their lives for the King who sacrificed his life for them.

CHAPTER 8

MISSION ACCOMPLISHED, THOUGH KING FOREVER

HEBER CARLOS DE CAMPOS JR.

There is a long, ongoing debate regarding the duration of Christ's three-fold office. Since the office of mediator has been regarded by some as a single position held by Christ with three distinct functions,[1] one could ask rather broadly: Does the office of mediator continue in the eternal state, or does it cease? Would we still need a prophet in eternity since the eschatological reality prophesied has come? Would we still need a priest if there is no sin barrier? Would we need a king if the enemies have been overcome? On the other hand, could we say that Christ would let go of any glorious function once history reaches its grand finale? Do we not step out of orthodoxy by saying that Christ would not be king anymore in any sense of the term?

---

1. Donald Macleod, "The Work of Christ," in *Reformation Theology: A Systematic Summary*, ed. Matthew Barrett (Wheaton, IL: Crossway, 2017), 348. Zacharias Ursinus mentions the prophetical, sacerdotal, and regal as the three "parts of the office of the mediator." Zacharias Ursinus, *Commentary on the Heidelberg Catechism* (Phillipsburg, NJ: P&R, n.d.), 170. However, it is not uncommon to see early writers on this topic refer to the three offices of Christ, since distinct Old Testament men occupied these duties without accumulating even two of them. Cf. Westminster Shorter Catechism, 23; William Ames will say on one aphorism that "the office . . . is threefold" and in the next aphorism will talk about the "number and order of offices" in Christ. William Ames, *The Marrow of Theology*, trans. John Dykstra Eusden (Grand Rapids: Baker, 1997), 1.19.10–11, 132. Hence, the tradition does not rule out the language of "the three offices of Christ," and it could be used as synonymous to "the threefold office of the mediator."

These questions are not merely theoretical because Scripture brings information that could sustain either position. Some passages speak of a priesthood after the order of Melchizedek that is eternal (Ps 110:4; Heb 7:24). Even though the Levitical priesthood was called perpetual (Exod 40:12–15), the epistle to the Hebrews informs us that it did have an end. As for royalty, several passages point to a kingdom without end (2 Sam 7:13, 16; Pss 45:6; 89:35–37; Dan 2:44; 7:14; Luke 1.33; Rev 11:15), but other passages present a sense of conclusion to the kingdom (1 Cor 15:24–28; Heb 2:5–8). Even if the biblical witness seems to favor the idea of a perennial office, how does one interpret the concept of Christ "[delivering] the kingdom" at the end (1 Cor 15:24 ESV; cf. Dan 7:18, 27a)?

This issue of Christ's kingship and its eschatological goal is not merely an academic exercise with no applications to the life of the church.[2] In my Brazilian context, the topic is helpful to address cultural and ecclesiastical issues that touch upon the threefold relationship in creation: with God, with neighbor, and with nature.

First, in regard to God, Christ's regal office was not self-appointed but appointed by God (Heb 5:4–5, quoting Ps 2:6–7; Phil 2:9–11),[3] as the very nature of the office requires (i.e., to have authority delegated by a superior, to speak in the name of a superior authority). Thus, the common praise to "crown him with many crowns" may positively mean honor (recognition), but negatively, it loses the element of authority transferal that is involved in crowning. When democracy is considered the unquestionable social structure as it is in Brazil, it becomes hard to understand how we should behave in a spiritual monarchy, when Christ is appointed the ruler by God, not the people. Christ is not even "made king in our hearts," as expressed by some songs back home, for our surrender does not transfer authority but only submits to it. In practice, we extol the king, but we never crown him.

---

2. Application of the threefold office is prevalent within the Reformed tradition. For specific application of Christ's kingly office, see the Heidelberg Catechism, 31; Westminster Shorter Catechism, 26; Westminster Larger Catechism, 43–45.

3. This historical appointment to the office of king should not be confused with Eternal Functional Subordination of the Son. There is no discussion going on here about ontological issues, neither are we specifically addressing eternal relationships in the economic trinity, but merely the historical fulfillment of the exaltation of Christ often referred to in coronation language.

FROM SOFANIT T. ABEBE

The Ethiopian Orthodox Church affirms the teaching of Christ's threefold office. A treatise titled *Mazgaba Haymanot* ("Treasure of the Faith") articulates the Church's doctrine on christological themes: "[Christ] being priest and prophet, and king as well, he baptized Adam and his progeny with his blood; he saved him, he set him free; he drew him close to himself; and he offered him to his father as peace offering."[a] In this affirmation of Christ's reconciliatory work that has reinstated sinners to the glory of being at peace with God, the *Treasure of the Faith* acknowledges the important idea of Christ's identity as the kingly priest who with authority and power defeated the power of evil and death, setting sinners free. In the affirmation that Christ draws redeemed humanity to himself, the biblical idea of union with Christ might be seen to be at play here. At any rate, it is as the prophetic and priestly king that Christ accomplishes his task of setting humanity free. Christ is king forever. Similar to the Brazilian context, it bears remembering that our songs and heart should dance to the rhythm of surrender, harmonizing with the majestic authority of Christ the king. We do not crown him with many crowns; we do not "enthrone him as king" or confer authority to him, as some of our Ethiopian songs might imply.

---

[a] *Mazgaba Haymanot*, 17.

Second, regarding relationships with neighbors, an increasing desire to establish social power on top of previous appeals for equality is growing in Brazilian culture, and these social issues need to be looked at with Christ's mediatorial rule in mind. Conservative Christians in general do not side with agendas of power for political reasons: because of the oppressive suffocation of any contrary opinion, a social harm recognized even by non-Christians. But they have not realized that Christians have a deeper gospel reason, based on Christ's kingship, to be countercultural: gospel social ethics go even deeper in submission to one another. In the kingdom they are made servants (Matt 20:25–28) who not only consider their brothers and sisters superior to themselves (Phil 2:3–4) but even let go of their freedoms to live as servants of God to others in the public square (1 Pet 2:16). Until the true King returns, they should honor the earthly king (2:17). Their only oppressive attitude should be against their sinful selves, and they should face evildoers as sojourners and exiles (2:11–12), unattached to the social liberties they may lose in this foreign land.

FROM ELIZABETH W. MBURU

Siding with agendas of power is common in many African nations, particularly because ethnicity often tends to overshadow Christian identity. This extends to politics. Many heads of state as well as other political leaders are often elected on the basis of ethnic affiliation rather than ideology. There is the view that if the leader is from one's ethnic group, then he will bring prosperity to that group. And in most cases, this tends to be true. Those that end up amalgamating power and wealth in a particular government are often those that come from the ethnic group represented by the head of state. Negative ethnicity escalates during electioneering periods, and this extends even to the church.

Third, as the secular call to save the environment has been proclaimed louder and louder over the years, Western culture has voiced that humanity ruins a perfect natural world wherever it touches, but ironically burdens the same humanity to become earthly redeemers. Christians who appreciate the cultural mandate and want to be good stewards of natural resources tend to forget that we do not live under the creational atmosphere of Genesis 2. Fallen reality experiences the rebellious nature of creation (Gen 3:17–19) in opposition to our attempt at productivity, eager for freedom from its bondage (Rom 8:20–22). That mission to liberate creation from corruption is not ours. That is why the writer of Hebrews applies Psalm 8 not to humanity in general but to Christ as he endeavors to reestablish human dominion over all things (Heb 2:5–8). And that is part of the official mission with which he was entrusted. When we understand that an officer is in the position of being accountable to the one who entrusted him with a mission (1 Cor 15:24), we shape our expectation about our relationship with creation.

FROM SOFANIT T. ABEBE

The Ethiopian Orthodox Church's Forest Protection Initiative has received the *2023 ACT Alliance Climate Resilience Award.* The phenomenon of clearing land for agriculture has resulted in the eradication of much of the country's forests in highland Ethiopia. What remains is mostly what are known as "church forests." There are concentric circles of purity to keep ritual impurity away—an aspect of Jewish religiosity that may predate the arrival of Christianity to Ethiopia in the fourth century. Out of a desire to maintain a rigorous system of purity and pollution in the church site and surrounding areas, Orthodox churches preserve forests in their efforts to maintain the church as a conduit of God's physical appearance. Perhaps the Orthodox Church's forest conservation emanates from the role creation plays in the book of Enoch. Jewish apocalyptic authors decried injustice and the pollution of the earth with evil and impurity even as they expressed hope of an end to this world and for life beyond this world. However, in this they did not imply that a faithful response would be indifference to the welfare of this world in the here and now. If they hoped for the destruction of the world, it was because this seemed to be the only way to bring an end to evil. In Revelation, the expectation of cosmic destruction by no means made the conduct of the Roman empire acceptable or tolerable in the present. On the contrary, John's visions of destruction are a cry of protest and a subversive response in allegiance to Christ. Thus, the end-times vision of Revelation should not be understood as a quietist acceptance of the status quo of the environment or any socio-political system. Rather, what the New Testament calls us for is to subversively labor to end social and environmental injustice that continues to propagate inhabitable spaces for human beings in Africa, South Asia, and Latin America. This labor is a faithful response to Christ the King through whose victory and in whose Spirit we decry violence and oppression wherever it rears its head.

Now that the debate has been introduced and possible applications have been raised, this essay will develop the thesis asserting why the consummation is not less glorious to Christ as the officer, but more so. To explain why his duty ends, it will first explore three aspects of the nature of the threefold office as applied to the king: its human nature, its redemptive purpose, and its historical apex. Then it will draw important lessons from the two passages that imply a finished task: Hebrews 2 and 1 Corinthians 15. Lastly, it will propose how this eschatological perspective may impact church life and the hope of things to come.

CHRIST'S ROYAL OFFICE: DOES IT END?

This debate splits the opinion among the Reformed. Since our focus is on the royal office, we will restrain the arguments used to prove greater continuity or discontinuity between Christ's kingship now and after his second coming. Herman Bavinck comments that John Calvin, David Pareus, and Johann Heinrich Alting said that Christ's kingship was "economic and temporary," while Petrus van Mastricht, Bernardinus De Moor, and Campegius Vitringa admitted there would be change in the manner of governing but believed in the perpetuity of Christ's kingship.[4] Other Reformed scholastics who favored the end of the mediatorial kingdom are Wilhelmus à Brakel and John Gill,[5] while the majority sustained the eternity of Christ's mediating rule (Johannes Wollebius, Thomas Ridgley, Johann Heinrich Heidegger, Francis Turretin),[6] especially in opposition to the Socinian claim to a kingdom that ends. In the nineteenth and twentieth centuries, Reformed dogmaticians such as John Dick and Charles Hodge believe the mediatorial government of the universe lasts until its objective is accomplished,[7] while Robert Lewis Dabney and Herman Hoeksema contend for an eternal mediatorial dominion.[8]

---

4. Bavinck, *RD* III.482n165–66.

5. Wilhelmus à Brakel, *The Christian's Reasonable Service*, ed. Joel R. Beeke, trans. Bartel Elshout, vol. 1 (Grand Rapids: Reformation Heritage, 1995), 564; John Gill, *A Body of Doctrinal and Practical Divinity* (Paris, AR: Baptist Standard Bearer, 1989), 448.

6. Johannes Wollebius, *The Abridgment of Christian Divinitie*, trans. Alexander Ross (London: Printed by T. Mabb for Joseph Nevill, 1660), 165; Thomas Ridgley, *A Body of Divinity: Wherein the Doctrines of the Christian Religion Are Explained and Defended* (New York: Carter, 1855), 575; Johann Heinrich Heidegger *apud* Heppe, *Reformed Dogmatics*, 484; Francis Turretin, *Institutes of Elenctic Theology* vol. 2, trans. George Musgrave Ginger (Philipsburg, NJ: P&R, 1997), XIV.xvii (p. 490–494).

7. John Dick, *Lectures on Theology*, vol. 3 (Edinburgh: Oliphint, 1834), 241–44; Charles Hodge, *Systematic Theology*, vol. 2 (New York: Scribner, 1872), 601.

8. Robert Lewis Dabney, *Systematic Theology* (repr., Edinburgh: Banner of Truth, 1985), 551–53; Herman Hoeksema, *Reformed Dogmatics* (Grand Rapids: Reformed Free, 1976), 365, 397.

Coming from the Reformed tradition myself, it is quite a challenge to face a question that is as unresolved as this one. However, it does not mean that it is useless to push the theological conversation forward. The arguments on both sides will be surveyed and analyzed in an attempt to find clues for a clearer statement about the future of the kingly office. Theological tradition does not always establish the matter unmistakably, but it still functions as a lens through which one looks at Scripture, the single authoritative source of theology. And since it is the purpose of this book to advance the conversation in different contextual settings, this essay will draw from previous insights and attempt to reshape some categories of this ancient faith in new contexts.

The thesis of this chapter is that the threefold relationship established in creation and broken in the fall (with God, neighbor, and nature—the so called "threefold mandate") is regained by the last Adam, and the kingly aspect of this mission (victory over enemies, rescue of prisoners, setting up the ethics of the kingdom, restoring the dominion over God's creation) has a consummation. When Christ frees humankind from demons to become servants of God, when he restores the order of relationships within humanity and over creation, he establishes an order in his first coming that advances toward a final fulfillment. This is not to say that at the eschaton mediation is over altogether, but it does mean that it enters a new stage where Scripture says more of its eternal glory than of its perennial functions.

The thesis above assumes a possible distinction between Christ's royal office and his broader mediation, which appears in Calvin but is not always distinguished by scholars. In his polemical response to Francesco Stancaro's denial of Christ's mediatorship according to his divine nature, Calvin asserts a mediation from eternity (creational) that is distinct from his mediation of reconciliation (after the fall). The first category unites creatures (including angels) to God so that they remain uncorrupted, and it occurred before his incarnation. The second is only possible if he is also divine (because of all that redemption accomplishes), and it "links the present state with the future," a possible reference to 1 Corinthians 15, which he mentions at the end of the paragraph.[9] But in making this distinction, Calvin never flattens the

---

9. Cf. Joseph Tylenda, "Christ the Mediator: Calvin Versus Stancaro," *Calvin Theological Journal* 7 (1972): 11–16.

difference between being the covenant head of the church from eternity and becoming king in history.[10] In fact, Calvin only mentions Christ's kingship once in passing because he is not discussing Christ's historical role of reconciliation in his response to Stancaro. On the other hand, it is the royal office as it is played out in history that is the focus of this chapter's thesis.

THE NATURE OF THE OFFICE APPLIED TO THE ROYAL DUTIES

This section will enlighten the concept of office and, thus, provide a few insights as to Christ's kingly office and the consummation. Three aspects of the office will be explored: its human nature, its redemptive purpose, and its historical apex. As the nature of the office is investigated, a foundation will be laid out to respond to the question of whether he is forever king or if his kingly office ends.

First, *the mediatorial kingly office is proper to the incarnation.* That is, Christ is only an officer king when he is already incarnate. This assumes a distinction between his eternal divine dominion (historically called his essential, universal, or natural rule, where he rules the universe from eternity

---

10. Contra Stephen Edmondson, *Calvin's Christology* (Cambridge: Cambridge University Press), 143–47. Edmondson talks about these two as "layers of complexity" to Christ's mediatorship (p. 143) and assumes "his office as king or head" as being executed "from the beginning." Only the role of priest was added after the fall (p. 144). So, not only does he flatten the distinction between eternal mediation and "Christ's royal redemptive office" (p. 146), but he splits the threefold office by making the kingship eternal and the priesthood historical. On top of that, Edmondson never deals with Calvin's comments on 1 Corinthians 15:24–28 both in the commentary and in the *Institutes.* Richard Muller is more careful in his read of Calvin as he asserts an epistemological rather than an ontological change in the future, for though our epistemological incapacities are healed when sin is overcome, our ontological incapacity remains the same (finite man needs mediation to approach infinite God). Richard Muller, "Christ in the Eschaton: Calvin and Moltmann on the Duration of the *Munus Regium,*" *Harvard Theological Review* 74, no. 1 (1981): 37, 40–42. Muller refers to a passage of the *Institutes* (2.12.1) where Calvin briefly states "a necessary antelapsarian mediation," that is, a need for a Mediator even if humanity had not fallen into sin. This brief comment in the *Institutes* is coherent with his distinction in his writing against Stancaro's views. Edwin Chr. van Driel also distinguishes between the cosmic mediatorship fulfilled by the Word independent of his incarnation and the eschatological role of his kingship, which ends as the ascent to God has been reached, and thus, for Calvin, Christ's human nature plays no mediatorial role. Edwin Chr. van Driel, "'Too Lowly to Reach God without a Mediator': John Calvin's Supralapsarian Eschatological Narrative," *Modern Theology* 33, no. 2 (April 2017): 275–77, 284–86.

according to his divinity)[11] and his temporal mediatory domain. Scripture speaks of a beginning of the latter one (Ps 2:6–7) as he is invested unto this exalted position in his resurrection (Rom. 1:4).[12] This is how his office is to be under the authority delegated to him (e.g., judicial officer), his anointing being the public ceremony conferring him authority.[13] Christ already incarnate functions as an officer because he is called and established by the Father to execute certain functions (Ps 45:6–7; Isa 42:1; 61:1; Luke 4:16–24; John 3:17; Heb 1:8–9). Louis Berkhof notes how Hebrews 5, especially verse 1, teaches us that the priest is "chosen from among men," for he acts "on behalf of men in relation to God."[14] Deuteronomy 17 says that the king in Israel should be chosen "from among your brothers" (v. 15 ESV). In both passages there is an issue of identification between the officer and those to whom he ministers. This does not mean that Christ is a mediator only according to his humanity, as if to disjoint his divinity,[15] but it emphasizes that the role of an officer is typical of humanity (1 Tim 2:5).

The implication of the first statement is that *the office is temporal.* It has a beginning in time, as the Son enters human existence in history. This counters Herman Bavinck's claim that "under the Old Testament [dispensation], he was active as prophet, priest, and king."[16] If he means to argue

---

11. Richard Muller, *Dictionary of Latin and Greek Theological Terms, Drawn Principally from Protestant Scholastic Theology* (Grand Rapids: Baker, 1985), s.v. "regnum Christi," p. 260. The apostle John testifies that when Isaiah saw the Lord seated on the throne (Isa 6:1), the prophet had seen Christ (John 12:41). Thus, the Son of God was king before King Uzziah had died and continued his domain after the death of the human king, because his dominion has no end.

12. Romans 1:4 is not teaching some kind of adoptionism but speaks of an investiture to an exalted position. Because of the suffering on the cross (Heb. 2:9) and the triumph over evil, the rightful king is exalted in his resurrection and his kingdom is inaugurated on earth. There is no need to place the cross as the beginning of his reign in correction to the view that Christ became king is his resurrection, as Jeremy Treat does. Both the cross and his resurrection are victories of the king. Cf. Jeremy Treat, *The Crucified King: Atonement and Kingdom in Biblical and Systematic Theology* (Grand Rapids: Zondervan, 2014), 152.

13. The anointed becomes obliged to act the same way the authority over him would act. The king should be a servant, not an oppressor of the people (Deut 17:16–17), for he is not above the law (17:18–20), but he submits and represents the Legislator.

14. Louis Berkhof, *Systematic Theology: New Combined Edition* (Grand Rapids: Eerdmans, 1996), 361.

15. Turretin argues for a mediatorship according to both natures, a standard protestant position. Turretin, *Institutes of Elenctic Theology*, 14.2 (2:379–84); cf. Johann Gerhard, *Theological Commonplaces: On the Person and Office of Christ*, trans. Richard J. Dinda, ed. Benjamin T. G. Mayes (St. Louis: Concordia, 2009), 321–25.

16. Bavinck, *RD*, 3:365. Herman Witsius, Wilhemus à Brakel, and Louis Berkhof make the same claim. Cf. Herman Witsius, *The Economy of the Covenants between God and Man: Comprehending*

for the economic operation of the second person of the Trinity through Old Testament saints, it would still be the operation of God, not the operation of a subordinate office. Even if one were to use passages such as 1 Peter 1:19–20 to contend for an office of mediator in eternity,[17] one would need to be aware that it could be confusing the decree to atone with its historical execution, just like the seventeenth-century antinomians did with the doctrine of justification.[18] There is no doubt that the elect are covenantally united to Christ in eternity for salvation (Eph 1:4). However, this covenantal union should not be confused with the union with Christ through faith (3:17). In similar fashion, we should not mistake the operations of the Godhead in the Old Testament with the incarnate mediatorship of the Son.

Second, *Christ's office has a redemptive purpose.* There are many things that Christ as king does for his people as he frees them from the world to himself, governs them through officers and laws, bestows blessings upon the obedient and corrects them for their sins, protects and sustains them under temptations and sufferings, overcomes all their enemies, and orders all things for their good.[19] These are redemptive measures of the king, a typical emphasis of the Reformed tradition. William Ames introduces his chapter on the office of Christ with these words: "The office is that which he undertook in order to obtain salvation for men."[20] Francis Turretin states that the office of mediator "embraces all that Christ ought to do from his mission and calling towards an offended God and offending men, reconciling and again uniting them to each other."[21]

Since the office has a redemptive purpose, the implication is to see the kingly office as having a *mission of reconquest.* The task of the king is to take back what was usurped by the enemy. When Scripture says that the casting out of demons is proof that the kingdom has arrived (Matt 12:28), that Satan has fallen (Luke 10:18), and that such victory over evil happens through the

---

a Complete Body of Divinity, vol. 1 (repr., Phillipsburg, NJ: P&R, 1990), 2.3.2, 178–79; Brakel, *The Christian's Reasonable Service*, 1:564; Berkhof, *Systematic Theology*, 409–10.

17. Herman Hoeksema claims that "Christ is anointed from before the foundation of the world." Hoeksema, *Reformed Dogmatics*, 365.

18. Cf. Westminster Confession of Faith, 11.4.

19. Westminster Larger Catechism, 45. He also judges those who are not his people.

20. Ames, *The Marrow of Theology*, 1.19.1, 131.

21. Turretin, *Institutes of Elenctic Theology* vol. 2, XIV.v.1, 391.

work of the cross (John 12:31–33; Col 2:15; Heb 2:14; Rev 12:10–11), it is portraying the atonement with the language of conquest (the *Christus Victor* motif).[22] David, the warrior king who after his anointing defeats Israel's enemies before his ascension to the throne and who after the coronation advances the limits of the kingdom, functions as a type of Christ. For the son of David is also a warrior king who between his anointing (Luke 3:21–22; 4:18–21) and his ascension (Acts 2:33–35) constantly defeats spiritual forces to free captives and who after his ascension advances the limits of his kingdom through the work of the Spirit. However, this conquering theme has not been completed. Just like the reigning David still had to deal with a usurper (Absalom), the ascended Christ still has to crush those who want to ruin his kingdom.

Third, *the kingly office has an accomplishable mission.* The monarchical position occupied by the God incarnate has a historical development that goes from lesser glory to greater glory, from inauguration to consummation. If the anger of the judging King was somewhat shocking in the temple (John 2:13–17), much more horrendous will be his anger in his coming (Rev 6:15–17). If the king was first acclaimed by the Jerusalem inhabitants (Matt 21:1–9), much more recognized will he be when every knee shall bow and every tongue confess that he is Lord (Phil 2:9–11). This progression is partially explained with a view of mission that has an end to it. To affirm that the mission of the church is the Great Commission (to make disciples) and that it should not be confused with the greatest commandment (loving God above all) is helpful to get a sense of accomplishment, of a finished task. It does not mean that once the task is finished the church ceases to be church or goes into a mode of inertia, but we may deduce that it enters a different season of activity. Christ's kingly office may also have a sense of completion without Christ ceasing to act as a mediator.

The implication of an accomplishable mission is to affirm more clearly *the "already" and "not yet" state of the kingly office.* The tension between "already" and "not yet" is even applied to the New Testament allusions to Psalm 110:1. While Peter places angels and powers already subjected to him

---

22. Cf. Michael S. Horton, *Lord and Servant: A Covenant Christology* (Louisville: Westminster John Knox, 2005), 243–254.

(1 Pet 3:22), the author of Hebrews says Christ awaits such subjugation (Heb 10:12–13). While the Psalm places the overcoming of enemies as a promise from the Lord to the Messiah, Paul switches the order and makes the triumph to be a gift from Son to the Father (1 Cor 15:24–28). The consequence of the already aspect of the triumph is that Christians are protected from the evil one (1 John 5:18), but the not-yet aspect of the triumph reminds that he is still dangerous (1 Pet 5:8), and there is need to put on the armor of God (Eph 6:10–20). Needing protection from the devil is momentary. Once the problem of evil is solved (Rev 20:11–15), there will be no need for it.

Thus, the nature of the office conduces to an understanding of a human position of authority delegated by God that starts in time, of a redemptive purpose to regain what was usurped, and to accomplish such a mission to enter a new state of domain.

FROM ARUTHUCKAL VARUGHESE JOHN

The attribution of divine status was a widespread practice in various kingdoms, where kings were often regarded as deities, manifestations of gods, or, at the very least, semidivine. This stood in stark contrast to the guidance given to Israel in the Decalogue, which instructed them to abstain from worship of other gods. The command emphasized having no other gods besides Yahweh and prohibiting the creation of any carved images or representations of things in the heavens, on the earth, or in the waters below (Exod 20:3–5). In contrast to the customs of other kingdoms, the kings of Israel, along with the prophets and other leaders, derived their authority from God. As such, they were considered mere stewards of both God's people and the land. This understanding constantly critiqued human tendencies toward "monarchical absolutism," which consequently fostered a system that incorporated checks and balances to counteract any inclination toward absolute power within monarchies.

This historical backdrop of monarchies is crucial for grasping the context of the book of Revelation, especially as Caesar worship reached its peak throughout the Roman Empire. William Barclay illuminates this by noting that every individual in the Empire was obligated to appear before the authorities annually, offering a symbolic act of burning "a pinch of incense to the godhead of Caesar" and proclaiming, "Caesar is lord." Failure to conform to this ritual could result in persecution and even death.[a]

The central theme of the book of Revelation revolves around Christ's eternal kingship and the triumph of Jesus. The text unveils Christ's absolute authority, demonstrating his power over adversaries as the conquering king who vanquishes sin and death (5:5; 17:14). The Westminster Catechism succinctly states that the primary purpose of humanity is "to glorify God and to enjoy him forever," presenting a profound vision of God's glorification through the worship of Jesus. Revelation vividly portrays a triumphant Christ reigning supreme in the New Jerusalem. Early Christian writings emphasize the worship of Jesus, redirecting believers from veneration of other beings previously considered worthy of worship.

Consistent with prophetic declarations emphasizing exclusive worship of Yahweh, early Christian writings underscore the exclusive divinity ascribed to Jesus, reinforcing the monotheistic commitment of Jewish followers of Christ. This commitment kept them vigilant against the risk of worship being diverted toward a created object or being. The book of Revelation in particular portrays Jesus as the ultimate Judge, King, and Lord (1:5). His eternal reign is highlighted in 11:15, signifying the transformation of worldly kingdoms into the everlasting kingdom of our Lord and Messiah.

In 5:8–12, John explicitly portrays worship as directed toward Christ. The significance of Christ's sacrificial death is reiterated through the continued reference to the "slain lamb," acknowledged as deserving of worship. God establishes the cornerstone of his kingdom with the foundational work accomplished through Christ's atoning death. The hymn in 5:12, proclaiming loudly, "Worthy is the Lamb who was slain, to receive power and wealth and wisdom and might and honor and glory and blessing!" (NRSVue), epitomizes the majesty and grandeur of Christ.

Throughout the text, Jesus is identified as "the faithful witness, the firstborn from the dead, and the ruler of the kings of the earth" (1:5). His complete authority and power is expressed as John declares him to be "Lord of lords and King of kings" (17:14). The comprehensive power and righteous wrath of Jesus are vividly described in his roles as the judge and the king (19:11–16). As "the Alpha and the

Omega, the First and the Last," Jesus stands as the ultimate arbiter, judging each person according to their deeds (22:12–13).

ᵃ William Barclay, *The Revelation of John: The Daily Study Bible*, rev. ed., vol. 1 (Edinburgh: St Andrews Press, 1990), 15.

WHAT IS THE FINISHED TASK?

Two important New Testament passages that clearly speak of a future finished task of subjugation are Hebrews 2:5–8 and 1 Corinthians 15:24–28. The first passage says that the world was not subjected to angels, and then it quotes a section of Psalm 8. One may conclude that this is the writer's way of saying that the world was subjected to humankind. However, as the author of Hebrews interprets the Psalm at the end of verse 8, there is no application to us, only to Christ. Regarding Christ, Hebrews says that God "left nothing outside his control" (ESV). However, this is not a reference to his eternal divine dominion, or else other psalms would be much more appropriate to refer to rather than Psalm 8 (cf. Pss 24; 93; 99). Hence, this is the mediatorial kingship in which Christ becomes like us (Heb 2:14, 17) to help the ones he represents, not only as a priest (Heb 2:17–18) but as a mighty warrior king who frees the offspring of Abraham from slavery (Heb 2:15–16). This kingly mission already had an inaugural victory ("through death he might destroy the one who has the power of death, that is, the devil," v. 14 ESV), though there are things yet to accomplish ("At present, we do not yet see everything in subjection to him," v. 8 ESV).

The correlation between humanity in its original state and Christ the King is not hard to find. Christ is the king whose domain comes to redeem our failed vice-regency established by God in creation. The son of David came with the task of restoring human vice-regency over all the earth.[23] The subduing of the natural world has already been mentioned in this chapter.

---

23. Treat, *The Crucified King*, 150. Michael S. Horton asserts that "the messianic king is greater even than David not simply because he is divine, but also because he fulfills the human commission that Adam, Israel, and even David fell short of achieving." Michael S. Horton, *The Christian Faith: A Systematic Theology for Pilgrims on the Way* (Grand Rapids: Zondervan, 2011), 525.

The earth that was damned and filled with thorns and thistles, thus placed in enmity against us (Gen 3:17–19), will now became the New Earth, filled with righteousness (2 Pet 3:13). However, there is more about this subjection attained by Christ in our stead. Because humanity has been subdued by evil angels since the fall, it is possible to correlate Christ's exorcisms as a step toward establishing his people as the kingly judges of angels (1 Cor 6:3).[24] So the triumph over powers and principalities through the atonement (John 12:31–33; Col 2:13–15; cf. Matt 12:29; 1 John 3:8) also operates to reestablish the honored position of the redeemed to judge. His kingly office, therefore, has a specific mission to accomplish as the God-man restores humanity to its rightful domain.

FROM ARUTHUCKAL VARUGHESE JOHN

The book of Revelation not only presents a vivid portrayal of Christ's kingship but also emphasizes exclusive worship of Christ, accompanied by a clear prohibition on the worship of angels. This prohibition holds particular significance in a culture where the distinction between the creator and creation is often blurred, as in South Asia. Even though angels are created, their dual nature as both created and heavenly beings can cause confusion. This confusion is evident in the stern warning against worshiping angels, as articulated in the words of an angel in the Apocalypse of John (Rev 19:10 ESV): "Then I fell down at his feet to worship him, but he said to me, 'You must not do that! I am a fellow servant with you and your brothers who hold the testimony of Jesus. Worship God!'" For the South Asian context, where worship of cosmic forces is common, this passage suggests that we should not only refrain from worshiping idols crafted from earthly materials or human figures, even those of kings and emperors, but also from worshiping celestial beings such as angels.

In the human mind, especially in my culture that envisions the universe as an embedded cosmos, where individuals are nested within the community and

---

24. Anthony Hoekema says redemption is the positive aspect of the kingdom and judgment of the rebels is its negative aspect. Anthony Hoekema, *The Bible and the Future* (Grand Rapids: Eerdmans, 1979), 45–46.

the community within a cosmos encompassing gods and the spirits, there is a potential to elevate angels to a higher plane. This tendency arises from perceiving the universe as arranged in layers with angels occupying a higher deck within the worldview. Conversely, this same inclination may relegate Jesus to a lower status due to his humanity. The apostle John corrects this perspective by rightfully placing Jesus in an exalted position and also dismantles the stratified view of the cosmos in the process.

Even though "the glory of all angels to some extent resembles the glory of their Maker,"[a] the angel explicitly prohibits being worshiped and identifies himself with the worshiper as a "fellow servant." This recurring theme serves to underscore that the glory of God is exclusive and not to be shared with anyone else—be it angels or an earthly king who is self-absorbed in his greatness. All of them are mere agents and "fellow-servants" of God, just like the apostles who served as instruments to declare his revelation to the world. The intermediary role of the angel becomes evident in Jesus's direct testimony: "It is I, Jesus, who sent my angel to you with this testimony for the churches" (22:16 NRSVue), and "The one who testifies to these things says, 'Surely I am coming soon'" (22:20 NRSVue).

The highlight of John's revelation is to reject the worship of the beast (which will take a historical frame) and the veneration of angels. This revelation emphasizes that all earthly and heavenly positions are subordinate to God, whose kingdom is established through the redemptive work of Jesus Christ and his atoning death. The angel's question in 5:2, "Who is worthy to open the scroll and break its seals?" is met with the response in 5:3 stating, "No one in heaven or on earth or under the earth was able to open the scroll or to look into it" (ESV).

In short, Revelation portrays Jesus as the triumphant King, overcoming sin and death. Through vivid symbolism, it depicts his eternal reign, final judgment, and the establishment of God's kingdom. Jesus is hailed as the Lamb, King of kings, and Lord of lords, asserting his absolute authority and eternal sovereignty over all creation.

---

[a] Richard Bauckham, *The Climax of Prophecy: Studies on the Book of Revelation* (New York: T&T Clark, 1993), 131.

The second biblical passage that is significant for the present discussion is 1 Corinthians 15:24–28. The parallel between Adam and Christ guides the whole context, where Christ as the last Adam repairs the damage produced by the first Adam (15:22, 42–45). In the context of the bodily resurrection, death is described as the last enemy to be defeated (15:26). But alongside death, he will destroy every rule, authority, and power (15:24). That conquest is associated with the kingdom he has received (15:27), he is conducting (15:25), but that he will finally deliver (15:24). There is a finality to what he is doing, after he accomplishes his victory over death, and some kind of change represented in the language of "deliver[ing] the kingdom" (ESV) and the "Son subjecting himself under God" (15:24, 28). The creational language of Psalm 8 again appears in verse 27 to say that God placed this authority over all things under the last Adam. The language of Psalm 110 is also appropriated, but in reverse order (1 Cor 15:25): while the emphasis in Psalm 110 is on the honor placed by Yahweh on the Messiah (authority for the mission), in 1 Corinthians the anointed Adam honors God by subjecting all enemies under him and gives an ordered creation back to God (accomplished mission).

The Father covenantally assigned him a kingdom (Luke 22:29) and in this intra-Trinitarian covenant (traditionally called *pactum salutis*) the Son undertakes the kingly task and eventually demands his rewards (John 17:5; Heb 12:2). His economic subordination to the Father demands that he reports to him. The Mediator has always portrayed his mission as doing the will of the Father (John 4:34; 5:30; 6:38). Therefore, not only in his first coming does he say that he has accomplished the work he was given to do (John 17:2, 4), but his work is yet to accomplish the subjugation of all enemies before he comes to the Father and declares to have accomplished that as well (1 Cor 15:24–26). We must understand the present state of the kingdom as distinct from its future condition: "The kingdom is present now only in a provisional and incomplete state," says Anthony Hoekema, and in its present state the kingdom "is an object of faith, not of sight."[25] Therefore, there is a task that still needs to be accomplished and a formal presentation of victory

---

25. Hoekema, *The Bible and the Future*, 51, 52.

that needs to be displayed before the throne of God. So his mediatorial task is to present the redeemed to his divine self (Eph 5:27).

There is a historical debate between Reformed theologians regarding the length of Christ's mediatorial kingdom and the language in 1 Corinthians 15. On the discontinuity end of the spectrum John Dick contends the mediatorial kingdom ends with the salvation of the elect,[26] while on the opposite continuity side Robert Lewis Dabney believes the book of Revelation favors a continuous action of the mediator (Rev 7:17; 21:22–23) and 1 Corinthians 15 only teaches that the church is restored to the Father without severing Christ's headship.[27] In a more moderate expression of discontinuity, Calvin claims that Christ will be discharged of the office of mediator so that God will rule the church immediately, transferring the manner of his rule from his humanity to his divinity (a world without human hierarchies).[28] A nuanced version of continuity is found in Francis Turretin (only the administration is changed),[29] where in 1 Corinthians 15:24–28 the time reference ("until") doesn't mean the afterward is excluded (just like Matthew 28:20 doesn't mean Christ will not be with his disciples after consummation), a position shared by Thomas Ridley,[30] and the subjection to God is a presentation of the perfected church (just like Johannes Wollebius)[31] or a subordination of his humanity. Hodge and Berkhof stand in middle ground when they refer to classic bifurcations of the mediatorial kingdom[32] to establish a spiritual government of the church that is never ending while the dominion over the universe (an authority conferred for a special purpose) is handed over to the Father.[33]

Since this chapter is trying to account for the finished task of Christ's kingly office, it will attempt to be faithful to the tradition without being

---

26. Dick, *Lectures on Theology*, 3:241.

27. Dabney, *Systematic Theology*, 551–53.

28. John Calvin, *Institutes of the Christian Religion*, ed. John T. McNeill, trans. Ford L. Battles (Philadelphia: Westminster, 1960), 2.14.3, 5. Calvin, *Commentary on 1 Cor 15:24, 27*. For Richard Muller, Calvin's reference to the conclusion of Christ's earthly mediation does not mean termination of the office but perfecting of the mediatorial work (since humanity advances in the economy of salvation). Muller, "Christ in the Eschaton," 44, 45.

29. Turretin, *Institutes of Elenctic Theology*, 2:14.17.7, 9–12 (pp. 492–94).

30. Cf. Ridgley, *A Body of Divinity*, 575.

31. Wollebius, *The Abridgment of Christian Divinitie*, 165.

32. Cf. Richard Muller, *Dictionary of Latin and Greek Theological Terms, Drawn Principally from Protestant Scholastic Theology* (Grand Rapids: Baker, 1985), s.v. "regnum Christi" (pp. 260–61).

33. Hodge, *Systematic Theology*, 2:601-4; Berkhof, *Systematic Theology*, 410-11.

bound to one author or another. My response to the questions raised in the introduction start by establishing that mediation is broader than the office (contra Dick), and the current administration of Christ's royal office is different from the future of the office. But mediation doesn't occur merely according to his divinity (contra Calvin), for his humanity continues to display God's glory (Rev 21:23). If the previous section established that his mediatory domain has a beginning in time, if it has a mission to accomplish and its accomplishment progresses over time toward a consummation, then we should account for things that cease and things that remain in Christ's kingship. The time reference in 1 Corinthians 15 ("until") should not be undermined based on the everlasting presence of Christ after the fulfillment of the Great Commission (contra Ridgley and Turretin) because both passages differentiate between modes of being. In Matthew 28, his promise to be with them serves as security until his physical return, and thus in 1 Corinthians 15, we have to conclude different modes of dominion. Lastly, Christ's subjection to God in 1 Corinthians 15:28 cannot be a reference to the church as Christ's body (contra Wollebius and Turretin) because it is not the church but Christ alone who subjects all enemies under his feet (15:25).

There is no question that the redemptive economy of the office (which includes actions such as defeat of the enemies) ceases, for there is no need to continue them in eternity. In light of the context of Christ being the firstfruits of the redeemed resurrected (15:23), it does make sense to interpret the delivering of kingdom (15:24) as the presentation of the church to God (Calvin, Turretin). However, the deliverance seems to be more than that, for he is giving over dominion in order to be a subject (15:28).[34] So one could say that the representative task of regaining the dominion that Adam lost is a finished task that needs to cease. Christ fulfilling his mission of subverting enemies and giving the kingdom back to the Father is not less glorious; it is his glory! The redeemed will celebrate the accomplishments of the king forever and ever. Thus, the economy of the royal office ceases, but its glorious

---

34. Even if some interpreters prefer to say that Christ became subject to God according to his humanity, one could make the case that the submission of the Son in v. 28 is economic, not ontological. Cf. Leon Morris, *The Epistle of Paul to the Corinthians*, Tyndale New Testament Commentaries (Grand Rapids: Eerdmans, 1973), 217–18.

status remains. Christ does not need to be a human king over humans like the anointed kings were leaders over Israel under God; it is possible that all human hierarchies will cease (Calvin). That kind of mediation being over, he becomes a regent over creation like us (according to his humanity) governing over all (according to his divinity), even though Christ will necessarily rule over us as God-man because of the hypostatic union. He will continue to unite different types of regency, but not anymore to bridge the chasm between our chaotic ruling of this world and God's holy dominance. As Bavinck would say, the "mediatorship of reconciliation" ceases while the "mediatorship of union" remains forever.[35]

He continues to be the mediator, but not in the same sense. It is a perennial condescension, an eternal expression of God's approximation to his people, celebrated by the meal that recollects Christ as our rescuer (Mark 14:25). Christ remains a mediator, neither out of ontological necessity, for there is no basis to assert that innocent Adam had such a need, nor to sustain the blessings he acquired, a providential action that does not require that he be God-man. He became human to be our king forever (observe the Lamb on the throne in Rev 21:5; 22:1, 3) because it is his delight to be ours, and we will be enraptured by the beauty of our glorious king. Scripture does not reveal the many activities that Christ will uniquely operate according to his humanity, but it certainly exalts the glory of the accomplishment. God will be all in all, but not because Christ's humanity is not necessary anymore. With the completion of his mission, his incarnation finally conveys the unity with his people that he prayed for (John 17:24–26). God and man are forever united, and we are elevated to contemplate his glory and to be fully involved in divine love.

PERSPECTIVE FOR THIS LIFE AND HOPE FOR THINGS TO COME

This last section will briefly lay out how this eschatological perspective may impact church life in the present and Christian hope of things to come.

---

35. Bavinck, *RD*, 3:482.

The already/not yet reality of the kingdom impacts both their posture and expectations with very practical applications to the Brazilian evangelical culture. Their posture, in light of spiritual warfare described in Scripture, should be that of soldiers (1 Tim 6:12; 2 Tim 2:3–4; 4:7) who are in the position not of conquering warriors but of diplomatic ambassadors. The spiritual warfare frenzy of the 1990s sought to bind Satan several times, map out the demons of different regions, break hereditary curses, and influence noncharismatic churches into singing songs of conquest. A renewed understanding of their place in the battle became urgent. Their posture as the militant church in between "D-day" and "V-day," to use Oscar Cullmann's famous World War II analogy, is not of those who win the fight in the name of Jesus. Believers are not invading warriors; Christ is the warrior king who conquered what was rightfully his. Once he has invaded enemy territory and placed his people as embassies of the kingdom, they are not in attack mode, but in resistance (cf. Eph 6:11, 13, 14). They are ambassadors in enemy land (6:20), and their actions are merely diplomatic, for their only weapon of offense is the sword of the Spirit, which is the word of God (6:17). In the present age they announce the interests of the kingdom that is yet fully to come. As they represent the kingdom in diplomatic fashion, it advances by the power of the Spirit.

FROM SOFANIT T. ABEBE

Given the reality of Christ's victory over death and all evil, the New Testament calls Christians to appropriate his victory by bearing witness to his life, death, and resurrection. Living in submission to the reign of the slain Lamb means standing in allegiance to him. In Revelation, the way to conquer is portrayed as being through the word of witness (Rev 7:13–14). Christian witness—even to the point of death (cf. Rev 2:10; 12:10; 13:7; 14:13)—is radically interpreted as a potent symbol of victory against Satan. The place of Christians in enemy land is indeed that of ambassadors, but to their diplomatic tool kit, Paul assigns not only a shield of faith and the sword of the Spirit but also the radical claim that Christians share in the resurrection of Christ and the promise of his enthronement.

This is the foundation for Christians' participation in foreign lands. It is not merely diplomatic—it is in fact a call for resistance. Thus, Paul says, "Be strong in the Lord and in the strength of his might" (Eph 6:10 ESV). For Paul, God's power with which he is calling believers to be strengthened is linked to Christ's resurrection and enthronement. We see this when he prays in Ephesians 1:19–20 for his readers to know "what is the immeasurable greatness of [God's] power toward us who believe, according to the working of his great might" (ESV). Christ's resurrection power is indispensable to the church in the call to engage evil while living as ambassadors to Christ. Christ has triumphed over his enemies and ended their dominion "in the heavenly places" (Eph 6:12 ESV) when he was enthroned in the "heavenly places" (Eph 1:20 ESV). While Christians would not need to conquer a defeated enemy, they are still called to resist Satan and demonic beings (Eph 6:11, 13; 1 Pet 5:9). Paul and Peter urge us to do this despite the fact that Christ has already triumphed over them, ending their dominion "in the heavenly places." But until evil is completely eradicated, while living in the "not yet" of the here and now, we are soldier-ambassadors proclaiming the victories of Christ and resisting the enemy, shouting in unison *maranatha*, until evil's earthly dominion is eradicated when Christ the King returns.

Considering the identity of ambassadors who wait for their coming king, believers must have specific expectations. Until Christ's return, they live in this world as pilgrims, as people who don't belong (1 Pet 2:11) but have a calling to exercise the kingly office as ambassadors of the king (2 Cor 5:18–20). This language of ambassadors is an identity of those who live in a foreign land but function as representative authorities of the nation or kingdom they represent. But as ambassadors, as exiles, they will return to their homeland. So just like Christ's mission of subjugation has an end, so does their mission as ambassadors have an end. When that day arrives, Christ will establish a state of perfect dominion, and they shall reign on the earth with him (Rev 3:21; 5:10). There shouldn't be an understanding of entitlement to the land here and now, as assumed by the neo-Pentecostal health-and-wealth gospel, but there will be a future claim of the believer's inheritance. They will be crowned in Christ's heavenly kingdom (2 Tim 4:8, 18) because he has the authority to make them king with him.

When Christ's kingship is consummated, the threefold relationship established in creation will finally have been restored. Believers will have regained their place as servants under God (not having a kingdom of their own), in equality with their fellow brothers (not dominating over them), and in dominion of creation. However, this threefold restoration does not happen simultaneously and with the same intensity. The moment that they are in Christ, enmity against God is removed entirely, whereas it is removed gradually with their brothers and sisters and only at the end with the rest of creation. Just as God first makes people new creatures before placing them on New Heavens and New Earth, the restoration of the spiritual mandate (relationship with God) is a prerequisite of the restoration of the other mandates. The redeemed presently commune with God and with their brothers and sisters before they can have a smooth relationship with the natural world. Their insertion into the kingdom starts with submission to the divine King, then it restores their relationship with their fellow citizens of the kingdom, and finally they get to reign over all the earth. All of this happens through the office of King Jesus.

CHAPTER 9

IN STEP WITH
THE KING

Participation and the Reign of Christ

SOFANIT T. ABEBE

INTRODUCTION

The relationship between God and his chosen people is central to the Bible. In the Old Testament we see God using the ministry of kings as an instrument of his reign over a people he has chosen and called to communion.[1] For this reason kings are called to emulate God's goodness, leading the people as a shepherd leads his flock (Ps 78:72). They would be able to then put into effect God's covenant in the life of the people as God's representatives and symbols of his exclusive sovereignty. Having attained their kingly office by anointing, which signifies God's outpouring of the Holy Spirit and his enablement of the task set before them, kings were installed as instruments of God's reign

---

1. The notion of communion with God is an important theme in the Old Testament. Writing of the various sacrifices stipulated in the Pentateuch, John A. Davies notes that the rationale behind any sacrifice offered to God, including the offerings of oxen from which "the blood of the covenant" came in Exodus 24:5–6, is to render the worshiper "acceptable to YHWH" thus leading to the "establishment of a communion" (cf. Lev 1:3–4), cf. John A. Davies, *A Royal Priesthood: Literary and Intertextual Perspectives on an Image of Israel in Exodus 19.6* (London: T&T Clark, 2004), 120–21. The establishment of a communion is exactly what is anticipated in Exodus 24, which narrates the community's agreement to obey (24:3) and their consequent consecration through sprinkling with blood (v. 8), which culminated in their access to God; see Exod 24:10 LXX: "and they saw the place where the God of Israel stood," which is an expansion of the MT's "and they saw the God of Israel."

with a mediatory role. They represent the people before God, as Solomon did at the dedication of the temple (1 Kgs 8:22–53). For this reason, kings were not to consider their royalty as an end in itself but to act as mediators of the people. Despite the litany of ways they failed to carry out the task of governing, leading, and protecting their people, we learn from the Old Testament that the calling of the ancient kings of Israel was envisioned as a service to God, to glorify him and make known his glorious riches before his covenant people and Israel's neighboring nations.

FROM HEBER CARLOS DE CAMPOS JR.

Anointing is a rich biblical concept that has been partially and oftentimes mistakenly appreciated in evangelical circles. When Brazilian believers pray that God would anoint the preacher, they convey two ideas: that anointing is synonymous to supernatural power (partially correct) and that anointing is temporary (incorrect), as if the power would enter the preacher just before stepping up to preach and leave him as he sat down. I have learned with the biblical texts and with the rich confessional tradition that emanated from the Reformation that anointing is not only about power but first and foremost about authority. The anointing of a king was a public ceremony of declaration of authority to the people (1 Sam 10:1, 20–25; 16:13; 2 Sam 2:4; 1 Kgs 1:34, 39; 2 Kgs 11:12), and this explains why David struggles with and finally gives up the idea of dethroning Saul, the Lord's anointed (1 Sam 24:4–7; 26:8–10). David is not struggling with Saul's power but with his God-given authority. God is the only one who can give and take away this authority, as he did with Saul. The issue of authority being God-given seems to be in the background of David's prayer after sinning with Bathsheba: "Take not your Holy Spirit from me" (Ps 51:11 ESV). The Westminster Larger Catechism states that Christ's anointing of the Holy Spirit furnished him with "all authority and ability" (42). Christ is the supreme king furnished with all authority and power (Matt 28:18; Acts 10:38). And because we have been anointed as well (1 John 2:20), we should speak of an anointing that abides in us (2:27): not a temporary power but an authority that does not submit to proto-gnostic guardians of mysterious revelations. We have already been authorized and empowered by God to convey

> his truth. Hence, we do not pray for a new coming down of the Spirit in preaching but only that the anointing already residing will come to its effect and accordingly produce fruit by the power of the Spirit in us.

The ministry of Israel's kings to represent God as his witnesses and instruments of his reign announces and points to Christ the king who is the "one mediator between God and men, the man Christ Jesus" (1 Tim 2:5 ESV). In the New Testament we come to understand the significance of this twofold task of representing and bearing witness to God's reign on the one hand and representing the people and entering into God's presence in their name on the other, as encapsulated and perfected in the life and work of Jesus Christ.

Since the fourth century, the belief in and affirmation of the lordship of Jesus has been continuously practiced in Ethiopia. In what follows, I will explore what it means for an Ethiopian to think of Jesus of Nazareth as God's anointed, the *Christ*, the resurrected, ascended, and exalted King seated at the right hand of the Father. By employing a descriptive analysis of the notion of the *Atse* (the Amharic word for "emperor" or "king of kings") and related categories in relation to the imperial history of Ethiopia as well as aspects of the Ethiopian Orthodox *Tewahedo* Church's depiction of Christ's kingship and human participation in Christ's reign, my aim is to underline an appreciation of an Ethiopian reading of the New Testament's announcement of Jesus of Nazareth as king and the profound claim that those who believe in him also share in his reign.

To this end and reading from an Ethiopian perspective, I will begin my discussion by exploring the theme of kingship in the Old Testament to gain an appreciation of Christ's kingly ministry in the New Testament. Then, before addressing the issue of believers' participation in Christ's kingship, I will offer a brief discussion on the notion of believers' union with Christ. This foundational discussion will set the way for a descriptive analysis of an Ethiopian perspective on kingship in general and, specifically, Christ's identification as king as refracted through the lens of the imperial and ecclesiastical traditions of Ethiopia. These sections will draw out the contrasting aspect of Christ's incomparable supremacy as the Redeemer-King and the hope of glory for his chosen people over whom he reigns.

KINGSHIP IN THE BIBLE

The Old Testament

Kings were installed through anointing such that they held the title and office of "Anointed" (i.e., Messiah; see, e.g., Pss 2:2; 18:50; 20:6). An important feature of the messianic king is his victory over opponents (Ps 110:1–2; cf. Ps 45:5):

> The LORD says to my Lord:
>> "Sit at my right hand,
> until I make your enemies your footstool."

> The LORD sends forth from Zion
>> your mighty scepter.
>> Rule in the midst of your enemies![2]

The king's victory over his enemies is here attributed to his share in God's throne. This victory will ensure that the people would live in peace and prosperity (Ps 72:3–16).

Again, in Psalm 2:1–3, God's and the king's enemies cause intense opposition (cf. Pss 69:4; 109:3):

> Why do the nations rage
>> and the peoples plot in vain?
> The kings of the earth set themselves,
>> and the rulers take counsel together,
>> against the LORD and against his Anointed, saying,

---

2. Unless otherwise noted, Scripture quotes from this chapter come from the ESV.

> "Let us burst their bonds apart and
>   cast away their cords from us."

God overcomes the enemies by enthroning the king and installing him as his son (2:6–8):

> "As for me, I have set my King
>   on Zion, my holy hill."

> I will tell of the decree:
> The LORD said to me, "You are my Son;
>   today I have begotten you.
> Ask of me, and I will make the nations your heritage,
>   and the ends of the earth your possession.

The king is thus God's agent who shares in and represents God's rule (see also Ps 89:20–37; cf. 2 Sam 7:12–14). God will exalt him over his enemies and God's rule will be established, resulting in the bestowal of blessings, peace, and security over the people (Pss 2:8–10; 72:16–17; 101:5–8; 110:2; cf. Isa 9:7; 11:3–5; Jer 23:17; Dan 7:14; Mic 5:2–5; Zech 9:9–10).

Another important feature of the Davidic king is that he participates in God's divine kingship, not by nature but through grace. As Joshua Jipp notes, "The king participates in God's royal glory (Pss 3:4; LXX 20:7–8; LXX 44:4; LXX 61:9; LXX 62:4), receives his victories from the strength of the Lord (LXX Pss 20:2; 143:1, 10), is established by God's "right hand" (LXX Ps. 62:9), and is sheltered by God (LXX Pss 16:8; 60:5)."[3] In Psalm 24, glory is associated with God's presence and kingship. According to verses 7–10, God is the "King of Glory," who bestows his glory on the king (e.g., Ps 3:3). While not divine, the king was divinely gifted and was viewed as "the Lord's anointed, as God's own son, to be invested with God's authority and power to rule (Ps 2:6–9; LXX 88:27–29; 109:1–4; cf. 2 Sam 7:12–14)."[4]

---

3. Joshua Jipp, *Christ Is King: Paul's Royal Ideology* (Minneapolis: Fortress, 2015), 153.
4. Jipp, *Christ Is King*, 155.

FROM ARUTHUCKAL VARUGHESE JOHN

At times, we erroneously assume that grace only comes into play with the advent of Christ in the New Testament. However, its evident operation is observed in the Old Testament as well. This paper underscores a crucial point: the Davidic kingship is facilitated by grace rather than entitlement. However, there is nuanced understanding to be had. While David is king by the grace of God in the Old Testament, Christ the king serves as the direct and ultimate channel of grace to humanity in the New Testament.

Grace stands out as the defining characteristic that sets Christianity apart from other religions and ideologies. Joining a discussion among Oxford colleagues debating the uniqueness of Christianity, or the lack thereof, C. S. Lewis is said to have promptly interjected, "Oh, that's easy. It's grace!" This assertion resonates strongly within the multireligious landscape of India.

The Hindu tradition suggests three paths to salvation: *jñānā mārga*, *karma mārga*, and *bhakti mārga*. *Jñānā mārga* is Socratic in its prognosis, identifying the fundamental human problem as ignorance. Echoing Ramanuja's understanding, Raghavachar elucidates the *jñānā mārga* as a sphere where "the human self [functions] as a center of knowing by the exercise of that very knowing itself and by developing that potency to its fullness of actualization through the knowing of God."[a] In this context, achieving salvation is confined to those with access to knowledge, as in the case of a Brahmin, rendering it fundamentally restrictive. The *karma mārga* bears a resemblance to the Mosaic law, as salvation is achieved through one's deeds. Similar to the Mosaic law, one finds numerous ritual prescriptions governing the religious and cultural lives of Hindu believers. Here again only one who is resilient and enabled by the *guṇas* (nature), which determine one's character, can attain salvation through their actions. The third path to salvation is the *bhakti mārga*, where devotion to God is key. However, when devotion is primarily defined within the framework of works, one finds that the restrictive *guṇas* (nature) predetermine one's character and actions, making it inaccessible to all.

In this context, the distinctive nature of the Christian concept of grace, which is the opposite of just desserts, becomes evident. It is in Christ, who is "full of grace and truth" (John 1:14 NIV), that we find the fullness of grace. In human interactions, it may be surmised that when grace is emphasized, truth is often compromised, and conversely, when truth takes precedence, grace may be compromised. This highlights the ideal that both truth and grace are fully realized in Christ the king, the prototype for Christian believers.

---

[a] S. S. Raghavachar, "The Spiritual Vision of Rāmānujā," in *Hindu Spirituality: Vedas through Vedanta*, ed. Krishna Sivaraman (New York: Crossroad, 1989), 266.

Christ the King

When the New Testament identifies Jesus of Nazareth with the title *Christ* (Messiah), it indicates his kingly office such that Jesus is the "anointed one." This is further elaborated by linking the promised Davidic king of 2 Samuel 7:16 to Jesus, the one to whom God grants "the throne of his father David" (Luke 1:32). The New Testament also alludes to the Davidic shepherd of Ezekiel 34:23–24 when describing Jesus's identity as the "good shepherd" (John 10:11, 14). As Andreas Köstenberger notes, "Jesus saw himself as embodying the characteristics and expectations attached to this salvation-historical biblical figure."[5] Jesus is thus the anticipated ideal king who had succeeded in shepherding God's people in accordance with the will of God (cf. Matt 11:28; Luke 7:22; 15:4–5). He is the very antithesis of the self-centeredness and wickedness of the bad shepherds described in Ezekiel 34 and the many self-centric kings and emperors Ethiopian history attests to. He is the embodiment of the ideal shepherd-king who fulfilled the role of dying for his sheep and gathering the scattered flock (Isa 53:6).

While the Bible presents Jesus as the ideal shepherd-king, his kingship is stated as extending beyond the prototype set by David. Not only does Christ perfectly adhere to the Father's will, but he also gives his sheep a heart for God. In Ezekiel 34, following the appointment of the coming ideal Davidic king, God says, "I will make a covenant of peace with them" (34:25 NIV). The king to come will internalize the law and reconcile the flock with God (Isa 11:12, 16; 19:18–25). By mirroring divine rule in heaven,

---

5. Andreas J. Köstenberger, "John," in *Commentary on the New Testament Use of the Old Testament*, ed. G. K. Beale and D. A. Carson (Grand Rapids: Baker Academic, 2007), 462.

the king accomplishes the bestowal of God's gifts of "righteousness, rule over one's enemies, and internal peace and prosperity" to the people.[6] In other words, "sharing in God's rule places the king in the position of distributing to humanity the benefits of God's rule."[7] Not only does Christ accomplish this ideal, but he is also the agent through whom his people share in divine reign. Before we turn our attention to the role of the church in Christ's kingly ministry, let us first explore the relationship between Christ and believers.

UNION WITH CHRIST

Following Christ's ascension and the outpouring of the Holy Spirit, Jesus's followers were constituted as members of Christ's body, empowered to bear witness to Christ and proclaim the good news of reconciliation with God and redemption from sin through Jesus Christ. Believers are members of the in-Christ community, united to one another through the Holy Spirit. Paul describes this unity using language of the human body (1 Cor 12:12–26; Eph 4:1–16). Just as the body and all its different parts are united to the head, the church relates to Christ, the Head of the body, through a union effected by God. This is achieved through the Holy Spirit who is sent by the risen Christ and who indwells believers (John 17:21; Acts 2:33–36). Jesus Christ rules over his church as its only head and sovereign Lord. It is in this profound unity between Christ and his body the church that Christ rules over, governs and protects the Church.[8]

Through faith granted by the Spirit, believers are said to be "in Christ." This language of being in Christ has been discussed in terms of a unity with Christ. This union with Christ entails incorporation into the family of

---

6. Righteousness and justice are a feature of his reign; see Ps 72:1–4a and Isa 11:4–5. For victory over enemies, see Gen 49:10–12; Num 24:17–19; Ps 72:4b, 8–11. For peace and prosperity, see Pss 72:15–16; 132:15; 144:12–14; Isa 11:6–9.

7. Julien Smith, *Christ the Ideal King: Cultural Context, Rhetorical Strategy, and the Power of Divine Monarchy in Ephesians*, WUNT 2 (Tübingen: Mohr Siebeck, 2011), 175.

8. For an in-depth discussion of the kingly office of Christ and its impact on the church as seen through the unity of believers with Christ, see Robert Letham, *The Work of Christ: Contours of Christian Theology* (Downers Grove, IL: IVP, 1993), 75–87, 197–247.

God—not just as beneficiaries in Christ, but also an identification with Jesus himself (we will discuss below the notion of intercommunion, that is, mutual indwelling).

In expressing believers' union with Christ, the New Testament employs several images. One is that of baptism, which is presented as a fundamental change of identity that results from our being baptized into Christ's death and resurrection (Rom 6:1–23; cf. 1:3–4; 4:25; 1 Cor 15:35–36; 1 Pet 3:21–22; 2 Pet 3:5–7). What is Christ's is made ours by the Spirit so that Christ imparts himself to us (John 16:14).[9] While this would be how Ethiopian evangelicals would understand believers' participation in Christ, the ancient Ethiopian Orthodox Church would additionally signify partaking of the Lord's Supper as the means through which the Spirit would continually effect believers' unification with Christ.[10]

FROM ARUTHUCKAL VARUGHESE JOHN

The process of *theosis* is realized through the dual actions of God's two hands, as described by Irenaeus: Christ, the redeemer and the only Son of God, and the Holy Spirit, the sanctifier and the Lord who imparts life.

The saying of Jesus in the Sermon on the Mount, "Be perfect, therefore, as your heavenly Father is perfect" (Matt 5:48), is a call to perfection, where the human goal is to be in the likeness of God. Yet spiritual perfection is not achieved through the human will but is the result of the sanctifying work of the Holy Spirit in human beings. In the Eastern tradition, the Holy Spirit holds a prominent position in both theology and liturgy. This is evident through the inclusion of prayers for the Holy Spirit and the prayer of epiclesis. This is in contrast to the relatively recent focus on pneumatology, prompting the remark that the Holy Spirit had been overlooked, akin to being the Cinderella of theology in Western theological discourse and church practices.

---

9. Michael S. Horton, *Pilgrim Theology: Core Doctrines for Christian Disciples* (Grand Rapids: Zondervan, 2017).

10. See the eucharistic liturgy ("*Akuatêta Querbän*") in the Anaphora of Athanasius in Marcos Daoud, trans., *The Liturgy of the Ethiopian Church* (London: Kegan Paul, 2005) 138–58, esp. 150, 152, 155. For a descriptive analysis of the Anaphora, see Ernst Hammerschmidt, "Jewish Elements in the Cult of the Ethiopian Church," *Journal of Ethiopian Studies* 3, no. 2 (1965): 1–12.

Salvation, viewed as *theosis*, is sometimes rejected without thoughtful consideration due to perceived pantheistic implications. Understandably, the notion of human deification or divinization appears to blur the line between creator and creature, resembling the Hindu Advaitic perspective of *Aham Brahmasmi* (meaning "I am Brahman"), where an individual realizes their identity as Brahman. However, in the Eastern Church's understanding, *theosis* is not about erasing distinctions but rather communion with God, resulting in a godly nature.

Theosis is the inverse of incarnation. As Vladimir Lossky writes, "The Son has become like us by the incarnation; we become like Him by deification, by partaking of the divinity in the Holy Spirit."[a] For Lossky the story of God is not fully appropriated by limiting our theological reflection on the idea of redemption, as it would make "strange and abnormal" the patristic sentence, "God made Himself man, that man might become God." He clarifies, "The thought of union with God is forgotten because of our preoccupation solely with our own salvation; or rather, union with God is seen only negatively, in contrast with our present wretchedness."[b] *Theosis* is fundamentally the work of the Holy Spirit, which as Stavropoulos writes, "Only in the Holy Spirit will we reach the point of becoming gods, the likeness of God."[c]

The incarnation (descent; *katabasis*) of Christ enables *theosis* (ascent; *anabasis*) in the Spirit for human beings, thus locating the "essence of Christianity—an ineffable descent of God to the ultimate limit of our fallen human condition, even unto death—a descent of God which opens to men a path of ascent to the ultimate vision of the union of created beings with the divinity."[d] In short, the redemptive work of Christ is purposed to unite humans with God, enabling them to "may participate in the divine nature" (2 Pet 1:4).[e] Despite the unconventional characterization of God's nature as "energy," this concept encapsulates grace as an inherent and emanating aspect of God. Thus the prayer for the Holy Spirit in the liturgy of STECI reads as follows: "It is your Holy Spirit who shed abroad your love into our hearts. It is the Holy Spirit who enables us to be filled with the mind and life of Christ, and thus become like Jesus and to abide in the love of the Father. It is the Holy Spirit who strengthens us from above for our service and activities. . . . We pray to you oh Lord, that the Holy Spirit, who was sent upon your church on the day of Pentecost, may be given in His fullness unto us and to all the believers and that your church may thus be empowered."

ᵃ Vladimir Lossky, *In the Image and Likeness of God*, ed. J. H. Erickson (Crestwood, NY: St. Vladimir's Seminary Press, 1974), 109.

ᵇ Lossky, *In the Image and Likeness of God*, 98.

ᶜ Christophoros Stavropoulos, *Partakers of Divine Nature*, trans. S. Harakas (Minneapolis: Light of Life, 1976), 29.

ᵈ Lossky, *In the Image and Likeness of God*, 97.

ᵉ Leonid Ouspensky, *Theology of the Icon* (Crestwood, NY: St. Vladimir's Seminary Press, 1978), 215.

BELIEVERS' PARTICIPATION

Sonship and Viceregency

Humanity was destined to reign over creation as God's vice-regents (Gen 1:26–28; Ps 8:4–6). Through Adam's disobedience, however, sin and death reigned over humanity (Rom 5:12–21). The New Testament states that God's intention for humanity "is brought to fruition through the Messiah's cosmic rule and his extension of this rule to his people."[11] In Romans 1:4, Paul states that Jesus Christ was "declared to be the Son of God in power according to the Spirit of holiness by his resurrection from the dead." Christ's crucifixion and resurrection has inaugurated his reign. His enthronement to a position of leadership is not only over his people but the entire cosmos, entailing victory over his enemies.

Christ's kingship is extended to humanity because of his unique identity as God's royal messiah. As Jipp notes, "Every aspect of the Son's royal enthronement in Romans 1:4 has participatory consequences, as Paul conceptualizes humanity's salvation as participation in the constituent events of Christ's rule, namely, his sonship [cf. Rom 8:14–23, 29–30], resurrection life, receipt of the Spirit, and cosmic inheritance [Rom 1:3–4; cf. Pss 2: 7–8; 110:1]."[12] God's promise concerning the king in 2 Samuel 7:14 links the king as Israel's representative to God using kinship language. When Paul states

---

11. Jipp, *Christ Is King*, 194–95.
12. Jipp, *Christ Is King*, 187. Bracketed references added.

in Romans 8:15 that believers have received "the Spirit of adoption as sons," he indicates believers' participation in Christ's sonship as the children of God through the Spirit. In Galatians 4:6, Paul again links believers' sonship with that of Christ's by referring to "the Spirit of his Son": "Because you are sons, God has sent the Spirit of his Son into our hearts, crying, 'Abba! Father!'" Paul reiterates believers' participation in Christ in terms of a familial link with God in Romans 8:29. Thus, Paul implies that Israel's promises of sonship for God's installed king (2 Sam 7:12–14; Ps 2:7; LXX 88:26–27) are extended to the Messiah's people by virtue of the Spirit. Whereas Israel's Scriptures portrayed God's gift of the Spirit as establishing the king as holy, sacrosanct, and the locus of God's presence, so now Messiah Jesus shares the royal gift of the Spirit with all his people. Thus, those who share in the Messiah's sonship receive the *same Spirit and are described as "in the Spirit"* (Rom 8:9).[13]

This participation in Christ's sonship is contrasted in both Romans and Galatians with the tyrannical rule of sin and death (cf. Rom 8:12–17; Gal 6:4–7) thus indicating believers' freedom from the dominion of sin and entrance into participation in Christ's reign (Rom 8:17).

Triumph over Evil

Believers' participation in Christ's rule is on a scope that is both cosmic and eschatological (1 Cor 3:21–23). As the ideal king, Christ's reign is marked by opposition from cosmic powers and their earthly agents (Eph 1:20–23; cf. Ps 2). Humanity is also under captivity by the same enemies of Christ (Eph 2:1–5). Given Paul's direct citation of Psalms 109:1 and 8:7 LXX (Eph 1:20, 22), it is likely that the enemies of God and his anointed are understood by Paul through the lens of the Psalms' portrait of opposition to the anointed (Pss 2:2–3; 109:2–3; cf. Dan 7:27).[14]

However, according to Ephesians 6, the church is enabled by God's power to resist Satan and the powers of evil, who have been defeated through the resurrection of Christ (6:11, 13). In Romans when Paul states that the "God of peace will soon crush Satan under your feet" (16:20; cf. Ps 8:6; Gen 3:15),

---

13. Jipp, *Christ Is King*, 190–91.
14. Jipp, *Christ Is King*, 200–201.

he is indicating that through the death, resurrection, and enthronement of Christ, believers have been reinstated to the role of reigning over the entire cosmos (Eph 2:6–7). It also depicts God's intention to have believers participate in his eschatological triumph over Satan along with suffering (Rom 8:35), rulers and powers (8:38), and death (8:36, 38).[15] Through Christ and as the children of God, believers become conquerors over evil through their participation in Christ's triumph (Rom 8:37).[16]

CHRIST THE KING: AN ETHIOPIAN PERSPECTIVE

Present day Ethiopia has the historical backdrop of three consecutive dynasties that ruled the country until 1974 when the last Emperor was deposed by a Communist coup: (1) the *Axumite* dynasty, which ran from the first through the seventh centuries AD, (2) the *Zagwe* dynasty from the eighth through the thirteenth centuries, and (3) the Solomonic dynasty, claiming descent from the biblical King Solomon and the Queen of Sheba, which occurred from 1270 to 1974.

In addition to this historical background that frames the lived religiosity of both Orthodox and Protestant Christianity, there are commentaries for every book of the Bible that originated in Gondar, Ethiopia's capital from 1635 to 1855. With oral tradition as their most likely origin, these commentaries were first written in the Amharic language by imperial decree in 1681. The term *Andəmta* is an Amharic word related to the particle *andəm* meaning "or." It is a key technical term used to introduce an alternative meaning to a word or concept in the biblical text that needs more than one explanation. The main objective of the *Andəmta* is "to get to the heart of the texts under analysis [and] to discover the 'mystery' contained, or indeed hidden, in the depths of the texts."[17] Interpretations offered in the *Andəmta* thus stand in

---

15. Jipp, *Christ Is King*, 197.
16. Jipp, *Christ Is King*, 197.
17. Tedros Abraha, "Andəmta," *Encyclopaedia Aethiopica*, ed. Siegbert Uhlig (Wiesbaden: Harrassowitz, 2003–14), 258

the Antiochene literary interpretive tradition on the one hand and the *sensus plenior* alongside an allegorical interpretation on the other. In all this the Ethiopian context is brought to the forefront.[18]

The cultural context of centuries of imperial rule and a violent reaction to perceived or real imperial hegemony that began in 1974 continues to shape the Ethiopian social imaginary, as do the popular *Andǝmta* commentaries. In what follows, I will explore the biblical notion of Christ's kingly office as refracted through a formative segment of Ethiopia's long history and the country's ancient Christian heritage. To this end, as well as toward the chapter's overall aim to highlight an appreciation of Christ's unique kingship, a contrast will be drawn between historical and cultural notions of kingship and the biblical depiction of Christ's kingship, where the latter is discussed in conversation with the *Andǝmta*.

Atse: *God's Representative, Emperor of Ethiopia, King of Kings, of the Tribe of Judah*

According to Ethiopia's fourteenth-century foundation legend known as the *Kebra Nagast* ("Glory of the Kings"), kings traced their origins to Menilik II, who they claim is the son the Israelite king Solomon had with Makda, the Queen of Sheba. Ethiopia's 1955 Constitution claims that kings were distant relatives of Jesus himself, and so their title bears a tribal identification with Jesus: ዘእም ነገደ ይሁዳ (*ze'em nagada Yihuda*, "of the tribe of Judah").[19] According to the *Fetha Nagast* or the "Law of Kings" (c. 1270), the divine appointment of the king is expressed through a biblical quotation: "Thou shalt in any way set him king over thee whom the Lord thy God shall choose, one from among thy brethren shalt thou set king over thee."[20] Not only a divine appointment but also vice-regency is claimed by the *Atse*, who is said to be a representative of God.

---

18. See Afework Hailu, *Jewish Cultural Elements in the Ethiopian Orthodox Täwaḥado Church* (Piscataway, NJ: Gorgias, 2020), 301; contra Roger W Cowley, *Ethiopian Biblical Interpretation: A Study in Exegetical Tradition and Hermeneutics* (Cambridge: Cambridge University Press, 1989), 373, who sees a purely literary interpretation with no allegory.

19. Steven Kaplan, "Solomonic Dynasty," in Uhlig, *Encyclopaedia Aethiopica*, 690.

20. Deuteronomy 17:15 as quoted in the *Fetha Nagast*, cf. Pankhurst 1966

FROM HEBER CARLOS DE CAMPOS JR.

Sofanit's history of Ethiopian rulers clearly highlights the importance of tracing lineage as a testament to one's rightful claim to the throne. The Old Testament also had a concern for lineage to prove kingship. Being in the line of David allowed any king of Judah to pray for God's blessing and be heard, while the kings of the Northern Kingdom did not have the same rightful claim. This explains why there are constant changes in dynasties in the North. As we move to the New Testament, we are introduced to a lineage of faith as descendants of Abraham in Christ (Gal 3:29); being in the family gives us the right to royal inheritance (Gal 4:7). In fact, according to the doctrine of Christ's threefold office, one could argue that we are the many kings who descend from Sarah (Gen 17:16). Thus, we should never assert that the Old Testament worked merely with material and concrete blessings (e.g., many blood descendants) and the New Testament works with abstract blessings (e.g., faith). As readers of Scripture who notice continuity in the way the New Testament appropriates passages of the Old Testament, we should argue for seminal promises in the Old Testament both expanding and blessing the descendants, in addition to being fulfilled in majestic fashion in the New Testament. But those promises of the Old Testament also had to be appropriated in faith, since not every descendant by blood was equally blessed. Such reading of Scripture facilitates our understanding of why the analogy of descendants of God in Christ is abundant in the New Testament and often the basis for the blessings we receive.

Although this Solomonic model of kingship entailed a close link between church and state with kings perceived to be defenders of the Christian faith, relations with the church were not always smooth. The kings often clashed with monks who criticized their behavior and fiercely argued that "even the ruler was subject to Christian norms."[21] Thus, while the national narratives (the *Fetha Nagast* and the *Kebra Nagast*) and Christian art glorified the emperors, they have a complex legacy where their efforts to

---

21. Kaplan, "Solomonic Dynasty," 691.

modernize Ethiopia and unify its diverse people under a common goal is tainted with nepotism, tribalism, and the ruthless quest to subjugate and domineer. A common adage that perhaps highlights such sentiments and the yearning for social justice is a particularly poignant lament that defined the rule of Ethiopia's last emperor: *daha tabadala feteh taguadada* (the poor are oppressed, and justice is trampled upon). This stands in stark contrast with the biblical motif of the shepherd-king that was fulfilled, perfected, and revealed by Jesus Christ.

Christ: Redeemer-King and Our Hope of Glory

Christ's supremacy above all kings and earthly systems of governance is depicted not only in the cosmic dimension of his reign, but he is the preeminent creator and goal of the cosmos. In Colossians 1:15–17, Paul says: "He is the image of the invisible God, the firstborn of all creation. For by him all things were created, in heaven and on earth, visible and invisible, whether thrones or dominions or rulers or authorities—all things were created through him and for him. And he is before all things, and in him all things hold together." Christ's kingship is also incomparable to the monarchical systems of humanity because of the corporate participation of the church as his body in his mediatorial kingly task. Paul continues in Colossians 1: "He is the head of the body, the church. He is the beginning, the firstborn from the dead, that in everything he might be preeminent. For in him all the fullness of God was pleased to dwell, and through him to reconcile to himself all things, whether on earth or in heaven, making peace by the blood of his cross." In exercising his kingly functions and prerogatives, Christ did so as our mediator. As Paul put it, God, in Christ, "has delivered us from the domain of darkness and transferred us to the kingdom of his beloved Son, in whom we have redemption, the forgiveness of sins" (Col 1:13–14). The post-resurrection Christ, enthroned and installed at God's right hand, is the one who died on the cross for our redemption. By his atoning death, peace and the gift of reconciliation are ensured (1:20).

While some view the Ethiopian monarchs as great leaders who brought stability and security from foreign domination and exploitation, ensuring that Ethiopia never experienced the unspeakable horrors of colonialism and the trans-Atlantic slave trade, others criticize them for the violence they used to maintain power and for the pain they inflicted on various minority and non-Christian communities in the kingdom. What is considered just and upright is ultimately subservient to the monarch's innate desire to consolidate power and find legitimation. This renders all earthly monarchs suspect to self-serving domination and control.

Christ's model of kingship is one of humility and service in stark contrast to the Ethiopian model of kingship. This point is emphasized in Ephesians 1:3–14 where Paul lists the spiritual blessings we have in Christ that are put into effect by the Holy Spirit. Our election (1:4) and adoption as the children of God (1:5) are because of the blood of Jesus Christ through whom we have received redemption and the forgiveness of our sins (1:7). Christ is the mediatorial king who has purchased our redemption through his sacrificial death on the cross, according to the riches of God's grace that was lavished on us (1:8). Paul then states that God has subjected all things under Christ's headship (1:10). In Christ, "we have obtained an inheritance" (1:11) as his chosen people, having believed in him and being sealed by the Holy Spirit (1:13–14), who guarantees our glorification. This depiction of the salvation we have received is summarized in 1 Corinthians 1:30, where Paul identifies believers as being in Christ, that is, united with Christ, "who became to us wisdom from God, righteousness and sanctification and redemption."

FROM HEBER CARLOS DE CAMPOS JR.

Our Lord Jesus Christ shocked his disciples, who were either asking for power and authority or indignant at the ones who asked for it. He taught them that in his kingdom, the ones who are great are those who become servants and slaves to their brothers and sisters just like he did (Matt 20:20–28). This concept of "humbled royalty" is totally countercultural. But it is the way of the gospel. In the kingdom of God, the path to greatness is always a path of humility (Phil 2:5–11). This was the trajectory of Christ, the king first despised and later exalted. But Christ taught Peter that he would open the way for him to go through the same path (John 13:36). That is why the exalted Christ called Peter to follow him into a path of suffering (John 21:18–19). Peter takes this teaching and appeals to all his readers who share Christ's sufferings to embrace this suffering in the name of Christ as a blessing (1 Pet 4:12–14). But the blessing is not in the suffering itself, but in our Christian identity being clearly revealed and in the glory that awaits us. Therefore, we should understand that kingdom reality in this life is marked by service and suffering. We should embrace a calling to be despised in the name of Christ while we make his name great, not ours. This means that more than fighting for our own dignity, we strive to extol his dignity. More than nurturing high self-esteem, we nurture a high esteem for our king.

Everything we have received when we trusted our risen Lord is given to us out of the riches of his glory. Christ died for us. To make us alive with him and to seat us with him in the heavenly places, Christ united himself to us through the Holy Spirit by faith. For this reason, Paul says, "For you have died, and your life is hidden with Christ in God. When Christ who is your life appears, then you also will appear with him in glory" (Col 3:3–4). Paul can thus say "Christ in you, the hope of glory" (Col 1:27). Not only does Christ reign to give to others the gifts of peace, justice, and love, but he has also incorporated those who pledge allegiance to him into his own kingly office and his identity as king! When Peter writes about believers being "partakers of the divine nature" (2 Pet 1:4), he describes it in terms of personal intercommunion, that is, the mutual indwelling with the triune God believers have in Christ (see, e.g., John 14:20, 23). This means that our union with Christ and the intercommunion we have in Christ is effected by the Holy Spirit through faith, which is a conviction the Holy Spirit gives to us about the truth of Christ's gospel.[22] Our unity in Christ and participation in his kingly ministry is thus on the basis of God's grace. Unlike the familial nature of kingly succession in the past and ethnic favoring and nepotism among rulers in today's Ethiopia, believers are beneficiaries of Christ's gift, and we are also participants in the Giver, irrespective of our familial link, race, ethnicity, or socioeconomic status. "There is neither Jew nor Greek,

---

22. Berkhof, *Systematic Theology*, 503.

there is neither slave nor free, there is no male and female, for you are all one in Christ Jesus" (Gal 3:28).

Participation in Christ's Kingly Office

To an Ethiopian contemplating Christ's resurrection, ascension, and session in relation to the Holy Spirit and the life of the church, several ecclesiastical and cultural aspects come to mind. To affirm the notion of the kingship of Christ and its exercise over the church is to physically experience, to some degree, the burning incense of the Ethiopian Orthodox Tewahdo Church's liturgical service and the sound of chants and prayers in Ethiopic (Ge'ez), the church's ancient liturgical language. These features are evoked when reading of the union believers have with Christ and encountering the New Testament's profound teaching that Jesus Christ assumed true humanity, accomplishing our salvation through his death and resurrection (Luke 1:35; John 1:1–3, 14; Heb 2:14–18; 4:14–5:10) as our representative (Rom 5:12–21).

Like Paul, the Ethiopian also conceives of this union in terms of Christ's kingly ministry and in close conjunction with baptism (see the section below; cf. Rom 6:1–22; 1 Cor 10; Col 2:11–13). Although baptism and the notion of union with Christ is understood and articulated differently among the country's Orthodox, Lutheran, Baptist, independent Reformed, Pentecostal and New Apostolic Reformation circles, it is nevertheless connected to the kingly office of Christ through the praxis of the Lord's Supper.

In the New Testament, the triune God's indwelling of believers is discussed within a temporal framework of an "already" and "not yet" reality. Not only was the Spirit sent to the church by Christ with the Father on the Day of Pentecost, but he is also an aspect of the life of the church in the here and now. The presence and work of the Holy Spirit is an aspect of the church in the present and in a continuous sense. Furthermore, it is in the future, at Christ's return, that the Spirit's fullness will be revealed. Thus, as the body of Christ built on the foundation of Christ's death on the cross and the fact of his resurrection, the church is brought into being by the Spirit.

The life of the church, made possible and enlivened by the Holy Spirit, is an aspect of Christ's kingly ministry. The new life that Christ lives in us through his Spirit leads us to glorify God and continue what Paul calls our "ministry of reconciliation." All this is from God, who through Christ reconciled us to himself and gave us the ministry of reconciliation. In Christ, God was reconciling the world to himself, not counting their trespasses against them, and entrusting to us the message of reconciliation (2 Cor 5:18–19). In bearing witness to Christ the king and proclaiming the gospel, the church participates in Christ's kingly ministry of bringing those who belong to him under his headship. In the present, while awaiting the complete eradication of all evil, the church has a role within the advancing conquest of Christ as he "progressively subjugates his enemies, his Spirit working through his church."[23]

FROM HEBER CARLOS DE CAMPOS JR.

When the issue of participation in Christ's kingly office comes to the fore, it is of the utmost importance to distinguish how one mirrors the other and how they differ. Regarding the royal priesthood (1 Pet 2:9), there is certainly a way we function similarly to Christ the king. However, because his authority is intrinsic (received from his divine self) and not derived like ours, we must establish how Christ's office is unique. On the one hand, the universal priesthood of believers should lead to a universal kingship of believers. Scripture says that we shall reign with him (Rev 3:21; 5:10), we shall have our task of dominion and our ability to govern new creation restored. However, such dominion is "not yet" visible because Christ's work has not been consummated. Therefore, we must observe the differences between our performance and Christ's in the time between Christ's first and second coming, lest we rob him of his unique glory. And how could we rob him of his glory? Whenever we highlight the language of coparticipation, as if we were building, expanding, bringing, or establishing the kingdom, we give the impression that we are helpers and partners of the supreme Lord to advance his dominion. The language of building the kingdom alongside Jesus is unhelpful because it does not match the language of Scripture, where we see, enter, inherit,

---

23. Letham, *The Work of Christ*, 222.

or seek the kingdom—verbs that diminish our active participation to espouse a more receptive mode. Second, the language of the church as partners to establish the kingdom portrays a nonexistent dichotomy. It is not as if Christ had his part in building the kingdom and we have our part. The glory in bringing the kingdom is reserved to Christ alone, the supreme king, and it is not shared with his royal family. The stories of victories over Jericho (Josh 6), the Midianites (Judg 7) and the Assyrians (2 Kgs 19) do not portray heroes fighting alongside God but show men who trusted in the victory God alone would bring. That is why the theological language of *union* with Christ and *participation* with him is so precise. It does not separate the glory of Christ's accomplishment from our benefits, but it also does not dichotomize Christ's work and our work in the kingdom.

Biblical Interpretation of the *Andemta*

After stating a doctrine of the functional subordination of the Son and stating that Paul alludes to Christ's obedience to death on the cross in 1 Corinthians 15:28, the *Andəmta* on 1 Corinthians goes on to offer a verse-by-verse interpretation of the rest of the chapter with cross references from other New Testament passages. In the commentary on verses 44–49, the authors state,

> The First Adam is earthly as his origin is from the dust of the earth. But the Second Adam, Christ, is heavenly as he came from heaven. Just like Adam is earthly, we too are earthly. But like Christ is heavenly, we too are heavenly. Just like we have embodied the earthly Adam, we will embody the heavenly Christ. For being like Adam is partaking in death, but being in Christ is life prevailing through holiness.[24]

Here an aspect of the church's engagement with Christ's kingly ministry through evangelization or discipleship is not mentioned. However, the commentary goes some way in exploring the impact of Christ's work on the church by alluding to the corporate dimension of Christ's reign over

---

24. Ethiopian Orthodox Church, *Saint Paul's Book: Its Reading with Interpretation* (Addis Ababa: BerhanenaSelam, 2007), 192–93. My translation.

death and the implication for believers when Paul identifies Christ as the second Adam and head of the new humanity inaugurated through his death and resurrection (Rom 5:12–21). To understand how union with Christ is conceptualized by Ethiopian Christians, especially as it relates to believers' participation in Christ's victorious reign over cosmic enemies, it is important to consider how texts like Ephesians 6:10–20 are interpreted. Paul writes, "In all circumstances take up the shield of faith, with which you can extinguish all the flaming darts of the evil one" (6:16). The *Andəmta* on this verse states that it is through baptism that believers are given a shield of faith by God, thereby identifying believers' participation in Christ's kingly office with union with Christ. In connection with Christ's exaltation and glorification, the Bible provides a spatial aspect of Christ's reign as extending over the entire cosmos and specifically as garnering the subjugation of demonic beings (Eph 1:21; 3:10; cf. Phil 2:9). For the Ephesian *Andəmta* writers, one role the church plays as a representative of Christ's reign is to engage in battle with the evil one by upholding their trust in Christ.

Elaborating on this, the authors state that baptism enables Christians to resist the devil and emerge victorious over the enemy, who has been defeated by Christ's death and resurrection. In attributing Christ's victory to believers and thus indicating the outworking of Christians' participation in Christ's kingly office, the authors develop the fiery image Paul uses in Ephesians 6:16. While the devil shoots "a continually flaming and poison-laced arrow" on believers, "the one to whom God reveals His wisdom takes up baptismal water onto himself and his shield so that the flame is quenched by the water, the poison washed off. Just so, those who have received power through their baptism will be able to gain victory over the devil."[25]

Ethiopic Liturgy

The Ethiopian Orthodox Tewahdo Church generally identifies partaking in the Lord's Supper as bestowing the grace that "makes possible the unification of the faithful with Christ."[26] This unification through the

---

25. *Saint Paul's Book*, 292. My translation.
26. Andualem Dagmawi, "Theosis: Some Ideas of Deification as Reflected throughout the Ethiopic Divine Liturgy," *Collectanea Christiana Orientalia* 6 (2009): 63.

eucharistic liturgy is effected by the Holy Spirit and it entails believers' active participation in the continued offering from the cosmos to God (Ps 24:1; Rom 8:22; 2 Cor 5:17).[27] This is evident in the anaphora of St. John Son of Thunder:

> We ... beseech thee, Lord our God, as this bread which was scattered among the mountains and the little hills, in the forests and the vales, being gathered together, became one perfect bread, likewise gather us together, through thy divinity, out of all evil thought of sin into thy perfect faith. As with the mixture of this wine with water, the one cannot be separated from the other, so let thy divinity be united with our humanity, and our humanity with your divinity.[28]

Further elucidating the Spirit's role in believers' partaking of divine likeness, especially holiness and immortality, a prayer recited before the Lord's Supper states, "Grant us to be united through thy Holy Spirit, and heal us by this oblation that we may live in thee for ever."[29]

In sum, what we in the Protestant tradition call believers' union with Christ is an important doctrine for Ethiopian Christians. In our brief discussion so far, we have seen that the Holy Spirit is identified as effecting believers' participation in Christ and the important role ascribed to baptism and partaking of the Lord's Supper.

CONCLUSION

To Ethiopian Christians contemplating the royal imagery of the Old Testament, the shepherd-king who acts as God's viceregent in perfect obedience to God is significant for understanding the identity and work of Christ.

Christ's Lordship contrasts with sovereigns in Ethiopia and beyond, who demand the sacrifice of others for their good and sometimes for the common

---

27. Dagmawi, "Theosis," 57.

28. Marcos Daoud, trans., *Liturgy of the Ethiopian Church* (Cairo: Egyptian, 1959), 123.

29. Daoud, *Liturgy*, 76.

good. The *Andəmta* commentaries on Ezekiel or the Psalms do not apply Scripture's royal discourse to Ethiopia's monarchs. However, as an Ethiopian I cannot help but think of how our country's long history of imperfect ways of conceiving and exercising leadership and power sharply contrast with the biblical ideal of the king.

Unfortunately, despite the claim of divine approval and a Davidic-messianic descent going back to Jesus of Nazareth, the battles won by Ethiopian kings and emperors never managed to result in the bestowal of peace and social harmony. While victorious kings and their close contacts amassed wealth and ever-increasing authority, tensions often propagated by the nobility resulted in endless cycles of warfare, internal schisms, and oppression for the majority of Ethiopians. Many of the ethnic tensions and violent otherings contemporary Ethiopia has been struggling with for the past fifty years can be attributed to leaders and powerful men who correspond to the evil shepherds of Ezekiel 34.

In this regard, the image of the ideal shepherd-king and the image of God's anointed invested with God's authority and power have the practical import of transforming our notion of power and leadership and our view of our contested past. Through the lens of the royal prerogatives of generosity, goodwill, and reconciliation contained in these passages, we can evaluate and learn from our emperors and kings. However, it is important to acknowledge that no Ethiopian king could have done right as tainted by the fall as we all are. Instead, their frailties and evil intents antithetically point toward Christ the king, the one who is greater than all kings, past and present.

CONCLUSION

MICHAEL S. HORTON, ELIZABETH W. MBURU,
AND JUSTIN S. HOLCOMB

Over these chapters we have attempted to communicate together the diversity of witnesses to the one savior of the world: our everlasting prophet, priest, and king. On the one hand, one may stress the universal singularity of this gospel while neglecting the different ways people hear and convey this truth. On the other hand, one may emphasize diversity to the point of creating microtheologies that threaten the "one Lord, one faith, one baptism" that forms "one holy, catholic, and apostolic church." Genuine catholicity means unity in diversity and diversity in unity. As editors of this volume, we want to leave the reader with a brief word of appreciation to our contributors for their rich instruction and for modeling the paradigm we have in mind for this project.

MANY VOICES

The chapters in this volume have revealed that the understanding of the threefold office of Christ as prophet, priest, and king is influenced, either positively or negatively, by factors that stem from cultural, social, political, religious, and ecclesiastical contexts.

More than a prophet. Some of the diversity in how people hear the gospel is due to religious convictions. In contexts where Islam is the dominant religion, for example, Jesus is viewed as a great prophet but certainly not God incarnate. Jesus (or Isa) prepared the way for the greatest of all prophets, Muhammad. There are also socio-cultural factors. While most contexts represented in this volume have a notion of the concept of prophethood, and indeed there is some overlap between their understanding and that of Christ as prophet, it is not a one-to-one correspondence. Thus, while this forms a useful bridge, there is often a language barrier that makes translating christological concepts, generally from English, extremely difficult. Finding equivalent words that communicate the same thing is often so challenging that new words often need to be coined. In this instance, the form *prophet* should be retained because of its familiarity to many contexts in the Global South. However, when the referent is Christ, it must be imbued with new meaning that truly reflects the superior nature of Christ's prophethood.

A sociopolitical lens also can affect the way people interpret this office. The liberative features of Christ's prophethood are crucial, especially for those living under oppressive and unjust regimes. At the same time, we should beware of assimilating the uniqueness of Jesus's ministry to modern movements, even ones that may be worthy of support.

Interestingly, in some ecclesiastical contexts, the prophetic ministry of the church is acknowledged while Christ's prophetic office hardly receives mention. This is compounded by a basic lack of knowledge of Christian doctrine. This is a serious oversight as it bifurcates the ministry of Christ and that of the Holy Spirit, and any continuity is either assumed or ignored. An accurate biblical-theological understanding of Christ's prophetic office would go a long way in providing a balanced and holistic Christology (and, by implication, ecclesiology).

More than a priest. In some religious contexts, sin is viewed as moral-ritual impurity. This governs how priesthood, which is at the top of the hierarchy of persons, is understood. Purity is inherent in the priesthood, and this makes it possible for them to pass it on. However, there is always the possibility of contracting impurity. While the definition of sin may differ, purification in many traditional religious contexts is an essential aspect of the priesthood. From this religious perspective, the nature and role of Christ's priesthood can easily be accessed. However, it would be difficult to understand how Christ's priesthood would not require the endless rituals and/or rites needed to maintain purity. While there are many overlapping elements, a biblical-theological lens is needed to confront this contextual understanding and to show that the priesthood of Christ is superior. The understanding that all enlightened individuals could attain to a universal priesthood is a positive aspect in some religious contexts and coheres with the biblical concept of the priesthood of all believers. Nevertheless, it is important to stress that the priesthood of Christ is qualitatively different from that of his followers.

A holistic worldview in many cultures means that the priest handles both spiritual and physical issues. He serves as a mediator between the physical and spiritual realms. This enhances the understanding of Christ as priest over all dimensions of life. What is different is that Christ operates from a position of authority, and not one of trying to appease the spirits and ancestors. In some other contexts, religiopolitical issues influence how the office of priest is understood. Traditionally, the priesthood was an office that could only be held by the emperor or high-ranking officials. Thus, mediation between the human and the divine had both spiritual and political dimensions. An understanding of this mediatorial role provides a useful bridge to understanding Christ's priesthood. Nevertheless, it misses the point that Christ is both the priest and the atoning sacrifice and that he transcends all political categories.

More than a king. Sociocultural issues from the different contexts represented present challenges in recognizing Christ's supremacy as divine king as they often bleed into ecclesiastical traditions and practices. In some contexts, many assumptions underlying traditional beliefs and practices are often incorporated, sometimes with positive effects but often with negative ones. So, for instance, the worldviews of holism and dynamism are a bridge to understanding the existence of both spiritual and physical dimensions of life. However, they also provide answers for defenses against malevolent spirits that often breed fear of the spirit realm. This is seen particularly in those denominations that flourish partly because of the continuity between their beliefs and practices and these worldviews. The recognition that Christ is sovereign even over these malevolent spirits is oftentimes difficult to grasp.

An accurate understanding of the ultimate power that Christ holds as king over both the physical and spiritual realms would provide a much-needed balance.

While these ideals have some positive features, overestimating them frequently leads to an overrealized rather than an "already"/"not yet" eschatology, which diminishes the nature and extent of Christ's divine reign. Thus, while continuity serves as a valuable bridge, unless it is interrogated and measured against the biblical narrative, the sovereignty of Christ will inevitably be overlooked and misunderstood. In other contexts, Christ's kingship is distorted by political systems, whether colonial empires, egalitarian democracies, or totalitarian regimes. Christ as a greater king than David—even more, surpassing and contrasting with the rulers of this passing age—gives us corrective lenses to resist conforming the biblical story of a king on a cross to another chapter in abusive lordship. Sometimes, therefore, it is precisely in the gospel's *difference* from one's contextual experience that its power is evident.

We must point out that contextual intrusions are present wherever the church exists. Those that are identified above have some overlap as well as differences across the different regions represented. The picture of Christ that emerges when understood through these contexts reveals facets that sometimes enhance and at other times detract from a right understanding. Ultimately, when read together and refracted through the lens of Scripture, they provide a more robust picture of Christ's threefold office.

ONE SONG

"Who do people say that the Son of Man is?" This episode in Matthew 16:13–20 stands out as a turning point in the disciples' recognition of Jesus's identity. Jesus is an unsubstitutable character in the story of Israel, the mighty deeds of Yahweh, which also happens to determine the history of the whole world. If Jesus had appeared in Athens, some might have said Hercules, Apollo, or Dionysus. However, to comprehend the question and Peter's response, we must step into a story that seems at first quite alien to all of us who did not belong to the original audience. While remaining very important, all our contexts must be subordinated to the story of Israel as the context of the good news. Even the title Son of Man can be understood only in the light of the book of Daniel and its interpretation in the Judaism of Jesus's day. And notice the candidates: "They said, 'Some say John the Baptist, others say Elijah, and others Jeremiah or one of the prophets'" (Matt 16:14 ESV). Who are these three figures anyway? And why would the people have associated Jesus with their ministries? With each of these names came a flood of associations familiar to the Jews of Jesus's day.

Jesus congratulates Simon Peter on answering correctly: "You are the Christ, the Son of the living God" (16:16 ESV). This response, too, is pregnant with resonances forged by the promise-making and promise-keeping Yahweh of Israel. The word *Christ* means Messiah or Anointed One. God sent his people many deliverers, but only one fulfilled the many prophecies going all the way back to Genesis 3:15, the savior who would defeat the serpent. And sometimes the angels are called sons of God; Israel itself is called "my son" (Hos 11:1). But all of these other "christs" and "sons" are mere types pointing toward one candidate. The definite article in Matthew 16:16 makes all the difference: Jesus is *the* Christ (*ho Christos*) and *the Son* of the living God (*ho Huios tou Theou tou zōntos*). How is it that the second person of the Trinity, of exactly the same essence as the Father and the Holy Spirit, was born in Bethlehem, crucified on Golgotha, and rose again for our salvation? Mary herself asked this question—"How will this be?"—when Gabriel brought her the announcement (Luke 1:34). It is the mystery of all mysteries: God in flesh, upholding all things by the word of his power even as he is thirsty; sovereign over all cosmic and political powers, even as he submits to cruelty and crucifixion to purchase the redemption of the ungodly.

Jesus could not have become incarnate just anywhere and anytime: "When the fullness of time had come, God sent forth his Son, born of woman, born under the law, to redeem those who were under the law, so that we might receive adoption as sons" (Gal 4:4–5 ESV). We have to be immersed in the unfamiliar particularity of Israel's history in order to see the impact of his being "the Christ, the Son of the living God" for the world (Matt 16:16 ESV). At the end of the day, there is no dynamic equivalent for

Jesus. He breaks all molds and fulfills the messianic mold of the Hebrew prophets.

As it turns out, all of us—everywhere and in all times—are "born under the law," condemned as transgressors (Gal 4:4). Yet the blessing of the Christ is as universal as the curse. Justified by Christ's righteousness as a gift, apart from the law, we now form a new nation, the body of Christ:

> Therefore remember that at one time you Gentiles in the flesh, called "the uncircumcision" by what is called the circumcision, which is made in the flesh by hands—remember that you were at that time separated from Christ, alienated from the commonwealth of Israel and strangers to the covenants of promise, having no hope and without God in the world. But now in Christ Jesus you who once were far off have been brought near by the blood of Christ. For he himself is our peace, who has made us both one and has broken down in his flesh the dividing wall of hostility by abolishing the law of commandments expressed in ordinances, that he might create in himself one new man in place of the two, so making peace, and might reconcile us both to God in one body through the cross, thereby killing the hostility. And he came and preached peace to you who were far off and peace to those who were near. For through him we both have access in one Spirit to the Father. So then you are no longer strangers and aliens, but you are fellow citizens with the saints and members of the household of God, built on the foundation of the apostles and prophets, Christ Jesus himself being the cornerstone, in whom the whole structure, being joined together, grows into a holy temple in the Lord. In him you also are being built together into a dwelling place for God by the Spirit. (Eph 2:11–22 ESV)

In addition, this singular message comes to diverse peoples across many times and places. Whether we recognize it or not, we all hear this message in our own skin, as it were, shaped by different cultural-linguistic, social, and personal histories. While affirming one catholic and evangelical faith, we also come from different traditions of Christ's body—Baptists, Presbyterians, Lutherans, Anglicans, and Independents. In these pages we have heard some of these differences. Whether it is cultural or ecclesial diversity, we can only grow together by listening to each other, learning from each other, deepening our own understanding of our distinctive convictions. In my own culture, Jesus has been adapted to nonbiblical narratives. "Who do people say that the Son of Man is?" Some say a cosmic therapist, moral teacher, miracle worker, or political mascot. If we do not know how we hear the gospel, it is difficult to interrogate presuppositions that keep us from understanding and embracing it truly. By hearing how these claims of Christ are heard in South Asian, East Asian, African, Middle Eastern, Central and South American, European, and North American environments, my awareness of my own worldview has been enriched. More importantly, my appreciation for Christ's threefold ministry has expanded.

Significantly, after Peter's confession, Jesus says,

> "Blessed are you, Simon Bar-Jonah! For flesh and blood has not revealed this to you, but my Father who is in heaven. And I tell you, you are Peter, and on this rock I will build my church, and the gates of hell shall not prevail against it. I will give you the keys of the kingdom of heaven, and whatever you bind on earth shall be bound in heaven, and whatever you loose on earth shall be loosed in heaven." (Matt 16:17–19 ESV)

A play on Peter's name, this "rock" on which Jesus builds his church is this simple confession of faith. By this very specific word of the gospel, Christ creates faith and builds his church. From the most particular—a fetus in the womb of a Jewish virgin—the sovereign Son of God spreads his reign of grace to every people on earth. Through this proclamation of Jesus as God's true and final prophet, priest, and king, the dungeons filled with Satan's prisoners are liberated. Refreshed by his word, baptized into him, and nourished by his table, emaciated souls raise their voices, singing, "You are the Christ, the Son of the living God"!

FOR FURTHER READING

Ames, William. "The Office of Christ," and "The Application of Christ." In *The Marrow of Theology*, translated by John D. Eusden, vol. 1, 131–34, and 149–52. Grand Rapids: Baker, 1997.

Aquinas, Thomas. *Summa Theologiae* I, question 22, article 1. Translated by Fathers of the Dominican Province. New York: Benzinger, 1947.

Bavinck, Herman. *Reformed Dogmatics.* Volume 3, *Sin and Salvation in Christ*, 367–68, 473–74. Grand Rapids: Baker, 1883–1901, 2006.

———. *Reformed Dogmatics.* Volume 4, *Holy Spirit, Church, and New Creation*, edited by John Bolt, translated by John Vriend, 685. Grand Rapids: Baker Academic, 2008.

Berkhof, Louis, *Systematic Theology*, 356–57. 1932. Repr., Grand Rapids: Eerdmans, 1996.

Berkouwer, G. C. *The Work of Christ*, 85–86. Grand Rapids: Eerdmans, 1965.

Beza, Theodore. *A Little Book of Christian Questions and Responses*, edited by Dikran Y. Hadidian, translated by Kirk M. Summers, Princeton Theological Monograph Series, 9. Eugene, OR: Pickwick, 1986.

———. *The Christian Faith.* London: James Dickson, 2016.

Calvin, John. *Institutes of the Christian Religion.* Edited by J. T. McNeill. Translated by Ford Lewis Battles. 2 vols. Philadelphia: Westminster, 1960. See book 2.15.

———. "Catechism of Geneva." In *Calvin: Theological Treatises*, edited by J. K. S. Reid, Library of Christian Classics, 95–96. 1954. Repr., Louisville: Westminster John Knox, 2006.

Cyril of Jerusalem. "Commentary on the Creed." In *The Catechetical Lectures of S. Cyril, Archbishop of Jerusalem, Translated, With Notes and Indices.* Oxford: Parker, Rivington, 1838.

Eusebius. *Ecclesiastical History*, 1.3. Translated by Arthur Cushman McGiffert. In *Nicene and Post-Nicene Fathers*, second series, vol. 1, edited by Philip Schaff and Henry Wace, 86. Buffalo, NY: Christian Literature, 1890.

Flavel, John. *Christ and His Threefold Office*. Grand Rapids: Reformation Heritage, 2021. See especially part 1.

The Heidelberg Catechism. Tiffin, OH: Good, 1879. See Question and Answer 31.

Hodge, A. A. "The Offices of Christ," Monergism, https://www.monergism.com/offices-christ.

Hubernius, Caspar. "A Comforting Sermon on the Resurrection of Christ, Useful for Those Weak in Faith to Read, 1525." In *Early Protestant Spirituality*, edited by Scott H. Hendrix and Bernard McGinn, translated by Scott H. Hendrix, Classics of Western Spirituality 113–14. Mahwah, NJ: Paulist, 2009.

John of Damascus. *An Exposition of the Orthodox Faith*, book 4, translated by E.W. Watson and L. Pullan. In *Nicene and Post-Nicene Fathers*, second series, vol. 9, edited by Philip Schaff and Henry Wace. Buffalo, NY: Christian Literature, 1899.

Luther, Martin. "On Christian Freedom (1520)." In *First Principles of the Reformation*, translated by H. Wace and C. A. Buckheim. Philadelphia, 1885.

Justin Martyr. *The Dialogue with Trypho*. Translated by Thomas B. Falls. Selections from the Fathers of the Church, Vol. 3. Revised and with a new introduction by Thomas P. Halton. Edited by Michael Slusser. Washington, DC: Catholic University of America Press, 2003. See chapter 86.

Schaff, Philip. *The Person of Christ: The Miracle of History*, 3–4. Michigan Historical Reprint Series. New York: Charles Scribner, 1866.

———. "Jesus Christ, Threefold Office Of: A Phrase Connoting the Functions of Christ as Prophet, Priest, and King." In *The New Schaff-Herzog Encyclopedia of Religious Knowledge*, vol. 6. Innocente-Liudger. https://www.ccel.org/s/schaff/encyc/encyc06/htm/iii.lvii.v.htm.

Sibbes, Richard. "The Sun of Righteousness." In *The Works of Richard Sibbes*. Edited by Alexander Grosart. Edinburgh: Banner of Truth, Repr. 2001.

Spurgeon, Charles H. "It Is Finished." In *Majesty in Misery*, volume 3, *Calvary's Mournful Mountain*, 218–20. Carlisle, PA: Banner of Truth, 2005.

Turretin, Francis. *Institutes of Elenctic Theology*, 3 volumes, edited by James T. Dennison Jr., translated by George Musgrave Giger, 292–93. Phillipsburg, NJ: P&R 1994.

Warfield, B. B. "The Glorified Christ." In *The Saviour of the World*, 185–86. 1916. Repr., Carlisle, PA: Banner of Truth, 1991.

Westminster Confession of Faith. Free Presbyterian Press, 1995. See Question 23.

LIST OF CONTRIBUTORS

SOFANIT T. ABEBE teaches the New Testament and Greek at Oak Hill College in London having previously served as lecturer and dean of students at the Ethiopian Graduate School of Theology, Ethiopia. She earned a PhD in New Testament and Christian origins from the University of Edinburgh. Sofanit is the author of *Apocalyptic Spatiality in 1 Peter and Selected 1 Enoch Literature: A Comparative Analysis* and coeditor of *Reading Hebrews and 1 Peter from Majority World Perspectives*.

HEBER CARLOS DE CAMPOS JR. is professor of historical theology at Andrew Jumper Graduate Center in Sao Paulo, Brazil, and director of the Jonathan Edwards Center Brazil. He holds a PhD in historical theology from Calvin Theological Seminary. Campos is the author of *Doctrine in Development: Johannes Piscator and Debates over Christ's Active Obedience*.

HAVILAH DHARAMRAJ is faculty in Old Testament at the South Asia Institute of Advanced Christian Studies in Bangalore, India. She earned a PhD in Old Testament from the University of Durham. Her areas of academic interest, in which she has published widely, are Old Testament narrative, reception-centered intertextuality that engages texts across the biblical canon, and comparative literature, which converses biblical texts with the sacred texts of other faiths.

NELSON MORALES FREDES is professor of New Testament and dean/provost at the Seminario Teológico Centroamericano in Guatemala. He received his PhD in Theological Studies and New Testament at Trinity International

University. He is the author of *Poor and Rich in James: A Relevance Theory Approach to James's Use of the Old Testament*, the coauthor of *Introducción al griego bíblico*, and the editor of *Buenas Nuevas desde América Latina*.

JUSTIN S. HOLCOMB is the bishop of the Episcopal Diocese of Central Florida and teaches theology and apologetics at Reformed Theological Seminary. He earned a PhD from Emory University. He is the author, coauthor, or editor of more than twenty books on theology, abuse, and biblical studies, including *Know the Creeds and Councils*, *Know the Heretics*, and *Rid of My Disgrace*. He is also the series editor for the Know series with Zondervan and the Christian Theologies series with New York University Press.

MICHAEL S. HORTON is the J. Gresham Machen Professor of Systematic Theology and Apologetics at Westminster Seminary California, founder and editor-in-chief of Sola Media, and host of the *White Horse Inn*, a weekly roundtable podcast on theology and culture. He earned a PhD from Wycliffe Hall, Oxford and Coventry University. He is the author of more than thirty books, including *Justification: Volumes 1 and 2* in Zondervan Academic's New Studies in Dogmatics and *The Christian Faith: A Systematic Theology for Pilgrims on the Way*.

WILSON JEREMIAH is a full-time lecturer in systematic theology at Southeast Asia Bible Seminary in Malang, East Java, Indonesia. He earned his PhD from Trinity Evangelical Divinity School. He is a Langham scholar who is committed to equipping a new generation of Bible teachers and serving the global church through training more pastors to become pastor-theologians.

ARUTHUCKAL VARUGHESE JOHN is professor of theology and the dean of faculty at the South Asia Institute of Advanced Christian Studies, Bengaluru, India. He received his PhD in philosophy from the University of Madras in Kierkegaard studies. He is the author of *Indian Secularism and Religious Freedom: Mapping the Cross-Pressures* as well as *Truth and*

Subjectivity, Faith and History: Kierkegaard's Insights for Christian Faith. In addition to his role at SAIACS, he is an associate with Oxford House Research, a networking team member with the International Fellowship for Mission as Transformation, and a member of the Theology Working Group with the Lausanne Movement. Varughese is also an ordained minister of the St. Thomas Evangelical Church of India.

ELIZABETH W. MBURU is an associate professor of New Testament and Greek at Africa International University, Kenya, and the Langham Literature Regional Coordinator, Anglophone Africa. She holds a PhD in New Testament from Southeastern Baptist Theological Seminary. Her research and publishing interests are primarily in the areas of New Testament, Intercultural Hermeneutics, Bible Translation, and Culture and Worldview Studies. She is the author of several works, including *Qumran and the Origins of Johannine Language and Symbolism* and *African Hermeneutics*, and has edited several projects.

WAGEEH MIKHAIL is Christianity and Islam director of engagement with scholar leaders and formerly the director of the Center for Middle Eastern Christianity at Evangelical Theological Seminary in Cairo. He holds a PhD in Arab Christian Theology from the University of Birmingham and master's degrees in theology from Westminster Theological Seminary and Calvin Theological Seminary. He has served within the Presbyterian Church and seminary in Egypt. Dr. Mikhail has published and translated seven books covering a wide range of theological topics.

THOMAS PARK has been a theological educator in Taiwan since 2021. His role is to assist CELC (China Evangelical Lutheran Church) with theological education and help start a Lutheran theological seminary in Chiayi, Taiwan. He holds a PhD in missiology from Concordia Theological Seminary. He previously served as a theology professor at Concordia University and as a pastor in Lutheran congregations in Minnesota, Wisconsin, Indiana, California, Montreal, and Seoul. He belongs to the Lutheran Church–Missouri Synod (LCMS).

SHAO KAI ("ALEX") TSENG earned his DPhil from the University of Oxford. He is a Taiwanese-Canadian scholar currently serving as research professor of philosophy at Zhejiang University, China. He has published extensively in Chinese, English, and German in areas ranging from theology and philosophy to musicology.

SCRIPTURE INDEX

Genesis

1:26–28 240
2 210
2–3 120
2:4–25 157
2:10–14 157
2:15 158
2:17 123
3:1–5 116
3:6 123
3:14–15 123
3:15 . . . . 11, 241, 259
3:17–19 . . . . 210, 221
3:18 123
3:24 157
12:1–3 25
12:2 170
14 155
14:13 155
14:18 . . . . 82, 156
14:18–20 . . . . 82, 83
14:19–20 156
14:22 156
14:24 156
15 11
15:18 169
17:16 244
18:1–33 15
19:1 15
21:27–30 156
24:7 . . . . 13, 15
32:22–32 15
34:15 5
49:10–12 237

Exodus

7:1–2 8
13:21 7
15 170
17:6 17
18:12 156
19 12
20 12
20:3–5 218
20:19 5
20:19–21 12
23:23 15
24 230
24:1–11 156
24:3 230
24:5–6 230
24:8 230
24:10 (LXX) 230
24:16 . . . . 6, 7
25:18–22 157
25:40 84
28 128
28:1 158
29:21 122
32–34 13
32:34 15
33:2 15
33:22 17
34:29 6
40:12–15 208
40:35 6
40:38 7

Leviticus

1:3–4 230
2:2 154
2:3 154
2:9 154
2:10 154
2:16 154
8–9 128
8:34 128
9:23–24 128
13–14 151
13:45 134
13:46 134
14:2 135
14:3 135
14:4–31 135
15 . . . . 135, 137
15:30 136
16 84
18 130
21 . . . . 116, 146
21:1–3 137
21:11 137
21:12 137
21:21 . . . . 145, 153

Numbers

6:24–26 161
12:6–8 4
18:5 153
19 . . . . 136, 137
19:12 137
24:17–19 237
36:13 3

Deuteronomy

17 215
17:15 . . . . .215, 243
17:16–17 215
18:5 3
18:9–22 4
18:14–15 12
18:14–22 . . . . 3, 4
18:15 . . . . . . 4, 7, 16, 62, 71
18:15–18 174
18:15–22 . . . . 12, 25
18:16 5
18:17–18 12
18:18 . . . . 4, 7, 71
18:22 4
21:23 142
34:10 . . . . 4, 5
34:12 16

Joshua

6 250
18:2 3

Judges

7 250

1 Samuel

2:12–17 130
7 176
8 176
10:1, 20–25 231
13:7–14 115
15:29 82
16:13 231
24:4–7 231
26:8–10 231

2 Samuel

2:4 231
6:3–8 122
6:12–19 82
7 11
7:1–4 169
7:5–8 169
7:5–16 169

7:8 169
7:8–11 170
7:9–11 170
7:11 170
7:11–16 170
7:12 170
7:12–14 . . . . 234, 241
7:13 . . . . .170, 171, 208
7:14 . . . . .171, 240
7:15 171
7:16 . . . . .208, 236
7:17 171
8:18 82
13:20 15
16:1–2 172
17:27–29 156

1 Kings

1:34, 39 231
5–6 170
8 82
8:22–53 231
12:33 115
13:18 . . . . 13, 15

2 Kings

4:32–37 8
9:13 173
11:12 231
19 250

1 Chronicles

21:16 15
22:2–5 170
28:2–3, 63 170

2 Chronicles

26:16–21 115

Psalms

2 241
2:1–3 233
2:2 233
2:2–3 241
2:6–7 . . . . .208, 215

2:6–8 234
2:6–9 234
2:7 241
2:7–8 240
2:8–10 234
3:3 234
3:4 234
8 . . . . .210, 220
8:4–6 240
8:6 241
8:7 (LXX) 241
16:8 (LXX) 234
18:50 233
20:2 (LXX) 234
20:6 233
20:7–8 (LXX) 234
24 . . . . .220, 234
24:1 . . . . 185, 252
24:7–10 234
33:6 10
44:4 (LXX) 234
45:5 233
45:6 208
45:6–7 215
46:4 157
51:11 231
60:5 (LXX) 234
61:9 (LXX) 234
62:4 (LXX) 234
62:9 (LXX) 234
69:4 233
72:1–4a 237
72:3–16 233
72:4b, 8–11 237
72:15–16 237
72:16–17 234
74 13
74:9–12, 21–22 14
76:2 155
78:72 230
88:26–27 (LXX) 241
88:27–29 (LXX) 234
89:20–37 234
89:35–37 208
93 220

99 220
99:6. 82
101:5–8 234
109:1. 241
109:1–4 234
109:2–3 241
109:3. 233
110 . . . . .81, 83, 223
110:1. . . . . 83, 84, 217, 240
110:1–2 233
110:1, 4 81
110:2. 234
110:4 . .82, 83, 84, 156, 208
110:4–7 82
110:5. 83
118 173
132:15 237
143:1 (LXX),
  10 (LXX) 234
144:12–14. 237

Isaiah
2:2. 179
2:6. 12
5 17
6:1. 215
8:14. 17
8:18. 19
9:7. 234
11:3–5 234
11:4–5 237
11:6–9 237
11:12, 16 236
19:18–25 236
24:18–19, 23. 191
25:6–8 179
30:18–26. 25
40 5
42 5
42:1. 215
44:6–8 10
44:8 17
49 5
52:13–53:12 8
53 89

53:4–6 143
53:6. 236
55:11. 10
61 5
61:1. . . . . . . 184, 190, 215
62:11. 172
63:9. 15
65:17. 183

Jeremiah
6:13. 129
23 . . . . .15, 18, 25
23:16–17 11
23:17. 234
23:18. 15
23:18–22. 12
23:29 10
27:9. 12
29:8. 12
31 11
31:31–34 . . . . .84, 85
31:31–37 179
50:36 12

Ezekiel
16:60, 63 14
24:14. 82
34 . . . . . . 15, 18, 236, 253
34:11–31 . . . . .15, 18
34:23–24. 236
34:25 236
47:1. 157
47:1–12 157

Daniel
2:44 208
7 . . . . .8, 176
7:14. . . . . .208, 234
7:18. 208
7:27. 241
7:27a 208
12:2. 8

Hosea
6:9. 129

11:1. 259

Joel
2:28–32 . . . . .25, 179

Amos
3:7. 11

Micah
3:11. 129
5:2–5 234

Zephaniah
3:4. 129

Zechariah
3 15
3:1–3. 15
3:1–10 15
6:12–13 82
9:9. 172
9:9–10 . . . . .172, 234
10:2. 12
13:2. 133

Malachi
1:6. 129
1:6–14 146
3:1. . . . . 8, 15
4:5. . . . . .6, 8, 62

Matthew
1:1. 171
1:22. 14
2:1–12 190
2:2. 189
2:13, 16 191
3:1–13 17
3:17. 16
4:2. 158
4:4. . . . . 19, 91
5:1–7:29. 73
5:14–16 35
5:17. 14
5:17–7:27. 17

5:21 73
5:21–48 73
5:22 73
5:27 73
5:27–30 73
5:27–32 74
5:28 73
5:31 73
5:31–32 73
5:32 73
5:33 73
5:34 73
5:38 73
5:39 . . . . 73, 196
5:43 73
5:44 . . . . 73, 196
5:48 238
6:9–10 . . . . 159, 194
6:11–13 159
7:28–29 17
7:29 14
9:18 137
9:25 137
11:1–19 17
11:3 190
11:5 190
11:28 236
12:1–8 75
12:9–14 74
12:28 216
12:29 221
12:32 178
13:16–17 74
13:24–43 186
13:28 186
13:30 186
13:49 178
14:6 180
14:19–21 172
15:1 171
16:13–20 258
16:14 . . . . 16, 259
16:16 259
16:17–19 261
17:1–13 5

17:5 16
17:10–13 17
17:11 180
17:23 189
19:1–12 74
19:3–12 74
19:28 . . . . 178, 180
20:20–28 246
20:22 177
20:25 196
20:25–28 . . . . 177, 209
20:26–28 196
20:28 173
21 17
21:1 171
21:1–9 217
21:1–11 171
21:4 172
21:4–5 172
21:6–7 172
21:8 173
21:9 173
21:11 . . . . 14, 172, 174
21:12–17 . . . . 17, 189
21:18–22 17
21:33–42 17
21:43–44 17
21:45–46 18
21:46 14
22:15–22 195
22:44 81
24 14
24:3 178
25:35–40 190
26:6–13 . . . . 184, 191
26:17–29 142
26:64–66 20
27:27 142
27:52 138
27:62 142
28 225
28:11–15 76
28:16–20 20
28:18 . . . . 185, 231
28:20 224

Mark
1:1–3 45
1:11 7
1:23–27 133
1:24 134
1:27 133
1:34 133
1:41 . . . . 134, 135
1:42 135
2:7 20
2:23–28 75
3:1–6 74
3:5 75
3:11 134
3:22–30 134
4:19 178
5 135
5:1 135
5:2–13 134
5:3 134
5:9 134
5:13 134
5:20 135
5:28 136
5:35 137
6:4 16
6:14–16 16
7:1–23 132
7:24–25 134
7:37 165
8:27–28 16
8:29 7
8:38 . . . . 6, 178
9:1–13 6
9:2 5
9:2–13 5
9:5–6 6
9:7 7
9:8 7
9:9 7
9:10 7
9:11 8
9:11–12 6
9:20 134
9:26 134

9:31................ 189
9:37................. 6
9:45................. 6
10 177
10:30 178
10:35–45 178
11:7................ 172
11:10.............. 173
12:36 81
14:12–25 142
14:25............... 226
14:29–31 186
15:2................ 189
15:16.............. 142
15:42 142

Luke
1:11–38 15
1:32................ 236
1:33................ 208
1:34................ 259
1:35...........184, 248
1:46–48............. 72
1:46–55 72
1:47–55 190
1:50................ 72
1:50–51a 72
1:51–53 72
1:51b............... 72
1:52................ 72
1:53................ 72
1:54................ 72
2:1–7 190
2:7................. 158
2:34................ 191
2:40 158
2:52................ 158
3:21–22 217
4:16–24 215
4:18...........184, 191
4:18–21 217
4:21................ 184
4:25................ 191
4:31–37, 41 191
5:12–14 151

5:12–16 191
6:1–5 75
6:6–11 74
6:7................. 75
7:15................ 138
7:16................ 14
7:21................ 191
7:22................ 236
7:48–49 17
8:26–39 191
8:49................ 137
9:28................. 6
9:28–36 5
9:37–42 191
10:2................ 33
10:18............... 216
10:23–24............ 74
10:31–32 137
13:28 189
13:33............... 14
15:4–5 236
17:20–21 184
18:1–8 191
18:30............... 178
18:35–43........... 191
19:14............... 176
19:35............... 172
19:38 173
20:35 178
20:42 81
20:46–47........... 191
21:1–4 191
21:6................ 189
22:7–23 142
22:19 160
22:29 223
23:54 142
24:19 14
24:25–27.........18, 178
24:27 6
24:45–47............ 76
24:48–49............ 76

John
1:1–3............16, 248

1:1–4 158
1:1–5............... 10
1:11................ 114
1:14........ 158, 235, 248
1:17................ 16
1:21–23 14
1:29.............88, 144
1:32................ 184
1:33................ 184
1:45................ 5, 6
2:13–17 217
2:19–21 111
3:2................. 14
3:8................. 198
3:16................ 89
3:17................ 215
4:19................ 14
4:25................. 5
4:34................ 223
5:15, 18............. 20
5:30................ 223
5:39................ 18
5:45–47 5
6:14.............. 14, 174
6:38................ 223
7:40................ 14
8:12................ 204
9:17................ 14
10:11, 14 236
10:18............... 89
10:33............... 20
11:25............... 204
11:39............... 138
12:13 173
12:31–33 .... 217, 221
12:32 ....87, 177
12:41 215
13 178
13:36 246
14–16 20
14:6...........18, 19, 204
14:17............... 198
14:20, 23 247
15:13–15 .... 117, 124
15:18............... 124

16:14 238
17:2, 4 223
17:5 . . . . 7, 223
17:9 89
17:15 41
17:21 237
17:24–26 226
18:10–11 186
18:11 196
19:15 176
19:20–21 189
19:31 142
19:42 142
20:22 25
21:18–19 247

Acts

1:8 76
2:17 179
2:17–21 25
2:22–24 176
2:33–35 217
2:33–36 237
2:34–36 81
3:2, 5 4
3:6 183
3:18–24 16
3:21 180
3:22–23 5
3:22–24 8
4:2 18
4:12 183
7:37 5
8:16 183
9 162
9:15 183
9:20 18
10:38 . . . . 190, 231
17:22 162
17:22–31 162
17:28 163
17:30–31 163
17:32–34 164
20:27 32
22:28 162

Romans

1:1–3 18
1:3–4 . . . . 238, 240
1:4 . . . . 215, 240
1:26–27 123
2:15 131
3:20 90
3:26 88
4:25 . . . . 19, 238
5:1 179
5:12–21 . . . . 240, 248, 251
5:20 91
6:1–22 248
6:1–23 238
7 185
8:9 241
8:12 179
8:12–17 241
8:14–23 240
8:15 . . . . 184, 241
8:17 241
8:18–25 . . . . 180, 184
8:20–22 210
8:22 252
8:23 184
8:28–30 201
8:29 . . . . 29, 241
8:29–30 240
8:35 242
8:36 242
8:37 242
8:38 242
9:33 17
10:1–17 20
14:17 194
16:20 241

1 Corinthians

1:2 184
1:30 246
2:6 178
3:21–23 241
6:3 221
10 248
10:4 17

10:11 178
10:16 160
12:3 10
12:12–26 237
12:13 124
15 . . . . . 212, 213, 224, 225
15:22 . . . . 90, 223
15:23 225
15:24 . . 208, 210, 223, 225
15:24–26 223
15:24–28 . . . 208, 214, 218,
220, 223, 224
15:25 . . . . 223, 225
15:26 223
15:27 223
15:28 . . . . . . 223, 225, 250
15:35–36 238
15:42–45 223
15:44–49 250
15:56–57 89

2 Corinthians

1:20 10
2:14 202
3:7, 13 7
3:18 202
4:4 . . . . 24, 179
4:5 18
4:16 180
5:17 . . . 183, 185, 195, 252
5:18–19 249
5:18–20 228
5:20 . . . . 25, 183
5:21 183

Galatians

1:4 . . . . 178, 179
3:8 25
3:13 142
3:28 . . . . 124, 248
3:29 244
4:4 260
4:4–5 . . . . 19, 259
4:6 241
4:7 244

6:4–7 241
6:16................. 25

Ephesians
1:3–11 179
1:3–14 246
1:4............216, 246
1:4–5 89
1:5................. 246
1:7............184, 246
1:8................. 246
1:9–10 197
1:10................ 246
1:11................ 246
1:13–14 ....195, 246
1:19–20 228
1:20...........228, 241
1:20–23 241
1:21............178, 251
1:22............... 241
2:1.................. 90
2:1–5 241
2:6–7 242
2:11–22 260
3 196
3:6................. 197
3:10.............. 251
3:17............... 216
4 64
4:1–16 237
4:4................ 119
4:5–6 119
4:11..............32, 64
4:24 ....29, 184
4:30............... 184
5:1–2.............. 194
5:16............... 201
5:27............... 224
6 241
6:10............... 228
6:10–20 ....218, 251
6:11....... 227, 228, 241
6:12............... 228
6:13....... 227, 228, 241
6:14............... 227

6:16................. 251
6:17................ 227
6:20................ 227

Philippians
1:6................. 201
2:3–4 209
2:3–8 183
2:5.................. 88
2:5–11 246
2:7................. 117
2:8................. 193
2:8–11 181
2:9................. 251
2:9–11 ..... 193, 208, 217
3:4–6 162
3:5................ 162
4:6................. 159

Colossians
1:13–14 245
1:15............... 24
1:15–16 16
1:15–17 ....10, 245
1:16–17 205
1:20.............. 245
1:27.............. 247
2:6–7 65
2:11–13 248
2:13–15 ....89, 221
2:15..............75, 217
3:3–4 247
3:10............... 29
3:17.............. 183
4:5................. 201

1 Thessalonians
5:23–24 184

1 Timothy
2:5............215, 232
3:15................ 33
4:1................. 179
5:17................ 32
6:12............... 227
6:19............... 178

2 Timothy
2:3–4 227
3:1................. 179
4:7................. 227
4:8, 18 228

Philemon
15–16.............. 199

Hebrews
1:1–4 45
1:2............... 19, 179
1:3...............24, 84
1:4................. 85
1:8................. 15
1:8–9 215
1:13................ 81
2 212
2:5–8 ...... 208, 210, 220
2:8................. 220
2:9................. 215
2:13................ 19
2:14...........217, 220
2:14–18 248
2:15–16 220
2:17.............83, 220
2:17–18 220
3:1–6 16
3:2, 5 4
4:14–5:10........83, 248
4:14–7:28......... 84
4:15........131, 155, 158
5 215
5:1................. 215
5:4–5 208
5:5–10 82
5:6–10 81
5:9................. 85
6:4–5 179
6:5................ 178
6:19–7:28 82
7 ....91, 155, 156
7:4–9 82
7:11................ 145
7:11–12 85

7:11–18. 84
7:11–28 81
7:17. 155
7:21–26 85
7:24. . . . . 165, 208
7:26. 143
7:27–28 85
7:28. 85
8:1. 84
8:1–6 . . . . 83, 84
8:1–13 16
8:2. 84
8:3. 85
8:4. 85
8:5. 84
8:6. 85
8:10–12 85
8:13. 85
9:1–11 111
9:8–11 111
9:11. . . . . 111, 143
9:15. 85
9:26–28 111
10:1. 124
10:1–23 94
10:2. 84
10:8–10 158
10:10. 85
10:11–23 159
10:12–13 218
10:18. 84
10:20 111
11:19. 8
12:2. . . . . 84, 194, 223

James
5:16. 159

1 Peter
1:2. 191
1:10–12 18
1:11. 14
1:19–20 216

1:20. 89
2:1–10 25
2:4–10 191
2:8. 17
2:9. . . . . 29, 249
2:9–10 161
2:11. . . . . 186, 228
2:11–12 210
2:12–14 186
2:15. 186
2:16. 209
2:17. 210
2:21. . . . . 183, 194
2:21–23 183
2:24 143
3:14–15 195
3:15. . . . . 118, 164
3:21–22 238
3:22. 218
4:12–14 . . . . 183, 247
5:8. 218
5:9. 228

2 Peter
1:4. . . . . 239, 247
1:21. 8
2:20. 186
3:3. 179
3:5–7 238
3:10–13 186
3:12. 194
3:13. 221

1 John
1:1. 27
1:1–4 20
1:5. 143
2:20. 231
2:20–22 20
2:27. 231
3:2. 195
3:8. 221
5:18. 218

Jude
3 65

Revelation
1:4–8 19
1:5. 219
1:6. 193
2:10. 227
3:14. 19
3:21. . . . . 228, 249
5 91
5:2. 222
5:3. 222
5:5. 219
5:6. 87
5:8–12 219
5:9. 176
5:9–10 193
5:10. . . . . 193, 228, 249
5:12. 219
6:15–17 217
7:10. 87
7:13–14 227
7:17. 224
11:15. . . . . 208, 219
12:10. 227
12:10–11 217
13:7. 227
14:13. 227
17:14. 219
19:10. 221
19:11–16 219
20:6 193
20:11–15 218
21:1–22:5. 158
21:5. 226
21:22–23. 224
21:23 225
22:1, 3 226
22:5. 193
22:12–13. 220
22:16. 222
22:20 222

SUBJECT INDEX

Aaron, 8, 12, 128
'Abd al-Malik Ibn Marwān, 50
'Abd al- Raḥmān ibn 'Abd al- Malik ibn
    Ṣāliḥ al- Hāshimī, 51–52
Abimelek, 156
Abraham, 155, 244
Abrahamic covenant, 11
Abram, 155, 156
absolution, 160
Adam
    as earthly, 250
    entrance of sin and death to the world
        through, 90, 240
    as image of God, 29, 90
    Jesus as last, 88, 92, 213, 223
    Jesus as new, 19
    as prototype of the priesthood, 157
    rejection of God as King, 90, 91
    second, 158
Africa
    churches in, 23, 40
    and divinity of Jesus, 49–50
    ethnic identity vs. Christian identity in,
        23, 210
    mediatory role of priests in, 129, 152
    need for contextualized theology in,
        40–41
    prophets in, 64
    retribution theology in, 95
    sacrifice in, 95, 121
    view of Jesus in, 49–50, 63–64
    view of sin in, 121
    worldview in, 23, 40, 152

age to come, the, 178–79, 180–81
al-Baṣrī, 'Ammār. See Baṣrī, 'Ammār al-
al-Ṭabranī, Ibrāhīm. See Ṭabranī, Ibrāhīm al-
already and not yet. See now and not yet
Alting, Johann Heinrich, 212
Ames, William, 216
amulets, 146–47, 146n3
Ancient of Days, the, 6
Andal, 111–12
Andəmta tradition, 186–87, 192, 193,
    242–43, 250–51, 253
angels, 15, 24, 186–87, 213, 221–22, 259
anointing
    Brazilian view of, 231
    of Jesus, 24, 32, 87, 165, 184, 191, 215,
        231, 236
    of Old Testament kings, 226, 230, 231,
        233–34
    as prophets, 20
    purpose of, 231–32
    as symbolizing the presence of the Holy
        Spirit, 184, 230, 231
Anselm of Canterbury, 108
Antigonus, 116
antikingdom, the, 66, 67
apostles, the, 18, 19–20, 64, 163, 183, 222
Aquinas, Thomas, 103, 149
Arab Christians, 59–61
Arabic language, development of, 50
Aramaic Levi, 129, 130
archetypal theology, 113n20
Arianism, 186
ark of the covenant, 122, 122n3, 155, 157, 169

Athanasius, 103
atonement
    Christ as sacrifice of, 85, 105, 141, 158,
        165, 219, 245, 248, 257
    Confucian view of 95
    Day of, 84, 155, 165
    as example of sacrifice, 182
    as greatest difficulty of religion, 94, 123
    rituals of, 128, 136, 154–55
    triumph over principalities and powers
        through, 221
atonement theories, 87–88
Atse, the, 243
Augsburg Confession, the, 160
Augustine, 188
Balirāja, 204
baptism
    of Jesus, 7, 16, 184
    as union of believers with Christ, 238,
        248, 251
Barclay, William, 218
Barnard, Jody, 157
Barreda, Juan José, 74
Barth, Karl, 148, 149
Bartholomew, Craig, 36
Barzillai, 156
Baṣrī, 'Ammār al-, 51
Bavinck, Herman
    and Adam, 29n28
    and the church as Christ's prophetess,
        23, 32–33, 37
    and the church's spiritual power and
        authority, 26–35
    and confessional statements, 34–35
    and duration of Christ's kingly office,
        212, 215, 226
    and the ecclesial offices, 30–32, 31n31
    and interrelation of theology and the
        church, 26
    and the *munus triplex*, 27–28, 29–30,
        30n29
    and preaching, 33, 33n39
    and Reformed theology, 43n59, 107
    and the rule of faith, 33–34, 41
    and universals, 107
    vocation of, 26

Beaty, Katelyn, 65
Beelzebul, 134
Belgic Confession, the, 103
Bellah, Robert, 77
benediction, 161
Berkhof, Louis, 215, 224
bhakti tradition, 111–12
Bond Kristen Tionghoa (BKT), 22n5
Bouillard, Henri, 114n23
Brakel, Wilhelmus à, 212
Brazil, 208, 209–10, 231
Brueggemann, Walter, 69, 70
Būshī, Būlus al-, 56
Calvin, John, 201, 212, 213, 214n10, 224,
        225, 226
Canons of Dort, 108
Chao, Charles, 103
Chen, Chao-Ying, 101
China
    confessional reformed theology in, 110–15
    Marxism in, 100, 101–2
    social hierarchy in, 123, 124
    and transcendence, 100, 104, 108, 109
    view of priestly office in, 95, 97–105,
        107–11, 115, 124
    See also Confucianism
Chinese Christian Union, the, 22n5
"Christus Victor," 88
church, the
    in Africa, 23
    as the body of Christ, 27, 88, 119, 124,
        248, 260
    as creation of the Holy Spirit, 26
    as diminishing social hierarchy, 124
    grace as defining characteristic of, 235
    in Indonesia, 22, 22nn4–6
    invisible, 27
    as justified, 88
    as kingdom of priests, 92
    kingly office of, 25
    marks of the, 25, 30
    members of as ambassadors and witnesses,
        227–28
    offices of, 25, 30–32, 31n31
    priestly office of, 25, 92

prophetic office of, 23, 25, 28, 29, 32–33,
    35–36
sharing in reign of Jesus, 24, 32, 92, 232,
    237, 240–42, 245, 247–52
and theology, 26, 39
triumph of over evil, 241–42, 251
union of with Jesus, 24, 232, 237–38,
    239, 246, 247–48, 250
visible, 27
Cole, R. Alan, 6
conciliarism, 41
concursus Dei, doctrine of, 154
Confucianism
    ancestor worship in, 97, 145, 149n8
    and atonement, 95
    and heaven, 97, 98, 99, 100, 101, 109
    as a religion, 131
    and rituals, 97, 98
    and sanctification, 95
    scholastic school, 99, 100
    school of the heart, 99–100, 114
    and supreme political ruler as Son of
        Heaven, 97–99, 100, 102, 117
    and transcendence, 93, 100, 101, 104,
        108, 109, 117
    view of good and evil in human nature, 97
    view of priestly office, 95, 97–105,
        107–11, 115, 124
    view of sin, 131
    See also China
Congar, Yves, 114n23
Council of Chalcedon, 106
crucifixion, 75, 76, 78, 142, 189, 193, 240,
    259
Cyprian's dictum, 27, 27n23
Dabney, Robert Lewis, 212, 224
Damaris, 164
Daniel, 6, 189
Daniélou, Jean, 114
Darmaputera, Eka, 39–40
David
    Jesus as king greater than, 169, 236
    humiliation of prior to exaltation, 183
    as king by grace, 235
    and now and not yet kingdom, 189
    as prophet, 117

and Saul, 231
as servant, 170, 183
triumphant return of, 172
as true theocratic king, 169–70
as a type of Christ, 217
Davidic covenant, the, 11, 170–71
Day of Atonement, the, 84, 155, 165
De Moor, Bernardinus, 212
Delitzsch, Franz, 5
demons, 133–34
Di, 98, 99
Dick, John, 212, 224, 225
Dionysius, 164
disability, prohibition of in priesthood,
    145–46
divinity
    of Jesus, 49–50, 53, 104–6, 108–9, 111,
        124, 141, 158, 187, 213, 219
    of kings, 218–19
divorce, 73–74, 74n41
docetism, 105
Dort, Canons of, 108
ectypal theology, 113, 113n20
Eden, Garden of, 157–58
Edmonson, Stephen, 214n10
Eisenstadt, Shmuel N., 175
Elijah, 6, 8, 16, 17, 117, 153
Ellingworth, Paul, 83
Escobar, Samuel, 63
Ethiopia
    Andəmta tradition in, 186–87, 192, 193,
        242–43, 250–51, 253
    and baptism, 238, 248, 251, 252
    dynasties in, 242
    forest conservation in, 211
    liturgy of, 251–52
    view of Christ's threefold office, 209
    view of the cross, 193
    view of human kingship, 232, 243–46,
        247, 252–53
    view of the kingdom of God, 186–87,
        192, 193, 206
    view of the kingship of Jesus in, 186–87,
        192, 193, 232, 242–53
    yearning for social justice in, 192, 193,
        206, 245

ethnic identity, 23
Eve, 90
exorcisms, 133–34, 139
Fadiman, Anne, 148
Fetha Nagast, the, 243
Feuerbach, Ludwig, 100–101
Fifth Ecumenical Council, the, 103
Formula of Concord, the, 106
France, R. T., 171, 173, 174
Gaozi, 97
Gay, Craig, 114
gef, 192
Genus Aposlesticum, 106–7
Genus Maiestatetiticum, 106
Gereja Reformed Injili Indonesia (GRII), 43–44, 44n62
German Mass, the, 140–41
Ghassānids, the, 61
ghost money, 149–50, 149n8
Gill, John, 212
God
    absolute power of, 149
    breaking into human history, 71, 72
    cloud signifying presence of, 7
    communion with, 230, 230n1
    final judgment of, 191, 206, 217
    grace of, 239, 246, 247
    humans created in image of, 29, 29n28, 88, 90, 195
    inverted kingdom of, 190, 192
    Jesus as image of, 24, 29, 29n28, 30n29, 189, 245
    as king, 11, 176, 234
    kingdom of. *See* kingdom of God
    as Lord of Hosts, 169
    markers of kingdom of, 190–94
    potentia ordinata of, 149, 154
    as revealed through Christ's priestly ministry, 89
    as the Rock of Israel, 17
    speech as method of action of, 9–10, 11
    as wrathful judge, 139–40
governmental theory, the, 87, 91
grace
    covenant of, 11
    as defining characteristic of Christian church, 235
    Jesus as source of, 235–36
    of God, 239, 246, 247
Great Commission, the, 217, 225
"great divorce," 37
Grondona, Mariano, 203
Hare, John, 123
Hasmoneans, the, 116
Hayek, Michel, 46
heaven, Chinese views of, 97, 98, 99, 100, 101, 109
Hebrews, letter to the, 83
Heidegger, Johann Heinrich, 212
Heidegger, Martin, 101
Henry, Carl, 77, 113
Herod the Great, 116
Hiestand, Gerald, 37
Ḥīra, 61
Hirsch, Emanuel, 148
Hmong, the
    documents of, 127
    sacrifices among, 148
    shamanism among, 127, 147–50, 151, 152
    view of sin, 131
Hodge, Charles, 212, 224
Hoekema, Anthony, 223
Hoeksema, Herman, 212
Holy Spirit
    church and theology as fruits of activity of, 26, 248, 252
    divinity and humanity of, 186–87
    miracles performed through, 48
    presence of upon Jesus, 184
    presence of upon Mary, 184
    prominent position of in Eastern tradition, 238
    prophethood of Christ through agency of, 24–25
    prophetism as gift of, 65
    sending of, 16, 159, 237, 248
    and unity of believers with Jesus, 237, 239–40, 252
    as working to bring about effect of God's word, 10

hosanna, 173
human nature, Chinese views of, 97
Hyrcanus II, 116
impurity
    and association with death, 132–33
    corpse, 136–38, 139, 142
    and demons, 133–34, 139
    and genital flow, 132–33, 135–36, 137, 139
    hierarchy of, 133
    lepra, 134–35, 137, 138, 142
    moral, 120, 256
    ritual, 120, 132, 256
India
    astrologers in, 98–99
    bhakti tradition in, 111–12
    exorcisms in, 134
    impurity in, 133, 135–36, 137, 142
    menstruation as unclean in, 135–36
    outcastes in, 122, 134
    patriarchy in church of, 109, 110
    priests in, 98–99, 109–10, 111–12, 115,
        124, 125–27, 128
    purity gradient in, 122, 124–25
    rituals in, 126, 128
    shamanism in, 147, 150–51
    and transcendence, 109–10
    view of angels in, 221–22
    view of Jesus in, 99
    view of the kingdom of God, 200, 203–5
    view of salvation in, 235, 239
individual, emergence of concept of, 174–75
Indonesia
    administration of sacraments in, 42–43
    Chinese churches in, 22, 22nn4–6,
        36n44, 37, 42
    evangelicals in, 22, 22n4
    and Jesus as prophet, 65
    move to Pentecostal and charismatic
        churches in, 36n44
    need for confessional churches in, 41–43
    need for contextualized theology in,
        39–40, 42, 43
    need for evangelistic training in, 38
    need for theologians in, 22, 22n6, 37, 39
    and prophetism as gift of the Holy Spirit
        in, 65

New Order in, 22–23n7
    ordination of women in, 42, 42n57
    prophetic ministry of church in, 36–44
indulgences, 140
inequality, 123–24
Injil, the, 45, 50
intercommunion, 238, 247
Irenaeus, 238
Isaiah, 117
Ishmael, 56
Islam
    and bhakti tradition, 112
    connection to Arabic language, 50
    importance of in the early Christian world,
        59–60, 60n24
    view of Jesus, 45, 46–49, 50–51, 58,
        58n22, 256
    view of Mary, 46, 47, 48
    view of Moses, 49
Israel, ancient
    fear of God among, 139
    impurity in, 132–33, 135, 136–37
    kings of as deriving authority from God,
        218, 232
    moral lapses among priesthood in, 130,
        131
    priests in, 128, 129–31
    purity gradient in, 121–22, 125
    rituals in, 126–27, 128, 129–30
James, 6, 177
Jeremiah, 117
Jeroboam of the Northern Kingdom, 115
Jesus
    anointing of, 24, 32, 87, 165, 184, 191,
        215, 231, 236
    Arab Christian view of, 50–57
    authority of, 14, 183, 185, 205, 208–9,
        215, 219, 222, 228, 257
    baptism of, 7, 16, 184
    believers as sharing in reign of, 232, 237,
        240–42, 247, 248–52
    believers called to emulate, 182–83, 187,
        194
    birth of, 71, 72, 72n36, 189, 190
    blessing of, 161
    as coming from the Father, 14, 17

as creator, 45–46, 55, 56, 57, 59, 104, 105, 183, 205, 245

death of, 75–76, 75n48, 78, 107–8, 111, 142, 143, 176, 193, 245

divine glory of, 6, 7

divinity of, 49–50, 53, 104–6, 108–9, 111, 124, 141, 158, 187, 213, 219

as embodying hope, 187, 189, 192, 232, 247

as eternal sacrifice, 85, 87, 88–89, 91

exorcisms by, 133–34, 139, 221

falling of Holy Spirit upon, 184

as fulfillment of prophetic writings, 14–15, 18, 62, 81, 85, 171–74, 184, 259

God's public acknowledgement of, 7, 16, 55

at God's right hand, 82, 83, 84, 106, 176, 194, 232, 245

as the gospel of God, 51

as greatest prophet, 7–8, 10, 14–20, 45–46, 51–57, 73, 86, 256

healings by, 134–35, 142, 151, 164, 190, 191

as high priest, 83–86, 91, 104–5, 107, 111, 112, 130–39, 141, 143, 146, 147, 158, 164–65

holiness of, 131, 132, 134, 135, 136, 138–39, 142, 143

human nature of, 103–5, 106, 107–9, 111, 141, 158, 183, 187, 226, 248

humanity called to become prophets of, 25, 32, 92

humility of, 181, 246

as the image of God, 24, 29, 29n28, 30n29, 189, 245

Indian view of, 99

interaction of with fringes of society, 70–71, 190–91, 194

interaction of with impurity, 132, 133–39, 142, 190, 191

as judge, 92, 219–20, 222

as king greater than David, 169, 220n23, 258

as king of the Jews, 172, 189

as king of kings, 219, 222, 232, 245, 253, 257

kingship of. *See* kingship, of Jesus

as the lamb of God, xiv, 88, 91, 144, 158, 219, 222, 227

as the lamb on a throne, 87–89, 226

as the last Adam, 88, 92, 213, 223, 250

Latin American view of, 47–48, 56, 60, 63, 64, 65–70

and liberation from Satan, 182, 191

as living embodiment of God's presence, 189–90

as Lord, 172, 181, 193, 195, 217, 219, 222, 237

as mediator between God and the people. *See* mediator, Jesus as

as Messiah, 62, 171, 173–74, 176, 177, 189, 190, 236, 240

miracles as demonstrating divine power of, 14, 46–48, 48n3, 51, 52–53, 54, 55, 57

Muslim view of, 45, 46–49, 50–51, 58, 58n22, 256

as the new Adam, 19

offices of king and priest combined in, 82, 83–84, 91

priestly office of. *See* priestly office, Jesus

as prophet like Moses, 3–5, 12, 16, 62, 71, 73

prophetic ministry of. *See* prophetic ministry, Jesus

resurrection of, 68n25, 75, 76, 77, 78, 163, 176, 179, 240

resurrections by, 137–38, 139, 142

as the rock of offense, 17

as sacrifice of atonement, 85, 105, 141, 158, 165, 219, 245, 248, 257

sending the Holy Spirit, 16, 159, 237, 248

servant imagery of, 170, 173, 177–78, 246

as sinless, 141, 146, 155, 158, 159, 165

as son of David, 173, 176

as the Son of God, 47, 53–56, 105, 107–8, 134, 176, 240, 259

as the Son of Man, 258–59

as source of grace, 235–36

as speaking God's words, 4, 7, 12, 14, 17, 62

suffering of, 6, 7–8, 18, 173, 183, 193

support of women, 73–74, 78, 191

as temple, 17, 94, 111, 144, 158, 189–90

threefold nature of. *See* threefold nature, Jesus

transfiguration of, 5–7, 16

triumphal entry of, 171–74

union of believers with, 232, 237–38, 239, 246, 247–48, 250

as the way to God, 19, 111

as the Word of God, 15, 18–19, 45, 46, 51, 53–55, 57–59, 158

worship of, 219, 221, 222

John (apostle), 6, 177

John of Damascus, Saint, 58

John the Baptist, 8, 14, 17, 184, 190

Johns, Brenda, 151

Joseph, 183

Joshua, 3

Joshua the high priest, 15

Jubilees, 130

justification, 19, 179, 216

Kant, Immanuel, 94, 94n3

Kebra Nagast, the, 243

Keil, Carl Friedrich, 5

Kibiru, Mugo wa, 64

Kim, Andrew, 96

Kinda, 61

kingdom of God

building bridges between cultures and, 203–5

cruciform nature of, 192–92, 196

as establishing the meaning and goal of history, 205–6

Ethiopian view of, 186–87, 192, 193, 206

Gentiles included in, 196–97

humility as greatness in, 246

Jesus as beginning of, 184, 189, 196, 215, 222, 240

Indian view of, 200, 203–5

as inverted, 190–92, 196

miracles as markers of, 190

new identity of believers within, 184–85

as now and not yet, 182, 183–86, 187, 188–89, 217–18, 223–24, 227, 248, 258

and social transformation, 194, 200–203

kings, Old Testament

as anointed by God, 218, 230, 231, 232, 233–34

call to emulate God, 230, 232, 234

mediatory role of, 230–31

participation of in God's kingship through grace, 234, 235

role of lineage in, 244

kingship, generally

emergence of secular concept of, 174–75

Ethiopian view of, 232, 243–46, 247, 252–53

Jesus's redefinition of, 176–78

Old Testament. *See* kings, Old Testament

New Testament, 236

kingship, of Jesus

Brazilian view of, 208

duration of, 207, 208, 209, 212–16, 214n10, 219, 222, 224–26

finished task of, 220–21, 223–26

Ethiopian view of, 186–87, 192, 193, 232, 242–53

historical apex of, 212, 214, 217–18

human nature of, 212, 214–16, 220

in believers' hearts, 194–95

in the church, 196–97

in the world, 197–200

Israel's rejection of, 176

and liberation from Satan, 182, 186–87, 191, 213, 216

redefinition of, 176–78, 189–90

redemptive purpose of, 212, 216–17

and restoring humanity to its rightful domain, 92, 180–81, 184, 213, 220–21, 249

in the book of Revelation, 221–22

and salvation, 190

and subjugation of the earth, 220–21, 223

Korea

economic power of, 146

and Jesus's divine and human natures, 106

negative pastoral leadership in churches of, 95–96

shamanism in, 95–96, 102, 127, 131–32, 139, 145–47, 146nn2–3, 150–52
view of priests, 139
view of sin, 131–32
Köstenberger, Andreas, 236
Küng, Hans, 114n23
Ladd, George Eldon, 188
last days, the, 179–80
Last Supper, the, 142
Latin America
  need for biblically trained pastors in, 33–34, 38–39
  need for contextualized theology in, 41–42
  need for teaching of Christian doctrine (theology) in, 38–39
  percentage of Christians in, 60
  view of Jesus in, 47–48, 56, 60, 63, 64, 65–70
Lazarus, 138
Leibniz, G. W., 117
Lewis, C. S., 235
lineage, biblical importance of in kingship, 244
Long, V. Philips, 154
Lord's Supper, the, 92, 106, 160, 179, 238, 248, 251–52
Lossky, Vladimir, 239
Lot, 155, 187
Löwith, Karl, 101, 205
Lu, Luke, 107
Lubac, Henri de, 114n23
Lugalzagesi, 116
lust, 73, 73n40
Luther, Martin, 140, 141, 161, 188
Macedonianism, 186
Magnificat, the, 72, 72n34, 78
Mahābali, 204
Maine, Henry J. S., 123
Makda, 243
Manāthirs, the, 61
mantrawadi, the, 134, 147
Marcion of Sinope, 144
Marcionism, 144–45
Marxism, 100–101

Mary
  Holy Spirit coming upon, 184
  and the *Magnificat*, 72, 72n34, 78
  as mother of God, 105, 107, 108
  Muslim view of, 46, 47, 48
Mastricht, Petrus van, 212
materialism, 100, 131, 206
Mbiti, John, 121
mediator, Jesus as
  in prophetic office, 4, 10, 15, 17, 24, 28–29, 62, 117
  in priestly office, 82, 85, 89, 92, 99, 107, 110–11, 120, 165
  in kingly office, 215, 216, 232, 236–37, 245, 246
Meenakshi, 125
Melchizedek, 82, 84, 155–56
Mencius, 97
Menilik II, 243
menstruation, as impure, 132–33, 135–36
messenger formula, the, 169–70
messianic expectation, 4, 5, 170, 172
messianic prophecy, 172, 184
messianic secret, 7
Milgrom, Jacob, 121
ministry of reconciliation, 249
miracles
  as criteria of true prophets, 48n3, 71
  as demonstrating divine power of Christ, 14, 46–48, 48n3, 51, 52–53, 54, 57, 190
  as God's way of working through nature, 154
  as markers of God's kingdom, 190
  as prophetic actions, 74–75, 74n43, 153
  as present today, 48
  vs. magic, 153
missionaries, 227–28
Moab, 3
Moffitt, David, 157
moral conscience, 187
moral influence theory, the, 87
Moses
  farewell addresses of, 3
  as mediator, 12, 13, 15, 153

miracles of, 154
Muslim view of, 49
as prophet, 3, 8, 12, 16
transfiguration of, 6, 7
at the transfiguration of Jesus, 6, 16
Mottin, Jean, 152
mudang, 146, 146n2
Muhammad, 53, 56, 256
munus triplex, 27, 29–30, 30n29, 31
Mu'tazilah, the, 58
Nathan, 117, 169, 171
naturalism, 148, 154
Nawās, Dhū al-, 61
Nestorianism, 108, 187
new covenant, 11, 17, 20, 84, 85, 179
New Heavens and New Earth, 183, 229
Nicaea, Second Council of, 60n24
Niebuhr, H. Richard, 201
Noah, 187
nominalism, 148–49
nouvelle theology, 114, 114n23
now and not yet, 182, 183–90, 217–18,
    223–24, 227, 248, 258
Núñez, Emilio Antonio, 63
Oakley, Francis, 175
Onam festival, 201
Owen, John, 104, 105
Pancasila, 40, 40n52
Pannenberg, Wolfhart, 101
parable of the weeds, 186–87
Pareus, David, 212
Paul, 18, 162–64, 228
Pei-Jung, Fu, 98
Peter, 5, 6–7, 177, 180, 186, 228, 246–47,
    261
Peterson, David, 84–85
Philip, 5
Phule, Jyotirao Govindrao, 204
Prayaschitta, 126
prayer
    for the Holy Spirit, 238, 239
    intercessory 159–60
    Lord's, 159, 194
    of the Church, 159–60
present age, the, 178, 179, 188, 227

priesthood, the
    choosing of priests, 145, 146, 153, 154,
        215
    high, 154–55
    intercessory prayer of, 159
    as mediator between holiness and
        sinfulness, 120, 128, 134, 153, 215,
        257
    offering forgiveness, 160
    offering sacrifices, 152–53
    to provide access to God, 120
    preventing pollution of the sanctuary,
        120, 127, 128, 137, 142, 153
    profiteering among, 130
    prohibition against disabilities among,
        145–46, 153
    purity and, 256–57
    responsibilities of, 152–55
    restriction from corpse impurity of, 137,
        139
    and sacrifices, 152–54, 155, 158–59
    sexual offenses among, 130
priesthood of all believers, 111, 114, 117,
    161, 249, 257
priestly office, Jesus
    beginning of, 157
    Christ's human nature in, 109
    as continued through the church, 161
    as distinct from his kingly office, 110–11
    duration of, 207, 208, 212, 214n10
    as exercised in heaven, 85
    healing as part of, 151
    interceding for us, 159, 165
    New Testament on, 83–86
    Old Testament on, 81–83
    presuppositions of doctrine of, 89–91
    and priesthood of all believers, 111
prophetic imagination, 69–70, 71, 78
prophetic ministry, Jesus
    African view of, 63–64
    crucifixion and, 75–76, 75n48, 78
    and denunciation of the antikingdom,
        66–67
    duration of, 207
    Indonesian view of, 65

Latin American view of, 63, 64, 65–70
miracles and, 74–75, 74n43
New Testament examples of, 71–76
political aspect of, 66–68
resurrection and, 75, 76, 77, 78
prophets
as ambassadors, 11–12
as attorneys, 10–14, 15
biblical vs. other, 9–10, 11–12
criteria of true, 71
as divinely inspired, 4, 8, 9, 71
false, 11, 12, 15, 18
Holy Spirit and, 65, 71
humanity as, 25, 32, 92
outside of ancient Israel, 4, 9
as performing miracles, 153
requirements for, 3
sorcery and divination among, 4, 9, 11, 12
prosperity gospel, 102
purity
gradient of, 122
inherent to the priesthood, 256–57
ritual vs. moral, 120, 128, 129
Rahner, Karl, 114
Ram-Rajya, 200
Ratzinger, Joseph, 114n23
reformation, 202
Reformed Evangelical Church of
Indonesia, 43–44, 44n62
resurrection
by Jesus, 137–38, 139, 142
of Jesus, 68n25, 75, 76, 77, 78, 163, 176,
179, 240
retribution theology, 95
Reymond, Robert, 113
Ricci, Matteo, 98
Ridgley, Thomas, 212, 224, 225
Rock of Israel, the, 17
Ross, Allen, 82
Ryrie, Charles, 48n3
sacred contagion, 122
sacrifice
in Africa, 95, 121
among the Hmong, 148
Old Testament, 127, 154, 155, 158–59

rationale behind, 230n1
salvation. *See* theosis
Samaritans, the, 5
Samuel, 115
Sarah, 244
Saul, 115, 162, 231
Schmitt, Carl, 101
Scholastic School, the, 99
Schrock, David, 157
Scotus, Duns, 149
Second Great Awakening, the, 175
Segundo, Juan Luis, 66, 67, 67n19, 68n25
Seleucids, the, 115–16
Seminari Alkitab Asia Tenggara (SAAT),
21, 21n2, 44n61
Sermon on the Mount, 17, 73
shamanism
among the Hmong, 147–50, 151–52
in India, 147, 150–51
in Korea, 95–96, 102, 127, 131–32, 139,
145–47, 146nn2–3, 150–52
natural vs. supernatural in, 154
and the prosperity gospel, 102
sacrifices in, 148, 152
in Taiwan, 149, 152
and the theology of the glory, 102
shamans
becoming, 151, 153
combined prophet and priestly roles of,
153
as mediating between the natural and the
supernatural, 153–54
as performing magic, 153–54
responsibilities of, 151–52
similarity to Old Testament priests, 152,
153, 164
Simon the Leper, 184
sin, 121, 131, 132, 256
Sinai covenant, 3, 11, 13, 14
Sobrino, Jon, 66–67, 66n12
Solomon, 117, 231, 243
South Asia. *See* India
Stancaro, Francesco, 213
Staupitz, Johann von, 140
Stephen, 5

Strecker, David, 151
Suazo, David, 64, 69–70, 71, 74, 76, 78
sufism, 112
Sundareshwara, 125
supernaturalism, 148
Sutanto, Gray, 40
Symbol of Chalcedon, the, 103, 104
syncretism, 40–41
tabernacle, the, 84, 143, 170
Ṭabranī, Ibrāhīm al-
    conversions following debate of, 52, 52n8
    defense of Christianity by, 51–52
    and the eternity of God's Word, 58–59
    and Jesus as the Son of God, 53, 54,
        55, 57
    and the miracles of Jesus, 47–48, 52–53,
        54, 55, 57
    and the supremacy of Jesus over all
        prophets, 46, 51–57, 59
    trials by fire and poison of, 52, 52n8
Tagore, Rabindranath, 118
Taiwan, 149, 152
Taylor, Mark C., 195
Testament of Levi, the, 130
theologians
    need for in Indonesia, 22, 22n6, 37
    need for in Latin America, 38–39
    pastors as, 37, 38, 39–40
    shrinking need for in the West, 37
theology
    archetypal, 113n20
    Bavinck's views on, 26
    in context, xv–xiv
    of the cross, 102
    definition of, 24n11
    ectypal, 113, 113n20
    of the glory, 102, 178
    liberation, 66, 68
    nouvelle, 114, 114n23
    retribution, 95
theosis, 238, 239
Thiessen, Matthew, 133, 135, 136, 138
threefold mandate, the, 213
threefold nature, Jesus
    Brazilian view of, 208, 209

duration of, 207–9, 213
    Ethiopian view of, 209
Tillard, J.-M. R., 114
Tong, Stephen, 43, 43n60, 44, 44n61, 103,
    104, 107
transcendence
    Christian view of, 100, 103–4, 110
    Confucian view of, 93, 100, 101, 104,
        108, 109, 117
    Indian view of, 109–10
transfiguration, 5, 6, 7, 16
Trinity Evangelical Divinity School, 21n2
triumphal entry, the, 171–74
tur, 206
Turretin, Francis, 212, 216, 224, 225
Tyre, 134
Ubuntu, 23
Uzzah, 122
Uzziah, 115
Vāmana, 204
Van den Toren, Benno, 164
Van Gelder, Craig, 25–26
VanGemeren, Willem, 71, 73n37
Vannoy, J. Robert, 170
Vitringa, Campegius, 212
vocation, 77–78
von Balthasar, Hans Urs, 114n23
Weber, Max, 131, 153, 197
Weber, Stuart K., 173
Wilson, Todd, 37
Wolff, Christian, 117
Wollebius, Johannes, 212, 224, 225
Woodberry, Robert, 202
Word of God, the
    eternity of, 58–59
    Jesus as, 15, 18–19, 45, 46, 51, 53, 54, 55,
        57–59, 58n22
    Quranic view of, 58, 58n22
Wright, N. T., 70, 75, 196
Xu, Ximian, 39, 42–43
Xunzi, 97, 101
Yangming, Wang, 99
Yuming, Jia, 103
Zechariah, messianic prophecy of, 172
Zongsan, Mou, 100